LOGIC AND KNOWLEDGE

BERTRAND RUSSELL

O.M., F.R.S.

Fellow of Trinity College, Cambridge

Logic
and
Knowledge

ESSAYS
1901–1950

EDITED BY
ROBERT CHARLES MARSH

CAPRICORN BOOKS
G. P. PUTNAM'S SONS NEW YORK

FIRST PUBLISHED 1956
SECOND IMPRESSION 1964
THIRD IMPRESSION 1966
FOURTH IMPRESSION 1968

Reprinted by arrangement
with George Allen and Unwin Ltd. and
The Macmillan Company, New York
CAPRICORN BOOKS EDITION 1971

Third Impression
SBN: 399-50146-0

PRINTED IN THE UNITED STATES OF AMERICA

PREFACE

THE ten essays in this volume represent work extending through fifty years in the life of one of the great philosophers of our times. All of these essays are representative, and several can be regarded as among the most important of his writings. None the less, only one of these papers has previously been available in a hard-cover edition, authorized by Lord Russell, and available through the normal channels of the book trade. Indeed, most of these papers have previously been available only in libraries with unusually full periodical collections, and this in itself would serve as ample justification for reprinting them in book form.

Two collections of essays with partly overlapping contents are all we have had, up to now, to preserve the shorter writings of Russell's most productive decades of work in logic, mathematics, and the theory of knowledge. Nothing included in *Philosophical Essays* (1910) or *Mysticism and Logic* (1918) appears here, and an examination of all three books is necessary for a comprehensive view of Russell's papers of the early years of the century. The period which marked the transition to the neutral monism of *An Analysis of Mind* (1921)—in other words, Russell's philosophical activity (apart from social philosophy) during and immediately after the 1914–18 war—has previously been difficult to study. The appearance here of three papers from those years, none of them previously available in an authorized edition, should serve to fill this troublesome gap in the chronology of Russell's available works.

It is the editor's belief that what is ultimately desired is a comprehensive edition of Russell's shorter writings arranged on a chronological basis by subject, eliminating only journalistic pieces of limited interest. Such a project is beyond the means of a commercial publisher, in all probability, but it deserves the attention of those interested in preserving in an appropriate form the writings which—for the most part—linked one of our most distinguished contemporaries with his audience.

Selection has been difficult, and I do not expect everyone to agree with my choices. I have reprinted the three papers of Russell which are starred in Church's *Bibliography of Symbolic Logic*. These are technical but important. To include them I was forced to omit

a group of papers which appeared originally in French in the
Revue de Métaphysique et de Morale which are still among the best
general discussions of the problems they raise. I regret that I had
to make such a choice, but I do not regret the choice that I made.
The reader who is not prepared to cope with mathematical logic
will, nonetheless, find in certain of the other essays writing as
lucid and readable as any of Russell's more popular works.

I was introduced to Russell's philosophy by Professor Arthur H.
Nethercot at Northwestern University in 1944. In 1951 I took a
doctorate at Harvard University with a thesis on Russell's philosophy, and since that year I have had the pleasure, from time to
time, of discussing philosophical questions with Lord Russell himself. In the production of this book, I alone am responsible for its
contents and the views expressed in the introductory remarks
which preface each of the essays. Lord Russell has been consulted
on all matters relating to the text of the papers, and these, to the
best of my knowledge, are here issued in the form which he wishes
to be taken as final and definitive. For this aid, and for many other
kindnesses, I am greatly in his debt.

The first paper has not been reset entirely: the greater part of
the symbols are reproduced here by means of photo-engraving
from the original edition. For that reason slight variations may be
found in the typography of the English text and the symbolic
material, since it has not been possible to duplicate exactly the type
faces of Peano's Italian printer. There is no instance, however, in
which this is likely to introduce an element of ambiguity. In resetting the second paper we have followed the style of the *Principia
Mathematica* rather than the earlier typographical conventions
Russell used in the initial publication of this essay. It was Lord
Russell's desire that we take advantage of the resetting of the paper
to introduce these minor revisions. The dates given for the papers
are those of initial *publication*. In most instances the paper was
written in the same year or that immediately preceding publication.

The scarcity of some of the papers now made generally available
here can be seen from the fact that only one copy of the text of the
lectures on logical atomism was known to exist in the whole of
Cambridge, and when this disappeared from the University library
during the preparation of the book it was necessary for me to
borrow the missing material from the library of the University of

Bristol. I am greatly in debt to Bristol for the consideration shown me in making the original edition of these lectures freely available to me. Because of this kindness, future students of philosophy will be spared the inconvenience of inter-library loans or the necessity of resorting to theft.

This collection was planned shortly after I first went to Cambridge in 1953 and was eventually seen through the press during my second period there in 1954–56. I shall always associate Cambridge with a wonderful sense of having achieved freedom from departmentalism, so that I might function, not as a philosopher, or a musician, or an educator, but as a thinker with the right to do whatever he feels to be important.

Mr. Walter Beard of George Allen and Unwin undertook supervision of the production of the book. He has been obliged to deal with some vexing problems, and his contribution to the volume is not to be underestimated. I am grateful to him for the assistance he has given me, and for the effective but unobtrusive manner in which he attended to difficulties.

Trinity College,   ROBERT CHARLES MARSH
Cambridge.

CONTENTS

PREFACE   page v

1901   *The Logic of Relations*   1

1905   *On Denoting*   39

1908   *Mathematical Logic as Based on*   57
        The Theory of Types

1911   *On the Relations of Universals and Particulars*   103

1914   *On the Nature of Acquaintance*   125

1918   *The Philosophy of Logical Atomism*   175

1919   *On Propositions: what they are and how they*   283
        mean

1924   *Logical Atomism*   321

1936   *On Order in Time*   345

1950   *Logical Positivism*   365

I AM grateful to Mr. Robert Marsh for the industry, patience and accuracy which he has displayed in the following reprints of some of my less well-known writings. In regard to a considerable part of this volume he has undertaken the laborious work of collating versions which differed owing to difficulties arising from war-time censorship. Of many of the articles copies were not easily available and he has had much trouble in finding the material. Mr. Marsh has, in my opinion, shown good judgment in selecting what to reprint and also in his elucidatory introductions. It is not for me to judge whether it is worth while to perpetuate the record of what I thought at various times, but if any historian of bygone lucubrations should wish to study my development he will find this volume both helpful and reliable.

BERTRAND RUSSELL

The Logic of Relations

In his autobiographical essay MY MENTAL DEVELOPMENT *Russell says: 'The most important year in my intellectual life was the year 1900, and the most important event in that year was my visit to the International Congress of Philosophy in Paris.'* He travelled to Paris with Whitehead, his former teacher and then colleague, and they were both struck by the skill shown in the discussion of mathematical and logical problems by Peano and his pupils. Impressed, Russell went home to master Peano's works and particularly his notation. Its influence on the later Russell-Whitehead notation of the* PRINCIPIA MATHEMATICA *is fairly easily traced.*

THE LOGIC OF RELATIONS *was written in 1900 and published the following year. It was composed in Peano's notation, although it represents work contemporary with the writing of much of the* PRINCIPLES OF MATHEMATICS *in which Russell uses an early form of the notation developed fully in the* PRINCIPIA MATHEMATICA. *Those unfamiliar with Peano's symbols will find a concise and admirable discussion of the system in Jörgen Jörgensen's standard rok,* A TREATISE OF FORMAL LOGIC, *Copenhagen and London, 1931, Vol. I, p. 176 ff. The Peano notation is actually not difficult to read if one knows that of the* PRINCIPIA MATHEMATICA, *and the paper is therefore reproduced in its original form.*

Russell's first publication was in 1895, the year following his first period of residence at Cambridge. It is of no particular interest, although his mathematical investigations during the following four years led to publications that repay examination. However it is with this paper that we see clearly the appearance in philosophy of a creative mind of the first order, and on its publication (in the year in which he was twenty-nine) Russell's eventual position as a 'thinker of reputation' seems to have been assured. Asked what idea in the paper he now feels to be the most important, Russell replied 'my definition of cardinal number'—which here appeared in print for the first time.

It was largely on the basis of this paper and next but one in this collection that Russell was elected a Fellow of the Royal Society in 1908.

**The Philosophy of Bertrand Russell*, Evanston and Cambridge, 1944 *et seq.*, p. 12.

THE LOGIC OF RELATIONS

With some Applications to the Theory of Series

This paper first appeared in French in Peano's *Rivista di Matematica* [*Revue de Mathématiques*] Vol. VII, pp. 115–48, Turin, 1900–01. The translation is by R.C.M. and has been revised and corrected by Lord Russell.

CONTENTS

		page
§1	*General Theory of Relations*	5
§2	*Cardinal Numbers*	10
§3	*Progressions*	15
§4	*Finite and Infinite*	23
§5	*Compact Series*	26
§6	*Fundamental Series in a Compact Series*	30

THE LOGIC of relations, which we find in the works of Peirce and Schröder, is difficult and complicated to so great a degree that it is possible to doubt its utility. Since they lack the distinction between ϵ and $\supset$, these authors consider a class as a simple sum of individuals. For that reason, a relation for them is like a sum of pairs of individuals. It follows from this that the fundamental properties of relations are expressed by very long formulae of summation, the significance of which is not made very evident by the notation. It is, however, the logic of relations which must serve as a foundation for mathematics, since it is always types of relations which are considered in symbolic reasoning; that is, we are not required to consider such and such particular relation, with the exception of those which are fundamental to logic (like ϵ and $\backsim$), but rather relations of a certain type—for example, transitive and asymmetrical relations, or one-one relations. I point out in the present paper that it is possible to simplify the logic of relations enormously by making use of Peano's notation, knowledge of which is assumed in the following text. However it will appear that the logic of Peano is hardly complete without an explicit introduction to relations. Of the basic concepts, take for example the definition of *function* (1). The signs xu and ux, which appear on the right in that definition, are not made self-explanatory by the preceding text. The juxtaposition of two letters has not hitherto possessed any meaning other than logical multiplication, which is not involved here. The fact is that the definition of *function* is not possible except through knowing a new primitive idea, that of *relation*. We may observe, for example, the following consequence. From the definition cited, and from P§20 P9·4, §22 P2·4, §23 P1·02, P2·0, we derive

$$a, b\varepsilon\ N_0\ .\backsim.\ a+b = ab = a\times b$$

This consequence shows that the notation adopted has need of modification. I shall give a more complicated notation from which we cannot derive an equivalent conclusion. I believe, moreover, that the introduction of relations gives occasion for a simplification and generalization of many mathematical theories; and it permits us to give *nominal* definitions whenever definitions are possible.

In the following text, I have adopted some of the sumbols of Schröder, for example, Ř, o', 1'. I have not succeeded in making myself conform to the rule of formulation, to put all symbols in a line, and in the case of relations I have had to distinguish between RP and R∩P. Otherwise I have adopted all that is given in the logic of Peano, and at the same time the notation Elm suggested by Padoa [*Rivista di Matematica*, Vol. VI, p. 117]; however I have distinguished ϱu, where u is a class contained in the range of a relation R, from $\varrho\cap u$. For that reason the logical product of a class u and a class represented by a Greek letter is always indicated by $\varrho\cap u$, or $\pi\cap u$ etc., and not by ϱu or $u\varrho$. [See §1, Prop. 1·33·34·35·36].

§1. GENERAL THEORY OF RELATIONS

✱ 1·0 *Primitive idea*: Rel = Relation

·1 $R\epsilon$ Rel .⊃: xRy .=. x has the relation R with y.

·21 $R\varepsilon$ Rel .⊃. $\varrho = x\mathfrak{z}\{\exists y\mathfrak{z}(xRy)\}$ Df

·22 $R\varepsilon$ Rel .⊃. $\breve{\varrho} = x\mathfrak{z}\{\exists y\mathfrak{z}(yRx)\}$ Df

If R is a relation, ϱ can be called the *domain* of the relation R, that is to say, the class of terms which have that relation with a single term, or with several terms. I always use (except for the relations which are met with in the formulary) capital letters for relations and the corresponding small Greek letters for the domain of the relations. In definitions ·21 ·22 the letter R is assumed to be variable, that is to say, α shall be the domain of a relation A, β of a relation B, etc. I regard $\mathfrak{z}$ as a primitive idea of the sort that permits me to put this sign before propositions which are not reducible without its aid to the form $x\epsilon\alpha$.

·31 $R\varepsilon$ rel . $x\varepsilon\varrho$.⊃. $\breve{\varrho}x = y\mathfrak{z}(xRy)$ Df

·32 $x\varepsilon\breve{\varrho}$.⊃. $\varrho x = y\mathfrak{z}(yRx)$ Df

·33 $R\varepsilon$ rel. $u\varepsilon$ Cls . $u\supset\varrho$.⊃. $\breve{\varrho}u = y\mathfrak{z}\{\exists u\cap x\mathfrak{z}(xRy)\}$ Df

·34 $\breve{u\varrho} = y\mathfrak{z}\{x\exists u .\supset x . xRy\}$ Df

·35 $u\supset\breve{\varrho}$.⊃. $\varrho u = y\mathfrak{z}\{\exists u\cap x\mathfrak{z}(yRx)\}$ Df

·36 $u\breve{\varrho} = y\mathfrak{z}\{x\exists u .\supset x . yRx\}$ Df

·4 $R\varepsilon$ rel .⊃. $\exists\varrho$.=. $\exists\breve{\varrho}$

·5 $\exists R$.=. $\exists\varrho$ Df

·6 $R,R'\varepsilon$ rel .⊃∴ $R\supset R'$.=: $xRy \supset x,y. xR'y$ Df

·61 $R=R'$.=: $R\supset R'$. $R'\supset R$ Df

·7 $R\varepsilon$ rel .⊃. $\exists$ rel $\cap$ $R'\mathfrak{z}$ $(xR'y .=. yRx)$ Pp

·71 $R\varepsilon$ rel .⊃. rel $\cap$ $R'\mathfrak{z}(xR'y .=. yRx)$ ε Elm

    [R_1,R_2 ε rel $\cap$ $R'\mathfrak{z}(xR'y .=. yRx)$.⊃∴ $xR_1y .=. yRx : xR_2y .=. yRx.\therefore$

                   ⊃: $xR_1y .=. xR_2y : ⊃. R_1 = R_2$]

·72 $R\varepsilon$ rel .⊃. $\breve{R} = \imath$ rel $\cap$ $R'\mathfrak{z}(xR'y .=. yRx)$ Df

·8 $\exists$ rel$\cap R\mathfrak{z}(\varrho = \iota x . \breve{\varrho} = \iota y)$ Pp

This Pp is of great importance, chiefly in arithmetic. It affirms that between any two individuals there is a relation which does not hold for any other pair of individuals . It does not need a hypothesis, since x and y are not subject to any limitation. However one can limit it to the case where x and y are different, since the case where x and y are identical is derived from this by relative multiplication.

·9 $R\varepsilon$ rel .ɔ. $\breve{\breve{R}} = R$

[$x\breve{\breve{R}}y$.=. $y\breve{R}x$.=. xRy]

·91 $R, S\varepsilon$ rel . $R = \breve{S}$.ɔ. $\breve{\varrho} = \sigma$. $\varrho = \breve{\sigma}$

$R = \breve{S}$.=. $\breve{R} = S$

·93 $R_1, R_2\varepsilon$ rel .ɔ∴ $x(R_1\cup R_2)y$.=: xR_1y .∪. xR_2y	Df
·94 $K\varepsilon$ Cls'rel .ɔ. $\cup$'$K = R\mathfrak{z}\{xRy$.=. $\mathfrak{z}K \cap R'\mathfrak{z}(xR'y)\}$	Df
·95 $\cup$'$K \varepsilon$ rel	Pp
·96 $R_1, R_2\varepsilon$ rel .ɔ∴ $x(R_1\cap R_2)y$.=: xR_1y . xR_2y	Df
·97 $K\varepsilon$ Cls'Rel .ɔ. $\cap$ '$K = R\mathfrak{z}\{xRy$.=: $R'\varepsilon K$.ɔR'. $xR'y\}$	Df
·98 $\cap$'$K \varepsilon$ rel	Pp
✳ 2·1 $R_1, R_2\varepsilon$ rel .ɔ: $x\, R_1R_2\, z$.=. $\mathfrak{z}\, y\mathfrak{z}(xR_1y . yR_2z)$	Df
·11 $R_1R_2\, \varepsilon$ rel	Pp

It is necessary to distinguish $R_1\cap R_2$, which signifies the logical product, from R_1R_2, which signifies the relative product. We have $R_1\cap R_1 = R_1$, but not in general, $R_1R_1 = R_1$; we have $R_1\cap R_2 = R_2\cap R_1$, but not in general $R_1R_2 = R_2R_1$. For example, *grandfather* is the relative product of *father* and *father* or of *mother* and *father*, but not of *father* and *mother*.

·12 $R\varepsilon$ rel .ɔ. $R^2 = RR$	Df
·13 $R, S\varepsilon$ rel .ɔ. $(\breve{RS}) = \breve{S}\breve{R}$	

[$x(\breve{RS})y$.=. $yRSx$.=. $\mathfrak{z}\mathfrak{z}\varepsilon$ $(yRz$. $zSx)$.=. $\mathfrak{z}z\varepsilon$ $(x\breve{S}z$ $z\breve{R}y)$.=. $x\breve{S}\breve{R}y$]

·2 Transitive = tr = rel$\cap R\mathfrak{z}(R^2\supset R)$ Df

When one has $R^2\supset R$, one has $xRy.yRz.\supset.xRz$.

·3 $R\varepsilon$ rel .ɔ∴ $R^2 = R$.=: xRz .=. $\mathfrak{z}y\mathfrak{z}(xRy . yRz)$

If R is a relation which yields a series (which requires that R be transitive and contained in diversity), $R^2 = R$ gives the condition for that series to be compact (*überall dicht*) that is to say it contains a term between any two of its terms. (See §5 below.)

·4 $R\varepsilon$ rel .⊃: x-Ry .=. -(xRy) Df

·5 -$R\ \varepsilon$ rel Pp

·6 $(\text{-}\breve{R}) = \text{-}(\breve{R})$

I have not found the relative addition of Peirce and Schröder necessary. Here is its definition:

Let R and S be relations: their relative sum is a relation P such as

$$xPy .=. x\text{-}Rz .⊃_z. zSy : z\text{-}Sy .⊃_z. xRz \qquad \text{Df}$$
$$xPy .=. -\exists(-\varrho x \cap -\sigma y) .=. -|x(-R\text{-}S)y|$$

yielding

* 3·1 $\varepsilon\varepsilon$ rel **Pp**

This Pp says that ε is a relation. In this case I have been obliged to abandon the rule of using capitals for relations.

·2 $e = x\mathfrak{z}|\exists y\mathfrak{z}(x\varepsilon y)|$ Df [e = individual]

·3 $\breve{e} = x\mathfrak{z}|\exists y\mathfrak{z}(y\varepsilon x)|$ Df [$e = \text{Cls-}\iota\wedge$]

·4 $\breve{e} ⊃ e$ [$y\varepsilon\breve{e} .⊃. y\varepsilon\text{Cls} .⊃. y\varepsilon e$]

·5 $x\varepsilon\breve{e}y .=. \exists z\mathfrak{z}(x\varepsilon z . y\varepsilon z)$

·51 $x\varepsilon\breve{e}y .=. \exists z\mathfrak{z}(z\varepsilon x . z\varepsilon y) .=. x,y\varepsilon\text{Cls} . \exists xy$

·6 $y\varepsilon\text{Cls'Cls} .⊃. \smile'y = x\mathfrak{z}(x\varepsilon'y)$

·7 $R\varepsilon$ rel : $x\varrho z .⊃_x. y\mathfrak{z}(xRy) = x$:⊃. $R = \breve{\varepsilon}$

[$x\varepsilon\varrho .⊃_x : xRy .=. y\varepsilon x .⊃.\therefore R = \breve{\varepsilon}$]

·8 $u,v\varepsilon\text{Cls-}\iota\wedge .⊃. \exists$ rel $\cap R\mathfrak{z}(xRy .=. x\varepsilon u . y\varepsilon v)$

[Prop 1·8 .⊃. $\exists$rel $\cap P\mathfrak{z}(\iota u = \pi . \iota v = \breve{\pi})$

$P\varepsilon$ rel . $\iota u = \pi . \iota v = \breve{\pi} .⊃::$

$x\varepsilon u . y\varepsilon v .=_{x,y}. x(\varepsilon P\breve{\varepsilon})y .\therefore x\text{-}\varepsilon u .\smile. y\text{-}\varepsilon v .=_{x,y}. -|x(\varepsilon P\breve{\varepsilon})y| ::⊃. \text{Prop}]$

This proposition proves that, if u, v are two non-null classes, there is a relation which holds between all terms of u and all terms of v, but which does not hold between any other pair of terms.

·81 $u\varepsilon\text{Cls-}\iota\wedge .⊃. \exists$ rel $\cap R\mathfrak{z}(\varrho = u : x\varepsilon u .=_x. xRu)$

[Prop 1·8 .⊃. $\exists$ rel$\cap P\mathfrak{z}(\pi = \iota u . \breve{\pi} = \iota u) :⊃.\therefore$

$x\varepsilon u .⊃_x. x(\varepsilon P)u : x\text{-}\varepsilon u .⊃_x. -x(\varepsilon P)u .⊃.\therefore \text{Prop}]$

·82 $u\varepsilon\text{Cls-}\iota\wedge .⊃. \varepsilon u = \imath$ rel $\cap R\mathfrak{z}(\varrho = u : x\varepsilon u .=_x. xRu)$ Df

The relation ϵ_u is the relation ϵ for the class u alone. It is formed by the relative product of ϵ with the relation which holds only between u and u.

✳ 4·1 *Primitive idea*: 1' = identity

This symbol is given in the notation of Schröder. I do not use the symbol = for the identity of individuals, since it has another usage for the equivalence of classes, of propositions, and of relations.

> ·2　1' ε Rel　　　　　　　　　　　　　　　　　　　　　Pp
> ·3　0' = -1'　　　　　　　　　　　　　　　　　　　　　　　　Df

o' is diversity. It is a relation as a consequence of Prop 2·5.

> ·31　x 1' x　　　　　　　　　　　　　　　　　　　　　　　　Pp
>
> ·32　1' $\mathtt{o}$ $\breve{1}$'　　　　　　　　　　　　　　　　　　　　　　　　　Pp
>
> ·33　R ε rel . xRy . y 1' z .$\mathtt{o}$. xRz　　　　　　　　Pp
>
> ·34　1'^{2} $\mathtt{o}$ 1'　　　　　　[Prop 4·33 .$\mathtt{o}$. Prop]
>
> ·4　1' = $\breve{1}$'
>
> 　[$x\breve{1}'y$.=. y1'x　|1|　　　　|1| . Prop·32 .$\mathtt{o}$. x1'y　|2|
>
> 　|2| .$\mathtt{o}$. $\breve{1}$' $\mathtt{o}$ 1'　|3|　　　　|3| . Prop·32 .$\mathtt{o}$. Prop]
>
> ·41　1'^{2} = 1'
> 　[x1'y . y1'y .$\mathtt{o}$. x1'^2y :$\mathtt{o}$. 1' $\mathtt{o}$ 1'^{2}　　　　　　　|1|
> 　|1| . Prop·34 .$\mathtt{o}$. Prop]
>
> ·42　0' = $\breve{0}$'
> 　[Prop·3·4 .$\supset$. Prop]
>
> ·5　R,Pε rel .$\mathtt{o}$: R$\breve{\mathrm{P}}$ $\mathtt{o}$ 0' .=. $\breve{\mathrm{R}}$P $\mathtt{o}$ 0'
>
> 　[R$\breve{\mathrm{P}}$ $\mathtt{o}$ 0' .=: xRy . $y\breve{\mathrm{P}}z$.$\mathtt{o}_{x,y,z}$. x0'z :
>
> 　　　　=. -$\exists$ $(x,y)$$\mathtt{g}$($xRy$. $y\breve{\mathrm{P}}x$)
>
> 　　　　=. -$\exists$ $(x,y)$$\mathtt{g}$($y\breve{\mathrm{R}}x$. xPy)
>
> 　　　　=: $y\breve{\mathrm{R}}x$. xPz .$\mathtt{o}_{x,y,z}$. y0'z :=. $\breve{\mathrm{R}}$P $\mathtt{o}$ 0']
>
> **✳ 5·1**　Nc+1 = Rel $\cap$ Rz|xRy . xRz .$\mathtt{o}_{x}$. y1'z|　　Df
> ·11　1+Nc = Rel $\cap$ Rz|yRx . zRx .$\mathtt{o}_{x}$. y1'z|　　Df
>
> ·2　Rε Nc+1 .=. $\breve{\mathrm{R}}$$\varepsilon$ 1+Nc
> ·3　1+1 = (Nc+1)$\cap$(1+Nc)　　　　　　　　　　　　Df

Nc+1 is the class of many-one relations. The symbol Nc+1

indicates that, if we have xRy, when x is given, there is only one possible y, but that, when y is given, there is some cardinal number of x's, which satisfies the condition xRy. Similarly, $1 \rightarrow Nc$ is the class of the converses of many-one relations, and $1 \rightarrow 1$ is the class of one-one relations.

·31 $Nc \rightarrow 1 = Rel \cap R\tilde{\jmath}(x\varepsilon\varrho \mathbin{\supset}_{\cdot_x} \cdot \breve{\varrho}x \varepsilon Elm)$

·32 $1 \rightarrow Nc = Rel \cap R\varepsilon(x\varepsilon\breve{\varrho} \cdot \mathbin{\supset}_x \cdot \varrho x \varepsilon Elm)$

·4 $1' \varepsilon 1 \rightarrow 1$
 [Prop 4·34·4 .ɔ. Prop]

·5 $R\varepsilon 1 \rightarrow 1 \mathbin{.\supset.} \breve{R} \varepsilon 1 \rightarrow 1$

·6 $R\varepsilon 1 \rightarrow Nc \mathbin{.\supset.} R\breve{R} \mathbin{\supset} 1'$

One does not have $R\breve{R} = 1'$, since the domain of $R\breve{R}$ is the same as that of R, which is in general only a part of the domain of $1'$.

 [$xR\breve{R}y \mathbin{.\supset.} \exists z\tilde{\jmath}(x,y\varepsilon \varrho z) : R\varepsilon 1 \rightarrow Nc \mathbin{.\supset.} \varrho z \varepsilon Elm \mathbin{.\therefore\supset.} Prop$]

·7 $R,S\varepsilon 1 \rightarrow 1 \mathbin{.\supset.} RS \varepsilon 1 \rightarrow 1$

·8 $R,S\varepsilon Nc \rightarrow 1 \cdot u\varepsilon Cls \cdot u\mathbin{\supset}\varrho \cdot \breve{\varrho}u \mathbin{\supset}\sigma \cdot RS = P \mathbin{.\supset.} \breve{\sigma}(\breve{\varrho}u) = \breve{\pi}u$

 [$x\varepsilon u \cdot y \; 1' \; 1x\breve{\varrho} \mathbin{.\supset.} y\varepsilon\sigma \mathbin{.\supset:} z \; 1' \; 1y\breve{\sigma} \mathbin{.\supset.} xRSz \mathbin{.\therefore\supset.} \breve{\sigma}(\breve{\varrho}u) \mathbin{\supset} \breve{\pi}u$ |1|

  $x\varepsilon u \cdot xRSz \mathbin{.\supset.} \exists \sigma \neg y\tilde{\jmath}(xR y \cdot ySz) \mathbin{.\supset.} y\breve{\varrho}u \cdot z\varepsilon\breve{\sigma}(\breve{\varrho}u) :$

  $\breve{\supset.} \breve{\pi}u \mathbin{\supset} \breve{\sigma}(\breve{\varrho}u)$ |2|

 |1| . |2| .ɔ. Prop]

✱ 6·1 $S\varepsilon Nc \rightarrow 1 \cdot R = S\breve{S} \mathbin{.\supset.} R^2\mathbin{\supset}R \cdot R = \breve{R}$

 [$xRz \mathrel{.=.} \exists y\tilde{\jmath}(xSy \cdot zSy)$ |1|

  $zRw \mathrel{.=.} \exists v\tilde{\jmath}(zSv \cdot wSv)$ |2|

  $S\varepsilon Nc \rightarrow 1 \cdot zSy \cdot zSv \mathbin{.\supset.} y1'v$ |3|

  $|\dot{1}|.|2|.|3| \mathbin{.\supset.} xRz \cdot zRw \mathbin{.\supset.} \exists y\tilde{\jmath}(xSy \cdot wSy) \mathbin{.\supset.} xRw \mathbin{:\supset.} R^2 \mathbin{\supset} R$ |4|

  $xRz \mathrel{.=.} \exists y\tilde{\jmath}(xSy \cdot zSy) \mathrel{.=.} \exists y\tilde{\jmath}(zSy \cdot xSy) \mathrel{.=.} zRx \mathbin{:\supset.} \breve{R} = R$ |5|

  |4|.|5| .ɔ. Prop]

·2 $R\varepsilon rel \cdot R^2\mathbin{\supset}R \cdot R = \breve{R} \cdot \exists R \mathbin{.\supset.} \exists Nc \rightarrow 1 \cap S\tilde{\jmath}(R = S\breve{S})$

 [$xSu \mathrel{.=.} x\varepsilon\varrho \cdot u = \breve{\varrho}x \mathbin{:\supset:}$

  $xSu \cdot ySu \mathrel{.=.} x,y\varepsilon\varrho \cdot u = \breve{\varrho}x = \breve{\varrho}y \mathbin{.\supset.} xRy \mathbin{:\supset.} S\breve{S} \mathbin{\supset} R$ |1|

  $R^2\mathbin{\supset}R \cdot R = \breve{R} \cdot \exists R \mathbin{.\supset:} \varrho x \mathbin{.\supset}_x \cdot x\varepsilon \breve{\varrho} x$ |2|

  |2| . Hp|1| .ɔ: $xRy \mathbin{.\supset.} x,y\varepsilon \breve{\varrho}x \mathbin{.\supset.} x\breve{S}\varrho x \cdot y\breve{S}\varrho x \mathbin{.\supset.} x\breve{S}\breve{S}y \mathbin{:\supset.} R\mathbin{\supset}\breve{S}\breve{S}$ |3|

  |1| . |3| .ɔ. Prop]

P6·2 is the converse of P6·1. It affirms that all relations which are transitive, symmetrical, and non-null can be analysed as products of a many-one relation and its converse, and the demonstration gives a way in which we are able to do this, without proving that there are not other ways of doing it. P6·2 is presupposed in the definitions by abstraction, and it shows that in general these definitions do not give a single individual but a class, since the class of relations S is not in general an element. For each relation S of this class, and for all terms x of R, there is an individual that the definition by abstraction indicates; but the other relations S of that class do not in general give the same individual. This will be explained better in the applications, for example in the following section. Meanwhile, we can always take the class $\breve{\varrho}x$, which appears in the demonstration of Prop 6·2, as the individual indicated by the definition by abstraction; thus for example the cardinal number of a class u will be the class of classes similar to u.

§2. CARDINAL NUMBERS

✱   1·1 $u,r\,\varepsilon\,\text{Cls}\,.\,\mathbin{\cdot}\!\,:\;u\,\text{sim}\,v\,.\!=\!.\,\exists\,1\dotplus1\cap R\!s(u\!\supset\!\varrho\,.\,\breve{\varrho}.u\!=\!r)$ Df

For the definition of $\breve{\varrho}u$ see 1 Prop 1·33.

·11   sim ε rel   Pp

To affirm that a term of constant value, such as 'sim', belongs to this or that class, we always need some Pp.

·2 $u\,\varepsilon\,\text{Cls}\,.\,\mathbin{\cdot}\!\,.\,u\,\text{sim}\,u$
    [$1'\,\varepsilon\,1\dotplus1:R\!=\!1'\,.\,\mathbin{\cdot}\!\,.\,u\!\supset\!\varrho\,.\,\breve{\varrho}u\!=\!u\!:\!\mathbin{\cdot}.$ Prop]
·21 $u,\,v\,\varepsilon\,\text{Cls}\,.\,\mathbin{\cdot}\!:u\,\text{sim}\,v\,.\!=\!.\,v\,\text{sim}\,u$
    [§1 Prop 5·5 .:. Prop]
·22 $u,\,v,\,w\,\varepsilon\,\text{Cls}\,.\,\mathbin{\cdot}\!\,:u\,\text{sim}\,v\,.\,v\,\text{sim}\,w\,.\mathbin{\cdot}\!.\,u\,\text{sim}\,w$
    [§ 1 Prop 5·7 .:. Prop.]
·3 $\exists\,\text{Nc}\dotplus1\cap S\!s(\text{sim}=S\breve{S})$
    [1.11·2·21·22. § 1 Prop 6·2 .:. Prop]
·4 $S=\text{Nc}\dotplus1\cap S\!s\,(\text{sim}=S\breve{S})$ Df

See the note at the end of §1. If we wish to define cardinal number by abstraction, we can only define it as a class of classes, of which each has a one-one correspondence with the class 'cardinal number' and to which belong every class that has such a correspondence. This results from proposition ·52 and ·54 below.

·5 $S \varepsilon \mathsf{S}$.ɔ. $\sigma =$ Cls [sim $= S\breve{S} : u\varepsilon$ Cls .ɔu . u sim u :ɔ.
    $u\varepsilon$ Cls .ɔu. ꓱ $x\mathsf{э}(uSx)$]

·51 $S, S' \varepsilon \mathsf{S}$.ɔ. $S\breve{S}'$ ε $1\rightarrow 1$

[$x\breve{S}S'y$. $x\breve{S}S'y'$.=. ꓱ Cls $\cap$ $u\mathsf{э}(uSx$. uS $y)$. ꓱ Cls $\cap$ $u'\mathsf{э}(u'Sx$. $u'S'y')$ |1|

uSx . $u'Sx$.ɔ. u sim u' .ɔ. u $S'\breve{S}'u'$.ɔ. ꓱ $y''\mathsf{э}(uS'y''$. $u'S'y'')$ |2|

|1| . |2| . $S, S' \varepsilon$ Nc$\rightarrow$1 .ɔ. $y1'y''$. $y'1'y''$.ɔ. $y1'y'$.ɔ. $\breve{S}S'$ ε Nc$\rightarrow$1 |3|

|3| .ɔ. $\breve{S}'S$ ε Nc$\rightarrow$1 .ɔ. $\breve{S}$ S' ε $1\rightarrow$Nc |4| |3|.|4| .ɔ. Prop]

·52 $S, S' \varepsilon \mathsf{S}$.ɔ. $\breve{\sigma}$ sim $\breve{\sigma'}$

[$x\varepsilon\sigma$.ɔ. ꓱ Cls $\cap$ $u\mathsf{э}$ (uSx) |1|
Prop 1·5 . $u\varepsilon$Cls .ɔ. ꓱ σ $\cap$ $y\mathsf{э}(uS'y)$ |2|

|1| . |2| .ɔ: $x\varepsilon\breve{\sigma}$.ɔx. ꓱ$\breve{\sigma'}$ $\cap$ $y\mathsf{э}(x\breve{S}S'y)$ |3|

|3| .ɔ: $y\varepsilon\breve{\sigma'}$.ɔy. ꓱ$\breve{\sigma}$ $\cap$ $x\mathsf{э}(x\breve{S}S'y)$ |4|

|3| . |4| . Prop 5·1 .ɔ. Prop]

·53 $S \varepsilon$ rel . $R \varepsilon$ $1\rightarrow$Nc . $\breve{\sigma}$ ɔ ϱ .ɔ. $SR\breve{R}\breve{S} = S\breve{S}$

[$\breve{\sigma}$ ɔ ϱ .ɔ: $x Sy$.ɔx,y. ꓱ$z\mathsf{э}(yRz)$ |1|

$R \varepsilon$ $1\rightarrow$Nc .ɔ: yRz . $z\breve{R}y'$.ɔ. $y1'y'$ |2|

|1| . |2| .ɔ. $SR\breve{R} = S1'$ |3|

|3| . § 1 Prop 4·33 .ɔ. $SR\breve{R} = S$.ɔ. Prop]

·54 $S \varepsilon \mathsf{S}$. k sim $\breve{\sigma}$.ɔ. ꓱ$\cap$ $S'\mathsf{э}(k = \breve{\sigma'}.)$

[k sim $\breve{\sigma}$.=. ꓱ $1\rightarrow 1$ $\cap$ $R\mathsf{э}(k\varrho\breve{\sigma}$. $\varrho k = \breve{\sigma})$ |1|
|1| . Prop 1·5 .ɔ:$u\varepsilon$ Cls .ɔu. ꓱ $k\cap x\mathsf{э}(uSRx)$ |2|

$S \varepsilon$ Nc$\rightarrow$1 . $R \varepsilon$$\rightarrow$1 .ɔ: SR ε Nc$\rightarrow$1 |3|
Prop ·53 .ɔ. SR $\breve{R}\breve{S} = S\breve{S} =$ sim |4|
|2| . |3| . |4| . ɔ . Prop]

Propositions ·52 and ·54 prove that all classes which form the domains of different relations of the class S are similar (sim), and that all classes similar to one of them belong to this class of classes. The arithmetic of cardinal numbers applies in its entirety to each of these classes; but to develop the theory of finite numbers completely, one needs mathematical induction. (See §4.)

❋   2.   S$\varepsilon$$\varsigma$.$\mathfrak{o}$::

·1 $u,v\varepsilon$ Cls .$\mathfrak{o}$: $\imath\breve{\sigma}u > \imath\breve{\sigma}v$.=. -($usimv$) . $\exists$Cls$w\mathfrak{z}$ ∩ ($w$sim$v$. $w\mathfrak{o}u$)   Df

·2 $\imath\breve{\sigma}u < \imath\breve{\sigma}v$.=. $\imath\breve{\sigma}v > \imath\breve{\sigma}u$ Df

·3 $u=\bigwedge . v=\bigwedge$.$\mathfrak{o}$. u sim v

  [Rε 1→1 . $u=\bigwedge$.$\mathfrak{o}$. $u\mathfrak{o}\varrho$. $\varrho u = \bigwedge$ |1|

  |1| . $v=\bigwedge$. Prop 1·1 .$\mathfrak{o}$. Prop]

·4   O$\sigma = \imath\breve{\sigma}\bigwedge$ Df

·5 $\imath x$ sim $\imath y$

  [§1 Prop 1·8 .$\mathfrak{o}$. Prop]

·6 u sim $\imath x$.$\mathfrak{o}$. $u\varepsilon$ Elm

  [u sim $\imath x$.=. $\exists$ 1→1 ∩ R$\mathfrak{z}$($u\mathfrak{o}\varrho$. $\breve{\varrho}u = \imath x$)

  Rε1→1 . $u\mathfrak{o}\varrho$. $\breve{\varrho}u = \imath x$.$\mathfrak{o}$: $y,z\varepsilon u$.$\mathfrak{o}$. yRx . zRx .$\mathfrak{o}$. y1'z .$\mathfrak{o}$. $u\varepsilon$ Elm]

·61 u,v ε Elm .$\mathfrak{o}$. u sim v

  [$u\varepsilon$ Elm . $x\varepsilon u$.$\mathfrak{o}$. u sim $\imath x$ |1|

  $v\varepsilon$ Elm . $y\varepsilon v$.$\mathfrak{o}$. v sim $\imath y$ |2|

  |1| . |2| . Prop 2·5 .$\mathfrak{o}$. Prop]

·7 $1_\sigma = \imath\breve{\sigma}$ ∩ $x\mathfrak{z}$($u\varepsilon$ Elm .$u\mathfrak{c}$. uSx)   Df

❋   3·1   Rε rel . $u\mathfrak{o}\varrho$.$\mathfrak{o}$. $u\varepsilon$ Elm

  $\exists$ rel ∩ R'$\mathfrak{z}$|ϱ'=u : xR'y .=$_{x,y}$. $x\varepsilon u$. xRy|

Hp. §1 Prop 3·8 .$\mathfrak{o}$. $\exists$ rel ∩ R''$\mathfrak{z}$| $\varrho'' = u . \breve{\varrho}'' = \breve{\varrho}u$: $x\varepsilon u$. $y\varepsilon \breve{\varrho}u$.=$_{x,y}$. xR''y|

  R''εrel : xR''y .=$_{y,x}$. $x\varepsilon u$. $y\varepsilon \breve{\varrho}u$: R∩R'' = R' :$\mathfrak{o}$:

  xR'y .=. $x\varepsilon u$. $y\varepsilon \breve{\varrho}u$. xRy .=. $x\varepsilon u$. xRy :$\mathfrak{o}$. Prop]

·11   Rε rel . $u\mathfrak{o}\varrho$.$\mathfrak{o}$. rel ∩ R'$\mathfrak{z}$ |xR'y .=. $x\varepsilon u$. xRy| $\mathfrak{z}$Elm

[R$_1$,R$_2$$\varepsilon$rel∩R'$\mathfrak{z}$|$xR'y$.=.$x\varepsilon u$.$xRy$|.$\mathfrak{o}$: xR$_1y$.=. $x\varepsilon u$. xRy.=.xR$_2y$:$\mathfrak{o}$. Prop]

P·1·11 point out that one can always find a relation the domain of which is a limited portion of that of a given relation, and equivalent to the given relation in that portion.

·12   Rε rel . $u\mathfrak{o}\varrho$.$\mathfrak{o}$. R$u = \imath$ Rel ∩ R'$\mathfrak{z}$|xR'y .=. $x\varepsilon u$. xRy|

                                                 Df

·2 $u,u'\varepsilon$ Cls . u sim u' .$\mathfrak{o}$. $\exists$ 1→1 ∩ R$\mathfrak{z}$($\breve{\varrho}=u$. $u'=\breve{\varrho}$)

  [u sim u' .$\mathfrak{o}$. $\exists$ 1→1 ∩ R$\mathfrak{z}$($u\mathfrak{o}\varrho$. $\breve{\varrho}u = u'$) |1|

  |1| . Prop3·1 .$\mathfrak{o}$. Prop]

·3 $u,v,u',v'\varepsilon$ Cls . $uv=\bigwedge$. $u'v'=\bigwedge$. u sim u' . v sim v' .$\mathfrak{o}$.

    $u\smile v$ sim $u'\smile v'$

[$u \sin u'$. Prop·2 .ɔ. Ǝ 1∔1 ⌢ Rɜ($u=\varrho$. $u'=\tilde{\varrho}$)

$v \sin v'$. Prop·2 .ɔ. Ǝ 1∔1 ⌢ R ɜ($v=\varrho'$. $v'=\tilde{\varrho'}$)

$uv=\bigwedge$. $u'v'=\bigwedge$. P= R∪R' .ɔ. $\pi=u\smile v$. $\tilde{\pi}=u'\smile v'$. Pɛ 1∔1 .ɔ. Prop]

·4 $k\varepsilon$ Cls' 1∔1 : $R_1,R_2 \varepsilon k$. R_1 0' R_2 .ɔ $\underset{R_1,R_2}{.}$. $\varrho_1 \frown \varrho_2 = \bigwedge$.

$\varrho_1 \frown \varrho_2 = \bigwedge$:ɔ. $\smile'k \, \varepsilon \, 1∔1$

[$x(\smile'k)y$.≡. Ǝ $k\frown$ Rɜ(xRy) .ɔ. Ǝ $k\frown$ Rɜ($x\varepsilon\varrho$)

$R_1,R_2 \varepsilon k$. R_1 0' R_2 $\underset{R_1,R_2}{.}$. $\varrho_1 \frown \varrho_2 = \bigwedge$:ɔ: Ǝ $k\frown$ Rɜ($x\varepsilon\varrho$) .ɔ$_x$ ᴧ $k\frown$ Rɜ($x\varepsilon\varrho$) ɛ Elm :

ɔ.·. Rεk . $x\varepsilon\varrho$.ɔ: $x(\smile'k)y$.≡. xRy .·.ɔ. Prop]

3·41 Rε 1∔1 . $\varrho,\tilde{\varrho}$ ɛ Cls'Cls : xRy .ɔx,y. $x \sin y$:

$x,x'\varepsilon\varrho$. x0'x'.ɔx,x'. $xx'=\bigwedge$: $y,y'\tilde{\varepsilon}\tilde{\varrho}$ .y0'y'.ɔy,y'. $\varrho\varrho'=\bigwedge$:ɔ. $\smile'\varrho$ sim $\smile'\tilde{\varrho}$

[xRy .ɔx,y. $x$sim$y$:ɔ: xRy .ɔ. Ǝ 1∔1 ⌢ R'ɜ($x=\varrho'$. $y=\tilde{\varrho}'$)

$x\varepsilon\varrho$.ɔx. R$_x$ ɛ 1∔1 ⌢ R'ɜ($x=\varrho'$. $\tilde{\iota}\varrho x=\tilde{\varrho}'$) : $k=$ 1∔1 ⌢ R''ɜ|ƎϱE ⌢ xɜ(R''1'R$_x$)|:

P= $\smile'k$. Prop 3·4 :ɔ. Pε 1∔1 . $\pi=\smile'\varrho$. $\tilde{\pi}=\smile'\tilde{\varrho}$.ɔ. Prop]

This proposition gives the foundation of arithmetical addition, in a form which permits the addition of an infinite number with finite or infinite numbers.

3·5 $u\varepsilon$ Cls . $x,y\varepsilon u$.ɔ. $u\smile\iota x$ sim $u\smile\iota y$

[$u\smile\iota x\smile\iota y$ sim $u\smile\iota x\smile\iota y$. ιx sim ιy . Prop 3·3 .ɔ. Prop]

·51 $u,v\varepsilon$ Cls . u sim v . $x\varepsilon u$. $y\varepsilon v$. ⊃. $u\smile\iota x$ sim $v\smile\iota y$

[Rε 1∔1 . $u=\varrho$. $v=\tilde{\varrho}$. xRy .ɔ. Prop |1|

Rε 1∔1 . $u=\varrho$. $v=\tilde{\varrho}$. -(xRy) .ɔ.·. Ǝ $v\frown z\varepsilon$(xRz) : xRz .ɔ$_z$. y0'z .·.

ɔ. $u\smile\iota x$ sim $v\smile\iota z$ |2|

Prop3·5 .ɔ. $v\smile\iota z$ sim $v\smile\iota y$ |3|

:|1.:2:.;3| .ɔ. Prop]

·52 $u,r\varepsilon$ Cls . $x\varepsilon u$. $y\varepsilon v$.ɔ: u sim v .≡. $u\smile\iota x$ sim $v\smile\iota y$

✳ 4. Sεg .⊃::

·1 $m,n\varepsilon\tilde{\sigma}$.⊃. $m∔n = \tilde{\iota\sigma} \frown x\mathsf{ɜ}\{uSm$. vSn . $uv=\bigwedge$.ɔu,v. $u\smile v$ S$x\}$

' Df

This definition depends on Prop 3·3.

·2 $k\bar{\sigma}\sigma$.ɔ. $\Sigma k = \bar{\imath\sigma} \cap p\mathfrak{Z}\{u\varepsilon$ Cls'Cls . u sim k : $x,y\varepsilon u$.ɔx,y. $xy = \wedge$

    : $\exists\, 1 \rightarrow 1 \cap R\mathfrak{Z}(u = \varrho$. $k \bar{=} \varrho : x\varepsilon u$. xRy .ɔx. xSy) :ɔu. $\surd{}'u\, Sp\}$

                                                          Df

This definition depends on Prop 3·41. It is important to note that this defines the sum of a finite or infinite class of finite or infinite numbers; but it is necessary for all these numbers to be different, because otherwise, one cannot define them as a class of numbers but only as numbers of classes. For the case where there are some equal numbers in the summation, different considerations are required, and especially multiplication, which I do not develop here in order to avoid excess length.

·3 $1_\sigma 0' 0_\sigma$

    [uS$1\dot{\sigma}$.ɔ. $u\varepsilon$ Elm : vS0σ .ɔ. $v = \wedge$: $\wedge$-ε Elm :ɔ. Prop]

This proposition proves that for any relation whatsoever of the class S, 1σ differs from 0σ.

·4 $x\bar{\varepsilon}\sigma$.ɔ. $x + 1_\sigma = \bar{\imath\sigma} \cap y\mathfrak{Z}\{uSx$. $z = \varepsilon u$.ɔu,z. $u \cup \iota z\, Sy\}$ Df

·41 $x\varepsilon\bar{\sigma} \rightarrow \iota 0_\sigma$.ɔ.$x - 1_\sigma = \bar{\imath\sigma} \cap y\mathfrak{Z}\{uSx$. $z\bar{\varepsilon}u$.ɔu,z. $u \rightarrow \iota z\, Sy\}$ Df

This definition depends on Prop 3·51.

4·5 $x\varepsilon\,\bar{\sigma} \rightarrow \iota 0_\sigma$. ɔ: $x - 1_\sigma\, 1'x$.=. $\sigma 1'x + 1_\sigma$

    [$x - 1_\sigma\, 1'\, x$. uS $x - 1_\sigma$. vSx .ɔ. u sim v |1|

    |1| . Prop 3·52 .ɔ.·. $z = \varepsilon u$. $w - \varepsilon v$.⊃: u sim v .=. $u \cup \iota z$ sim $v \cup \iota w$.·.

    ɔ: $x - 1_\sigma\, 1'\, x$.=. $x\, 1'\, x + 1_\sigma$]

·6 $x\varepsilon\,\bar{\sigma} \rightarrow \iota 0_\sigma$.ɔ: $x - 1_\sigma\, 0'\, x$.=. $x\, 0'\, x + 1_\sigma$

    [·5 . Transp .ɔ. Prop]

Propositions ·5 and ·6 prove that if the number of a class is identical with the number of a class which is obtained by subtracting a term from the given class, then this number is also identical to the number of the class which is obtained by adding a term to the given class, and vice versa. Since we have proved (4·3) that 1σ is different from 0σ, we have the means of proving that in the class of numbers which obey mathematical induction, starting from 0σ, two successive numbers are never equal. To develop this subject, it is necessary to examine the theory of progressions, that is, of the series of which the ordinal number is ω.

§3. PROGRESSIONS

✱ 1.1 $\omega = \text{Cls} \cap u \ni \{ \exists 1 \dot{+} 1 \cap R \ni (u \ni \varrho \, . \, \varrho \breve{u} \ni u \, . \, \exists \, u \dot{-} \varrho \breve{u} :$

        $s\varepsilon \, \text{Cls} \, . \, \exists \, su \dot{-} \varrho \breve{u} \, . \, \varrho \breve{(su)} \ni s \, . \, \ni s \, . \, u \ni s \}$ **Df**

This is a definition of the ordinal number ω, or rather, if one wishes, a definition of the class of denumerable classes. The ordinal numbers are, in effect, classes of series. The class ω is the simplest of the classes of infinite series. Since the definition does not presuppose numbers, it will be good to give to this type of series a name which does not imply numbers. Therefore I call this the class of *progressions*. Here is the definition in words: ω is the class of the classes u such that there is a one-one relation R such that u is contained in the domain of R, and that the class of terms to which the different u's have the relation R is contained in u, without being identical with u, and which, if s is any class whatsoever to which belongs at least one of the terms of u to which any u does not have the relation R, and to which belongs all terms of u to which a term of the common portion of u and s has the relation R, then the class u is contained in the class s.

  ·11 $R\varepsilon 1 \dot{+} 1 \, . \, \breve{\varrho} \ni \varrho \, . \, \exists \varrho \dot{-} \breve{\varrho} \, . \, \ni \, .$

   $\omega \varrho = u \ni \{ u \ni \varrho \, . \, \varrho \breve{u} \ni u \, . \, \exists \, u \dot{-} \varrho \breve{u} : s\varepsilon \text{Cls} \, . \, \exists \, su \dot{-} \varrho \breve{u} \, . \, \varrho \breve{(su)} \ni s \, . \, \ni s \, . \, u \ni s \}$ **Df**

$\omega \varrho$ is the class of progressions of which R is the generating relation.

  ·12 $u\varepsilon\omega \, . \, \ni \, . \, \text{Rel}u = 1 \dot{+} 1 \cap R \ni (u\varepsilon \, \omega \varrho)$ **Df**

  ·13 $\text{Induct} = \therefore \, u\varepsilon\omega \, . \, R\varepsilon \, \text{Rel}u \, . \, \ni : s\varepsilon \, \text{Cls} \, . \, \exists \, su \dot{-} \varrho \breve{u} \, . \, \breve{\varrho} \, (su)$

        $\ni s \, . \, \ni s \, . \, u \ni s$ **Df**

  ·2 $u\varepsilon\omega \, . \, R\varepsilon \, \text{Rel}u \, . \, \ni \, . \, u \dot{-} \varrho \breve{u} \, \varepsilon \, \text{Elm}$

     $[\, x\varepsilon \, u \dot{-} \varrho \breve{u} \, . \, s = \iota x \cup \varrho \breve{u} \, . \, \ni \, . \, \breve{\varrho} (su) \ni s \, . \, \exists s \dot{-} \varrho \breve{u}$ |1|

     $|1| \, . \, \text{Induct} \, . \, \ni \, . \, u \ni s \, . \, \ni \, . \, u \ni \iota x \cup \varrho \breve{u} \, . \, \ni \, . \, u \dot{-} \varrho \breve{u} \ni \iota x \, . \, \ni \, . \, \text{Prop} \,]$

$R\varepsilon \, 1 \dot{+} 1 \, . \, \breve{\varrho} \ni \varrho \, . \, \exists \varrho \dot{-} \breve{\varrho} \, . \, u\varepsilon\omega \varrho \, . \, \ni \, : :$

  ·3 $\text{O}u = \iota(u \dot{-} \varrho \breve{u})$ **Df**

  ·31 $x\varepsilon u \, . \, \ni \, . \, \text{scq}x = \iota \varrho x$

  ·4 $P\varepsilon \, \text{Rel} \, . \, \ni \, . \, \text{PO}_u = 1'_\pi$ **Df**

  ·5 $P\varepsilon \, \text{Rel} \, . \, n\varepsilon u \, . \, \ni \, . \, \text{Pscq}n = P_n P$ **Df**

P1·4·5 define by induction the finite powers of relations. This definition is effected by means of the terms of u. In the theory of progressions one cannot do without the powers of relations; therefore, if one wishes to make that theory independent of numbers, it is necessary to define the powers in a manner which does not introduce numbers. The symbols $1'\pi$ signifies identity in the class π, and the null relation everywhere else. See §2 Prop 3·12.

·6 $1u = \imath\tilde{\varrho}\,(0u)$ Df

·7 $P\varepsilon\,1\dotplus1\,.\,\supset.\,P^{1u} = P$
     $[P^{1u} = 1'\pi P = P\,]$

1·8 $P\varepsilon\,1\dotplus1\,.\,a\varepsilon u\,.\,\supset.\,P^a\,\varepsilon\,1\dotplus1$
      $[P^{0u}\varepsilon\,1\dotplus1$ |1|
      $P\varepsilon 1\dotplus1\,.\,§1\text{Prop}\,5·7\,.\,\supset:\,a\varepsilon u\,.\,P^a\,\varepsilon\,1\dotplus1\,.\,\supset.\,P^{seqa}\,\varepsilon 1\dotplus1$ |2|
      $|1|.|2|\,.\,\text{Induct}\,.\,\supset.\,\text{Prop}\,]$

·81 $x\varepsilon u\,.\,0_u\,R^x z\,.\,\supset.\,x1'z$
      $[\,x1'0_u\,.\,0_u\,R^x\,z\,.\,\supset.\,z1'0_u$ |1|
      $0_u\,R^x\,x\,.\,\supset.\,0_u\,R^{seqx}\,seqx$ |2| $|1|.|2|\,.\,\text{Induct}\,.\,\supset.\,\text{Prop}\,]$

·82 $v\varepsilon\omega\,.\,R'\varepsilon\text{Relv}\,.\,x\varepsilon u\,.\,0_v\,R'^x z\,.\,\supset.\,z\varepsilon v$
      $[\,x1'0_u\,.\,0_v\,R'^x z\,.\,\supset.\,z1'0_v\,.\,\supset.\,z\varepsilon v$ |1|
      $0_v\,R'^x z\,.\,z\varepsilon v\,.\,\supset.\,0_v\,R'^{seqx}\,seqx\,.\,seq\,z\,\varepsilon v$ |2|
      $|1|.|2|\,.\,\text{Induct}\,.\,\supset.\,\text{Prop}\,]$

1·9 $v\varepsilon\omega\,.\,R'\varepsilon\,\text{Relv}'\,.\,\supset.\,\exists\,1\dotplus1\,\cap\,P\mathfrak{z}\{u=\pi\,.\,v=\tilde{\pi}:\,x,y\varepsilon u\,.$
      $x R y\,.\,\supset.\,x,y\,.\,\imath\,\tilde{\pi}\,x\,R'\,\imath\tilde{\pi}y\}$

This proposition affirms that two progressions are always two similar series, that is to say that one can find a one-one relation of which the domain is one of the two progressions, and of which the converse relation has the other progression for its domain, and which is such that terms which precede in one series correspond to terms which precede in the other, and vice versa.

[§ 1 Prop 1·8 .⊃. $\exists$ rel $\cap$ P$_0\mathfrak{z}(\pi_0 = \imath 0_u\,.\,\tilde{\pi}_0 = \imath 0 v)$ |1|
Prop 81 .⊃: $x\varepsilon u\,.\,0_u\,R^x\,z\,.\,\supset.\,z\varepsilon u$ |2|
Prop 82 .⊃: $x\varepsilon u\,.\,0_v\,R'^x\,z'\,.\,\supset.\,z'\varepsilon v$ |3|

$|1|\,.\,|2|\,.\,|3|\,.\,\supset:\,x\varepsilon u\,.\,z\tilde{R}^x\,P_0 R'^x\,z`\,.\,\supset.\,x\varepsilon u\,.\,z'\varepsilon v\,.\,z1'x$ |4|

§1 Prop 5·7 . §3 Prop 1·8 .⊃. $\tilde{R}^x\,P_0 R'^x\,\varepsilon\,1\dotplus1$ |5|

$|4|.|5|\,.\,Q = \text{rel}\,\cap\,F\mathfrak{z}|\exists u\,\cap\,x\mathfrak{z}(F = \tilde{R}^x\,P_0\,R'^x\,)|\,.\,P = \smile Q\,.\,\supset\,\therefore$

$P\varepsilon\,1\dotplus1\,.\,u=\pi\,.\,v=\tilde{\pi}:\,x,y\varepsilon u\,.\,x R y\,.\,\supset_{x,y}.\,\imath\pi x R'\imath\pi y\,\therefore\,\supset.\,\text{Prop}\,]$

1·91 $u'\,\text{sim}\,u\,.\,\supset.\,u'\varepsilon\omega$

In this proposition we prove that any class similar to a progression is itself a progression. If P is the one-one relation between u and u', and R the generating relation of u, then $\breve{P}RP$ is the generating relation of u'.

[$u'\mathrm{sim}u$.ɔ. ꓱ 1→1 ∧ P'ꙅ(uɔπ' . π̆'u = u') |1|

Pꙅ 1→1 . uɔπ . π̆u = u' : xꙅu .ɔₓ. x' = iπx . seqx' = iπ(seqx) :ɔ.

x'P̆x . xR seqx . seqx P seq x' .ɔ. x' P̆RP seq x' |2|

Hp |2| . P̆RP = R' .ɔ. R'ꙅ 1→1 . ϱ̆'u ɔu' |3|

Hp |3| . x₀' = iπ0ᵤ .ɔ. x₀' = iu̯–ϱ̆'u' |4|

Hp |3| . ꙅꙅ Cls . iu'–ϱ̆'u' ꙅꙅ . ϱ̆'(u'ꙅ) ɔꙅ ,ɔ.˙.

0ᵤ (Pꙅ)ꙅ : x(Pꙅ)u'ꙅ .ɔₓ . seqx (Pꙅ) u'ꙅ |5|

|5| . Induct .ɔ: xꙅu ,ɔₓ. x̯(Pꙅ)u'ꙅ |6|

Hp |5| . |6| . Pꙅ 1→1 .ɔ: x'ꙅu' .ɔ x'. x'ꙅꙅ |7|

|3| . |4| . |7| .ɔ. Prop]

✻ 2. ´Rꙅ1→1 . ϱ̆ ɔ ϱ . ꓱ ϱ̆–ϱ . uꙅ ωϱ . ɔ:꞉

·1   ϱ̆u ꙅ ωϱ

[Prop1·91 : R' = R̆RR .ɔ. ϱ̆u ꙅ ωϱ' |1|
|1| . R'ɔR .ɔ. Prop]

·11   xꙅu .ɔ.   ϱ̆ˣu ꙅ ωϱ

[u = ϱ⁰ᵤ u . Prop 2·1 . Induct .ɔ. Prop]

Note. ϱ̆ˣu = yꙅ| ꓱuꙆꙅ (zRˣ y)|.

·12   xꙅu .ɔ. x0' seq x

[ꓱu–ϱu . u –ϱu ꙅ Elm .ɔ. 0ᵤ 0'1ᵤ |1|

Prop 11 . xꙅu .ɔ. ϱ̆ˣuꙅωϱ . x1'0ϱ̆ˣ u |2|
|1| . |2| .ɔ: xꙅu ,ₓ. x0' seqx]

P2·11 proves that we can omit as many terms as we wish at the beginning of a progression without its ceasing to be a progression: P2·12 proves that any term of a progression differs from its successor.

·13   vɔ–v . ɔ. ꓱv–ϱ̆v

[vɔ ϱ̆v .ɔ.˙. 0ᵤ –ꙅv : ꙅx u–v .ɔₓ. seqx –ꙅv |1|

|1| . Induct .ɔ. –ꓱu∩ꓱꙅ .ɔ. v = ⋀ |2|

|2| .ɔ: vɔu . ꓱv .ɔ. ꓱv–ϱ̆v . u∩ɔv :ɔ. Prop]

2·14   vɔu . ꓱv . ϱ̆vɔv .ɔ. vꙅ ωϱ.

[Prop 2·13 .ɔ. ꓱv–ϱ̆v |1|

Hp .ɔ. ϱ̆vɔv |2|

vɔu . uɔϱ .ɔ. vɔϱ |3|

xꙅv . ϱ̆vɔv ɔ v .ɔ. seq x ɔv :ɔ: xꙅv .ɔₓ. ϱ̆ˣu ɔ ɔv :ɔ: ꓱx v–ϱ̆v .ɔ. v = ϱ̆ˣ u |4|
|4| . Prop 2·11 .ɔ. Prop]

$\cdot 15 \quad x \varepsilon \varrho u \, . \, \supset \, . \, x0'0u$

$[\, x \varepsilon \varrho u \, . 0u - \varepsilon \, \widetilde{\varrho} u \, . \supset . \, \text{Prop} \,]$

$\cdot 16 \quad x, z \varepsilon u \, . \, y \varepsilon \varrho u \, . \, x \mathrm{R}^y z \, . \supset . \, x0'z$

$[\, u' = \widetilde{\varrho}^x u \, . \supset . \, u_{,\varepsilon \varrho} \omega \, . \, x = 0_u \, . \, z \varepsilon u' \quad |1| \quad\quad |1| \, . \, \text{Prop } 2 \cdot 15 \, . \supset . \, \text{Prop} \,]$

This proposition proves that the same term can never recur in a progression; every term differs from all preceding terms.

$\cdot 2 \quad a, b \varepsilon u \, . \, \supset . \, \exists u \cap c \mathfrak{z}(a \mathrm{R}^b c)$

$[\, b1'0u \, . \supset . \, a \mathrm{R}^b a \quad\quad\quad\quad\quad\quad\quad\quad\quad\quad\quad\quad |1|$

$a \mathrm{R}^b c \, . \, c \varepsilon u \, . \supset . \, a \mathrm{R}^{\mathrm{seq} b}_{\mathrm{seq} c} \, . \, \mathrm{seq} c \, \varepsilon u \quad\quad\quad\quad\quad |2|$

$|1| \, . \, |2| \, . \, \text{Induct} \, . \supset . \, \text{Prop} \,]$

$\cdot 21 \quad a, b \varepsilon u \, . \, \supset . \, u \cap c \mathfrak{z}(a \mathrm{R}^b c) \, \varepsilon \, \text{Elm}$

$[\, \text{Prop } 1 \cdot 8 \, . \supset . \, \text{Prop} \,]$

$\cdot 3 \quad a, b \varepsilon u \, . \, \supset . \, a {+} b = \iota u \cap c \mathfrak{z}(a \mathrm{R}^b c) \quad\quad\quad\quad\quad\quad \text{Df}$

$\cdot 4 \quad a, b, x \varepsilon u \, . \, \supset . \, \exists u \cap y \mathfrak{z} \{ x (\mathrm{R}^a)^b y \}$

$[\, b1'0u \, . \supset . \, x (\mathrm{R}^a)^b x \quad\quad\quad\quad\quad\quad\quad\quad\quad\quad\quad |1|$

$x (\mathrm{R}^a)^b y \, . \, \exists u \cap z \mathfrak{z}(y \mathrm{R}^a z) \, . \supset . \, \exists u \cap z \mathfrak{z} | x (\mathrm{R}^a)^b \mathrm{R}^a z |$

$\supset . \, \exists u \cap z \mathfrak{z} | x (\mathrm{R}^a)^{\mathrm{seq} b} z | \quad\quad\quad\quad\quad\quad\quad\quad\quad |2|$

$|1| \, . \, |2| \, . \, \text{Induct} \, . \supset . \, \text{Prop} \,]$

$\cdot 41 \quad a, b \varepsilon u \, . \, \supset . \, (\mathrm{R}^a)^b \, \varepsilon 1 {+} 1$

$[\, (\mathrm{R}^a \, 0_x \, \varepsilon \, 1' {+} 1 \quad\quad\quad\quad\quad\quad\quad\quad\quad\quad\quad\quad\quad |1|$

$(\mathrm{R}^a)^b \, \varepsilon \, 1 {+} 1 \, . \, \S 1 \text{Prop } 5 \cdot 7 \, . \supset . \, (\mathrm{R}^a)^{\mathrm{seq} b} \, \varepsilon \, 1 {+} 1 \quad\quad |2|$

$|1| \, . \, |2| \, . \, \text{Induct} \, . \supset . \, \text{Prop} \,]$

$\cdot 42 \quad a, b, x \varepsilon u \, . \, \supset . \, u \cap y \mathfrak{z} \{ x (\mathrm{R}^a)^b y \} \, \varepsilon \, \text{Elm}$

$[\, \text{Prop } 2 \cdot 41 \, . \supset . \, \text{Prop} \,]$

$\cdot 43 \quad a, b, x \varepsilon u \, . \, \supset . \, x {+} ab = \iota u \cap y \mathfrak{z} \{ x (\mathrm{R}^a)^b y \} \quad\quad\quad \text{Df}$

$\cdot 44 \quad\quad\quad\quad\quad\quad\quad ab = 0u {+} ab \quad\quad\quad\quad\quad\quad\quad\quad \text{Df}$

$\cdot 45 \quad\quad\quad\quad\quad ab \, 1'c \, . \supset . \, x {+} ab \, 1' \, x {+} c \quad\quad [\, \text{Induct} \,]$

$\cdot 46 \quad\quad\quad\quad\quad ab \, 0'c \, . \supset . \, x {+} ab \, 0' \, x {+} c \quad\quad [\, \text{Induct} \,]$

$\cdot 47 \quad\quad\quad\quad\quad ab \, 1'c \, . = . \, x {+} ab \, 1' \, x {+} c$

$\quad\quad\quad\quad\quad\quad\quad\quad\quad\quad\quad [\, \text{Prop } 2 \cdot 45 \cdot 46 \, . \supset . \, \text{Prop} \,]$

$\cdot 48 \quad a \varepsilon u \, . \, \supset . \, a {+} 0_u = a$

$\quad\quad\quad\quad\quad\quad\quad [\, a {+} 0_u = \iota u \cap x \mathfrak{z}(a \mathrm{R}^{0u} x) = a \,]$

$\cdot 49 \quad a \varepsilon u \, . \, \supset . \, 0_u {+} a = a$

$\quad\quad\quad\quad\quad\quad\quad [\, \text{Prop } 1 \cdot 81 \, . \supset . \, \text{Prop} \,]$

2·5　$a, b \varepsilon u$.⊃. $R^a R^b = R^{a+b}$

[$R^a R^{0u} = R^a = R^{a + 0u}$　　　　　　　　　　　　　　|1|

$R^a R^b = R^{a+b}$.⊃. $R^a R^{seqb} = R^a R^b R = R^{a+b}R = R^{seq(a+b)}$　|2|

$a + seqb = \imath u \cap x_3 (aR^{seqb}x) = \imath u \cap x_3 ; \exists\, y_3(aR^b y \,.\, yRx)\,|$

　　　$= \imath u \cap x_3 ; \imath u \cap (a, y)_3 (O_u R^a \, a \,.\, a R^b \, y \,.\, yRx)\,|$　|3|

|3| . Hp; |2| .⊃. $a + seqb = \imath u \cap x_3 ; \exists\, u \cap y_3 (O_u R^{a+b}y \,.\, yRx)$

　　　　　　　　$= seq(a+b)$　　　　　　|4|

|2| . |4| ;⊃. $R^a R^b = R^{a,+b}$.⊃. $R^a R^{seqb} = R^{a+seqb}$　|5|

|1| . |5| . Induct .⊃. Prop]

·51　$a, b, x \varepsilon u$.⊃. $(x+a)+b = x+(a+b)$

[$(x+a)+b = \imath u \cap z_3 ; \exists\, u \cap y_3(xR^a y \,.\, yR^b z)\,|$

　　　$= \imath u \cap z_3 (xR^a R^b z)$　　　　　　　|1|

|1| . Prop 2·5 .⊃. $(x+a)+b = \imath u \cap z_3(xR^{a+b}z) = x+(a+b)$]

·52　$a, b, x \varepsilon u$.⊃. $x+a+b = (x+a)+b$　　　　Df

·53　$a, b \varepsilon u$.⊃. $a+b = b+a$

[$O_u + O_u = O_u + O_u$　|1|　　$O_u + 1_u = 1_u = 1_u + O_u$　|2|

$a + 1_u = 1_u + a$. ⊃ : $seq a + 1_u = (a+1_u) + 1_u = (1_u + a) + 1_u$　|3|

Hp |3| . |3| . Prop 2·52 .⊃. $seq a + 1_u = 1_u + (a+1_u) + 1_u = 1_u + seq a$　|4|

|2| . |4| . Induct .⊃. $a + 1_u = 1_u + a$　　　　|5|

|3| . $a + b = b + a$.⊃. $a + seqb = a + b + 1_u = a + 1_u + b = 1_u + a + b = 1_u + b + a$

　　　　$= b + 1_u + a = seqb + a$　　|6|

|1| . |6| . Induct .⊃. Prop]

·6　$a \varepsilon u$.⊃. $a 1 u = a$

[$a 1_u = \imath u \cap x_3 ; O_u (R^a)^{1u}x| = \imath u \cap x_3 ; O_u R^a x| = O_u + a = a$]

·60　$a \, 0_u = 0_u a = a$

·61　$a, b \varepsilon u$.⊃. $a(b+1_u) = ab + a$

[$a(O_u + 1_u) = a 1_u = a = a 0_u + a$　　　　　|1|

$a(b+1_u) = ab + a$.⊃.

$a(seqb + 1_u) = \imath u \cap x_3 ; O_u (R^a)^{seqb + 1_u}x$

　　　$= \imath u \cap x_3 ; \exists\, u \cap y_3(O_u R^{ab+a}y \,.\, yR^a x)\,|$

　　　$= \imath u \cap x_3 ; O_u R^{ab+a+a}x|$

　　　$= \imath u \cap x_3 ; O_u R^{aseqb+a}x| = aseqb + a$　|2|

|1| . |2| . Induct .⊃. Prop]

·611　$a, b \varepsilon u$.⊃. $(b+1_u)a = ba + a$

[$(b+1_u)O_u = O_u = bO_u + O_u$　　　　　|1|

$(b+1_u)a = ba + a$.⊃.

$(b+1_u)(a+1_u) = \imath u \cap x_3 ; O_u R^{(b+1u)(a+1u)}x|$

　　　$= \imath u \cap x_3 ; \exists\, y_3(O_u R^{(b+1u)a}y \,.\, yR^{b+1u}x)\,|$

　　　$= \imath u \cap x_3 ; \exists\, y_3(O_u R^{ba+a}y \,.\, yR^{b+1u}x)\,|$

　　　$= ba + a + b + 1_u = ba + b + a + 1_u$　|2|

Prop 2·61 .⊃. $ba + b + a + 1_u = b(a+1_u) + a + 1_u$　|3|

|2| ; |3| .⊃. $(b+1_u)a = ba + a$.⊃. $(b+1_u)(a+1_u) = b(a+1_u) + a + 1_u$ |4|

|1| . |4|. Induct .⊃. Prop]

2·62 $a,b,c\varepsilon u$.⊃. $a(b+c) = ab+ac$

$a(b+0_u) = ab = ab+a0_u$ |1|

$a(b+c) = ab+ac$.⊃. $a(b+c+1_u) = a(b+c)+a = ab+ac+a$ |2|

Prop 2·61 .⊃. $ab+ac+a = ab+a(c+1_u)$ |3|

Prop 2·53 .⊃. $ab+ac+a = ac+ab+a = ac+a(b+1_u) = a(b+1_u)+ac$ |4|

;2| .|3| .|4| .⊃: $a(b+c) = ab+ac$.⊃. $a(b+c+1_u) = ab+a(c+1_u) = a(b+1_u) +ac$ |5|

|1| : |5|. Induct . ⊃ . Prop]

·63 $a,b,c\varepsilon u$.⊃. $(b+c)a = ba+ac$

[$(b+c)0_u = 0_u = b0_u +c0_u$ |1|

$(b+c)a = ba+ca$.⊃. $(b+c)(a+1_u) = (b+c)a+b+c = ba+ca+b+c$

$= ba+b+ca+c$ |2|

Prop 2·61 .⊃: $ba+b = b(a+1_u)$. $ca+c = c(a+1_u)$ |3|

|2| .|3| .⊃: $(b+c)a = ba+ca$.⊃. $(b+c)(a+1_u) = b(a+1_u)+c(a+1_u)$ |4|

|1| . |4|. Induct .⊃. Prop]

·64 $a,b\varepsilon u$.⊃. $ab = ba$

[$a0_u = 0_u = 0_u\, a$ |1|

$ab = ba$.⊃. $a(b+1_u) = ab+a = ba+a = (b+1_u)a$ |2|

|1| . |2|. Induct .⊃. Prop]

We have now proved the formal laws of addition and multiplication: the associative law of addition in P2·51, the commutative law of addition in P2·53, the distributive law in ·62 and ·63, and the commutative law of multiplication in ·64. The associative law of multiplication results immediately (as for all relational products) from the same law for the logical products. In all that precedes we have never presupposed numbers: the entire theory applies to every progression. Hence follows in a general form all the arithmetic of finite numbers.

✱ 3. Rε 1+1 . ϱꞀϱ . Ꞁϱ=ϱ̃ . $u\varepsilon\omega\varrho$. $a,b,c\varepsilon u$.⊃::

·1 Pε 1+1 . yPz . xPseqaz .⊃. xP$^a y$

[x Pseq$a$ z .⊃. ⅎ $u\frown w\eth(x$P^a w . wP$z)$ |1|

Pε1+1 .⊃. $w\eth(w$P$z) \varepsilon$Elm |2|

|2| . $yP\eth$.⊃. $y\varepsilon w\eth(w$P$\eth)$.⊃. Prop]

·11 Pε 1+1 . xPy . xPseq$a$ z .⊃. y P$^a z$

Pseq$a$ = P$a+1u$ = P$1u+a$ = PPa |1|

|1| .⊃: xPseqaz . = . ⅎ$w\eth(x$Pw . wPa $z)$ |2,

|2| . $\overline{\pi}x\, \varepsilon$ Elm . xPy .⊃. $y\varepsilon w\eth(x$Pw . wPa z .⊃. Prop]

·12 $x\varepsilon\varrho\eth u$.⊃. $x-1$ $u = \imath$ $u\frown y\eth$ (seq$y=x$) Df

3·2 ∃ $u \cap x3(aR^x b \smile bR^x a)$

  [$O_u.R^b\, b$ |1|

  ∃ $\widetilde{e}u \cap x3(aR^x b)$. Prop 3·11 .⊃. $x{-}1_u\, \varepsilon\, u\cap y3(seqa\, R^y b)$ |2|
  $aR^{Ou}b$.⊃. $bR^{1u}seqa$.ε. ∃ $u \cap y3(bR^y\, seqa)$ |3|
  ∃ $u \cap x3(bR^x a)$. $z3u\, \varepsilon\, x3(bR^x a)$.⊃. $bR^{s3q^x}seqa$
                                    ⊃. ∃ $u\cap y3(bR^y\, seqa)$ |4|

  |2|.;|3|.|4| .⊃. ∃ $u \cap x3(aR^x b \smile bR^x a)$.⊃. ∃ $u \cap y3(seqa\, R^y b \smile b\, R^y seqa$ |5|
  |1|.|5| Induct .⊃. Prop]

·21 $O_u\, \varepsilon\, u \cap x3(aR^x b \smile bR^x a)$.⊃. $a1'b$

·22 $O_{u}{=}\varepsilon\, u \cap x3(aR^x b \smile bR^x a)$.⊃. ∃ $\widetilde{\varrho}u\,{\frown}x3(aR^x b \smile bR^x a)$

·3 $a{>}b$.=. ∃ $\widetilde{\varrho}u \cap x3(bR^x a)$ **Df**

·31 $a{<}b$.=. ∃ $\widetilde{\varrho}u \cap x3(aR^x b)$ **Df**
·32 $a1'b$.⌣. $a{>}b$.⌣. $a{<}b$ [Prop 3·2 .⊃. Prop]
·33 $a{>}b$.⊃. ¬$(a{<}b)$

  [$a{>}b$. $a{<}b$.=. $\exists\widetilde{\varrho}u{\frown}(x,y)3(aR^x b . bR^y a$.⊃. $\exists\widetilde{\varrho}u \cap x{+}y3(aR^{x+y}a)$
          ⊃. ¬(Prop 2·16) |1|
  |1| .⊃.·. Prop 2·16 .⊃. $a{>}b$.⊃. ¬$(a{<}b)$.⊃. Prop]

·34 $a{<}b$.⊃. ¬$(a{>}b)$
·35 $a{<}b = b{>}a$ [Prop 3·3·31 .⊃. Prop]
·36 $a{<}b$.⊃. $ac{<}bc$
·37 $a{>}b$.⊃. $ac{>}bc$

❋ 4. $R\varepsilon\ 1{\div}1$. $\widetilde{\varrho}\varrho$. $\exists\widetilde{\varrho}{=}\varrho$. $u\varepsilon\omega_\varrho$. $a,b,c\varepsilon\widetilde{\varrho}u$.⊃:.

·1 aBc .=. $ab{=}c$ **Df**
·11 $B\varepsilon\ Rel$
  [$x\varepsilon u$.⊃. $c3(xb{=}c)\varepsilon$ Elm |1|

  |1| . §1 Prop 1·8 .⊃: $xb{=}c$.⊃$_a$. $\exists Rel\cap R_{ab}3(\varrho_{ab}{=}ix . \widetilde{\varrho}_{ab}{=}ic)$ |2|
  $K_b = Rel\cap R_b3|\exists u\cap x3(xb{=}c . \varrho{=}ix . \widetilde{\varrho}{=}ic)|$. $R_b = \smile' K_b$.⊃.
        $aR_b\, c$.=.$ab{=}c$.⊃. $R_b\, 1'B$ |3|
  |3| . §1 Prop 1·95 .⊃. Prop]

2 $B\varepsilon\ 1{\div}1$
  [$b1'1_u$.⊃. $B\varepsilon1{\div}1$ |1|
  $B\varepsilon1{\div}1$. $d1'seqb$.⊃. $D\varepsilon1{\div}1$ |2|
  |1| . |2| . Induct .⊃. Prop]

·3 $d\varepsilon\widetilde{\varrho}\, u$.⊃: $aB\widetilde{C}d$.=. ∃ $u \cap n3|ab{=}n . dc{=}n|$.=. $bA\widetilde{D}c$

·4 $B\widetilde{C}\varepsilon\ 1{\div}1$
  [$B,C\varepsilon1{\div}1$.⊃. Prop]

4·5 $H\varepsilon\ Nc{\div}1$.⊃: $xOp_H = y$.=. xHy **Df**
·51 $Op = p3|(p{=})\ \varepsilon\ Nc{\div}1|$ **Df**

In mathematics we are accustomed to speak of operations rather than many-one relations. Df 4·5·51 are for the purpose of permitting us to use our accustomed language. The relation between a many-one relation and an operation is explained in these definitions: the operation coming after a sign of equality signifies the corresponding relation.

·6 $r_u = q3\{ ꓱ \, \varrho u \cap (x,y)3(q= \mathrm{Op}x\, \bar{ɤ})\}$ Df

·61 $b/c = \mathrm{Op}_B \, \bar{\sigma}$ Df

P4·6·61 give the general definition of operations which correspond to rational numbers. It is important to remark that according to this definition no rational number can be identified with a whole number, since the rational numbers are operations on whole numbers, whereas the whole numbers are not.

·7 $ab/(ac) = a/c$ [Prop 4·3 .ɔ. Prop]

·71 $a\mathrm{B}\breve{\mathrm{A}}b$ [$a\mathrm{B}ab$. $b\mathrm{A}ab$.ɔ. Prop]

·72 $q,q'ɛr$.ɔ. ꓱ $u\cap (x,y,z)3(q= x/z$. $q'= y/z)$

[$q=m/n$. $q'=m'/n'$. Prop 4·7 .ɔ. $q= mn'/(nn')$. $q'= m'n/(nn')$.ɔ. Prop]

·73 $q= x/z = x'/z'$. $q'= y/z = y'/z'$. $x<y$.ɔ. $\breve{x}'<\breve{y}'$

[Prop 3·36 .ɔ. Prop]

·74   ,   , $x>y$.ɔ. $x'>y'$

[Prop 3·37 .ɔ. Prop]

·8 $q,q'ɛ \, ru$.ɔ∴ $q\mathrm{M}q'$.=: $q= x/z$. $q'= y/z$.ɔx,y,z. $x<y$ Df

·81 $\mathrm{M} \, ɛ \, \mathrm{Rel}$

[This P is proved by the method of Prop 4·11, but the proof is long.]

·9 $q,q'ɛru$. $q\mathrm{M}q'$.ɔ. ꓱ $ru \cap q''3(q\mathrm{M}q''$. $q''\mathrm{M}q')$

[$q=a/c$. $q'=b/c$. -$(a\mathrm{R}b)$.ɔ. q M seq$a$ /c . seq$a$ /c M b/c ¦1¦

$q=a/c$. $q'=b/c$. $a\mathrm{R}b$. $d_{\mathrm{s}}\varrho^2x$.ɔ. $q= ad/(cd)$. $q'=bd/(cd)$. -$(ad\mathrm{R}bd)$ ¦2¦

¦1¦.¦2¦ .ɔ. Prop]

·91 $\mathrm{M}^2 = \mathrm{M}$ [Prop 4·9 . §1 Prop 2·3 .ɔ. Prop]

To avoid confusions, I have designated by M the relation of being smaller among the rational numbers. We wish to demonstrate that this relation is equal to its square, which proves that it gives rise to a compact series. In §5 we shall develop the general theory of these series.

✳ 5. $\mathrm{R}ɛ \, 1{+}1$. $\breve{\varrho}\varrho\varrho$. ꓱ $\varrho\bar{\varrho}$. $u\varepsilon\omega\varrho$. $a,b,c,d\varepsilon u$.ɔ::

·1 $+a = \mathrm{Op}_\mathrm{R^a}$ Df   ·11 $-a = \mathrm{Op}_{\bar{\mathrm{R}}^a}$ Df

·2 $\breve{\mathrm{R}}a = (\breve{\mathrm{R}}a)$ ¦ Induct ¦

·3 $+u = \hat{x}\hat{\jmath}\{\exists u\frown y\hat{\jmath}(x \; 1' \; +y)\}$ Df

·31 $-u = \hat{x}\hat{\jmath}\{\exists u\frown y\hat{\jmath}(x \; 1' \; -y)\}$ Df

·32 $\pm u = +u \smile -u$ Df

·4 $q,q'\varepsilon r_u \;.\supset.\; q(D/C)q' \;.=:\; q= a/c \;.\; q'= b/c$

─A $\varrho^2 u \frown (x,y,z)\hat{\jmath}(a{=}xz \;.\; c{=}yz \;\smile\; b{=}xz \;.\; c{=}yz) \;.\supset.\; a{+}d{=}b$ Df

·41 $+d/c = \mathrm{Op}_{D/C}$ Df   ·42 $-d/c = \mathrm{Op}_{(\breve{D} C)}$ Df

·5 $+r_u = \hat{x}\hat{\jmath}\{\exists u\frown (y,z)\hat{\jmath}(x= +y/z)\}$ Df

.51 $-r_u = \hat{x}\hat{\jmath}\{\exists u\frown(y,z)\hat{\jmath}(x= -y/z)\}$ Df

$+r_u$ is the class of positive rationals, which are operations on rationals without signs. The classes u, r_u, $+u$, $+r_u$ mutually exclude each other: no term of one of these four belongs to any of the three others.

§4. FINITE AND INFINITE

✱   1·1   Cls infin $=$ Cls $\frown u\hat{\jmath}\{\exists u\frown x\hat{\jmath}(u{-}\iota x \; \mathrm{sim} \; u)\}$ Df

·11   Cls fin $=$ Cls $-$ Cls infin   Df

·2   Cls infin $=$ Cls$\frown u\hat{\jmath}\{x\varepsilon u \;.\supset_x.\; u{-}\iota x \; \mathrm{sim} \; u\}$

[§2 Prop 3·5 .⊃: $x,y\varepsilon u$.⊃. $u{-}\iota x \; \mathrm{sim} \; u{-}\iota y$:⊃. Prop]

·21   Cls infin $=$ Cls$\frown u\hat{\jmath}\{u{-}\iota x \; \mathrm{sim} u\}$

[Prop 1·2 . $x\varepsilon u$.⊃. $u{-}\iota x \; \mathrm{sim} \; u$ |1|

$x{-}\varepsilon u$.⊃. $u{-}\iota x = u$.⊃. $u{-}\iota x \; \mathrm{sim} u$ |2|

|1| . |2| .⊃. Prop]

·22   Cls fin $=$ Cls $\frown u\hat{\jmath}\{x\varepsilon u \;.\supset_x.\; {-}(u{-}\iota x \; \mathrm{sim} \; u)\}$

[Prop 1·1·11 .⊃. Prop]

·3 $u\varepsilon$ Cls infin . $x{-}\varepsilon u$.⊃. $u \smile \iota x \;\varepsilon$ Cls infin

[Hp . $y\varepsilon u$.⊃. $u{-}\iota y \; \mathrm{sim} u$ |1|

|1| . §2 Prop 3·3 .⊃. $u \mathrm{sim} \; u\smile\iota x$.⊃. Prop]

·31 $u \smile \iota x \;\varepsilon$ Cls fin . $x{-}\varepsilon u$.⊃. $u\varepsilon$ Cls fin

[Prop 1·3 . Transp .⊃. Prop]

·4 $u\varepsilon$ Cls . $u\smile \iota x \;\varepsilon$ Cls infin . $x{-}\varepsilon u$.⊃. $u\varepsilon$ Cls infin

[$u\smile\iota x \;\varepsilon$ Cls infin . $x{-}\varepsilon u$.⊃. $u \smile \iota x \; \mathrm{sim} u$ |1|

|1| . $y\varepsilon u$. §1 Prop 3·51 .⊃. $u \; \mathrm{sim} \; u{-}\iota y$.⊃. Prop]

·41 $u\varepsilon$ Cls fin . $x{-}\varepsilon u$.⊃. $u\smile\iota x \;\varepsilon$ Cls fin

[Prop 1·4 . Transp .⊃. Prop]

·5 $u\varepsilon$ Cls . $x{-}\varepsilon u$.⊃: $u\varepsilon$ Cls fin .=. $u\smile\iota x \;\varepsilon$ Cls fin

[Prop 1·31·41 .⊃. Prop]

·6 $\Lambda\varepsilon$ Cls fin

[$u\varepsilon$ Cls infin .⊃. $\exists u$:⊃. Prop]

1·61   Elm ⊃ Cls fin

[$u\varepsilon$ Elm .⊃$_u$. ꓱ$x\vartheta(u=\iota x)$: Prop 1·41 . $\bigwedge\varepsilon$ Cls fin :⊃. Prop]

·7 $u\varepsilon$ Cls fin .⊃. ꓱ-u Pp

✱ 2.   S𝜀ꙅ .⊃::

·1 $\breve{\sigma}$ infin = $\breve{\sigma}$(Cls infin)   Df

·11 $\breve{\sigma}$ fin = $\breve{\sigma}$(Cls fin)   Df

·12 $\breve{\sigma}$ fin = $\breve{\sigma}$- $\breve{\sigma}$ infin   [S𝜀 Nc+1 .⊃. Prop]

·2 $x\varepsilon \breve{\sigma}$fin .=. $x+1_\sigma \varepsilon \breve{\sigma}$ fin   [Prop 1·5 .⊃. Prop]

·21 $x\varepsilon \breve{\sigma}$fin .=. $x0'x + 1_\sigma$

[Prop 1·22 . §2 Prop 4·6 .⊃. Prop]

·3   R$_\sigma$ = $\imath$Rel ∧ R$\vartheta\{xRy$.=. $x\varepsilon \breve{\sigma}$ fin . $y=x+1_\sigma\}$ Df

·31   R$_\sigma$ 𝜀 1+1   [§2 Prop 3·52 . S𝜀 Nc+1 .⊃. Prop]

·32   R$_\sigma$ ⊃ 0'   [Prop 2·21 .⊃. Prop]

·33   ϱ$_\sigma$ = $\breve{\sigma}$ fin

[$x\varepsilon$ ϱ$_\sigma$. uSx .⊃. $u\varepsilon$ Cls fin |1|

|1| . Prop 1·7 .⊃. ꓱ-u .⊃. ꓱεϱ$_\sigma$ x .⊃. Prop]

·34   ϱ$_\sigma$ = $\breve{\sigma}$ fin - $\iota 0_\sigma$

[$x\varepsilon \breve{\sigma}$ fin . uSx . $x0'0_\sigma$.⊃. ꓱu .⊃: $y\varepsilon u$.⊃. u-ιy Sιϱ$_\sigma$ x :⊃. Prop]

·35 $\breve{\sigma}$ fin 𝜀 Cls infin

[$\breve{\sigma}$ fin = ϱ$_\sigma$. $\breve{\sigma}$ fin - $\iota 0_\sigma$ = $\breve{\varrho}_\sigma$. ϱ$_\sigma$ sim $\breve{\varrho}_\sigma$.⊃. Prop]

✱ 3.   S𝜀ꙅ .⊃::

·1 $s\varepsilon$ Cls . 0$_\sigma$ 𝜀s . ϱ$_\sigma$ $(s ∧ \breve{\sigma}$ fin) ⊃s .⊃. $\breve{\sigma}$ fin ⊃ s Pp

·11   Induct = Prop 3·1   Df

One may, if one wishes, define the finite numbers by mathematical induction, and take as Pp definition 1·1. But I have not succeeded in deducing one of these P's from the other. If one has defined an infinite class by the property of containing a part that is similar to itself, one cannot succeed in demonstrating that the part which one obtains by removing a single individual is similar to the entire class, and this has fatal consequences for the theory of finite numbers. If one then defines an infinite class by the property of remaining similar to itself when one adds to it a term which does not belong to it, one excludes the class of all individuals [the universal class], since one can add nothing to that class. For

these reasons I have adopted the definition 1·1 with the two Pp
1·7 and 3·1.

3·2 $\bar{\sigma}$ fin ε ω
[Prop 2·3·31·33·34·3·1 . §3 Prop 1·1 .ɔ. Prop]

·3 $\bar{\rho}$ fin = Cls ∩ $u\mathfrak{z}$ {$\mathfrak{z}\mathfrak{z}$ ∩ S$\mathfrak{z}(u = \bar{\sigma}$fin)}   Df

·31 $\bar{\rho}$ fin = ω

[Prop 3·2 .ɔ. $\bar{\rho}$ fin ɔ ω ¦1¦

Rε 1→1 . $u = \varrho$. $\bar{\sigma}$ fin = $\bar{\varrho}$. P= RRɔ$\bar{R}$.ɔ. $u\varepsilon$ ω_π ¦2¦

§2 Prop 1·54 .ɔ. $u\varepsilon$ $\bar{\rho}$ fin   ¦3¦   ¦1¦ . ¦2¦ . ¦3¦ .ɔ. Prop]

We have now proved that any class similar to the finite cardinal
numbers is a progression, and vice versa. From that we deduce
that all the consequences of §3 apply to finite numbers.

·4 $u\varepsilon$ Cls fin .ɔ. $\mathfrak{z}$ ∩ ω ∩ $v\mathfrak{z}(u$ ɔ $v)$

[$u=\Lambda$.ɔ: $v\varepsilon\omega$.ɔ$_u$. $u\mathfrak{z}v$ ¦1¦
§2 Prop 3·5 . §3 Prop 1·91 .ɔ: $u\mathfrak{z}$Elm . $v'\varepsilon\omega$.ɔ. $v'-\iota x$ ∪∩ $\varepsilon\omega$
                                            .ɔ. $\mathfrak{z}$ ∩ ω ∩ $v\mathfrak{z}(u\mathfrak{z}v)$ ¦2¦
$u\varepsilon$ Cls fin . $v\varepsilon\omega$. $u\mathfrak{z}v$. uSx . $y-\varepsilon u$.ɔ.
    $u\wedge\iota y$ ε Cls fin . $u\wedge\iota y$ S $x+1\sigma$. $u\wedge\iota y$ ɔ $v\wedge\iota y$ ¦3¦
Prop 3·31 . Prop 2·35 . Prop 1·1·3 . §3 Prop 1·91 .ɔ. $v\wedge\iota y$ $\varepsilon\omega$ ¦4¦
¦3¦.¦4¦ .ɔ: $u\varepsilon$ Cls fin . $v\varepsilon\omega$. $u\mathfrak{z}v$. uSx . $y-\varepsilon u$.ɔ.
    $u\wedge\iota y$ ε Cls fin . $v\wedge\iota y\varepsilon\omega$. $u\wedge\iota y$ ɔ $v\wedge\iota y$. $u\wedge\iota y$ S $x+1\sigma$ ¦5¦
¦1¦ : ¦2¦ . ¦5¦ . Induct :ɔ. Prop]

·41 $u\varepsilon$ Cls fin .ɔ. $\mathfrak{z}$ ∩ ω ∩ $v\mathfrak{z}${$u\supset v$. $\mathfrak{z}$ ∩$v\wedge x\mathfrak{z}(y\varepsilon u$.=. $y<x$)}

For the definition of $y < x$ see §3 Prop 3·31.

[$u=\Lambda$. $v\varepsilon\omega$.ɔ: $y\varepsilon u$.=. $y<0_v$ ¦1¦
$u\varepsilon$Elm . Prop3·4 .ɔ. $\mathfrak{z}$ ∩ ω ∩ $v\mathfrak{z}(u\varepsilon v)$ ¦2¦
$v\varepsilon\omega$. $u\varepsilon v$. §3 Prop 2·11 .ɔ. ιu ∪ $v\wedge\mathfrak{z}$ $(z>u)$ $\varepsilon\omega$
                . $\mathfrak{z}v'$ ∩ $x\mathfrak{z}(y\varepsilon u$.=. $y<x$)¦   ¦3¦
$v\varepsilon\omega$. $u\varepsilon$ Cls fin . $u\mathfrak{z}v$. $\mathfrak{z}v$ ∩ $x\mathfrak{z}(y\varepsilon u$.=. $y<x)$. $z-\varepsilon u$.ɔ::
v ∪ $\iota z\varepsilon\omega$. u ∪ ιz ε Cls fin . u ∪ ιz ɔ $v\wedge\iota z$.·. $x\varepsilon u$: $y<x$.=. $y\varepsilon u$.·.ɔ.
$\mathfrak{z}\omega$ ∩ $v'\mathfrak{z}$ ¦$v\varepsilon v'$. $v'-v = \iota z$. $x\varepsilon u$: $y\varepsilon$ ∪∩ ιz .=. $y<x$ ¦   ¦4¦
¦1¦ . ¦2¦ . ¦4¦ . Induct .ɔ. Prop   ]

·42   Cls fin = Cls ∩ $u\mathfrak{z}${$\mathfrak{z}\omega$ ∩ $v\mathfrak{z}$ [$u\supset v$. $\mathfrak{z}v$ ∩ $x\mathfrak{z}$ ($y\varepsilon u$.=. $y<x$))]}

We deduce that any finite class may be well ordered.

·5 $u\varepsilon$ Cls fin .ɔ. =$\mathfrak{z}$ Cls ∩ $v\mathfrak{z}$ ($v\mathfrak{z}u$. $\mathfrak{z}u-v$. $u$sim$v$)

[SεS . vSx . $u-v$Sy .ɔ. uS $x+y$ ¦1¦
§3 Prop 2·16 .ɔ. $x+y$ 0' x .ɔ. Prop]

·51   Cls infin = Cls ∩ $u\mathfrak{z}$ {$\mathfrak{z}$ Cls ∩ $v\mathfrak{z}$ ($v\mathfrak{z}u$. $\mathfrak{z}u-v$. $u$sim$v$)}

[Prop 1·1: 3·51 . Transp :ɔ. Prop]

P3·51 gives the customary definition of infinity, from which, however, it does not appear possible to deduce P1·1.

3·6 $u,v\varepsilon$ Cls fin .⊃. $u\smallfrown v$ ε Cls fin

[$v\supset u$.⊃. $u\smallfrown v = u$.⊃. Prop |1|

    $u\varepsilon v$.⊃. $u\smallfrown v = v$.⊃. Prop |2|

    $\exists u{-}v$. $\exists v{-}u$. $S\exists y$. $u S x$. $v{-}u S y$.⊃. $u\smallfrown v$ $Sx{+}y$ |3|

    |3| . §3 Prop 2.2 .⊃. Prop |4|

    |1| . |2| . |4| .⊃. Prop]

·61 $u\varepsilon$ Cls infin . $v\varepsilon$Cls .⊃. $u\smallsmile v\varepsilon$ Cls infin

[$x\exists u$. $u\varepsilon$ Cls infin .⊃. $u\text{sim}u{-}\imath x$.⊃. $u\smallsmile v\text{sim}u\smallsmile v{-}\imath x$.⊃. Prop }

·62 $u\smallsmile v\varepsilon$Cls fin .⊃. $u,$ $v\varepsilon$Cls fin

[Prop 3.61 . transp .⊃. Prop]

§5. COMPACT SERIES

1·1 $R\varepsilon$ Rel . $R\supset 0'$. $R^{2} = R$.⊃. $\Phi_{R} = $ Cls $\smallfrown u\exists\{u\supset\varrho\breve\varrho$.∴.

          $x,y\varepsilon u$.⊃$_{x,y}$. x1'y .∨. xRy .∨. yRx .∴.

          $x,y\varepsilon u$. xRy .⊃$_{x,y}$. $\exists u\smallfrown z\exists(xRz$. zRy)}   Df

·11 $\Phi = $ Cls $\smallfrown u\exists\{$ $\exists$rel $\smallfrown R\exists(R\supset 0'$. $R^{2} = R$. $u\varepsilon$ Φ_{R})}   Df

These P's give the definition of a compact series. If R is a continuous relation contained in diversity and equal to its square, and if u is a class contained in the logical sum of the domain of R with that of $\breve R$, and if two different u's always have one of the two relations R, $\breve R$, and if between two u's there is always a third u, then u is a Φ_{R}. The class Φ is the class of all compact series for all relations which give rise to such series.

·2 $R\varepsilon$ Rel . $R\supset 0'$. $R^{2} = R$: $x\varepsilon$ $\varrho\breve\varrho$. ⊃$_x$.ϱx ∨$\imath x$ ∨ $\breve\varrho x$ $= \varrho\breve\varrho$: .⊃.

        $\varrho,$ $\breve\varrho,$ $\varrho\smallsmile\breve\varrho\varepsilon$ Φ_{R}

3     $R\varepsilon$ Rel . $R\supset 0'$. $R^{2} = R$. $u\varepsilon\Phi_{R}$. $\exists u = \breve\varrho u\supset$.⊃. $u{-}\breve\varrho u\varepsilon$ Elm

[$x\varepsilon u{-}\breve\varrho u$. $y\varepsilon u{-}\imath x$: xRy .∨. yRx :⊃. xRy .⊃. $y\varepsilon\breve\varrho u$]

·4 $R\varepsilon$ Rel . $R\supset 0'$. $R^{2} = R$.⊃. $\Phi_{R} = \Phi_{\breve R}$

·5 $R\varepsilon$Rel . $R\supset 0'$. $R^{2} = R$. $S\varepsilon 1{\leftarrow}1$. $\sigma\varepsilon$ Φ_{R} .⊃. $\sigma\varepsilon$ $\Phi_{\breve SRS}$

[$x\varepsilon\sigma$. y1'$\imath\sigma x$.⊃. $y\breve Sx$ (1)

   $x'\varepsilon\breve\varrho x$. y1'$\imath\sigma x'$.⊃. $x'Sy'$. xRx' .⊃. $xRSy'$ (2)

   (1) . (2) .⊃. $y\breve S$ RSy' . $y'\varepsilon$ σ (3)

   y $\breve S RS$ y' . y' $\breve S RS$ y'' .⊃. $y\breve SRS\breve SRS$ y'' (4)

   $S\varepsilon 1{\leftarrow}1$. $R^{2} = R$.⊃. $\breve SRS\breve SRS \supset \breve SRS$ (5)

$(4) . (5) .\ni. (\breve{S}RS)^2 \ni \breve{S}RS$ (6)

$y \breve{S}RS y'' .\ni. \exists \frown (x',x'') \, \imath \, (y\breve{S}x . xRx'' . x''Sy'')$ (7)

$(7) \vdash. R^2 = R . S\imath 1+1 .\ni. \exists \sigma \frown (x,x',x'') \, \imath \, (y\breve{S}x . xRx' . x'S\breve{S}x . x'Rx'' .$
$\qquad\qquad\qquad\qquad\qquad\qquad\qquad\qquad x''Sy'')$ (8)

$(8) .\ni. \breve{S}RS \ni (\breve{S}RS)^2$ (9)

$(6) . (9) .\ni. (\breve{S}RS)^2 = \breve{S}RS$ (10)

$R\ni 0' . S\imath 1+1 .\ni. \breve{S}RS \ni 0'$ (11)
$(8) . (10) . (11) .\ni. \text{Prop}$]

This P gives a method by means of which we obtain a new compact series by correlation with a given compact series. It proves that every class similar to a compact series is itself a compact series in respect to a certain relation. We have the more general theorem: given P, a relation such that $P\ni 0'.P^2 \ni P$, the class of series of the same type of order as π is the class of the domains of the relations P' such that there is a one-one relation S such as $P' = \breve{S}PS\pi = \sigma$. This theorem applies to series of all types without any exception. I omit the proof to avoid excess length.

·6 $R\varepsilon\text{Rel} . R\ni 0' . R^2 = R . u\breve{\varepsilon}\Phi_R. P = Ru\frown \varrho u .\ni. u\varepsilon\Phi_P. u = \pi\breve{\cup}\pi '$

For the definition of $Ru\frown\varrho u$, see §2 Prop $3\cdot 12$.

❋ 2. $P\varepsilon \text{Rel} . P\ni 0' . P^2 = P . u = \pi\breve{\cup}\pi . u\varepsilon \Phi_P .\ni::$
·1 $\quad v\varepsilon\text{Cls} . v\ni u .\ni. \pi(\pi v) = \pi v$
$[\quad \pi v = \bigwedge .\ni. \pi(\pi v) = \bigwedge .\ni. \pi(\pi v) = \pi v$ (1)
$\quad \exists \pi v .\ni.\therefore x\varepsilon\pi v .\ni. \exists v\frown y\imath (xPy):$ (2)
$\qquad (2) . P^2 = P .\ni. \exists u\frown z\imath (xPz . zPy) .\ni. x\varepsilon\pi(\pi v):$ (3)
$\qquad x\varepsilon\pi(\pi v) .\ni. \exists u\frown z\imath \mid \exists v\frown y\imath (xPz . zPy) \mid$
$\qquad\qquad .\ni. \exists v\frown y\imath (xPy) .\ni. x\varepsilon\pi v$ (4)
$\quad (1) . (3) . (4) .\ni. \text{Prop}$]
·2 $\quad v\varepsilon\text{Cls} . v\ni u .\ni. \breve{\pi}(\breve{\pi}v) = \breve{\pi}v$
·3 $\quad pu = \text{Cls}\frown v\imath \mid v\ni u . \pi v = v . \exists v . \exists u = v \mid$ Df
·4 $\quad \breve{p}u = \text{Cls}\frown v\imath \mid v\ni u . \breve{\pi}v = v . \exists v . \exists u = v \mid$ Df

pu corresponds to what Peano calls the class of segments [*Rivista di Matematica*, Vol .VI, p. 133, §8, P·o]. I shall call pu the class of lower segments, $\breve{p}u$ that of upper segments.

·5 $v\varepsilon$ Cls . $v \circ u$. $\exists$ $v \frown \pi$. $\exists$ $u \bullet \pi v$.ɔ. πv ε pu

[$\exists v \frown \pi$.ɔ. $\exists \pi v$ (1)   Prop 2·1 .ɔ. $\pi(\pi v) = \pi v$ (2)
(1) . (2) . $\exists u \bullet \pi v$.ɔ. Prop·]

2·51 $v\varepsilon$Cls . $v \circ u$. $\exists v \frown \pi$. $\exists u \bullet \pi v$.ɔ. πv ε pu
·6 $v,v'\varepsilon pu$.ɔ: $v \circ v'$.ᴠ. $v' \circ v$

[.$v,v'\varepsilon pu$. $\exists v'\bullet v$.ɔ. $\exists v'\frown v \pi$.ɔ: $x\varepsilon v$.ɔ$_x$. $\exists v'\frown y\varepsilon$ (xPy) :   (1)
(1) . $v'\varepsilon pu$.ɔ: $x\varepsilon v$.ɔ$_x$. $x\varepsilon v'$:ɔ. $v \circ v'$ (2)
$\exists v \bullet v'$.ɔ. $v' \circ v$ (3)   (2) . (3) .ɔ. Prop]

For the definition of $\breve{v\pi}$, see §1 Prop 1·34.

·61 $v,v'\varepsilon \breve{pu}$.ᴄ: $v \circ v'$.ᴠ. $v' \circ v$
·7 uTv' .=. $v,v'\varepsilon pu$. $v \circ v'$. $v \bullet\!=\! v'$ Df
·71 $T\varepsilon$ Rel

[§1 Prop 3·82 .ɔ: $v,v'\varepsilon pu$.=. $v\varepsilon_{pu} \breve{e}_{pu} v'$ (1)   (ɔ) εRel   (2)
(=) εRel   (3)

(1) . (2) . (3) . §1 Prop 1·98 . Prop 2·5 .ɔ. $(\varepsilon_{pu}\breve{e}_{pu}) \frown (ɔ) \frown (\bullet\!=\!)$ εRel   (4)

(4) .T= $(\varepsilon_{pu}\breve{e}_{pu}) \frown (ɔ) \frown (\bullet\!=\!)$.ɔ. Prop]

The P's (2) and (3) of this proof are the Pp, which we should have had to introduce in §1, if we had wished to make a complete logic; (2) affirms that the inclusion of a class in a class is a relation, and (3) affirms that the equality of classes is a relation.

·72 $T \circ 0'$. $T^2 \circ T$
·73 $T^2 = T$

[vTv' .ɔ. $\exists v'\bullet v$.ɔ. $\exists \pi v'\bullet v$.ɔ. $\exists v' \frown (x,y)\varepsilon$ $(x,y\bullet\varepsilon v$. $x0'y)$ (1)
(1) . xPy .ɔ. $vTx\pi x$. $\pi xTv'$ (2)   (1) . yPx .ɔ. $vT\pi y$. $\pi yTv'$ (3)
(1) . (2) . (3) .ɔ. Prop]
·8 pu ε Φ_T [Prop 1·1.2·71·72·73 :ɔ. Prop]

We have now proved that the class of lower segments is a compact series by reference to T. Similarly it is proved that the class of upper segments is a compact series.

✱ 3. $P\varepsilon$ Rel . $P \circ 0'$. $P^2 = P$. $u = \pi\frown\pi : x\varepsilon u$.ɔ. $\pi x \cup \iota x \cup \pi x = u$:ɔ::
·1 $\tau\varepsilon pu$.ɔ. $\tau v = pu \frown x\exists (xT\breve{v})$ [$\tau v \circ \tau$. $\tau \circ pu$.ɔ. Prop]
·2 w ε Cls . $w \circ pu$.ɔ. $\tau w = pu \frown x\exists\{\exists w \frown y\exists (xTy)\}$
·21 $w\tau = pu \frown x\exists\{y\varepsilon w$.ɔ$_x$. $xTy\}$

For the definition of $w\tau$, see §1 Prop 1·36.

·3 w $\varepsilon\mathrm{Cls}$. $w \circ pu$.ɔ. $\upsilon^{\epsilon}w \circ u$

$w\varepsilon\mathrm{Cls}$. $w \circ pu$. $\exists w$. $\exists \, pu - w$. $\exists u - \upsilon^{\epsilon}w$.ɔ·.

·4 $\upsilon^{\epsilon}w \, \varepsilon \, pu$

[$x\varepsilon\upsilon^{\epsilon}w$.=. $\exists \, w \wedge v\varepsilon(x\varepsilon w . v\varepsilon \, pu)$.=. $\exists w \wedge v\varepsilon; \exists v \wedge y\varepsilon(xPy)$ ·:

.=. $\exists \, \upsilon^{\epsilon}w \wedge y\varepsilon(xPy)$.=. $x\varepsilon \, \pi(\upsilon^{\epsilon}w)$:=. $\upsilon^{\epsilon}w = \pi(\upsilon^{\epsilon}w)$]

3·5 $\tau w = \tau(\upsilon^{\epsilon}w)$

[$v\varepsilon \, \tau w$.=. $v\varepsilon pu$. $\exists \, w \wedge z\varepsilon(v\varepsilon z)$ (1) $z\varepsilon w$.ɔ. $z\varepsilon \circ i(\upsilon^{\epsilon}w)$ (2)

(1) . (2) .ɔ. $v\varepsilon \, \tau w$.ɔ. $v\varepsilon pu$. $v\varepsilon \, \tau(\upsilon^{\epsilon}w)$:ɔ. $\tau w \circ \tau(\upsilon^{\epsilon}w)$ (3)

$v\varepsilon \, \tau(\upsilon^{\epsilon}w)$.ɔ. $v\circ \upsilon^{\epsilon}w$. $v - = \upsilon^{\epsilon}w$.ɔ. $\exists \, \upsilon^{\epsilon}w - v$

.ɔ. $\exists \, w \wedge z\varepsilon(vTz)$.ɔ. $v\varepsilon \, \tau w$:ɔ. $\tau(\upsilon^{\epsilon}w) \circ \tau w$ (4)

(3) . (4) .ɔ. Prop]

This P proves that, if w is a class of segments of a compact series, the class of segments contained in a variable term of w is the same as the class of segments contained in the logical sum of the class of classes w. When the class w has no maximum, we deduce that the logical sum of w is the higher limit of w: the class w has, therefore, always either a maximum or an upper limit. (See P3·6·7·8 which follow.) Half of the analogous theorem is demonstrated for the lower limit and the logical product in Prop 3·51.

·51 $\tau(\cap^{\epsilon}w) \circ w\tau$

[$x\varepsilon w$.ɔ: $\cap^{\epsilon}w \circ x$ (1)

(1) . $z \, T \cap^{\epsilon}w$.ɔ: $x\varepsilon w$.ɔ$_x$. $z Tx$:ɔ. $z\varepsilon \, w\tau$.ɔ. Prop]

One cannot prove that $\tau(\cap^{\epsilon}w) = w\tau$. This theorem will only be true when w has a minimum; in the contrary case, the lower limit of w will be $\cap^{\epsilon}w$, and will belong in certain cases to the class $w\tau$, but not the class $\tau(\cap^{\epsilon}w)$.

·6 $\exists pu \wedge x\exists(\tau w = \tau x)$ [Prop 3·5 .ɔ. Prop]

·7 $\lambda^{\epsilon}w = \imath pu \wedge x\exists(\tau w = \tau x)$ Df

·8 $v\varepsilon pu$.ɔ. $\exists \mathrm{Cls} \wedge w\exists(w \circ pu$. $v = \lambda^{\epsilon}w)$ [$w = \imath v$]

P3·6·8 prove that pu is perfect for upper limits, but not necessarily for lower limits. $\lambda^{\epsilon}w$, as just defined, is not always a limit, since it is the maximum if there is one. The segments which compose the class pu are defined by any classes contained in u. In the next section we shall examine the segments and limits which are obtained by using exclusively what Cantor calls fundamental series.
[*Rivista di Matematica*, Vol. V, p. 157.]

§6. FUNDAMENTAL SERIES IN A COMPACT SERIES

Fundamental series are series of type ω, each of which ascend or descend continuously within the compact series which contain them. In the first case $(1\cdot1)$ I call the fundamental series *progression*; in the second case $(1\cdot2)$ I call it *regression*. As for the compact series, it is not subject to any condition except for it to be compact; I do not decide, for example, whether it is denumerable or continuous or neither one nor the other.

✳   1. $P\varepsilon$ Rel $.$ $P\cup0'$ $.$ $P^2=P : x\varepsilon\, \pi\widetilde{\pi}\,.\circ.\,\pi x\cup\iota x\cup\widetilde{\pi}x=$

$$\pi\widetilde{\pi}:u{=}\pi\smile\widetilde{\pi}:\circ::$$

$\cdot1$ $\omega_P = \omega\cap v3\{v\circ u:\mathrm{R}\varepsilon\mathrm{Rel}_v.\,x,y\varepsilon v\,.\,x\mathrm{R}y\,.\circ_{x,y}.\,x\mathrm{P}y\,\}$ Df

$\cdot2$ $\omega_{\widetilde{P}} = \omega\cap v3\{v\circ u:\mathrm{R}\varepsilon\mathrm{Rel}_u.\,x,y\varepsilon v\,.\,x\mathrm{R}y\,.\circ_{x,y}.\,y\mathrm{P}x\,\}$ Df

If v is a progression, Rel$_v$ is the class of generating relations of that progression (§3 Prop $1\cdot12$). In the present case, one can admit as a generating relation only a relation which satisfies the given condition. Such a relation, if it exists, is unique. We must not confuse ω^P and ω_π. See §3 Prop $1\cdot11$.

$\cdot3$ $\pi\omega = x3\{\,\text{э}\,\omega_P\cap v3(x{=}\pi v)\}$ Df

$\cdot31$ $\omega\widetilde{\pi} = x3\{\,\text{э}\,\omega_P\cap v3(x{=}\widetilde{v}\pi)\}$ Df

$\cdot4$ $\widetilde{\pi}\omega = x3\{\,\text{э}\,\omega_{\widetilde{P}}\cap v3(x{=}\widetilde{\pi}v)\}$ Df

$\cdot41$ $\omega\pi = x3\{\,\text{э}\,\omega_{\widetilde{P}}\cap v3(x{=}v\pi)\}$ Df

We must not confuse $\pi\omega$ and *pu*. [§5 Prop $2\cdot3$]: *pu* is the class of all the lower segments of *u*, $\pi\omega$ is the class of lower segments which define progressions. These two classes are identical in most cases, but I do not know any proof that they are always so.

$\cdot5$ $v\varepsilon\,\omega_P\,.\circ.\,v\circ\pi v$ [$x\varepsilon v\,.\circ.\,x\,\mathrm{P}\,\mathrm{seq}x\,.\circ.\,x\varepsilon\,\pi v$]

$\cdot51$ $v\varepsilon\,\omega_{\widetilde{P}}\,.\circ.\,v\circ\,\widetilde{\pi}v$

$\cdot6$ $v\varepsilon\,\omega_P\,.\circ.\,\widetilde{v}\pi = u\text{-}\pi v$

[$x\varepsilon\,\widetilde{v}\pi\,.\circ.\,x\varepsilon\,u\text{-}\pi v$ (1)

$x\varepsilon\,u\text{-}\pi v\,.\circ.\,\text{-}\widetilde{\exists}v\cap y3(x\mathrm{P}y)\,.\circ.\cdot.\,y\varepsilon v\,.\circ_y:y1'x\,.\cup.\,y\mathrm{P}x$ (2)

$y1'x\,.\circ.\,x\mathrm{P}\mathrm{seq}y\,.\circ.\,x\varepsilon\pi v$ (3)

(2) $.$ (3) $.\circ.\cdot.\,x\varepsilon u\text{-}\pi v:\circ:y\varepsilon v\,.\circ_y.\,y\mathrm{P}x:\circ.\,x\varepsilon v\widetilde{\pi}$ (4)

(1) $.$ (4) $.\circ.$ Prop]

$\cdot61$ $v\varepsilon\,\omega_{\widetilde{P}}\,.\circ.\,\dot{v}\pi = u\text{-}\widetilde{\pi}v$

·7 $\pi\omega \supset pu$ ·71 $\overline{\pi}\omega \supset \overline{p}u$

·8 $v.v'\varepsilon\,\omega_P.\supset: \pi v \supset \pi v' .\backsim. \pi v' \supset \pi v$ [§5 Prop 2·6 .⊃. Prop]

·81 $v,v'\varepsilon\,\omega_{\overline{P}}.\supset: \overline{\pi}v \supset \overline{\pi}v' .\backsim. \overline{\pi}v' \supset \overline{\pi}v$ [§5 Prop 2·61 .⊃. Prop]

✳ 2. $P\varepsilon$ Rel . $P\supset0'$. $P^2 = P : x\varepsilon\pi\supset\pi .\supset_x. \pi x \smile \iota x\smile\pi x =$
$$\pi\smile\pi : u = \pi\smile\pi . v,v'\varepsilon\,\omega_P :\supset::$$

·1 $x\varepsilon v .\supset_x. \exists v' \frown y\exists(xPy . yP\text{seq}x) \supset: \backsim\exists v' \frown v\overline{\pi}$
[Hp : $k\varepsilon\omega .\supset_k. \exists k .\supset. \exists v' \frown y\exists|\exists v \frown x\exists(xPy . y P \text{seq}x)$ |

Rε Rel$_v$, R'εRel$_{v'}$, §3 Prop 2·11 , $x\varepsilon v$, $y\varepsilon v'$, xPy . $yP\varepsilon\text{seq}x .\supset. \overline{\varrho}^x v, \overline{\varrho}^y v'\varepsilon\omega_P$ (1)

Hp (1) . $y'\varepsilon v'$. $x'\varepsilon\overline{\varrho}^x v$. $x'Py'$. y P seq $x' .\supset. y'\varepsilon\overline{\varrho}^y v'$ (2)

$\exists \overline{\varrho}^y v' \frown y'\varepsilon(\text{seq}x' P y'' . y'' P \text{seq seq}x') .\supset: \text{seq}y' 1' y'' .\backsim. \text{seq}y' P y'' :$
$.\supset. \text{seq}y' P \text{seq seq}x'$ (3)

(2) . (3) .⊃.∵ $z\varepsilon v' .\supset_z: z\varepsilon \pi v .\supset. \text{seq}z\varepsilon \pi v$ (4)   Hp .⊃. $0_{v'}\varepsilon \pi v$ (5)

(4) . (5) . Induct .⊃. $v'\supset \pi v .\supset.$ Prop]

Since this demonstration is a little complicated, I shall repeat it in words. The P affirms that if two progressions v,v' are such that between any two consecutive terms of v whatsoever one always finds at least a term of v', then there is not any term of v' which follows all terms of v. Let x be a term of v, and y a term of v' between x and seq x. Then the terms of v which do not precede x form a progression $\overset{\smile}{\varrho}{}^x v$, and the terms of v' which do not precede y form a progression $\overset{\smile}{\varrho}{}^y v'$. If then x' is any term whatever of $\overset{\smile}{\varrho}{}^x v, y'$ a term of v' between x' and seq x', one deduces that y' is a term of $\overset{\smile}{\varrho}{}^y v$. Now there is a term y'' of $\overset{\smile}{\varrho}{}^y v'$ which goes between seq x' and seq seq x' and such a term must be seq y' or succeed seq y'; thus seq y must precede seq seq x'. It follows then, if z is a v' which precedes any v, then seq z is also a v' which precedes any v., But by the hypothesis there is some v' which precedes v, therefore the first term of v' must precede v. We deduce by induction that all terms of v' precede some terms of v, that is to say, that no term of v' follows all terms of v.

2·2   Hp Prop 2·1 .⊃. $\pi v = \pi v'$
[$x\varepsilon\pi v' .\supset. \exists v' \frown y\exists(xPy)$ (1)
(1) . $v'\supset\pi v .\supset: x\varepsilon\pi v' .\supset_x. x\varepsilon\pi v .\supset. \pi v'\supset\pi v$ (2)
$x\varepsilon\pi v .\supset. \exists v \frown y\exists(xPy) .\supset. \exists v' \frown z\exists(xPz) .\supset. x\varepsilon\pi v' :\supset. \pi v\supset\pi v'$ (3)
(2) . (3) .⊃. Prop]

·3 $w\varepsilon$Cls . $w\supset u$. $\exists v \cap z\exists(w\supset\pi z): x\varepsilon v$.$\supset_x$. $\exists w \cap y\exists(xPy$. $yP\mathrm{seq}qx)$.

$w \cap y\exists(xPy$. $yP\mathrm{seq}qx)$ ε Elm : $v\bar\pi \supset \bar{w\pi}$.$\therefore\supset$. w ε wP

This P affirms that if v is a progression in a compact series u, and if w is a class contained within u and succeeding certain terms of v, and if there is a term of w, and one alone, between any two consecutive terms whatsoever of v, and if finally the terms which succeed all terms of v succeed also all terms of w, then w is a progression in u.

[Hp . §1Prop1·8 .$\supset$: $x\varepsilon v$.$\supset_x$. $\exists 1\text{-}1 \cap R_x \,\triangleright\!\!\mid\!ix=\varrho x$.$w \cap y\exists(xPy$. $yP\mathrm{seq}qx)=\bar\varrho x$ $\mid$

$x\varepsilon v$.$\supset_x$. $R_x = \mathord{\mathrm{i}}1\text{-}1 \cap R_x \,\triangleright\!\!\mid\!ix = \varrho x$. $w \cap y\exists(xPy$. $yP\mathrm{seq}qx) = \bar\varrho x$ $\mid$:

$R_w\varepsilon$Rel $\cap$ R'$\triangleright\!\mid aR'b$.$=$. $\exists v \cap x\exists(aR_x b)\mid$. §3Prop2·16 :$\supset$. $R_w\varepsilon$ 1÷1   (1)

$R\varepsilon$Rel$_v$: $x\varepsilon v$.$\supset_x$. $w_x = \mathord{\mathrm{i}}\!\mathord{\mathrm{i}}\, y\exists(xPy$. $yP\mathrm{seq}qx)$: $\mathrm{seq}qw_x = w_{\mathrm{seq}qx}$:$\supset$. $xR_{1v}w_x$.$\supset$.

$w_x \breve{R}_{1v}$ R$\mathrm{seq}qx$. $\mathrm{seq}qx$ R$_{1v}\mathrm{seq}qw_x$:$\supset$. $w_x \breve{R}_{1v}$ R $R_{1v}\mathrm{seq}qw_x$ (2)

w_x P$\mathrm{seq}qx$. $\mathrm{seq}qx$ P$\mathrm{seq}qw_z$.$\supset$. w_z P$\mathrm{seq}qw_z$ (3)

$x\varepsilon v\text{-}\mathord{\mathrm{i}}0_v$.$\supset$. w_0 Px .$\supset$. $-(w\bar\supset\pi x)$ (4)

(4) . Hp .$\supset$. $w\bar\supset\pi 0_v$ (5)

$v\bar\pi\supset w\bar\pi$.$\supset$: $y\varepsilon w$.$\supset_y$. $\exists v \cap x'\exists(yP\mathrm{seq}qx')$ (6)

Hp (6) . §3Prop. 2·11 .$\supset$. $v \cap x'\exists(yP\mathrm{seq}qx')$ εwP   (7)

$y\varepsilon w$. $v \cap x'\exists(yP\mathrm{seq}qx') = v'$. $x = 0$ v' .$\supset$. $y = w_r$ (7)

§1 Prop5·7 . (1) . R' $= \breve{R}_{1v}$ RR_w .$\supset$. R'ε1÷1 . $w_0 = \mathord{\mathrm{i}}\!\mathord{\mathrm{i}}\,\mathord{\mathord{\mathrm{i}}}\!-\varrho'w$ (8)

$z\varepsilon$Cls . w_0 $z\varepsilon$: $x\varepsilon v$. w_x $z\varepsilon$.$\supset_x$. $\mathrm{seq}qw_x$ $z\varepsilon$:$\supset$: $x(R_{1v}\varepsilon)z w$.$\supset_x$. $\mathrm{seq}qx(R_{1v}\varepsilon)z w$ (9)

(9) . Hp(9) . Induct .$\supset$: $x\varepsilon v$.$\supset_x$. $x(R_W\varepsilon)$ $z w$ (10)

Hp (9) . (10) . $R_W\varepsilon$1÷ .$\supset$: w_x $z w$.$\supset_w$. w_z $z\varepsilon$ (11)

(7) . (8) . (11) .$\supset$. Prop]

·4 $\exists w$P $\cap w\exists(vw = \bigwedge$. $\pi v = \pi w)$ [Prop2·3 .$\supset$. Prop]

·5 $\exists v\bar\pi \cap z\exists(\pi z = \pi v)$.$\supset$. $v\bar\pi \cap z\exists(\pi z = \pi v)$ εElm

[$\pi z = \pi v$. zPz' .$\supset$. $\pi z' - = \pi v$ (1)

$\pi z = \pi v$. z'Pz .$\supset$. $\pi z' - = \pi v$ (2)   (1) . (2) .$\supset$. Prop]

·6 $\exists v\bar\pi\cap z\exists(\pi z = \pi v)$.$\supset$. $l'v = v\bar\pi \cap z\exists(\pi z = \pi v)$ Df

·61 $w\varepsilon w\exists\bar p$. $\exists w\pi\cap z\exists(\bar\pi z=\bar\pi w)$.$\supset$. $l_\bullet w=w\pi\cap z\exists(\bar\pi z=\bar\pi w)$ Df

$l'v$ and $l_\bullet w$, as just defined, are true limits, while $\lambda'v$ and $\lambda_\bullet v$ of the section preceding are either limits or maxima or minima. Since $l'v$ belongs to the class $v\pi$, $l'v$ cannot belong to the class v, which, moreover, by definition, has no maximum. Likewise $l_\bullet w$

does not belong to the class *w*, which has no minimum. If a
ωP or a $\omega\breve{\text{P}}$ possesses a limit, it is only possible to have one, but
it is possible not to have any at all. In the derived classes, $\pi\omega$,
$\omega\pi$, $\overset{\text{o}}{\omega}\pi$, $\overset{\text{o}}{\pi}\omega$, on the other hand, one can demonstrate the existence
of limits, as we have seen.

✳ 3 PεRel . P$\ni$O' . P^2=P . $u = \overline{\pi\upsilon}$: $x\varepsilon u$.$\ni_x$.$\pi x u$ $\iota x\overline{\pi} x = u$:$\ni$: :

·1 $a,b\varepsilon u$. aPb .$\ni$. $\overline{A}\omega$p $\cap$ $v$$\overline{3}(\overline{\pi v}\overline{\ni\pi}a$. πv $\ni\pi b)$

This P affirms that one can find a progression all the terms of
which are contained between two given terms of the compact
series *u*.

[$x\varepsilon u$. xPb . P^2 = P .$\ni$. $\overline{A}u\cdot y$$\overline{3}(xPy$. $yPb)$ (1)

§ 1 Prop 1·8 Rε1$\dashv$1 . $\breve{\varrho} \ni \varrho$. $\overline{A}\varrho$-ϱ . $v'\varepsilon w_\varrho$.$\ni$. $\overline{A}$ 1$\dashv$1$\cap$R$_0$ $\overline{v'}3(\varrho_0 = \iota O v'$.

$a\breve{\text{P}}\iota\varrho_0$. $\breve{\iota}\varrho_0$ P$b)$ (2)

§1 Prop1·8 . (1) . Hp(2) . $x\varepsilon v'$.$\ni$: $\overline{A}$1$\dashv$1$\cap$R$_x$ $\overline{v'}3(\varrho_x = \iota x$. $a\breve{\text{P}}\iota\varrho_x$. $\breve{\iota}\varrho_x$ P$b)$.$\ni$.

$\overline{A}$1$\dashv$1 $\cap$ R $_{\text{seq}x}$$\overline{v'}3$ (ϱ $_{\text{seq}x}$ = ιseq$x$. $\breve{\iota}\varrho$ x $\breve{\text{P}}\iota\varrho$ $_{\text{seq}x}$. $\breve{\iota}\varrho_{\text{se}}$ $_{\text{q}x}$P$b)$ (3)

(2).(3). Induct .$\ni$: $x\varepsilon v'$.$\ni_x$.$\overline{A}$1$\dashv$1$\cap$R$_x$ $\overline{v'}3(\varrho_x = \iota x$. $a\breve{\text{P}}\iota\varrho_x$.$\breve{\iota}\varrho_x$ $\breve{\text{P}}\iota\varrho$ $_{\text{seq}x}$. $\breve{\iota}\varrho$ $_{\text{seq}x}$P$b)$ (4)

$x\varepsilon v'$.$\ni_x$. S$_x$ ε1$\dashv$1$\cap$R$_x$ $\overline{v'}3(\varrho_x = \iota x$. $a\breve{\text{P}}\iota\varrho_x$. $\breve{\iota}\varrho_x$ $\breve{\text{P}}\iota\varrho$ $_{\text{seq}x}$. $\breve{\iota}\varrho$ $_{\text{seq}x}$P$b)$:

S = Rel $\cap$ R''$\overline{3}$|$\overline{A}v'\cap x3$(R'' = S$_x$)$\}$. R' = $\cup$'S .$\therefore$.$\ni$.

R'ε1$\dashv$1 . ϱ' = v' . $\breve{\varrho}'$simv' . $\overline{\pi\varrho'}$ $\ni$ $\overline{\pi}a$. $\pi\breve{\varrho}'$ $\ni$ πb (5)

(5) . § 3 Prop 1·91 .$\ni$. $\varrho'\varepsilon\omega$P   (6)   (5) . (6) .$\ni$. Prop]

In the above proof, one first takes any progression whatsoever
v' of which the generating relation is R. One takes any term whatsoever between *a* and *b* and establishes a relation Ro_v', which holds
uniquely between the first term of *v'* and the term which one takes
between *a* and *b*. Then one proves by induction that for any term
x of *v'*, one can find a relation R$_x$ which holds only between *x* and
a single term between *a* and *b*, which precedes the only term with
which seq *x* has the relation R seq *x*. Thus one takes the logical
sum R' of the relations R$_x$ for all the values of *x* for whichever *x*
is a *v*, and one demonstrates that the domain of $\breve{\text{R}}$' is a progression

in *u*, of which all the terms are found between *a* and *b*. The process which one has used can be described as 'counting without numbers'.

3·11　$a,b \varepsilon u$. aPb .ɔ. $\exists \omega \bar{P} \frown v \bar{s} (\pi v \, ɔ \, \pi a \, . \, \pi v \, ɔ \, \pi b)$

　　[§ 5 Prop 1·4 . § 6 Prop 3·1 .ɔ. Prop]

·2　$\pi \omega \, \varepsilon \, \Phi$

　　[$v,v' \varepsilon \omega P$. $\pi v T \pi v'$. $a,b \varepsilon \pi v' \cdot \pi v$. aPb . Prop 3·1 .ɔ.

　　　　$\exists \omega P \frown v'' \bar{s} (\pi v'' \, ɔ \, \pi a \, . \, \pi v' \, ɔ \, \pi b)$.ɔ. $\exists \omega P \frown v'' \bar{s} (\pi v T \pi v'' \, . \, \pi v'' T \pi v')$.ɔ. Prop]

For the definition of T, see §5 Prop 2·7.

·21　$\bar{\pi} \omega \varepsilon \Phi$

·3　$\bar{\omega} \bar{\pi} \, \varepsilon \, \Phi$

　　[Prop 1·6 .ɔ: $x,x' \varepsilon \bar{\omega} \bar{\pi}$.=. $u-x, u-x' \varepsilon \pi \omega$ (1)　(1). Prop 3·2 .⊃. Prop]

·31　$\omega \bar{\pi} \, \varepsilon \, \Phi$

·4　$\exists \pi \bar{\pi}$.ɔ. $\bar{\frown}' \pi \omega = \bar{\pi} \bar{\pi}$. $\bar{\frown}' \pi \omega \, \varepsilon \, \mathrm{Elm}$

　　[$x \varepsilon \, \pi \bar{\pi}$.ɔ: $v \varepsilon \, \omega P$.ɔ‚ $x \varepsilon \, \pi v$:ɔ. $x \varepsilon \, \bar{\frown}' \pi \omega$　　　　　　　　　　(1)

　　Prop 3·1·2 . $x \varepsilon \bar{\pi}$.ɔ. $\exists \, \omega P \frown v \bar{s} (x \varepsilon \, \bar{v \pi})$.ɔ. $x - \varepsilon \, \bar{\frown}' \pi \omega$　　　(2)

　　(1) . (2) . § 5 Prop 1·3 .ɔ. Prop]

·41　$\exists \pi \bar{\pi}$.ɔ. $\bar{\frown}' \bar{\pi} \omega = \bar{\pi} \bar{\pi}$. $\bar{\frown}' \bar{\pi} \omega \varepsilon \mathrm{Elm}$

·5　$\exists \pi \bar{\pi}$.ɔ. $\bar{\frown}' \omega \pi = \bar{\pi} \bar{\pi}$. $\bar{\frown}' \omega \pi \varepsilon \mathrm{Elm}$

　　[$x \varepsilon \pi \bar{\pi}$.ɔ: $v \varepsilon \omega \bar{P}$.ɔ‚ $x \varepsilon v \pi$:ɔ. $x \varepsilon \bar{\frown}' \omega \pi$　　　　　　　　(1)

　　$x \varepsilon \bar{\pi}$. Prop 3·11·31 .ɔ. $\exists \bar{\omega} \bar{P} \frown v \bar{s} (x \varepsilon \pi v)$.ɔ. $x - \varepsilon \bar{\frown}' \omega \pi$　　(2)　　(1) . (2) .ɔ. Prop]

·51　$\exists \pi \bar{\pi}$.ɔ. $\bar{\frown}' \bar{\omega \pi} = \bar{\pi} \bar{\pi}$. $\bar{\frown}' \omega \bar{\pi} \varepsilon \mathrm{Elm}$

·6　$\pi ɔ \bar{\pi}$.ɔ. $\bar{\frown}' \pi \omega = \wedge$　　　　　　　　Dem 3·4 N° (2) .ɔ. Prop]

·61　$\pi ɔ \bar{\pi}$.ɔ. $\bar{\frown}' \bar{\pi} \omega = \wedge$

·7　$\pi ɔ \bar{\pi}$.ɔ. $\bar{\frown}' \omega \pi = \wedge$

·71　$\bar{\pi} ɔ \bar{\pi}$.ɔ. $\bar{\frown}' \omega \pi = \wedge$

✱ 4　$P \varepsilon \mathrm{Rel}$. $P ɔ 0'$. $P^2 = P$. $u = \bar{\pi} \bar{\omega} \bar{\pi}$: $x \bar{\varepsilon} u$.ɔ‚$_x$. $x \omega x \bar{\omega} \pi x = u$.ɔ::

·1　$x T_1 y$.=. $x,y \varepsilon \pi \omega$. $x ɔ y$. $x - = y$　　　　　　　　　Df

·11　$x T_2 y$.=. $x,y \varepsilon \bar{\pi} \omega$. $x ɔ y$. $x - = y$　　　　　　　　　Df

·12　$x T_3 y$.=. $x,y \varepsilon \omega \pi$. $x ɔ y$. $x - = y$　　　　　　　　　Df

·13　$x T_4 y$.=. $x,y \varepsilon \omega \bar{\pi}$. $x ɔ y$. $x - = y$　　　　　　　　　Df

·2　$x \varepsilon \pi \omega$.ɔ. $\exists \, \omega T_1 \frown ɔ \bar{s} (1' z = x)$

　　[Prop 3·1 .ɔ: $y_1,y_2 \varepsilon u$. $y_1 P y_2$.ɔ‚$_{y_1,y_2}$. $\exists \pi \omega \frown m \bar{s} (\pi y_1 T_1 m$. $m T_1 \pi y_2)$　　(1)

　　(1) . Prop 2·1·3 . $v \varepsilon \omega P$. $x = \pi v$: $z \varepsilon v$.ɔ‚$_z$. $\bar{v}_x \varepsilon \pi \omega$. $\pi z T_1 v_z$. v_z $T_1 \pi (\mathrm{seq} z)$:

　　　$w = y_2 \vert \exists v \frown z \bar{s} (y 1' w_z) \vert$ . .ɔ. $w \varepsilon \omega T_1$ $1' w = x$]]

This P proves that any term of $\pi\omega$ (that is to say, all lower segments of u) is the upper limit of a progression of the terms of $\pi\omega$. If v is a progression in u, x a variable term of v, πv is the limit of the segments πx; but this fact does not suffice for the demonstration of 4·2, since one has no reason to believe that πx always belongs to the class $\pi\omega$, that is to say, that if x is a u, x is the upper limit of a progression in u.

$$.21 \quad x\varepsilon\,\omega\pi \;.\mathfrak{d}. \; \mathfrak{g}\,\omega\bar{T}_1 \,\cap\, z\mathfrak{z}(l_{,}\mathfrak{z}=x)$$

This P follows from Prop 3·11 as 4·2 follows from 3·1.

$$\cdot 22 \quad x\varepsilon\,\pi\omega \;.\mathfrak{d}. \; \mathfrak{g}\,\omega T_2 \,\cap\, z\mathfrak{z}(l'z=x)$$
$$\cdot 23 \quad x\varepsilon\,\omega\pi \;.\mathfrak{d}. \; \mathfrak{g}\,\omega\bar{T}_2 \,\cap\, z\mathfrak{z}(l_{,}\mathfrak{z}=x)$$
$$\cdot 24 \quad x\bar{\varepsilon}\,\pi\omega \;.\mathfrak{d}. \; \mathfrak{g}\,\omega T_2 \,\cap\, z\mathfrak{z}(l'\bar{z}=x)$$
$$\cdot 25 \quad x\varepsilon\,\mathfrak{z}\,\overline{\omega\pi} \;.\mathfrak{d}. \; \mathfrak{g}\omega\bar{T}_2 \,\cap\, z\mathfrak{z}(l\,\mathfrak{z}=x)$$
$$\cdot 26 \quad x\varepsilon\,\overline{\pi\omega} \;.\mathfrak{d}. \; \mathfrak{g}\omega T_1 \,\cap\, z\mathfrak{z}(l'\bar{z}=x)$$
$$\cdot 27 \quad x\varepsilon\,\mathfrak{z}\,\overline{\omega\pi} \;.\mathfrak{d}. \; \mathfrak{g}\omega\bar{T}_1 \,\cap\, z\mathfrak{z}(l_{,}\mathfrak{z}=x)$$

The demonstration of Prop ·22 to ·27 is similar to that of Prop 2. There are other propositions of the same form which we do not know how to demonstrate, and which do not always appear to be true. This is the proposition

$$x'\varepsilon\,\pi\omega \;..\mathfrak{d}. \; \mathfrak{g}\omega\bar{T}_1 \,\cap\, z\mathfrak{z}(l_{,}\mathfrak{z}=x')$$

$\cdot 3 \quad z\varepsilon\omega T_1 \;.\mathfrak{d}. \; l'z \,\varepsilon\,\pi\omega$
$[\; x\varepsilon z \;.\mathfrak{d}. \; xT\mathrm{seq}x \;.\mathfrak{d}. \; \mathfrak{z}u\wedge y\mathfrak{z}(xT\mathfrak{z}y \,.\, \mathfrak{z}yT\mathrm{seq}x) \qquad\qquad (1)$
$\mathrm{Prop}\ 2\cdot3 : x\varepsilon z : x\varepsilon z \;.\mathfrak{d}.\mathfrak{z}\; \mathfrak{r}_{,}\varepsilon u\wedge y\mathfrak{z}(xT\mathfrak{z}y \,.\, \mathfrak{z}yT\mathrm{seq}x) : \mathfrak{r} = \mathfrak{u}\mathfrak{z}\mathfrak{z}\mathfrak{z}\wedge z\mathfrak{z}(\mathfrak{r}l',\mathfrak{r}_{,}) : .\mathfrak{d}.$
$v\varepsilon\omega\ P \,.\, l'z = \pi v \;.\mathfrak{d}. \; \mathrm{Prop} \;]$
$.31 \quad z\varepsilon\,\omega\bar{T}_1 \;.\mathfrak{d}. \; l_{,}z\varepsilon\,\omega\pi$
$\cdot 32 \quad z\varepsilon\,\omega T_2 \;.\mathfrak{d}. \; l\,z\varepsilon\,\pi\omega$

$\cdot 33 \quad z\varepsilon\,\omega\bar{T}_2 \;.\mathfrak{d}. \; l'z\varepsilon\,\omega\pi$
$\cdot 34 \quad z\varepsilon\,\omega T_2 \;.\mathfrak{d}. \; l'\bar{z}\varepsilon\,\overline{\pi\omega}$
$\cdot 35 \quad z\varepsilon\,\omega\bar{T}_2 \;.\mathfrak{d}. \; l_{,}z\varepsilon\,\overline{\omega\pi}$
$\cdot 36 \quad z\varepsilon\,\omega T_1 \;.\mathfrak{d}. \; l'z\varepsilon\,\overline{\pi\omega}$
$\cdot 37 \quad z\varepsilon\,\omega\bar{T}_1 \;.\mathfrak{d}. \; l_{,}z\varepsilon\,\overline{\omega\pi}$

Here also there are eight other propositions of similar form which do not always appear to be true. Such is the proposition

$$z\varepsilon\,\omega\bar{T}_1 \;.\mathfrak{d}. \; l'z\varepsilon\,\pi\omega$$

Note to §6. We can now summarize the principal results of §6. A compact series (a Φ) is a series which has a term between any two of its terms. One such series is defined by a transitive relation P, which implies diversity, and which is such that $P^2 = P$. If xPy, one may say that x precedes y. If there are terms outside the series considered which have the relation P or $\breve{P}$ with other terms, one can always find another relation, equivalent to P in the series being considered, and such that all the terms which hold that relation or its converse belong to the series being considered. (§5 Prop 1·6.) In consequence, it is more simple, and no less general, to take as the type of a compact series the entire domain of a suitable relation and its converse.

Let u be one such series, P its generating relation. A progression in u is a series of type ω, contained in u, and such that one always has xP seq x, if x is a term of the progression. We call ωP the class of progressions in u. At the same time, $\omega\breve{P}$ is the class of regressions, that is to say, of series of type ω, for which $x\breve{P}$ seq x. One may construct a ωP and a $\omega\breve{P}$, of which all terms may be found between any two terms whatsoever of u.

Every class v contained in u defines four classes in u:

(1) πv, which contains all terms such that there is a v which succeeds them;

(2) $\breve{\pi}v$, which contains all terms such that there is a v which precedes them;

(3) $v\pi$, which contains all terms which precede any term of v;

(4) $v\breve{\pi}$, which contains all terms which succeed any term of v.

If v is a progression, (1) and (4) alone are important; for a regression (2) and (3) alone are important. If v is a progression, any term of u belongs to (1) or (4), and (1) does not have a last term; but one cannot know (in the general case) if (4) has a first term or not. One has some similar remarks if v is a regression.

One now advances the theory of segments, which constitutes a generalization of the theory of real numbers. One has four classes of segments:

(1) The class $\pi\omega$, which is formed of all the classes πv, where v is any ωP whatsoever;

(2) The class $\breve{\pi}\omega$, which is formed of all classes $\breve{\pi}v$, where v is any $\omega \breve{P}$ whatsoever;

(3) The class $\omega\pi$, which is formed of all the classes $v\pi$, where v is any $\omega\breve{P}$ whatsoever;

(4) The class $\omega\breve{\pi}$, which is formed of all the classes $v\breve{\pi}$, when v is any ωP whatsoever.

Each of these four classes is a Φ, of which the generating relation is derived from logical inclusion. Any term of $\omega\breve{\pi}$ is the product of u and the negation of the corresponding term of $\pi\omega$; and the same for $\breve{\pi}\omega$ and $\omega\pi$. The classes $\pi\omega$ and $\omega\pi$ may have common terms; for example, if u is the class of rational numbers, and v is a progression in u which does not have a rational limit, v' a regression which determines the same section (in the sense of Dedekind). If u is a series which satisfies Dedekind's postulate of continuity, $\pi\omega$ and $\omega\pi$ have not common terms; for then there is a third term in all classes which belong to the class $\omega\pi$, and in no class of $\pi\omega$.

In each of these four classes, $\pi\omega$, $\breve{\pi}\omega$, $\omega\pi$, $\omega\breve{\pi}$, one can construct a progression or a regression, which will always have a limit belonging to one of the four classes, but not always to the class which contains the same progression or regression. Further, any term of each of these four classes is the limit of certain progressions, or of certain regression, but not necessarily (so far as appears) of both; and the terms of the specified progressions or regressions do not have to belong to the same class as the term which is their limit. These results are summarized below:

Any term of		$\pi\omega$	is the limit of a progression in		$\pi\omega$		and a progression in		$\omega\breve{\pi}$
,,	,,	,,	$\breve{\pi}\omega$	,,	,,	,,	,, ,,	,,	,,	$\breve{\pi}\omega$	,, ,,	,,	,,	$\omega\pi$
,,	,,	,,	$\omega\pi$	,,	,,	,,	,, ,,	regression	,,	$\breve{\pi}\omega$	,, ,,	,,	,,	$\omega\pi$
,,	,,	,,	$\omega\breve{\pi}$	,,	,,	,,	,, ,,	,,	,,	$\pi\omega$	,, ,,	,,	,,	$\omega\breve{\pi}$

D

All progressions in $\pi\omega$ or in $\breve{\omega\pi}$ have a limit in $\breve{\pi\omega}$

,,   ,,   ,, $\breve{\pi\omega}$,, ,, $\breve{\omega\pi}$,, ,,   ,, $\breve{\pi\omega}$

,, regressions ,, $\pi\omega$,, ,, $\omega\pi$,, ,,   ,, $\omega\pi$

,,   ,,   ,, $\breve{\pi\omega}$,, ,, $\breve{\omega\pi}$,, ,,   ,, $\breve{\omega\pi}$

Thus:

$\pi\omega$ is identical to the class of limits of progressions in $\pi\omega$ or $\omega\pi$

$\breve{\pi\omega}$,,   ,,   ,, ,,   ,, ,,   ,, ,,   ,,   ,, $\breve{\pi\omega}$,, $\breve{\omega\pi}$

$\omega\pi$,,   ,,   ,, ,,   ,, ,,   ,, ,, regressions ,, $\pi\omega$,, $\omega\pi$

$\breve{\omega\pi}$,,   ,,   ,, ,,   ,, ,,   ,, ,,   ,,   ,, $\breve{\pi\omega}$,, $\breve{\omega\pi}$

We have not succeeded in proving that each of these four classes is a completely perfect series, but each of them is perfect either to the right or the left, that is to say, either for regressions or for progressions. The logical sum of $\pi\omega$ and $\omega\pi$, or of $\breve{\pi\omega}$ and $\breve{\omega\pi}$ is a perfect series, but in general that series will not be compact. For if there exists in u a progression v and a regression v' having the same limit in u (which is known to be possible), then πv and $v'\pi$ will be consecutive in the series $\pi\omega \cup \omega\pi$ for $v'\pi$ contains only a single term which does not belong to πv, namely the common limit. Therefore $\pi\omega \cup \omega\pi$ is not in general a continuous series.

We have not succeeded in proving that any progression or regression in u has a limit, because we do not know an example of a compact series of which no term is not a principal element (in the language of Cantor). We have not been able to prove that there are terms of $\pi\omega$ which are limits of regressions, etc.

One knows after Cantor how to prove all these theorems if u is a denumerable series [*Rivista di Matematica*, Vol. V, pp. 129-62]. We do not develop this subject, since it has been referred to previously by Cantor. In §6 we have only wished to deduce the results which are valid for all compact series, without introducing other conditions.

On Denoting

The volume of Mind *for* 1905 *appears superficially to be an out-dated collection of the sort of papers that usually fill journals issued by and for academic men. One would assume from it that the conflict between idealists and pragmatists over the nature of truth was the most important thing in the world. Embedded in this context of philo-sophic warfare and dwarfed by the seventy-eight page disquisition on 'Pragmatism v. Absolutism' that precedes it is a fourteen-page paper by Russell which he has called his finest philosophical essay. The editor of* Mind, *Professor G. F. Stout, regarded it as unusual and unconventional, but none the less had the sound judgment to print it. How many of his readers understood it remains an open question.*

On Denoting *is a milestone in the development of contemporary philosophy, revealing once more Russell's inventiveness and striking originality in thought. Ironically it contains a minor error. G. E. Moore has pointed out that Russell's 'shortest statement' at the close of the paper is faulty because of the ambiguity of the verb 'to write'. 'Scott is the author of* Waverley' *does not, therefore, have the same meaning as 'Scott wrote* Waverley', *since Scott (like blind Milton) may be the author of the work without being the person who literally wrote it for the first time. Russell has accepted this correction 'with equanimity'.* The right to feel patronizing about this slip is reserved by law to those who have done as much for philosophy as Russell and Moore.*

The fuller development of these ideas is the well-known theory of descriptions, the full statement of which was to come five years later with the publication of the first volume of the Principia Mathe-matica.

* *The Philosophy of Bertrand Russell*, Evanston and Cambridge, 1944 *et seq.*, p. 690. Moore's well-known essay is on p. 177 ff. of the same volume.

ON DENOTING

BY a 'denoting phrase' I mean a phrase such as any one of the following: a man, some man, any man, every man, all men, the present King of England, the present King of France, the centre of mass of the solar system at the first instant of the twentieth century, the revolution of the earth round the sun, the revolution of the sun round the earth. Thus a phrase is denoting solely in virtue of its *form*. We may distinguish three cases: (1) A phrase may be denoting, and yet not denote anything; e.g., 'the present King of France'. (2) A phrase may denote one definite object; e.g., 'the present King of England' denotes a certain man. (3) A phrase may denote ambiguously; e.g., 'a man' denotes not many men, but an ambiguous man. The interpretation of such phrases is a matter of considerable difficulty; indeed, it is very hard to frame any theory not susceptible of formal refutation. All the difficulties with which I am acquainted are met, so far as I can discover, by the theory which I am about to explain.

The subject of denoting is of very great importance, not only in logic and mathematics, but also in theory of knowledge. For example, we know that the centre of mass of the solar system at a definite instant is some definite point, and we can affirm a number of propositions about it; but we have no immediate *acquaintance* with this point, which is only known to us by description. The distinction between *acquaintance* and *knowledge about* is the distinction between the things we have presentations of, and the things we only reach by means of denoting phrases. It often happens that we know that a certain phrase denotes unambiguously, although we have no acquaintance with what it denotes; this occurs in the above case of the centre of mass. In perception we have acquaintance with the objects of perception, and in thought we have acquaintance with objects of a more abstract logical character;

but we do not necessarily have acquaintance with the objects denoted by phrases composed of words with whose meanings we are acquainted. To take a very important instance: there seems no reason to believe that we are ever acquainted with other people's minds, seeing that these are not directly perceived; hence what we know about them is obtained through denoting. All thinking has to start from acquaintance; but it succeeds in thinking *about* many things with which we have no acquaintance.

The course of my argument will be as follows. I shall begin by stating the theory I intend to advocate;* I shall then discuss the theories of Frege and Meinong, showing why neither of them satisfies me; then I shall give the grounds in favour of my theory; and finally I shall briefly indicate the philosophical consequences of my theory.

My theory, briefly, is as follows. I take the notion of the *variable* as fundamental; I use '$C(x)$' to mean a proposition† in which x is a constituent, where x, the variable, is essentially and wholly undetermined. Then we can consider the two notions '$C(x)$ is always true' and '$C(x)$ is sometimes true'‡. Then *everything* and *nothing* and *something* (which are the most primitive of denoting phrases) are to be interpreted as follows:

C (everything) means '$C(x)$ is always true';
C (nothing) means ' "$C(x)$ is false" is always true';
C (something) means 'It is false that "$C(x)$ is false" is always true'.§

Here the notion '$C(x)$ is always true' is taken as ultimate and indefinable, and the others are defined by means of it. *Everything*, *nothing*, and *something* are not assumed to have any meaning in isolation, but a meaning is assigned to *every* proposition in which they occur. This is the principle of the theory of denoting I wish

---

* I have discussed this subject in *Principles of Mathematics*, Chap. V, and § 476. The theory there advocated is very nearly the same as Frege's, and is quite different from the theory to be advocated in what follows.

† More exactly, a propositional function.

‡ The second of these can be defined by means of the first, if we take it to mean, 'It is not true that "$C(x)$ is false" is always true'.

§ I shall sometimes use, instead of this complicated phrase, the phrase '$C(x)$ is not always false', or '$C(x)$ is sometimes true', supposed *defined* to mean the same as the complicated phrase.

to advocate: that denoting phrases never have any meaning in themselves, but that every proposition in whose verbal expression they occur has a meaning. The difficulties concerning denoting are, I believe, all the result of a wrong analysis of propositions whose verbal expressions contain denoting phrases. The proper analysis, if I am not mistaken, may be further set forth as follows.

Suppose now we wish to interpret the proposition, 'I met a man'. If this is true, I met some definite man; but that is not what I affirm. What I affirm is, according to the theory I advocate:

'"I met x, and x is human" is not always false'.

Generally, defining the class of men as the class of objects having the predicate *human*, we say that:

'C (a man)' means '"$C(x)$ and x is human" is not always false'. This leaves 'a man', by itself, wholly destitute of meaning, but gives a meaning to every proposition in whose verbal expression 'a man' occurs.

Consider next the proposition 'all men are mortal'. This proposition* is really hypothetical and states that *if* anything is a man, it is mortal. That is, it states that if x is a man, x is mortal, whatever x may be. Hence, substituting 'x is human' for 'x is a man', we find:

'All men are mortal' means '"If x is human, x is mortal" is always true'.

This is what is expressed in symbolic logic by saying that 'all men are mortal' means '"x is human" implies "x is mortal" for all values of x'. More generally, we say:

'C (all men)' means '"If x is human, then $C(x)$ is true" is always true'.

Similarly

'C (no men)' means '"If x is human, then $C(x)$ is false" is always true'.

'C (some men)' will mean the same as 'C (a man)',† and

---

* As has been ably argued in Mr. Bradley's *Logic*, Book I, Chap. II.

† Psychologically 'C (a man)' has a suggestion of *only one*, and 'C (some men)' has a suggestion of *more than one*; but we may neglect these suggestions in a preliminary sketch.

'C (a man)' means 'It is false that "$C(x)$ and x is human" is always false'.

'C (every man)' will mean the same as 'C (all men)'.

It remains to interpret phrases containing *the*. These are by far the most interesting and difficult of denoting phrases. Take as an instance 'the father of Charles II was executed'. This asserts that there was an x who was the father of Charles II and was executed. Now *the*, when it is strictly used, involves uniqueness; we do, it is true, speak of '*the* son of So-and-so' even when So-and-so has several sons, but it would be more correct to say '*a* son of So-and-so'. Thus for our purposes we take *the* as involving uniqueness. Thus when we say 'x was *the* father of Charles II' we not only assert that x had a certain relation to Charles II, but also that nothing else had this relation. The relation in question, without the assumption of uniqueness, and without any denoting phrases, is expressed by 'x begat Charles II'. To get an equivalent of 'x was the father of Charles II', we must add, 'If y is other than x, y did not beget Charles II', or, what is equivalent, 'If y begat Charles II, y is identical with x'. Hence 'x is the father of Charles II' becomes: 'x begat Charles II; and "if y begat Charles II, y is identical with x" is always true of y'.

> Thus 'the father of Charles II was executed' becomes: 'It is not always false of x that x begat Charles II and that x was executed and that "if y begat Charles II, y is identical with x" is always true of y'.

This may seem a somewhat incredible interpretation; but I am not at present giving reasons, I am merely *stating* the theory.

To interpret 'C (the father of Charles II)', where C stands for any statement about him, we have only to substitute $C(x)$ for 'x was executed' in the above. Observe that, according to the above interpretation, whatever statement C may be, 'C (the father of Charles II)' implies:

> 'It is not always false of x that "if y begat Charles II, y is identical with x" is always true of y',

which is what is expressed in common language by 'Charles II had one father and no more'. Consequently if this condition fails, *every* proposition of the form '*C* (the father of Charles II)' is false. Thus e.g. every proposition of the form '*C* (the present King of France)' is false. This is a great advantage in the present theory. I shall show later that it is not contrary to the law of contradiction, as might be at first supposed.

The above gives a reduction of all propositions in which denoting phrases occur to forms in which no such phrases occur. Why it is imperative to effect such a reduction, the subsequent discussion will endeavour to show.

The evidence for the above theory is derived from the difficulties which seem unavoidable if we regard denoting phrases as standing for genuine constituents of the propositions in whose verbal expressions they occur. Of the possible theories which admit such constituents the simplest is that of Meinong.* This theory regards any grammatically correct denoting phrase as standing for an *object*. Thus 'the present King of France', 'the round square', etc., are supposed to be genuine objects. It is admitted that such objects do not *subsist*, but nevertheless they are supposed to be objects. This is in itself a difficult view; but the chief objection is that such objects, admittedly, are apt to infringe the law of contradiction. It is contended, for example, that the existent present King of France exists, and also does not exist; that the round square is round, and also not round, etc. But this is intolerable; and if any theory can be found to avoid this result, it is surely to be preferred.

The above breach of the law of contradiction is avoided by Frege's theory. He distinguishes, in a denoting phrase, two elements, which we may call the *meaning* and the *denotation*.† Thus 'the centre of mass of the solar system at the beginning of the twentieth century' is highly complex in *meaning*, but its *denotation* is a certain point, which is simple. The solar system, the twentieth century, etc., are constituents of the *meaning*; but the *denotation*

* See *Untersuchungen zur Gegenstandstheorie und Psychologie* (Leipzig, 1904) the first three articles (by Meinong, Ameseder and Mally respectively).

† See his 'Ueber Sinn und Bedeutung', *Zeitschrift für Phil. und Phil. Kritik*, Vol. 100.

has no constituents at all.* One advantage of this distinction is that it shows why it is often worth while to assert identity. If we say 'Scott is the author of *Waverley*', we assert an identity of denotation with a difference of meaning. I shall, however, not repeat the grounds in favour of this theory, as I have urged its claims elsewhere (loc. cit.), and am now concerned to dispute those claims.

One of the first difficulties that confront us, when we adopt the view that denoting phrases *express* a meaning and *denote* a denotation,† concerns the cases in which the denotation appears to be absent. If we say 'the King of England is bald', that is, it would seem, not a statement about the complex *meaning* 'the King of England', but about the actual man denoted by the meaning. But now consider 'the King of France is bald'. By parity of form, this also ought to be about the denotation of the phrase ' the King of France'. But this phrase, though it has a *meaning* provided 'the King of England' has a meaning, has certainly no denotation, at least in any obvious sense. Hence one would suppose that 'the King of France is bald' ought to be nonsense; but it is not nonsense, since it is plainly false. Or again consider such a proposition as the following: 'If *u* is a class which has only one member, then that one member is a member of *u*', or, as we may state it, 'If *u* is a unit class, *the u* is a *u*'. This proposition ought to be *always* true, since the conclusion is true whenever the hypothesis is true. But 'the *u*' is a denoting phrase, and it is the denotation, not the meaning, that is said to be a *u*. Now if *u* is *not* a unit class, 'the *u*' seems to denote nothing; hence our proposition would seem to become nonsense as soon as *u* is not a unit class.

Now it is plain that such propositions do *not* become non-

---

* Frege distinguishes the two elements of meaning and denotation everywhere, and not only in complex denoting phrases. Thus it is the *meanings* of the constituents of a denoting complex that enter into its *meaning*, not their *denotation*. In the proposition 'Mont Blanc is over 1,000 metres high', it is, according to him, the *meaning* of 'Mont Blanc', not the actual mountain, that is a constituent of the *meaning* of the proposition.

† In this theory, we shall say that the denoting phrase *expresses* a meaning; and we shall say both of the phrase and of the meaning that they *denote* a denotation. In the other theory, which I advocate, there is no *meaning*, and only sometimes a *denotation*.

sense merely because their hypotheses are false. The King in *The Tempest* might say, 'If Ferdinand is not drowned, Ferdinand is my only son'. Now 'my only son' is a denoting phrase, which, on the face of it, has a denotation when, and only when, I have exactly one son. But the above statement would nevertheless have remained true if Ferdinand had been in fact drowned. Thus we must either provide a denotation in cases in which it is at first sight absent, or we must abandon the view that the denotation is what is concerned in propositions which contain denoting phrases. The latter is the course that I advocate. The former course may be taken, as by Meinong, by admitting objects which do not subsist, and denying that they obey the law of contradiction; this, however, is to be avoided if possible. Another way of taking the same course (so far as our present alternative is concerned) is adopted by Frege, who provides by definition some purely conventional denotation for the cases in which otherwise there would be none. Thus 'the King of France', is to denote the null-class; 'the only son of Mr. So-and-so' (who has a fine family of ten), is to denote the class of all his sons; and so on. But this procedure, though it may not lead to actual logical error, is plainly artificial, and does not give an exact analysis of the matter. Thus if we allow that denoting phrases, in general, have the two sides of meaning and denotation, the cases where there seems to be no denotation cause difficulties both on the assumption that there really is a denotation and on the assumption that there really is none.

A logical theory may be tested by its capacity for dealing with puzzles, and it is a wholesome plan, in thinking about logic, to stock the mind with as many puzzles as possible, since these serve much the same purpose as is served by experiments in physical science. I shall therefore state three puzzles which a theory as to denoting ought to be able to solve; and I shall show later that my theory solves them.

(1) If *a* is identical with *b*, whatever is true of the one is true of the other, and either may be substituted for the other in any proposition without altering the truth or falsehood of that proposition. Now George IV wished to know whether Scott was the author of *Waverley*; and in fact Scott *was* the author of *Waverley*. Hence we may substitute *Scott* for *the author of 'Waverley'*, and thereby prove that George IV wished to know whether Scott was Scott.

Yet an interest in the law of identity can hardly be attributed to the first gentleman of Europe.

(2) By the law of excluded middle, either 'A is B' or 'A is not B' must be true. Hence either 'the present King of France is bald' or 'the present King of France is not bald' must be true. Yet if we enumerated the things that are bald, and then the things that are not bald, we should not find the present King of France in either list. Hegelians, who love a synthesis, will probably conclude that he wears a wig.

(3) Consider the proposition 'A differs from B'. If this is true, there is a difference between A and B, which fact may be expressed in the form 'the difference between A and B subsists'. But if it is false that A differs from B, then there is no difference between A and B, which fact may be expressed in the form 'the difference between A and B does not subsist'. But how can a non-entity be the subject of a proposition? 'I think, therefore I am' is no more evident than 'I am the subject of a proposition, therefore I am', provided 'I am' is taken to assert subsistence or being,* not existence. Hence, it would appear, it must always be self-contradictory to deny the being of anything; but we have seen, in connexion with Meinong, that to admit being also sometimes leads to contradictions. Thus if A and B do not differ, to suppose either that there is, or that there is not, such an object as 'the difference between A and B' seems equally impossible.

The relation of the meaning to the denotation involves certain rather curious difficulties, which seem in themselves sufficient to prove that the theory which leads to such difficulties must be wrong.

When we wish to speak about the *meaning* of a denoting phrase, as opposed to its *denotation*, the natural mode of doing so is by inverted commas. Thus we say:

The centre of mass of the solar system is a point, not a denoting complex;

'The centre of mass of the solar system' is a denoting complex, not a point.

Or again,

The first line of Gray's Elegy states a proposition.

* I use these as synonyms.

'The first line of Gray's Elegy' does not state a proposition. Thus taking any denoting phrase, say *C*, we wish to consider the relation between *C* and '*C*', where the difference of the two is of the kind exemplified in the above two instances.

We say, to begin with, that when *C* occurs it is the *denotation* that we are speaking about; but when '*C*' occurs, it is the *meaning*. Now the relation of meaning and denotation is not merely linguistic through the phrase: there must be a logical relation involved, which we express by saying that the meaning denotes the denotation. But the difficulty which confronts us is that we cannot succeed in *both* preserving the connexion of meaning and denotation *and* preventing them from being one and the same; also that the meaning cannot be got at except by means of denoting phrases. This happens as follows.

The one phrase *C* was to have both meaning and denotation. But if we speak of 'the meaning of *C*', that gives us the meaning (if any) of the denotation. 'The meaning of the first line of Gray's Elegy' is the same as 'The meaning of "The curfew tolls the knell of parting day",' and is not the same as 'The meaning of "the first line of Gray's Elegy".' Thus in order to get the meaning we want, we must speak not of 'the meaning of *C*', but of 'the meaning of "*C*",' which is the same as '*C*' by itself. Similarly 'the denotation of *C*' does not mean the denotation we want, but means something which, if it denotes at all, denotes what is denoted by the denotation we want. For example, let '*C*' be 'the denoting complex occurring in the second of the above instances'. Then

$$C = \text{'the first line of Gray's Elegy', and}$$

the denotation of *C* = The curfew tolls the knell of parting day. But what we *meant* to have as the denotation was 'the first line of Gray's Elegy'. Thus we have failed to get what we wanted.

The difficulty in speaking of the meaning of a denoting complex may be stated thus: The moment we put the complex in a proposition, the proposition is about the denotation; and if we make a proposition in which the subject is 'the meaning of *C*', then the subject is the meaning (if any) of the denotation, which was not intended. This leads us to say that, when we distinguish meaning and denotation, we must be dealing with the meaning: the meaning has denotation and is a complex, and there is not something other than the meaning, which can be called the complex, and be said to *have* both meaning and denotation. The right phrase, on the view in question, is that some meanings have denotations.

But this only makes our difficulty in speaking of meanings more evident. For suppose C is our complex; then we are to say that C *is* the meaning of the complex. Nevertheless, whenever C occurs without inverted commas, what is said is not true of the meaning, but only of the denotation, as when we say: The centre of mass of the solar system is a point. Thus to speak of C itself, i.e., to make a proposition about the meaning, our subject must not be C, but something which denotes C. Thus 'C', which is what we use when we want to speak of the meaning, must be not the meaning, but something which denotes the meaning. And C must not be a constituent of this complex (as it is of 'the meaning of C'); for if C occurs in the complex, it will be its denotation, not its meaning, that will occur, and there is no backward road from denotations to meanings, because every object can be denoted by an infinite number of different denoting phrases.

Thus it would seem that 'C' and C are different entities, such that 'C' denotes C; but this cannot be an explanation, because the relation of 'C' to C remains wholly mysterious; and where are we to find the denoting complex 'C' which is to denote C? Moreover, when C occurs in a proposition, it is not *only* the denotation that occurs (as we shall see in the next paragraph); yet, on the view in question, C is only the denotation, the meaning being wholly relegated to 'C'. This is an inextricable tangle, and seems to prove that the whole distinction of meaning and denotation has been wrongly conceived.

That the meaning is relevant when a denoting phrase occurs in a proposition is formally proved by the puzzle about the author of *Waverley*. The proposition 'Scott was the author of *Waverley*' has a property not possessed by 'Scott was Scott', namely the property that George IV wished to know whether it was true. Thus the two are not identical propositions; hence the meaning of 'the author of *Waverley*' must be relevant as well as the denotation, if we adhere to the point of view to which this distinction belongs. Yet, as we have just seen, so long as we adhere to this point of view, we are compelled to hold that only the denotation can be relevant. Thus the point of view in question must be abandoned.

It remains to show how all the puzzles we have been considering are solved by the theory explained at the beginning of this article.

According to the view which I advocate, a denoting phrase is essentially *part* of a sentence, and does not, like most single words, have any significance on its own account. If I say 'Scott was a man', that is a statement of the form '*x* was a man', and it has 'Scott' for its subject. But if I say 'the author of *Waverley* was a man', that is not a statement of the form '*x* was a man', and does not have 'the author of *Waverley*' for its subject. Abbreviating the statement made at the beginning of this article, we may put, in place of 'the author of *Waverley* was a man', the following: 'One and only one entity wrote *Waverley*, and that one was a man'. (This is not so strictly what is meant as what was said earlier; but it is easier to follow.) And speaking generally, suppose we wish to say that the author of *Waverley* had the property ϕ, what we wish to say is equivalent to 'One and only one entity wrote *Waverley*, and that one had the property ϕ'.

The explanation of *denotation* is now as follows. Every proposition in which 'the author of *Waverley*' occurs being explained as above, the proposition 'Scott was the author of *Waverley*' (i.e. 'Scott was identical with the author of *Waverley*') becomes 'One and only one entity wrote *Waverley*, and Scott was identical with that one'; or, reverting to the wholly explicit form: 'It is not always false of *x* that *x* wrote *Waverley*, that it is always true of *y* that if *y* wrote *Waverley* *y* is identical with *x*, and that Scott is identical with *x*'. Thus if '*C*' is a denoting phrase, it may happen that there is one entity *x* (there cannot be more than one) for which the proposition '*x* is identical with *C*' is true, this proposition being interpreted as above. We may then say that the entity *x* is the denotation of the phrase '*C*'. Thus Scott is the denotation of 'the author of *Waverley*'. The '*C*' in inverted commas will be merely the *phrase*, not anything that can be called the *meaning*. The phrase *per se* has no meaning, because in any proposition in which it occurs the proposition, fully expressed, does not contain the phrase, which has been broken up.

The puzzle about George IV's curiosity is now seen to have a very simple solution. The proposition 'Scott was the author of

Waverley', which was written out in its unabbreviated form in the preceding paragraph, does not contain any constituent 'the author of *Waverley*' for which we could substitute 'Scott'. This does not interfere with the truth of inferences resulting from making what is *verbally* the substitution of 'Scott' for 'the author of *Waverley*', so long as 'the author of *Waverley*' has what I call a *primary* occurrence in the proposition considered. The difference of primary and secondary occurrences of denoting phrases is as follows:

When we say: 'George IV wished to know whether so-and-so', or when we say 'So-and-so is surprising' or 'So-and-so is true', etc., the 'so-and-so' must be a proposition. Suppose now that 'so-and-so' contains a denoting phrase. We may either eliminate this denoting phrase from the subordinate proposition 'so-and-so', or from the whole proposition in which 'so-and-so' is a mere constituent. Different propositions result according to which we do. I have heard of a touchy owner of a yacht to whom a guest, on first seeing it, remarked, 'I thought your yacht was larger than it is'; and the owner replied, 'No, my yacht is not larger than it is'. What the guest meant was, 'The size that I thought your yacht was is greater than the size your yacht is'; the meaning attributed to him is, 'I thought the size of your yacht was greater than the size of your yacht'. To return to George IV and *Waverley*, when we say, 'George IV wished to know whether Scott was the author of *Waverley*', we normally mean 'George IV wished to know whether one and only one man wrote *Waverley* and Scott was that man'; but we *may* also mean: 'One and only one man wrote *Waverley*, and George IV wished to know whether Scott was that man'. In the latter, 'the author of *Waverley*' has a *primary* occurrence; in the former, a *secondary*. The latter might be expressed by 'George IV wished to know, concerning the man who in fact wrote *Waverley*, whether he was Scott'. This would be true, for example, if George IV had seen Scott at a distance, and had asked 'Is that Scott?'. A *secondary* occurrence of a denoting phrase may be defined as one in which the phrase occurs in a proposition p which is a mere constituent of the proposition we are considering, and the substitution for the denoting phrase is to be effected in p, not in the whole proposition concerned. The ambiguity as between primary and secondary occurrences is hard to avoid in language;

but it does no harm if we are on our guard against it. In symbolic logic it is of course easily avoided.

The distinction of primary and secondary occurrences also enables us to deal with the question whether the present King of France is bald or not bald, and generally with the logical status of denoting phrases that denote nothing. If 'C' is a denoting phrase, say 'the term having the property F', then

'C has the property ϕ' means 'one and only one term has the property F, and that one has the property ϕ'.*

If now the property F belongs to no terms, or to several, it follows that 'C has the property ϕ' is false for *all* values of ϕ. Thus 'the present King of France is bald' is certainly false; and 'the present King of France is not bald' is false if it means

'There is an entity which is now King of France and is not bald', but is true if it means

'It is false that there is an entity which is now King of France and is bald'.

That is, 'the King of France is not bald' is false if the occurrence of 'the King of France' is *primary*, and true if it is *secondary*. Thus all propositions in which 'the King of France' has a primary occurrence are false; the denials of such propositions are true, but in them 'the King of France' has a secondary occurrence. Thus we escape the conclusion that the King of France has a wig.

We can now see also how to deny that there is such an object as the difference between A and B in the case when A and B do not differ. If A and B do differ, there is one and only one entity x such that 'x is the difference between A and B' is a true proposition; if A and B do not differ, there is no such entity x. Thus according to the meaning of denotation lately explained, 'the difference between A and B' has a denotation when A and B differ, but not otherwise. This difference applies to true and false propositions generally. If '$a\,R\,b$' stands for 'a has the relation R to b', then when $a\,R\,b$ is true, there is such an entity as the relation R between a and b; when $a\,R\,b$ is false, there is no such entity. Thus out of any proposition we can make a denoting phrase, which denotes an entity if the proposition is true, but does not denote an entity

* This is the abbreviated, not the stricter, interpretation.

if the proposition is false. E.g., it is true (at least we will suppose so) that the earth revolves round the sun, and false that the sun revolves round the earth; hence 'the revolution of the earth round the sun' denotes an entity, while 'the revolution of the sun round the earth' does not denote an entity.*

The whole realm of non-entities, such as 'the round square', 'the even prime other than 2', 'Apollo', 'Hamlet', etc., can now be satisfactorily dealt with. All these are denoting phrases which do not denote anything. A proposition about Apollo means what we get by substituting what the classical dictionary tells us is meant by Apollo, say 'the sun-god'. All propositions in which Apollo occurs are to be interpreted by the above rules for denoting phrases. If 'Apollo' has a primary occurrence, the proposition containing the occurrence is false; if the occurrence is secondary, the proposition may be true. So again 'the round square is round' means 'there is one and only one entity x which is round and square, and that entity is round', which is a false proposition, not, as Meinong maintains, a true one. 'The most perfect Being has all perfections; existence is a perfection; therefore the most perfect Being exists' becomes:

'There is one and only one entity x which is most perfect; that one has all perfections; existence is a perfection; therefore that one exists'. As a proof, this fails for want of a proof of the premiss 'there is one and only one entity x which is most perfect'.†

Mr. MacColl (*Mind*, N.S., No. 54, and again No. 55, page 401) regards individuals as of two sorts, real and unreal; hence he defines the null-class as the class consisting of all unreal individuals. This assumes that such phrases as 'the present King of France', which do not denote a real individual, do, nevertheless, denote an individual, but an unreal one. This is essentially Meinong's theory, which we have seen reason to reject because it conflicts with the law of contradiction. With our theory of denoting, we are able to

* The propositions from which such entities are derived are not identical either with these entities or with the propositions that these entities have being.

† The argument can be made to prove validly that all members of the class of most perfect Beings exist; it can also be proved formally that this class cannot have *more* than one member; but, taking the definition of perfection as possession of all positive predicates, it can be proved almost equally formally that the class does not have even one member.

hold that there are no unreal individuals; so that the null-class is the class containing no members, not the class containing as members all unreal individuals.

It is important to observe the effect of our theory on the interpretation of definitions which proceed by means of denoting phrases. Most mathematical definitions are of this sort; for example '$m - n$ means the number which, added to n, gives m'. Thus $m - n$ is defined as meaning the same as a certain denoting phrase; but we agreed that denoting phrases have no meaning in isolation. Thus what the definition really ought to be is: 'Any proposition containing $m - n$ is to mean the proposition which results from substituting for "$m - n$" "the number which, added to n, gives m".' The resulting proposition is interpreted according to the rules already given for interpreting propositions whose verbal expression contains a denoting phrase. In the case where m and n are such that there is one and only one number x which, added to n, gives m, there is a number x which can be substituted for $m - n$ in any proposition containing $m - n$ without altering the truth or falsehood of the proposition. But in other cases, all propositions in which '$m - n$' has a primary occurrence are false.

The usefulness of *identity* is explained by the above theory. No one outside a logic-book ever wishes to say 'x is x', and yet assertions of identity are often made in such forms as 'Scott was the author of *Waverley*' or 'thou art the man'. The meaning of such propositions cannot be stated without the notion of identity, although they are not simply statements that Scott is identical with another term, the author of *Waverley*, or that thou art identical with another term, the man. The shortest statement of 'Scott is the author of *Waverley*' seems to be 'Scott wrote *Waverley*; and it is always true of y that if y wrote *Waverley*, y is identical with Scott'. It is in this way that identity enters into 'Scott is the author of *Waverley*'; and it is owing to such uses that identity is worth affirming.

One interesting result of the above theory of denoting is this: when there is anything with which we do not have immediate acquaintance, but only definition by denoting phrases, then the propositions in which this thing is introduced by means of a denoting phrase do not really contain this thing as a constituent, but contain instead the constituents expressed by the several words of the denoting phrase. Thus in every proposition that we can apprehend (i.e. not only in those whose truth or falsehood we can judge of, but in all that we can think about), all the constituents are really entities with which we have immediate acquaintance. Now such things as matter (in the sense in which matter occurs in physics) and the minds of other people are known to us only by denoting phrases, i.e. we are not *acquainted* with them, but we know them as what has such and such properties. Hence, although we can form propositional functions $C(x)$ which must hold of such and such a material particle, or of So-and-so's mind, yet we are not acquainted with the propositions which affirm these things that we know must be true, because we cannot apprehend the actual entities concerned. What we know is 'So-and-so has a mind which has such and such properties' but we do not know 'A has such and such properties', where A *is* the mind in question. In such a case, we know the properties of a thing without having acquaintance with the thing itself, and without, consequently, knowing any single proposition of which the thing itself is a constituent.

Of the many other consequences of the view I have been advocating, I will say nothing. I will only beg the reader not to make up his mind against the view—as he might be tempted to do, on account of its apparently excessive complication—until he has attempted to construct a theory of his own on the subject of denotation. This attempt, I believe, will convince him that, whatever the true theory may be, it cannot have such a simplicity as one might have expected beforehand.

Mathematical Logic as based on the Theory of Types

In this paper, originally published in the AMERICAN JOURNAL OF MATHEMATICS, Russell offers his celebrated approach to the solution of a set of classical mathematical and logical problems involving the appearance of contradiction. The doctrine of types (as he then called it) was 'put forward tentatively' in the second appendix to THE PRINCIPLES OF MATHEMATICS, a valuable discussion from the point of view of history, since it shows us these ideas in the form they took shortly after they first came to Russell in the opening years of the century, although (in the words of the Introduction he wrote to the second edition of the PRINCIPLES in 1937) as 'only a rough sketch'. The paper reprinted here gives us what was in effect the finished theory, although these ideas are better seen in the larger context in which they reappear in the first volume of the PRINCIPIA MATHEMATICA (1910).

The theory of types has played such an important role in modern philosophy that it is pointless to comment further on its significance, other than to say that this paper is one of Russell's finest and universally acknowledged to be a masterpiece of recent philosophic thought.

1908

MATHEMATICAL LOGIC AS BASED ON THE THEORY OF TYPES

THE following theory of symbolic logic recommended itself to me in the first instance by its ability to solve certain contradictions, of which the one best known to mathematicians is Burali-Forti's concerning the greatest ordinal.* But the theory in question seems not wholly dependent on this indirect recommendation; it has also, if I am not mistaken, a certain consonance with common sense which makes it inherently credible. This, however, is not a merit upon which much stress should be laid; for common sense is far more fallible than it likes to believe. I shall therefore begin by stating some of the contradictions to be solved, and shall then show how the theory of logical types effects their solution.

I. THE CONTRADICTIONS

(1) The oldest contradiction of the kind in question is the *Epimenides*. Epimenides the Cretan said that all Cretans were liars, and all other statements made by Cretans were certainly lies. Was this a lie? The simplest form of this contradiction is afforded by the man who says 'I am lying'; if he is lying, he is speaking the truth, and vice versa.

(2) Let w be the class of all those classes which are not members of themselves. Then, whatever class x may be, 'x is a w' is equivalent † to 'x is not an x'. Hence, giving to x the value w, 'w is a w' is equivalent to 'w is not a w'.

(3) Let T be the relation which subsists between two relations R and S whenever R does not have the relation R to S. Then,

* See below.

† Two propositions are called *equivalent* when both are true or both are false.

whatever relations R and S may be, 'R has the relation T to S' is equivalent to 'R does not have the relation R to S'. Hence, giving the value T to both R and S, 'T has the relation T to T' is equivalent to 'T does not have the relation T to T'.

(4) The number of syllables in the English names of finite integers tends to increase as the integers grow larger, and must gradually increase indefinitely, since only a finite number of names can be made with a given finite number of syllables. Hence the names of some integers must consist of at least nineteen syllables, and among these there must be a least. Hence 'the least integer not nameable in fewer than nineteen syllables' must denote a definite integer; in fact, it denotes 111,777. But 'the least integer not nameable in fewer than nineteen syllables' is itself a name consisting of eighteen syllables; hence the least integer not nameable in fewer than nineteen syllables can be named in eighteen syllables, which is a contradiction.*

(5) Among transfinite ordinals some can be defined, while others can not; for the total number of possible definitions is $\aleph_0$, while the number of transfinite ordinals exceeds $\aleph_0$. Hence there must be indefinable ordinals, and among these there must be a least. But this is defined as 'the least indefinable ordinal', which is a contradiction.†

(6) Richard's paradox‡ is akin to that of the least indefinable ordinal. It is as follows: Consider all decimals that can be defined by means of a finite number of words; let E be the class of such decimals. Then E has $\aleph_0$ terms; hence its members can be ordered as the 1st, 2nd, 3rd, ... Let N be a number defined as follows: If the nth figure in the nth decimal is p, let the nth figure in N be $p + 1$ (or 0, if $p = 9$). Then N is different from all the members of

---

* This contradiction was suggested to me by Mr. G. G. Berry of the Bodleian Library.

† Cf. König, 'Über die Grundlagen der Mengenlehre und das Kontinuum-problem', *Math. Annalen*, Vol. LXI (1905); A. C. Dixon, 'On "well-ordered" aggregates', *Proc. London Math. Soc.*, Series 2, Vol. IV, Part I (1906); and E. W. Hobson, 'On the Arithmetic Continuum', ibid. The solution offered in the last of these papers does not seem to me adequate.

‡ Cf. Poincaré, 'Les mathématiques et la logique', *Revue de Métaphysique et de Morale* (May, 1906), especially sections VII and IX; also Peano, *Revista de Mathematica*, Vol. VIII, No. 5 (1906), p. 149 ff.

E, since, whatever finite value n may have, the nth figure in N is different from the nth figure in the nth of the decimals composing E, and therefore N is different from the nth decimal. Nevertheless we have defined N in a finite number of words, and therefore N ought to be a member of E. Thus N both is and is not a member of E.

(7) Burali-Forti's contradiction* may be stated as follows: It can be shown that every well-ordered series has an ordinal number, that the series of ordinals up to and including any given ordinal exceeds the given ordinal by one, and (on certain very natural assumptions) that the series of all ordinals (in order of magnitude) is well ordered. It follows that the series of all ordinals has an ordinal number, Ω say. But in that case the series of all ordinals including Ω has the ordinal number $\Omega + 1$, which must be greater than Ω. Hence Ω is not the ordinal number of all ordinals.

In all the above contradictions (which are merely selections from an indefinite number) there is a common characteristic, which we may describe as self-reference or reflexiveness. The remark of Epimenides must include itself in its own scope. If *all* classes, provided they are not members of themselves, are members of w, this must also apply to w; and similarly for the analogous relational contradiction. In the cases of names and definitions, the paradoxes result from considering non-nameability and indefinability as elements in names and definitions. In the case of Burali-Forti's paradox, the series whose ordinal number causes the difficulty is the series of all ordinal numbers. In each contradiction something is said about *all* cases of some kind, and from what is said a new case seems to be generated, which both is and is not of the same kind as the cases of which *all* were concerned in what was said. Let us go through the contradictions one by one and see how this occurs.

(1) When a man says 'I am lying', we may interpret his statement as : 'There is a proposition which I am affirming and which is false'. All statements that 'there is' so-and-so may be regarded as denying that the opposite is always true; thus 'I am lying' becomes: 'It is not true of all propositions that either I am not affirming them or they are true'; in other words, 'It is not true for all propositions p that if I affirm p, p is true'. The paradox results

---

* 'Una questione sui numeri transfiniti', *Rendiconti del circolo matematico di Palermo*, Vol. XI (1897).

from regarding this statement as affirming a proposition, which must therefore come within the scope of the statement. This, however, makes it evident that the notion of 'all propositions' is illegitimate; for otherwise, there must be propositions (such as the above) which are about all propositions, and yet can not, without contradiction, be included among the propositions they are about. Whatever we suppose to be the totality of propositions, statements about this totality generate new propositions which, on pain of contradiction, must lie outside the totality. It is useless to enlarge the totality, for that equally enlarges the scope of statements about the totality. Hence there must be no totality of propositions, and 'all propositions' must be a meaningless phrase.

(2) In this case, the class w is defined by reference to 'all classes', and then turns out to be one among classes. If we seek help by deciding that no class is a member of itself, then w becomes the class of all classes, and we have to decide that this is not a member of itself, i.e., is not a class. This is only possible if there is no such thing as the class of all classes in the sense required by the paradox. That there is no such class results from the fact that, if we suppose there is, the supposition immediately gives rise (as in the above contradiction) to new classes lying outside the supposed total of all classes.

(3) This case is exactly analogous to (2), and shows that we can not legitimately speak of 'all relations'.

(4) 'The least integer not nameable in fewer than nineteen syllables' involves the totality of names, for it is 'the least integer such that all names either do not apply to it or have more than nineteen syllables'. Here we assume, in obtaining the contradiction, that a phrase containing 'all names' is itself a name, though it appears from the contradiction that it can not be one of the names which were supposed to be all the names there are. Hence 'all names' is an illegitimate notion.

(5) This case, similarly, shows that 'all definitions' is an illegitimate notion.

(6) This is solved, like (5), by remarking that 'all definitions' is an illegitimate notion. Thus the number E is *not* defined in a finite number of words, being in fact not defined at all.*

---

* Cf. 'Les paradoxes de la logique', by the present author, *Revue de Métaphysique et de Morale* (September, 1906), p. 645.

(7) Burali-Forti's contradiction shows that 'all ordinals' is an illegitimate notion; for if not, all ordinals in order of magnitude form a well-ordered series, which must have an ordinal number greater than all ordinals.

Thus all our contradictions have in common the assumption of a totality such that, if it were legitimate, it would at once be enlarged by new members defined in terms of itself.

This leads us to the rule: 'Whatever involves *all* of a collection must not be one of the collection'; or, conversely: 'If, provided a certain collection had a total, it would have members only definable in terms of that total, then the said collection has no total'.*

The above principle is, however, purely negative in its scope. It suffices to show that many theories are wrong, but it does not show how the errors are to be rectified. We can not say: 'When I speak of *all* propositions, I mean all except those in which "all propositions" are mentioned'; for in this explanation we have mentioned the propositions in which all propositions are mentioned, which we can not do significantly. It is impossible to avoid mentioning a thing by mentioning that we won't mention it. One might as well, in talking to a man with a long nose, say: 'When I speak of noses, I except such as are inordinately long', which would not be a very successful effort to avoid a painful topic. Thus it is necessary, if we are not to sin against the above negative principle, to construct our logic without mentioning such things as 'all propositions' or 'all properties', and without even having to say that we are excluding such things. The exclusion must result naturally and inevitably from our positive doctrines, which must make it plain that 'all propositions' and 'all properties' are meaningless phrases.

The first difficulty that confronts us is as to the fundamental principles of logic known under the quaint name of 'laws of thought'. 'All propositions are either true or false', for example, has become meaningless. If it were significant, it would be a proposition, and would come under its own scope. Nevertheless, some

---

* When I say that a collection has no total, I mean that statements about *all* its members are nonsense. Furthermore, it will be found that the use of this principle requires the distinction of *all* and *any* considered in Section II.

substitute must be found, or all general accounts of deduction become impossible.

Another more special difficulty is illustrated by the particular case of mathematical induction. We want to be able to say: 'If n is a finite integer, n has all properties possessed by o and by the successors of all numbers possessing them'. But here 'all properties' must be replaced by some other phrase not open to the same objections. It might be thought that 'all properties possessed by o and by the successors of all numbers possessing them' might be legitimate even if 'all properties' were not. But in fact this is not so. We shall find that phrases of the form 'all properties which *etc.*' involve *all* properties of which the '*etc.*' can be significantly either affirmed or denied, and not only those which in fact have whatever characteristic is in question; for, in the absence of a catalogue of properties having this characteristic, a statement about all those that have the characteristic must be hypothetical, and of the form: 'It is always true that, if a property has the said characteristic, then etc.' Thus mathematical induction is *prima facie* incapable of being significantly enunciated, if 'all properties' is a phrase destitute of meaning. This difficulty, as we shall see later, can be avoided; for the present we must consider the laws of logic, since these are far more fundamental.

II. ALL AND ANY

Given a statement containing a variable x, say '$x = x$', we may affirm that this holds in all instances, or we may affirm any one of the instances without deciding as to which instance we are affirming. The distinction is roughly the same as that between the general and particular enunciation in Euclid. The general enunciation tells us something about (say) all triangles, while the particular enunciation takes one triangle, and asserts the same thing of this one triangle. But the triangle taken is *any* triangle, not some one special triangle; and thus although, throughout the proof, only one triangle is dealt with, yet the proof retains its generality. If we say: 'Let ABC be a triangle, then the sides AB, AC are together greater than the side BC', we are saying something about *one* triangle, not about *all* triangles; but the one triangle concerned is absolutely ambiguous, and our statement consequently is also absolutely ambiguous. We do not affirm any one definite proposition, but an undetermined one of all the propositions resulting from supposing *ABC* to be this or that triangle. This notion of ambiguous assertion is very important, and it is vital not to confound an ambiguous assertion with the definite assertion that the same thing holds in *all* cases.

The distinction between (1) asserting any value of a propositional function, and (2) asserting that the function is always true, is present throughout mathematics, as it is in Euclid's distinction of general and particular enunciations. In any chain of mathematical reasoning, the objects whose properties are being investigated are the arguments to *any* value of some propositional function. Take as an illustration the following definition:

'We call $f(x)$ continuous for $x = a$ if, for every positive number σ, different from 0, there exists a positive number ϵ, different from 0, such that, for all values of δ which are numerically less than ϵ, the difference $f(a + \delta) - f(a)$ is numerically less than σ.'

Here the function f is *any* function for which the above statement has a meaning; the statement is *about f*, and varies as *f* varies. But the statement is not *about* σ or ϵ or δ, because *all* possible values of these are concerned, not one undetermined value. (In regard to ϵ, the statement 'there exists a positive number ϵ such that *etc.*' is the denial that the denial of '*etc.*' is true of *all* positive numbers.) For this reason, when *any* value of a propositional function is asserted, the argument (e.g., f in the above) is called a *real* variable; whereas, when a function is said to be *always* true, or to be not always true, the argument is called an *apparent* variable.* Thus in the above definition, f is a real variable, and σ, ϵ, δ are apparent variables.

When we assert *any* value of a propositional function, we shall say simply that we assert the *propositional function*. Thus if we enunciate the law of identity in the form '$x = x$', we are asserting the function '$x = x$'; i.e., we are asserting any value of this function. Similarly we may be said to deny a propositional function when we deny any instance of it. We can only truly assert a propositional function if, whatever value we choose, that value is true;

* These two terms are due to Peano, who uses them approximately in the above sense. Cf., e.g., *Formulaire Mathématique* (Turin, 1903), Vol. IV, p. 5.

similarly we can only truly deny it if, whatever value we choose, that value is false. Hence in the general case, in which some values are true and some false, we can neither assert nor deny a propositional function.*

If ϕx is a propositional function, we will denote by '$(x) \, . \, \phi x$' the proposition 'ϕx is always true'. Similarly '$(x, y) \, . \, \phi(x, y)$' will mean '$\phi(x, y)$ is always true', and so on. Then the distinction between the assertion of all values and the assertion of any is the distinction between (1) asserting $(x) \, . \, \phi x$ and (2) asserting ϕx where x is undetermined. The latter differs from the former in that it can not be treated as one determinate proposition.

The distinction between asserting ϕx and asserting $(x) \, . \, \phi x$ was, I believe, first emphasized by Frege.† His reason for introducing the distinction explicitly was the same which had caused it to be present in the practice of mathematicians; namely, that deduction can only be effected with *real* variables, not with apparent variables. In the case of Euclid's proofs, this is evident: we need (say) some one triangle ABC to reason about, though it does not matter what triangle it is. The triangle ABC is a *real* variable; and although it is *any* triangle, it remains the *same* triangle throughout the argument. But in the general enunciation, the triangle is an apparent variable. If we adhere to the apparent variable, we can not perform any deductions, and this is why in all proofs, real variables have to be used. Suppose, to take the simplest case, that we know 'ϕx is always true', i.e. '$(x) \, . \, \phi x$', and we know 'ϕx always implies ψx', i.e. '$(x) \, . \, \{\phi x$ implies $\psi x\}$'. How shall we infer 'ψx is always true', i.e. '$(x) \, . \, \psi x$'? We know it is always true that if ϕx is true, and if ϕx implies ψx, then ψx is true. But we have no premises to the effect that ϕx is true and ϕx implies ψx; what we have is: ϕx is *always* true, and ϕx *always* implies ψx. In order to make our inference, we must go from 'ϕx is always true' to ϕx, and from 'ϕx always implies ψx' to 'ϕx implies ψx', where the x, while remaining any possible argument, is to be the same in both. Then, from 'ϕx'

---

* Mr. MacColl speaks of 'propositions' as divided into the three classes of certain, variable, and impossible. We may accept this division as applying to propositional functions. A function which can be asserted is certain, one which can be denied is impossible, and all others are (in Mr. MacColl's sense) variable.

† See his *Grundgesetze der Arithmetik* (Jena, 1893), Vol. I, § 17, p. 31.

and 'ϕx implies ψx', we infer 'ψx'; thus ψx is true for any possible argument, and therefore is always true. Thus in order to infer '$(x) . \psi x$' from '$(x) . \phi x$' and '$(x) . \{\phi x$ implies $\psi x\}$', we have to pass from the apparent to the real variable, and then back again to the apparent variable. This process is required in all mathematical reasoning which proceeds from the assertion of all values of one or more propositional functions to the assertion of all values of some other propositional function, as, e.g., from 'all isosceles triangles have equal angles at the base' to 'all triangles having equal angles at the base are isosceles'. In particular, this process is required in proving *Barbara* and the other moods of the syllogism. In a word, *all deduction operates with real variables* (or with constants).

It might be supposed that we could dispense with apparent variables altogether, contenting ourselves with *any* as a substitute for *all*. This, however, is not the case. Take, for example, the definition of a continuous function quoted above: in this definition σ, ϵ, and δ must be apparent variables. Apparent variables are constantly required for definitions. Take, e.g., the following: 'An integer is called a *prime* when it has no integral factors except 1 and itself'. This definition unavoidably involves an apparent variable in the form: 'If n is an integer other than 1 or the given integer, n is not a factor of the given integer, for all possible values of n'.

The distinction between *all* and *any* is, therefore, necessary to deductive reasoning, and occurs throughout mathematics; though, so far as I know, its importance remained unnoticed until Frege pointed it out.

For our purposes it has a different utility, which is very great. In the case of such variables as propositions or properties, 'any value' is legitimate, though 'all values' is not. Thus we may say: 'p is true or false, where p is any proposition', though we can not say 'all propositions are true or false'. The reason is that, in the former, we merely affirm an undetermined one of the propositions of the form 'p is true or false', whereas in the latter we affirm (if anything) a new proposition, different from all the propositions of the form 'p is true or false'. Thus we may admit 'any value' of a variable in cases where 'all values' would lead to reflexive fallacies; for the admission of 'any value' does not in the same way create new values. Hence the fundamental laws of logic can be stated concerning *any* proposition, though we can not significantly say that they hold of *all* propositions. These laws have, so to speak, a particular enunciation but no general enunciation. There is no one proposition which *is* the law of contradiction (say); there are only the various instances of the law. Of any proposition p, we can say: 'p and not-p can not both be true'; but there is no such proposition as: 'Every proposition p is such that p and not-p can not both be true'.

A similar explanation applies to properties. We can speak of *any* property of x, but not of *all* properties, because new properties would be thereby generated. Thus we can say: 'If n is a finite integer, and if o has the property ϕ, and $m+1$ has the property ϕ provided m has it, it follows that n has the property ϕ'. Here we need not specify ϕ; ϕ stands for 'any property'. But we can not say: 'A finite integer is defined as one which has *every* property ϕ possessed by o and by the successors of possessors'. For here it is essential to consider *every* property,* not *any* property; and in using such a definition we assume that it embodies a *property* distinctive of finite integers, which is just the kind of assumption from which, as we saw, the reflexive contradictions spring.

In the above instance, it is necessary to avoid the suggestions of ordinary language, which is not suitable for expressing the distinction required. The point may be illustrated further as follows: If induction is to be used for defining finite integers, induction must state a definite property of finite integers, not an ambiguous property. But if ϕ is a real variable, the statement 'n has the property ϕ provided this property is possessed by o and by the successors of possessors' assigns to n a property which varies as ϕ varies, and such a property can not be used to define the class of finite integers. We wish to say: '"n is a finite integer" means: "Whatever property ϕ may be, n has the property ϕ provided ϕ is possessed by o and by the successors of possessors".' But here ϕ has become an *apparent* variable. To keep it a real variable, we should have to say: 'Whatever property ϕ may be, "n is a finite integer" means: "n has the property ϕ provided ϕ is possessed by o and by the successors of possessors".' But here the meaning of "n is a finite integer" varies as ϕ varies, and thus such a definition is impossible. This

* This is indistinguishable from 'all properties'.

case illustrates an important point, namely the following: 'The scope* of a real variable can never be less than the whole propositional function in the assertion of which the said variable occurs'. That is, if our propositional function is (say) 'ϕx implies p', the assertion of this function will mean 'any value of "ϕx implies p" is true', *not* ' "any value of ϕx is true" implies p'. In the latter, we have really '*all* values of ϕx are true', and the x is an *apparent* variable.

III. THE MEANING AND RANGE OF GENERALIZED
PROPOSITIONS

In this section we have to consider first the meaning of propositions in which the word *all* occurs, and then the kind of collections which admit of propositions about all their members.

It is convenient to give the name *generalized propositions* not only to such as contain *all*, but also to such as contain *some* (undefined). The proposition 'ϕx is sometimes true' is equivalent to the denial of 'not-ϕx is always true'; 'some A is B' is equivalent to the denial of 'all A is not B'; i.e., of 'no A is B'. Whether it is possible to find interpretations which distinguish 'ϕx is sometimes true' from the denial of 'not-ϕx is always true', it is unnecessary to inquire; for our purposes we may *define* 'ϕx is sometimes true' as the denial of 'not-ϕx is always true'. In any case, the two kinds of propositions require the same kind of interpretation, and are subject to the same limitations. In each there is an apparent variable; and it is the presence of an apparent variable which constitutes what I mean by a generalized proposition. (Note that there can not be a *real* variable in any proposition; for what contains a real variable is a propositional function, not a proposition.)

The first question we have to ask in this section is: How are we to interpret the word *all* in such propositions as 'all men are mortal?' At first sight, it might be thought that there could be no difficulty, that 'all men' is a perfectly clear idea, and that we say of all men that they are mortal. But to this view there are many objections.

* The *scope* of a real variable is the whole function of which 'any value' is in question. Thus in 'ϕx implies p' the scope of x is not ϕx, but 'ϕx implies' p.

(1) If this view were right, it would seem that 'all men are mortal' could not be true if there were no men. Yet, as Mr. Bradley has urged,* 'Trespassers will be prosecuted' may be perfectly true even if no one trespasses; and hence, as he further argues, we are driven to interpret such propositions as hypotheticals, meaning 'if anyone trespasses, he will be prosecuted'; i.e., 'if x trespasses, x will be prosecuted', where the range of values which x may have, whatever it is, is certainly not confined to those who really trespass. Similarly 'all men are mortal' will mean 'if x is a man, x is mortal, where x may have any value within a certain range'. What this range is, remains to be determined; but in any case it is wider than 'men', for the above hypothetical is certainly often true when x is not a man.

(2) 'All men' is a denoting phrase; and it would appear, for reasons which I have set forth elsewhere,† that denoting phrases never have any meaning in isolation, but only enter as constituents into the verbal expression of propositions which contain no constituent corresponding to the denoting phrases in question. That is to say, a denoting phrase is defined by means of the propositions in whose verbal expression it occurs. Hence it is impossible that these propositions should acquire their meaning through the denoting phrases; we must find an independent interpretation of the propositions containing such phrases, and must not use these phrases in explaining what such propositions mean. Hence we can not regard 'all men are mortal' as a statement about 'all men'.

(3) Even if there were such an object as 'all men', it is plain that it is not this object to which we attribute mortality when we say 'all men are mortal'. If we were attributing mortality to this object, we should have to say '*all men* is mortal'. Thus the supposition that there is such an object as 'all men' will not help us to interpret 'all men are mortal'.

(4) It seems obvious that, if we meet something which may be a man or may be an angel in disguise, it comes within the scope of 'all men are mortal' to assert 'if this is a man, it is mortal'. Thus again, as in the case of the trespassers, it seems plain that we are

---

* *Logic*, Part I, Chapter II.

† 'On Denoting', *Mind* (October, 1905). [The second paper in this volume. R.C.M.]

really saying 'if anything is a man, it is mortal', and that the question whether this or that is a man does not fall within the scope of our assertion, as it would do if the *all* really referred to 'all men'.

(5) We thus arrive at the view that what is meant by 'all men are mortal' may be more explicitly stated in some such form as 'it is always true that if x is a man, x is mortal'. Here we have to inquire as to the scope of the word *always*.

(6) It is obvious that *always* includes some cases in which x is not a man, as we saw in the case of the disguised angel. If x were limited to the case when x is a man, we could infer that x is a mortal, since if x is a man, x is a mortal. Hence, with the same meaning of *always*, we should find 'it is always true that x is mortal'. But it is plain that, without altering the meaning of *always*, this new proposition is false, though the other was true.

(7) One might hope that 'always' would mean 'for all values of x'. But 'all values of x', if legitimate, would include as parts 'all propositions' and 'all functions', and such illegitimate totalities. Hence the values of x must be somehow restricted within some legitimate totality. This seems to lead us to the traditional doctrine of a 'universe of discourse' within which x must be supposed to lie.

(8) Yet it is quite essential that we should have some meaning of *always* which does not have to be expressed in a restrictive hypothesis as to x. For suppose 'always' means 'whenever x belongs to the class i'. Then 'all men are mortal' becomes 'whenever x belongs to the class i, if x is a man, x is mortal'; i.e., 'it is always true that if x belongs to the class i, then, if x is a man, x is mortal'. But what is our new *always* to mean? There seems no more reason for restricting x, in this new proposition, to the class i, than there was before for restricting it to the class *man*. Thus we shall be led on to a new wider universe, and so on *ad infinitum*, unless we can discover some natural restriction upon the possible values of (i.e., some restriction given with) the function 'if x is a man, x is mortal', and not needing to be imposed from without.

(9) It seems obvious that, since all men are mortal, there can not be any *false* proposition which is a value of the function 'if x is a man, x is mortal'. For if this is a proposition at all, the hypothesis 'x is a man' must be a proposition, and so must the conclusion 'x is mortal'. But if the hypothesis is false, the hypothetical

is true; and if the hypothesis is true, the hypothetical is true. Hence there can be no false propositions of the form 'if x is a man, x is mortal'.

(10) It follows that, if any values of x are to be excluded, they can only be values for which there is no proposition of the form 'if x is a man, x is mortal'; i.e., for which this phrase is meaningless. Since, as we saw in (7), there must be excluded values of x, it follows that the function 'if x is a man, x is mortal' must have a certain *range of significance*,* which falls short of all imaginable values of x, though it exceeds the values which are men. The restriction on x is therefore a restriction to the range of significance of the function 'if x is a man, x is mortal'.

(11) We thus reach the conclusion that 'all men are mortal' means 'if x is a man, x is mortal, always', where *always* means 'for all values of the function "if x is a man, x is mortal".' This is an *internal* limitation upon x, given by the nature of the function; and it is a limitation which does not require explicit statement, since it is impossible for a function to be true more generally than for all its values. Moreover, if the range of significance of the function is i, the function 'if x is an i, then if x is a man, x is mortal' has the same range of significance, since it can not be significant unless its constituent 'if x is a man, x is mortal' is significant. But here the range of significance is again implicit, as it was in "if x is a man, x is mortal"; thus we can not make ranges of significance explicit, since the attempt to do so only gives rise to a new proposition in which the same range of significance is implicit.

Thus generally: '$(x) \cdot \phi x$' is to mean 'ϕx always'. This may be interpreted, though with less exactitude, as 'ϕx is always true', or, more explicitly: 'All propositions of the form ϕx are true', or 'All values of the function ϕx are true'.† Thus the fundamental *all* is 'all values of a propositional function', and every other *all* is derivative from this. And every propositional function has a certain

---

* A function is said to be significant for the argument x if it has a value for this argument. Thus we may say shortly 'ϕx is significant', meaning 'the function ϕ has a value for the argument x'. The range of significance of a function consists of all the arguments for which the function is true, together with all the arguments for which it is false.

† A linguistically convenient expression for this idea is: 'ϕx is true for all *possible* values of x', a possible value being understood to be one for which ϕx is significant.

range of significance, within which lie the arguments for which the function has values. Within this range of arguments, the function is true or false; outside this range, it is nonsense.

The above argumentation may be summed up as follows:

The difficulty which besets attempts to restrict the variable is, that restrictions naturally express themselves as hypotheses that the variable is of such or such a kind, and that, when so expressed, the resulting hypothetical is free from the intended restriction. For example, let us attempt to restrict the variable to *men*, and assert that, subject to this restriction, '*x* is mortal' is always true. Then what is always true is that if *x* is a man, *x* is mortal; and this hypothetical is true even when *x* is not a man. Thus a variable can never be restricted within a certain range if the propositional function in which the variable occurs remains significant when the variable is outside that range. But if the function ceases to be significant when the variable goes outside a certain range, then the variable is *ipso facto* confined to that range, without the need of any explicit statement to that effect. This principle is to be borne in mind in the development of logical types, to which we shall shortly proceed.

We can now begin to see how it comes that 'all so-and-so's' is sometimes a legitimate phrase and sometimes not. Suppose we say 'all terms which have the property ϕ have the property ψ'. That means, according to the above interpretation, 'ϕx always implies ψx'. Provided the range of significance of ϕx is the same as that of ψx, this statement is significant; thus, given any definite function ϕx, there are propositions about 'all the terms satisfying ϕx'. But it sometimes happens (as we shall see more fully later on) that what appears verbally as one function is really many analogous functions with different ranges of significance. This applies, for example, to 'p is true', which, we shall find, is not really one function of p, but is different functions according to the kind of proposition that p is. In such a case, the *phrase* expressing the ambiguous function may, owing to the ambiguity, be significant throughout a set of values of the argument exceeding the range of significance of any one function. In such a case, *all* is not legitimate. Thus if we try to say 'all true propositions have the property ϕ', i.e., ' "p is true" always implies ϕp', the possible arguments to "p is true" necessarily exceed the possible arguments to

ϕ, and therefore the attempted general statement is impossible. For this reason, genuine general statements about all true propositions can not be made. It may happen, however, that the supposed function ϕ is really ambiguous like "p is true", and if it happens to have an ambiguity precisely of the same kind as that of "p is true", we may be able always to give an interpretation to the proposition ' "p is true" implies ϕp'. This will occur, e.g., if ϕp is 'not-p is false'. Thus we get an appearance, in such cases, of a general proposition concerning *all* propositions; but this appearance is due to a systematic ambiguity about such words as *true* and *false*. (This systematic ambiguity results from the hierarchy of propositions which will be explained later on.) We may, in all such cases, make our statement about *any* proposition, since the meaning of the ambiguous words will adapt itself to any proposition. But if we turn our proposition into an apparent variable, and say something about *all*, we must suppose the ambiguous words fixed to this or that possible meaning, though it may be quite irrelevant which of their possible meanings they are to have. This is how it happens both that *all* has limitations which exclude 'all propositions', and that there nevertheless *seem* to be true statements about 'all propositions'. Both these points will become plainer when the theory of types has been explained.

It has often been suggested* that what is required in order that it may be legitimate to speak of *all* of a collection is that the collection should be finite. Thus 'all men are mortal' will be legitimate because men form a finite class. But that is not really the reason why we can speak of 'all men'. What is essential, as appears from the above discussion, is not finitude, but what may be called *logical homogeneity*. This property is to belong to any collection whose terms are all contained within the range of significance of some one function. It would always be obvious at a glance whether a collection possessed this property or not, if it were not for the concealed ambiguity in common logical terms such as *true* and *false*, which gives an appearance of being a single function to what is really a conglomeration of many functions with different ranges of significance.

The conclusions of this section are as follows: Every proposition

* E.g., by M. Poincaré, *Revue de Métaphysique et de Morale* (May, 1906).

containing *all* asserts that some propositional function is always true; and this means that all values of the said function are true, not that the function is true for all arguments, since there are arguments for which any given function is meaningless, i.e., has no value. Hence we can speak of *all* of a collection when and only when the collection forms part or the whole of the *range of significance* of some propositional function, the range of significance being defined as the collection of those arguments for which the function in question is significant, i.e., has a value.

IV. THE HIERARCHY OF TYPES

A *type* is defined as the range of significance of a propositional function, i.e., as the collection of arguments for which the said function has values. Whenever an apparent variable occurs in a proposition, the range of values of the apparent variable is a type, the type being fixed by the function of which 'all values' are concerned. The division of objects into types is necessitated by the reflexive fallacies which otherwise arise. These fallacies, as we saw, are to be avoided by what may be called the 'vicious-circle principle'; i.e., 'no totality can contain members defined in terms of itself'. This principle, in our technical language, becomes: 'Whatever contains an apparent variable must not be a possible value of that variable'. Thus whatever contains an apparent variable must be of a different type from the possible values of that variable; we will say that it is of a *higher* type. Thus the apparent variables contained in an expression are what determines its type. This is the guiding principle in what follows.

Propositions which contain apparent variables are generated from such as do not contain these apparent variables by processes of which one is always the process of *generalization*, i.e., the substitution of a variable for one of the terms of a proposition, and the assertion of the resulting function for all possible values of the variable. Hence a proposition is called a *generalized* proposition when it contains an apparent variable. A proposition containing no apparent variable we will call an *elementary* proposition. It is plain that a proposition containing an apparent variable presupposes others from which it can be obtained by generalization; hence all generalized propositions presuppose elementary propositions. In an elementary proposition we can distinguish one or more *terms* from one or more *concepts*; the *terms* are whatever can be regarded as the *subject* of the proposition, while the concepts are the predicates or relations asserted of these terms.* The terms of elementary propositions we will call *individuals*; these form the first or lowest type.

It is unnecessary, in practice, to know what objects belong to the lowest type, or even whether the lowest type of variable occurring in a given context is that of individuals or some other. For in practice only the *relative* types of variables are relevant; thus the lowest type occurring in a given context may be called that of individuals, so far as that context is concerned. It follows that the above account of individuals is not essential to the truth of what follows; all that is essential is the way in which other types are generated from individuals, however the type of individuals may be constituted.

By applying the process of generalization to individuals occurring in elementary propositions, we obtain new propositions. The legitimacy of this process requires only that no individuals should be propositions. That this is so, is to be secured by the meaning we give to the word *individual*. We may define an individual as something destitute of complexity; it is then obviously not a proposition, since propositions are essentially complex. Hence in applying the process of generalization to individuals we run no risk of incurring reflexive fallacies.

Elementary propositions together with such as contain only individuals as apparent variables we will call *first-order propositions*. These form the second logical type.

We have thus a new totality, that of *first-order propositions*. We can thus form new propositions in which first-order propositions occur as apparent variables. These we will call *second-order propositions*; these form the third logical type. Thus, e.g., if Epimenides asserts 'all first-order propositions affirmed by me are false', he asserts a second-order proposition; he may assert this truly, without asserting truly any first-order proposition, and thus no contradiction arises.

The above process can be continued indefinitely. The $n+1$th logical type will consist of propositions of order n, which will be

* See *Principles of Mathematics*, § 48.

such as contain propositions of order $n-1$, but of no higher order, as apparent variables. The types so obtained are mutually exclusive, and thus no reflexive fallacies are possible so long as we remember that an apparent variable must always be confined within some one type.

In practice, a hierarchy of *functions* is more convenient than one of propositions. Functions of various orders may be obtained from propositions of various orders by the method of *substitution*. If p is a proposition, and a a constituent of p, let 'p/aːx' denote the proposition which results from substituting x for a wherever a occurs in p. Then p/a, which we will call a *matrix*, may take the place of a function; its value for the argument x is p/aːx, and its value for the argument a is p. Similarly, if '$p/(a, b)$ː(x, y)' denotes the result of first substituting x for a and then substituting y for b, we may use the double matrix $p/(a, b)$ to represent a double function. In this way we can avoid apparent variables other than individuals and propositions of various orders. The *order* of a matrix will be defined as being the order of the proposition in which the substitution is effected, which proposition we will call the *prototype*. The order of a matrix does not determine its type: in the first place because it does not determine the number of arguments for which others are to be substituted (i.e., whether the matrix is of the form p/a or $p/(a, b)$ or $p/(a, b, c)$ etc.); in the second place because, if the prototype is of more than the first order, the arguments may be either propositions or individuals. But it is plain that the type of a matrix is definable always by means of the hierarchy of propositions.

Although it is *possible* to replace functions by matrices, and although this procedure introduces a certain simplicity into the explanation of types, it is technically inconvenient. Technically, it is convenient to replace the prototype p by ϕa, and to replace p/aːx by ϕx; thus where, if matrices were being employed, p and a would appear as apparent variables, we now have ϕ as our apparent variable. In order that ϕ may be legitimate as an apparent variable, it is necessary that its values should be confined to propositions of some one type. Hence we proceed as follows.

A function whose argument is an individual and whose value is always a first-order proposition will be called a first-order function. A function involving a first-order function or proposition as apparent variable will be called a second-order function, and so on. A function of one variable which is of the order next above that of its argument will be called a *predicative* function; the same name will be given to a function of several variables if there is one among these variables in respect of which the function becomes predicative when values are assigned to all the other variables. Then the type of a function is determined by the type of its values and the number and type of its arguments.

The heirarchy of functions may be further explained as follows. A first-order function of an individual x will be denoted by $\phi!x$ (the letters ψ, χ, θ, f, g, F, G will also be used for functions). No first-order function contains a function as apparent variable; hence such functions form a well-defined totality, and the ϕ in $\phi!x$ can be turned into an apparent variable. Any proposition in which ϕ appears as apparent variable, and there is no apparent variable of higher type than ϕ, is a second-order proposition. If such a proposition contains an individual x, it is not a predicative function of x; but if it contains a first-order function ϕ, it is a predicative function of ϕ, and will be written $f!(\psi!\hat{z})$. Then f is a *second-order predicative function*; the possible values of f again form a well-defined totality, and we can turn f into an apparent variable. We can thus define *third-order predicative functions*, which will be such as have third-order propositions for their values and second-order predicative functions for their arguments. And in this way we can proceed indefinitely. A precisely similar development applies to functions of several variables.

We will adopt the following conventions. Variables of the lowest type occurring in any context will be denoted by small Latin letters (excluding f and g, which are reserved for functions); a predicative function of an argument x (where x may be of any type) will be denoted by $\phi!x$ (where ψ, χ, θ, f, g, F or G may replace ϕ); similarly a predicative function of two arguments x and y will be denoted by $\phi!(x, y)$; a general function of x will be denoted by ϕx, and a general function of x and y by $\phi(x, y)$. In ϕx, ϕ can not be made into an apparent variable, since its type is indeterminate; but in $\phi!x$, where ϕ is a *predicative* function whose argument is of some given type, ϕ *can* be made into an apparent variable.

It is important to observe that since there are various types of propositions and functions, and since generalization can only be applied within some one type, all phrases containing the words 'all propositions' or 'all functions' are prima facie meaningless, though in certain cases they are capable of an unobjectionable interpretation. The contradictions arise from the use of such phrases in cases where no innocent meaning can be found.

If we now revert to the contradictions, we see at once that some of them are solved by the theory of types. Whercver 'all propositions' are mentioned, we must substitute 'all propositions of order n', where it is indifferent what value we give to n, but it is essential that n should have *some* value. Thus when a man says 'I am lying', we must interpret him as meaning: 'There is a proposition of order n, which I affirm, and which is false'. This is a proposition of order $n+1$; hence the man is not affirming any proposition of order n; hence his statement is false, and yet its falsehood does not imply, as that of 'I am lying' appeared to do, that he is making a true statement. This solves the liar.

Consider next 'the least integer not nameable in fewer than nineteen syllables'. It is to be observed, in the first place, that *nameable* must mean 'nameable by means of such-and-such assigned names', and that the number of assigned names must be finite. For if it is not finite, there is no reason why there should be any integer not nameable in fewer than nineteen syllables, and the paradox collapses. We may next suppose that 'nameable in terms of names of the class N' means 'being the only term satisfying some function composed wholly of names of the class N'. The solution of this paradox lies, I think, in the simple observation that 'nameable in terms of names of the class N' is never itself nameable in terms of names of that class. If we enlarge N by adding the name 'nameable in terms of names of the class N', our fundamental apparatus of names is enlarged; calling the new apparatus N', 'nameable in terms of names of the class N'' remains not nameable in terms of names of the class N'. If we try to enlarge N till it embraces *all* names, 'nameable' becomes (by what was said above) 'being the only term satisfying some function composed wholly of names'. But here there is a function as apparent variable; hence we are confined to predicative functions of some one type (for non-precative functions can not be apparent variables). Hence we have only to observe that nameability in terms of such functions is non-predicative in order to escape the paradox.

The case of 'the least indefinable ordinal' is closely analogous to the case we have just discussed. Here, as before, 'definable' must be relative to some given apparatus of fundamental ideas; and there is reason to suppose that 'definable in terms of ideas of the class *N*' is not definable in terms of ideas of the class *N*. It will be true that there is some definite segment of the series of ordinals consisting wholly of definable ordinals, and having the least indefinable ordinal as its limit. This least indefinable ordinal will be definable by a slight enlargement of our fundamental apparatus; but there will then be a new ordinal which will be the least that is indefinable with the new apparatus. If we enlarge our apparatus so as to include all possible ideas, there is no longer any reason to believe that there is any indefinable ordinal. The apparent force of the paradox lies largely, I think, in the supposition that if all the ordinals of a certain class are definable, the class must be definable, in which case its successor is of course also definable; but there is no reason for accepting this supposition.

The other contradictions, that of Burali-Forti in particular, require some further developments for their solution.

V. THE AXIOM OF REDUCIBILITY

A propositional function of *x* may, as we have seen, be of any order; hence any statement about 'all properties of *x*' is meaningless. (A 'property of *x*' is the same thing as a 'propositional function which holds of *x*'.) But it is absolutely necessary, if mathematics is to be possible, that we should have some method of making statements which will usually be equivalent to what we have in mind when we (inaccurately) speak of 'all properties of *x*'. This necessity appears in many cases, but especially in connexion with mathematical induction. We can say, by the use of *any* instead of *all*, 'Any property possessed by o, and by the successors of all numbers possessing it, is possessed by all finite numbers'. But we can not go on to: 'A finite number is one which possesses *all* properties possessed by o and by the successors of all numbers possessing them'. If we confine this statement to all first-order properties of numbers, we can not infer that it holds of second-order properties. For example, we shall be unable to prove that if *m*, *n* are finite numbers, then *m* + *n* is a finite number. For, with the above definition, 'm is a finite number' is a second-order property of m; hence the fact that $m+0$ is a finite number, and that, if $m+n$ is a finite number, so is $m+n+1$, does not allow us to conclude by induction that $m+n$ is a finite number. It is obvious that such a state of things renders much of elementary mathematics impossible.

The other definition of finitude, by the non-similarity of whole and part, fares no better. For this definition is: 'A class is said to be finite when every one-one relation whose domain is the class and whose converse domain is contained in the class has the whole class for its converse domain'. Here a variable relation appears, i.e., a variable function of two variables; we have to take *all* values of this function, which requires that it should be of some assigned order; but any assigned order will not enable us to deduce many of the propositions of elementary mathematics.

Hence we must find, if possible, some method of reducing the order of a propositional function without affecting the truth or falsehood of its values. This seems to be what common sense effects by the admission of *classes*. Given any propositional function ϕx, of whatever order, this is assumed to be equivalent, for all values of x, to a statement of the form 'x belongs to the class a'. Now this statement is of the first order, since it makes no allusion to 'all functions of such-and-such a type'. Indeed its only practical advantage over the original statement ϕx is that it is of the first order. There is no advantage in assuming that there really are such things as classes, and the contradiction about the classes which are not members of themselves shows that, if there are classes, they must be something radically different from individuals. I believe the chief purpose which classes serve, and the chief reason which makes them linguistically convenient, is that they provide a method of reducing the order of a propositional function. I shall, therefore, not assume anything of what may seem to be involved in the common sense admission of classes, except this: that every propositional function is equivalent, for all its values, to some predicative function.

This assumption with regard to functions is to be made whatever may be the type of their arguments. Let ϕx be a function, of any order, of an argument x, which may itself be either an individual or a function of any order. If ϕ is of the order next above x, we write the function in the form $\phi!x$; in such a case we will call ϕ a *predicative* function. Thus a predicative function of an individual is a first-order function; and for higher types of arguments, predicative functions take the place that first-order functions take in respect of individuals. We assume, then, that every function is equivalent, for all its values, to some predicative function of the same argument. This assumption seems to be the essence of the usual assumption of classes; at any rate, it retains as much of classes as we have any use for, and little enough to avoid the contradictions which a less grudging admission of classes is apt to entail. We will call this assumption the *axiom of classes*, or the *axiom of reducibility*.

We shall assume similarly that every function of two variables is equivalent, for all its values, to a predicative function of those variables, where a predicative function of two variables is one such that there is one of the variables in respect of which the function becomes predicative (in our previous sense) when a value is assigned to the other variable. This assumption is what seems to be meant by saying that any statement about two variables defines a relation between them. We will call this assumption the *axiom of relations* or the *axiom of reducibility*.

In dealing with relations between more than two terms, similar assumptions would be needed for three, four, . . . variables. But these assumptions are not indispensable for our purpose, and are therefore not made in this paper.

By the help of the axiom of reducibility, statements about 'all first-order functions of x' or 'all predicative functions of a' yield most of the results which otherwise would require 'all functions'. The essential point is that such results are obtained in all cases where only the truth or falsehood of values of the functions concerned are relevant, as is invariably the case in mathematics. Thus mathematical induction, for example, need now only be stated for all predicative functions of numbers; it then follows from the axiom of classes that it holds of *any* function of whatever order. It might be thought that the paradoxes for the sake of which we invented the hierarchy of types would now reappear. But this is not the case, because, in such paradoxes, either something beyond the truth or falsehood of values of functions is relevant, or expressions occur which are unmeaning even after the introduction of the axiom of reducibility. For example, such a statement as 'Epimenides asserts ψx' is not equivalent to 'Epimenides asserts $\phi ! x$', even though ψx and $\phi ! x$ are equivalent. Thus 'I am lying' remains unmeaning if we attempt to include *all* propositions among those which I may be falsely affirming, and is unaffected by the axiom of classes if we confine it to propositions of order n. The hierarchy of propositions and functions, therefore, remains relevant in just those cases in which there is a paradox to be avoided.

VI. PRIMITIVE IDEAS AND PROPOSITIONS OF SYMBOLIC LOGIC

The primitive ideas required in symbolic logic appear to be the following seven:

(1) Any propositional function of a variable x or of several variables $x, y, z, \ldots$ This will be denoted by ϕx or $\phi(x, y, z, \ldots)$

(2) The negation of a proposition. If p is the proposition, its negation will be denoted by $\sim p$.

(3) The disjunction or logical sum of two propositions; i.e., 'this or that'. If p, q are the two propositions, their disjunction will be denoted by $p \vee q$.*

(4) The truth of *any* value of a propositional function; i.e., of ϕx where x is not specified.

(5) The truth of *all* values of a propositional function. This is denoted by $(x) . \phi x$ or $(x) : \phi x$ or whatever larger number of dots may be necessary to bracket off the proposition.† In $(x) . \phi x$, x is called an *apparent variable*, whereas when ϕx is asserted, where x is not specified, x is called a *real variable*.

(6) Any predicative function of an argument of any type; this will be represented by $\phi ! x$ or $\phi ! a$ or $\phi ! R$, according to circum-

---

* In a previous article in this journal, I took implication as indefinable, instead of disjunction. The choice between the two is a matter of taste; I now choose disjunction, because it enables us to diminish the number of primitive propositions. [See 'The Theory of Implication', *American Journal of Mathematics*, Vol. XXVIII, 1906, pp. 159–202—R.C.M.]

† The use of dots follows Peano's usage. It is fully explained by Mr. Whitehead, 'On Cardinal Numbers', *American Journal of Mathematics*, Vol. XXIV, and 'On Mathematical Concepts of the Material World', *Phil. Trans. A.*, *Vol.* CCV, p. 472.

stances. A predicative function of x is one whose values are pro-positions of the type next above that of x, if x is an individual or a proposition, or that of values of x if x is a function. It may be described as one in which the apparent variables, if any, are all of the same type as x or of lower type; and a variable is of lower type than x if it can significantly occur as argument to x, or as argument to an argument to x, etc.

(7) Assertion; i.e., the assertion that some proposition is true, or that any value of some propositional function is true. This is required to distinguish a proposition actually asserted from one merely considered, or from one adduced as hypothesis to some other. It will be indicated by the sign '⊢' prefixed to what is asserted, with enough dots to bracket off what is asserted.*

Before proceeding to the primitive propositions, we need certain definitions. In the following definitions, as well as in the primitive propositions, the letters p, q, r are used to denote propositions.

$$p \supset q \, . = . \sim p \vee q \quad \text{Df.}$$

This definition states that '$p \supset q$' (which is read 'p implies q') is to mean 'p is false or q is true'. I do not mean to affirm that 'im-plies' can not have any other meaning, but only that this meaning is the one which it is most convenient to give to 'implies' in sym-bolic logic. In a definition, the sign of equality and the letters 'Df' are to be regarded as one symbol, meaning jointly 'is defined to mean'. The sign of equality without the letters 'Df' has a different meaning, to be defined shortly.

$$p \, . \, q \, . = . \sim (\sim p \vee \sim q) \quad \text{Df.}$$

This defines the logical product of two propositions p and q, i.e., 'p and q are both true'. The above definition states that this is to mean: 'It is false that either p is false or q is false'. Here again, the definition does not give the only meaning which can be given to 'p and q are both true', but gives the meaning which is most con-venient for our purposes.

$$p \equiv q \, . = . \, p \supset q \, . \, q \supset p \quad \text{Df.}$$

* This sign, as well as the introduction of the idea which it expresses, is due to Frege. See his *Begriffsschrift* (Halle, 1879), p. 1, and *Grundgesetze der Arithmetik* (Jena, 1893), Vol. I, p. 9.

That is, '$p \equiv q$', which is read 'p is equivalent to q', means 'p implies q and q implies p'; whence, of course, it follows that p and q are both true or both false.

$$(\exists x) . \phi x . = . \sim\{(x) . \sim\phi x\} \quad \text{Df.}$$

This defines 'there is at least one value of x for which ϕx is true'. We define it as meaning 'it is false that ϕx is always false'.

$$x = y . = : (\phi) : \phi ! x . \supset . \phi ! y \quad \text{Df.}$$

This is the definition of identity. It states that x and y are to be called identical when every predicative function satisfied by x is satisfied by y. It follows from the axiom of reducibility that if x satisfies ψx, where ψ is any function, predicative or non-predicative, then y satisfies ψy.

The following definitions are less important, and are introduced solely for the purpose of abbreviation.

$$(x, y) . \phi(x, y) . = : (x) : (y) . \phi(x, y) \quad \text{Df,}$$
$$(\exists x, y) . \phi(x, y) . = : (\exists x) : (\exists y) . \phi(x, y) \quad \text{Df,}$$
$$\phi x . \supset_x . \psi x := : (x) : \phi x \supset \psi x \quad \text{Df,}$$
$$\phi x . \equiv_x . \psi x := : (x) : \phi x . \equiv . \psi x \quad \text{Df,}$$
$$\phi(x, y) . \supset_{x, y} . \psi(x, y) := : (x, y) : \phi(x, y) . \supset . \psi(x, y) \quad \text{Df,}$$

and so on for any number of variables.

The primitive propositions required are as follows. (In 2, 3, 4, 5, 6, and 10, p, q, r stand for propositions.)

(1) A proposition implied by a true premise is true.

(2) $\vdash : p \lor p . \supset . p$.

(3) $\vdash : q . \supset . p \lor q$.

(4) $\vdash : p \lor q . \supset . q \lor p$.

(5) $\vdash : p \lor (q \lor r) . \supset . q \lor (p \lor r)$.

(6) $\vdash :. q \supset r . \supset : p \lor q . \supset . p \lor r$.

(7) $\vdash : (x) . \phi x . \supset . \phi y$;

i.e., 'if all values of $\phi \hat{x}$ are true, then ϕy is true, where ϕy is any value'.*

(8) If ϕy is true, where ϕy is any value of $\phi \hat{x}$, then $(x) . \phi x$ is true. This can not be expressed in our symbols; for if we write

---

* It is convenient to use the notation ϕx to denote the function itself, as opposed to this or that value of the function.

'$\phi y . \supset . (x) . \phi x$', that means '$\phi y$ implies that all values of $\phi \hat{x}$ are true, where y may have any value of the appropriate type', which is not in general the case. What we mean to assert is: 'If, however y is chosen, ϕy is true, then $(x) . \phi x$ is true', whereas what is expressed by '$\phi y . \supset . (x) . \phi x$' is: 'However y is chosen, if ϕy is true, then $(x) . \phi x$ is true', which is quite a different statement, and in general a false one.

(9) $\vdash : (x) . \phi x . \supset . \phi a$, where a is any definite constant.

This principle is really as many different principles as there are possible values of a. I.e., it states that, e.g., whatever holds of all individuals holds of Socrates; also that it holds of Plato; and so on. It is the principle that a general rule may be applied to particular cases; but in order to give it scope, it is necessary to mention the particular cases, since otherwise we need the principle itself to assure us that the general rule that general rules may be applied to particular cases may be applied (say) to the particular case of Socrates. It is thus that this principle differs from (7); our present principle makes a statement about Socrates, or about Plato, or some other definite constant, whereas (7) made a statement about a variable.

The above principle is never used in symbolic logic or in pure mathematics, since all our propositions are general, and even when (as in 'one is a number') we seem to have a strictly particular case, this turns out not to be so when closely examined. In fact, the use of the above principle is the distinguishing mark of *applied* mathematics. Thus, strictly speaking, we might have omitted it from our list.

(10) $\vdash : . (x) . p \vee \phi x . \supset : p . \vee . (x) . \phi x$;

i.e., 'if "p or ϕx" is always true, then either p is true, or ϕx is always true'.

(11) When $f(\phi x)$ is true whatever argument x may be, and $F(\phi y)$ is true whatever possible argument y may be, then $\{f(\phi x) . F(\phi x)\}$ is true whatever possible argument x may be.

This is the axiom of the 'identification of variables'. It is needed when two separate propositional functions are each known to be always true, and we wish to infer that their logical product is always true. This inference is only legitimate if the two functions take arguments of the same type, for otherwise their logical product is meaningless. In the above axiom, x and y must be of the same type, because both occur as arguments to ϕ.

(12) If $\phi x . \phi x \supset \psi x$ is true for any possible x, then ψx is true for any possible x.

This axiom is required in order to assure us that the range of significance of ψx, in the case supposed, is the same as that of $\phi x . \phi x \supset \psi x . \supset . \psi x$; both are in fact the same as that of ϕx. We know, in the case supposed, that ψx is true whenever $\phi x . \phi x \supset \psi x$ and $\phi x . \phi x \supset \psi x . \supset . \psi x$ are both significant, but we do not know, without an axiom, that ψx is true whenever ψx is significant. Hence the need of the axiom.

Axioms (11) and (12) are required, e.g., in proving

$$(x) . \phi x : (x) . \phi x \supset \psi x : \supset . (x) . \psi x.$$

By (7) and (11),

$$\vdash : . (x) . \phi x : (x) . \phi x \supset \psi x : \supset : \phi y . \phi y \supset \psi y,$$

whence by (12),

$$\vdash : . (x) . \phi x : (x) . \phi x \supset \psi x : \supset : \psi y,$$

whence the result follows by (8) and (10).

(13) $\vdash : . (\exists f) : . (x) : \phi x . \equiv . f ! x.$

This is the axiom of reducibility. It states that, given any function $\phi \hat{x}$, there is a predicative function $f ! \hat{x}$ such that $f ! x$ is always equivalent to ϕx. Note that, since a proposition beginning with '$(\exists f)$' is, by definition, the negation of one beginning with '(f)', the above axiom involves the possibility of considering 'all predicative functions of x'. If ϕx is *any* function of x, we can not make propositions beginning with '(ϕ)' or '$(\exists \phi)$', since we can not consider 'all functions', but only '*any* function' or 'all *predicative* functions'.

(14) $\vdash : . (\exists f) : . (x, y) : \phi(x, y) . \equiv . f ! (x, y).$

This is the axiom of reducibility for double functions.

In the above propositions, our x and y may be of any type whatever. The only way in which the theory of types is relevant is that (11) only allows us to identify real variables occurring in different contents when they are shown to be of the same type by both occurring as arguments to the same function, and that, in (7) and (9), y and a must respectively be of the appropriate type for arguments to $\phi\hat{z}$. Thus, for example, suppose we have a proposition of the form $(\phi) \cdot f!(\phi!\hat{z}, x)$, which is a second-order function of x. Then by (7),

$$\vdash : (\phi) \cdot f!(\phi!\hat{z}, x) \cdot \supset \cdot f!(\psi!\hat{z}, x),$$

where $\psi!\hat{z}$ is any *first*-order function. But it will not do to treat $(\phi) \cdot f!(\phi!\hat{z}, x)$ as if it were a first-order function of x, and take this function as a possible value of $\psi!\hat{z}$ in the above. It is such confusions of types that give rise to the paradox of the *liar*.

Again, consider the classes which are not members of themselves. It is plain that, since we have identified classes with functions,[*] no class can be significantly said to be or not to be a member of itself; for the members of a class are arguments to it, and arguments to a function are always of lower type than the function. And if we ask: 'But how about the class of all classes? Is not that a class, and so a member of itself?', the answer is twofold. First, if 'the class of all classes' means 'the class of all classes of whatever type', then there is no such notion. Secondly, if 'the class of all classes' means 'the class of all classes of type t', then this is a class of the next type above t, and is therefore again not a member of itself.

Thus although the above primitive propositions apply equally to all types, they do not enable us to elicit contradictions. Hence in the course of any deduction it is never necessary to consider the absolute type of a variable; it is only necessary to see that the different variables occurring in one proposition are of the proper relative types. This excludes such functions as that from which our fourth contradiction was obtained, namely: 'The relation R holds between R and S'. For a relation between R and S is necessarily of higher type than either of them, so that the proposed function is meaningless.

VII. ELEMENTARY THEORY OF CLASSES AND RELATIONS

Propositions in which a function ϕ occurs may depend, for their truth-value, upon the particular function ϕ, or they may depend

---

[*] This identification is subject to a modification to be explained shortly.

only upon the *extension* of ϕ, i.e., upon the arguments which satisfy ϕ. A function of the latter sort we will call *extensional*. Thus, e.g., 'I believe that all men are mortal' may not be equivalent to 'I believe that all featherless bipeds are mortal', even if men are co-extensive with featherless bipeds; for I may not know that they are coextensive. But 'all men are mortal' must be equivalent to 'all featherless bipeds are mortal' if men are coextensive with featherless bipeds. Thus 'all men are mortal' is an extensional function of the function 'x is a man', while 'I believe all men are mortal' is a function which is not extensional; we will call functions *intensional* when they are not extensional. The functions of functions with which mathematics is specially concerned are all extensional. The mark of an extensional function f of a function $\phi!\hat{z}$ is

$$\phi!x . \equiv_x . \psi!x : \supset_{\phi,\psi} :f(\phi!\hat{z}) . \equiv .f(\psi!\hat{z}).$$

From any function f of a function $\phi!\hat{z}$ we can derive an associated extensional function as follows. Put

$$f\{\hat{z}(\psi z)\} . = : (\exists\phi):\phi!x . \equiv_x . \psi x :f\{\phi!\hat{z}\} \quad \text{Df.}$$

The function $f\{\hat{z}(\psi z)\}$ is in reality a function of $\psi\hat{z}$, though not the same function as $f(\psi\hat{z})$, supposing this latter to be significant. But it is convenient to treat $f\{\hat{z}(\psi z)\}$ technically as though it had an argument $\hat{z}(\psi z)$, which we call 'the class defined by ψ'. We have

$$\vdash :. \phi x . \equiv_x . \psi x : \supset :f\{\hat{z}(\phi z)\} . \equiv .f\{\hat{z}(\psi z)\},$$

whence, applying to the fictitious objects $\hat{z}(\phi z)$ and $\hat{z}(\psi z)$ the definition of identity given above, we find

$$\vdash :. \phi x . \equiv_x . \psi x : \supset .\hat{z}(\phi z) = \hat{z}(\psi z).$$

This, with its converse (which can also be proved), is the distinctive property of classes. Hence we are justified in treating $\hat{z}(\phi z)$ as the class defined by ϕ. In the same way we put

$$f\{\hat{x}\hat{y}\psi(x, y)\} . = : (\exists\phi):\phi!(x, y) . \equiv_{x, y} . \psi(x, y) :f\{\phi!(\hat{x}, \hat{y})\} \quad \text{Df.}$$

A few words are necessary here as to the distinction between $\phi!(\hat{x}, \hat{y})$ and $\phi!(\hat{y}, \hat{x})$. We will adopt the following convention: When a function (as opposed to its values) is represented in a form involving $\hat{x}$ and $\hat{y}$, or any other two letters of the alphabet, the value of this function for the arguments a and b is to be found by substituting a for $\hat{x}$ and b for $\hat{y}$; i.e., the argument mentioned first is to be substituted for the letter which comes earlier in the alphabet, and the argument mentioned second for the later letter. This sufficiently distinguishes between $\phi!(\hat{x}, \hat{y})$ and $\phi!(\hat{y}, \hat{x})$; e.g.:

The value of $\phi!(\hat{x}, \hat{y})$ for arguments a, b is $\phi!(a, b)$.

,,	,,	,,	,,	,,	b, a ,, $\phi!(b, a)$.
,,	,,	$\phi!(\hat{y}, \hat{x})$	,,	,,	a, b ,, $\phi!(b, a)$.
,,	,,	,,	,,	,,	b, a ,, $\phi!(a, b)$.

We put

$$x\epsilon\phi!\hat{z}. = .\phi!x \quad \text{Df,}$$

whence

$$\vdash: .x\epsilon\hat{z}(\psi z). = :(\exists\phi):\phi!y.\equiv_y.\psi y:\phi!x.$$

Also by the reducibility-axiom we have

$$(\exists\phi):\phi!y.\equiv_y.\psi y,$$

whence

$$\vdash:x\epsilon\hat{z}(\psi z).\equiv.\psi x.$$

This holds whatever x may be. Suppose now we want to consider $\hat{z}(\psi z)\,\epsilon\hat{\phi}f\{\hat{z}(\phi!z)\}$. We have, by the above,

$$\vdash: .\hat{z}(\psi z)\,\epsilon\hat{\phi}f\{\hat{z}(\phi!z)\}.\equiv :f\{\hat{z}(\psi z)\}:$$
$$\equiv :(\exists\phi):\phi!y.\equiv_y.\psi y:f\{\phi!z\},$$

whence

$$\vdash: .\hat{z}(\psi z) = \hat{z}(\chi z).\supset :\hat{z}(\psi z)\epsilon x.\equiv_\kappa.\hat{z}(\chi z)\epsilon x,$$

where x is written for any expression of the form $\hat{\phi}f\{\hat{z}(\phi!z)\}$.

We put

$$cls = \hat{a}\{(\exists\phi).a = \hat{z}(\phi!z)\} \quad \text{Df.}$$

Here *cls* has a meaning which depends upon the type of the apparent variable ϕ. Thus, e.g., the proposition '*cls ϵ cls*', which is a consequence of the above definition, requires that '*cls*' should have a different meaning in the two places where it occurs. The symbol '*cls*' can only be used where it is unnecessary to know the type; it has an ambiguity which adjusts itself to circumstances. If we introduce as an indefinable the function '$\text{Indiv}!x$', meaning 'x is an individual', we may put

$$Kl = \hat{a}\{(\exists\phi).a = \hat{z}(\phi!z.\text{Indiv}!z)\} \quad \text{Df.}$$

Then *Kl* is an unambiguous symbol meaning 'classes of individuals'.

We will use small Greek letters (other than ϵ, ϕ, ψ, χ, θ) to represent classes of whatever type; i.e., to stand for symbols of the form $\hat{z}(\phi \,!\, z)$ or $\hat{z}(\phi z)$.

The theory of classes proceeds, from this point on, much as in Peano's system; $\hat{z}(\phi z)$ replaces $z \ni (\phi z)$. Also I put

$$\alpha \subset \beta \,.\, = \,:\, x\epsilon\alpha \,.\, \supset_x \,.\, x\epsilon\beta \quad \text{Df},$$
$$\exists \,!\, \alpha \,.\, = \,.\, (\exists x) \,.\, x\epsilon\alpha \quad \text{Df},$$
$$V = \hat{x}(x=x) \quad \text{Df},$$
$$\Lambda = x\{\sim(x=x)\} \quad \text{Df},$$

where Λ, as with Peano, is the null-class. The symbols $\exists$, Λ, V, like *cls* and ϵ, are ambiguous, and only acquire a definite meaning when the type concerned is otherwise indicated.

We treat relations in exactly the same way, putting

$$a\{\phi \,!\, (\hat{x}, \hat{y})\}b \,.\, = \,.\, \phi \,!\, (a,\, b) \quad \text{Df},$$

(the order being determined by the alphabetical order of x and y and the typographical order of a and b); whence

$$\vdash \,:.\, a\{\hat{x}\hat{y}\psi(x,\, y)\}b \,.\, \equiv \,:(\exists\phi) :\psi(x,\, y) \,.\, \equiv_{x,\,y} \,.\, \phi \,!\, (x,\, y) : \phi \,!\, (a,\, b),$$

whence, by the reducibility-axiom,

$$\vdash \,:\, a\{\hat{x}\hat{y}\psi(x, y)\}b \,.\, \equiv \,.\, \psi(a,\, b).$$

We use Latin capital letters as abbreviations for such symbols as $\hat{x}\hat{y}\psi(x,\, y)$, and we find

$$\vdash \,:.\, R = S \,.\, \equiv \,:\, xRy \,.\, \equiv_{x,\,y} \,.\, xSy,$$

where

$$R = S \,.\, = \,:\, f \,!\, R \,.\, \supset_f \,.\, f \,!\, S \quad \text{Df}.$$

We put

$$\mathrm{Rel} = \hat{R}\{(\exists\phi) \,.\, R = \hat{x}\hat{y}\phi \,!\, (x,\, y)\} \quad \text{Df},$$

and we find that everything proved for classes has its analogue for dual relations. Following Peano, we put

$$\alpha \cap \beta = \hat{x}(x\epsilon\alpha \,.\, x\epsilon\beta) \quad \text{Df},$$

defining the product, or common part, of two classes;

$$\alpha \cup \beta = \hat{x}(x\epsilon\alpha \,.\, \vee \,.\, x\epsilon\beta) \quad \text{Df},$$

defining the sum of two classes; and

$$-\alpha = \hat{x}\{\sim(x\epsilon\alpha)\} \quad \text{Df},$$

defining the negation of a class. Similarly for relations we put

$$R \mathbin{\dot\cap} S = \hat{x}\hat{y}(xRy \mathbin{.} xSy) \quad \text{Df},$$
$$R \mathbin{\cup} S = \hat{x}\hat{y}(xRy \mathbin{.} \mathbin{\vee} \mathbin{.} xSy) \quad \text{Df},$$
$$\mathbin{\dot-} R = \hat{x}\hat{y}\{\sim (xRy)\} \quad \text{Df}.$$

VIII. DESCRIPTIVE FUNCTIONS

The functions hitherto considered have been propositional functions, with the exception of a few particular functions such $R \mathbin{\dot\cap} S$. But the ordinary functions of mathematics, such as x^2, sin x, log x, are not propositional. Functions of this kind always mean 'the term having such-and-such a relation to x'. For this reason they may be called *descriptive* functions, because they *describe* a certain term by means of its relation to their argument. Thus 'sin $\pi/2$' describes the number 1; yet propositions in which sin $\pi/2$ occurs are not the same as they would be if 1 were substituted. This appears, e.g., from the proposition 'sin $\pi/2 = 1$', which conveys valuable information, whereas '$1 = 1$' is trivial. Descriptive functions have no meaning by themselves, but only as constituents of propositions; and this applies generally to phrases of the form 'the term having such-and-such a property'. Hence in dealing with such phrases, we must define any proposition in which they occur, not the phrases themselves.* We are thus led to the following definition, in which '$(\imath x)(\phi x)$' is to be read '*the* term x which satisfies ϕx'.

$$\psi\{(\imath x)(\phi x)\} \mathbin{.} = \mathbin{:} (\exists b) \mathbin{:} \phi x \mathbin{.} \equiv_{x} \mathbin{.} x = b \mathbin{:} \psi b \quad \text{Df}.$$

This definition states that 'the term which satisfies ϕ satisfies ψ' is to mean: 'There is a term b such that ϕx is true when and only when x is b, and ψb is true'. Thus all propositions about '*the* so-and-so' will be false if there are no so-and-so's or several so-and-so's.

The general definition of a descriptive function is

$$R\mathord{'}y = (\imath x)(xRy) \quad \text{Df};$$

that is, '$R\mathord{'}y$' is to mean 'the term which has the relation R to y'.

---

* See the above-mentioned article 'On Denoting', where the reasons for this view are given at length.

If there are several terms or none having the relation R to y, all propositions about $R'y$ will be false. We put

$$\mathrm{E}\,!\,(\imath x)\,(\phi x)\,.\,=\,:(\exists b):\phi x\,.\,\equiv_x.\,x=b\quad \mathrm{Df.}$$

Here '$\mathrm{E}\,!\,(\imath x)\,(\phi x)$' may be read 'there is such a term as the x which satisfies ϕx', or 'the x which satisfies ϕx exists'. We have

$$\vdash:.\,\mathrm{E}\,!\,R'y\,.\,\equiv\,:(\exists b):xRy\,.\,\equiv_x.\,x=b.$$

The inverted comma in $R'y$ may be read *of*. Thus if R is the relation of father to son, '$R'y$' is 'the father of y'. If R is the relation of son to father, all propositions about $R'y$ will be false unless y has one son and no more.

From the above it appears that descriptive functions are obtained from relations. The relations now to be defined are chiefly important on account of the descriptive functions to which they give rise.

$$\mathrm{Cnv}=\hat{Q}\hat{P}\{xQy\,.\,\equiv_{x,\,y}.\,yPx\}\quad \mathrm{Df.}$$

Here *Cnv* is short for 'converse'. It is the relation of a relation to its converse; e.g., of *greater* to *less*, of parentage to sonship, of preceding to following, etc. We have

$$\vdash.\,\mathrm{Cnv}'P=(\imath Q)\{xQy\,.\,\equiv_{x,\,y}.\,yPx\}.$$

For a shorter notation, often more convenient, we put

$$\breve{P}=\mathrm{Cnv}'P\quad \mathrm{Df.}$$

We want next a notation for the class of terms which have the relation R to y. For this purpose, we put

$$\overrightarrow{R}=\hat{a}\hat{y}\{a=\hat{x}(xRy)\}\quad \mathrm{Df,}$$

whence

$$\vdash.\,\overrightarrow{R}'y=\hat{x}(xRy).$$

Similarly we put

$$\overleftarrow{R}=\hat{\beta}\hat{x}\{\beta=\hat{y}(xRy)\}\quad \mathrm{Df,}$$

whence

$$\vdash.\,\overleftarrow{R}'x=\hat{y}(xRy).$$

We want next the *domain* of R (i.e., the class of terms which have the relation R to something), the *converse domain* of R (i.e., the class of terms to which something has the relation R), and the *field* of R, which is the sum of the domain and the converse domain. For this purpose we define the relations of the domain, converse domain, and field, to R. The definitions are:

$$D = \hat{a}\hat{R}\{a = \hat{x}((\exists y) . xRy)\} \quad \text{Df},$$
$$ Q = \hat{\beta}\hat{R}\{\beta = \hat{y}((\exists x) . xRy)\} \quad \text{Df},$$
$$C = \hat{\gamma}\hat{R}\{\gamma = \hat{x}((\exists y) : xRy . \vee . yRx)\} \quad \text{Df}.$$

Note that the third of these definitions is only significant when R is what we may call a *homogeneous* relation; i.e., one in which, if xRy holds, x and y are of the same type. For otherwise, however we may choose x and y, either xRy or yRx will be meaningless. This observation is important in connexion with Burali-Forti's contradiction.

We have, in virtue of the above definitions,

$$\vdash . D'R = \hat{x}\{(\exists y) . xRy\},$$
$$\vdash . Q'R = \hat{y}\{(\exists x) . xRy\},$$
$$\vdash . C'R = \hat{x}\{(\exists y) : xRy . \vee . yRx\},$$

the last of these being significant only when R is homogeneous. '$D'R$' is read 'the domain of R'; '$D'R$' is read 'the converse domain of R', and '$C'R$' is read 'the field of R'. The letter C is chosen as the initial of the word 'campus'.

We want next a notation for the relation, to a class a contained in the domain of R, of the class of terms to which some member of a has the relation R, and also for the relation, to a class β contained in the converse domain of R, of the class of terms which have the relation R to some member of β. For the second of these we put

$$R_\epsilon = \hat{a}\hat{\beta}\{a = \hat{x}((\exists y) . y\epsilon\beta . xRy)\} \quad \text{Df}.$$

So that

$$\vdash . R_\epsilon'\beta = \hat{x}\{(\exists y) . y\epsilon\beta . xRy\}.$$

Thus if R is the relation of father to son, and β is the class of Etonians, $R_\epsilon'\beta$ will be the class 'fathers of Etonians'; if R is the relation 'less than', and β is the class of proper fractions of the form $1 - 2^{-n}$ for integral values of n, $R_\epsilon'\beta$ will be the class of fractions less than some fraction of the form $1 - 2^{-n}$; i.e., $R_\epsilon'\beta$ will be the class of proper fractions. The other relation mentioned above is $(\breve{R})_\epsilon$.

We put, as an alternative notation often more convenient,

$$R``\beta = R_\epsilon`\beta \quad \text{Df.}$$

The *relative product* of two relations R, S is the relation which holds between x and z whenever there is a term y such that xRy and yRz both hold. The relative product is denoted by $R \mid S$. Thus

$$R \mid S = \hat{x}\hat{z}\{(\exists y) . xRy . yRz\} \quad \text{Df.}$$

We put also

$$R^2 = R \mid R \quad \text{Df.}$$

The product and sum of a class of classes are often required. They are defined as follows:

$$s`\kappa = \hat{x}\{(\exists a) . a\epsilon\kappa . x\epsilon a\} \quad \text{Df,}$$
$$p`\kappa = \hat{x}\{a\epsilon\kappa . \supset_a . x\epsilon a\} \quad \text{Df.}$$

Similarly for relations we put

$$\dot{s}`\lambda = \hat{x}\hat{y}\{(\exists R) . R\epsilon\lambda . xRy\} \quad \text{Df,}$$
$$\dot{p}`\lambda = \hat{x}\hat{y}\{R\epsilon\lambda . \supset_R . xRy\} \quad \text{Df.}$$

We need a notation for the class whose only member is x. Peano uses ιx, hence we shall use $\iota`x$. Peano showed (what Frege also had emphasized) that this class can not be identified with x. With the usual view of classes, the need for such a distinction remains a mystery; but with the view set forth above, it becomes obvious. We put

$$\iota = \hat{a}\hat{x}\{a = \hat{y}(y = x)\} \quad \text{Df,}$$

whence

$$\vdash . \iota`x = \hat{y}(y = x),$$

and

$$\vdash : E ! \dot{\iota}`a . \supset . \dot{\iota}`a = (\imath x)(x\epsilon a);$$

i.e., if a is a class which has only one member, then $\dot{\iota}`a$ is that one member.*

For the class of classes contained in a given class, we put

$$\text{Cl}`a = \hat{\beta}(\beta \subset a) \quad \text{Df.}$$

We can now proceed to the consideration of cardinal and ordinal numbers, and of how they are affected by the doctrine of types.

---

* Thus $\dot{\iota}`a$ is what Peano calls ιa.

IX. CARDINAL NUMBERS

The cardinal number of a class a is defined as the class of all classes *similar* to a, two classes being similar when there is a one-one relation between them. The class of one-one relations is denoted by $|\rightarrow|$, and defined as follows:

$$1\rightarrow1 = \hat{R}\{xRy \cdot x'Ry \cdot xRy' \cdot \supset_{x,y,x',y'} \cdot x=x' \cdot y=y'\} \quad \text{Df.}$$

Similarity is denoted by *Sim*; its definition is

$$Sim = \hat{a}\hat{\beta}\{(\exists R) \cdot R\epsilon1\rightarrow1 \cdot D'R=a \cdot D'R=\beta\} \quad \text{Df.}$$

Then $\overrightarrow{Sim}$ 'a is, by definition, the cardinal number of a; this we will denote by $Nc'a$; hence we put

$$Nc = \overrightarrow{Sim} \quad \text{Df.}$$

whence

$$\vdash \cdot Nc'a = \overrightarrow{Sim}\text{'}a.$$

The class of cardinals we will denote by NC; thus

$$NC = Nc''cls \quad \text{Df.}$$

o is defined as the class whose only member is the null-class, Λ, so that

$$0 = \iota'\Lambda \quad \text{Df.}$$

The definition of 1 is

$$1 = \hat{a}\{(\exists c): x\epsilon a \cdot \equiv_x \cdot x=c\} \quad \text{Df.}$$

It is easy to prove that o and 1 are cardinals according to the definition.

It is to be observed, however, that o and 1 and all the other cardinals, according to the above definitions, are ambiguous symbols, like *cls*, and have as many meanings as there are types. To begin with o: the meaning of o depends upon that of Λ, and the meaning of Λ is different according to the type of which it is the null-class. Thus there are as many o's as there are types; and the same applies to all the other cardinals. Nevertheless, if two classes a, β are of different types, we can speak of them as having the same cardinal, or of one as having a greater cardinal than the other, because a one-one relation may hold between the members of a and the members of β, even when a and β are of different types.

For example, let β be $\iota``\alpha$; i.e., the class whose members are the classes consisting of single members of $\alpha$. Then $\iota``\alpha$ is of higher type than α, but similar to α, being correlated with α by the one-one relation ι.

The hierarchy of types has important results in regard to addition. Suppose we have a class of α terms and a class of β terms, where α and β are cardinals; it may be quite impossible to add them together to get a class of α and β terms, since, if the classes are not of the same type, their logical sum is meaningless. Where only a finite number of classes are concerned, we can obviate the practical consequences of this, owing to the fact that we can always apply operations to a class which raise its type to any required extent without altering its cardinal number. For example, given any class α, the class $\iota``\alpha$ has the same cardinal number, but is of the next type above α. Hence, given any finite number of classes of different types, we can raise all of them to the type which is what we may call the lowest common multiple of all the types in question; and it can be shown that this can be done in such a way that the resulting classes shall have no common members. We may then form the logical sum of all the classes so obtained, and its cardinal number will be the arithmetical sum of the cardinal numbers of the original classes. But where we have an infinite series of classes of ascending types, this method can not be applied. For this reason, we can not now prove that there must be infinite classes. For suppose there were only n individuals altogether in the universe, where n is finite. There would then be 2^n classes of individuals, and 2^{2^n} classes of classes of individuals, and so on. Thus the cardinal number of terms in each type would be finite; and though these numbers would grow beyond any assigned finite number, there would be no way of adding them so as to get an infinite number. Hence we need an axiom, so it would seem, to the effect that no finite class of individuals contains all individuals; but if any one chooses to assume that the total number of individuals in the universe is (say) 10,367, there seems no *a priori* way of refuting his opinion.

From the above mode of reasoning, it is plain that the doctrine of types avoids all difficulties as to the greatest cardinal. There is a greatest cardinal in each type, namely the cardinal number of the whole of the type; but this is always surpassed by the cardinal number of the next type, since, if a is the cardinal number of one type, that of the next type is 2^a, which, as Cantor has shown, is always greater than a. Since there is no way of adding different types, we can not speak of 'the cardinal number of all objects, of whatever type', and thus there is no absolutely greatest cardinal.

If it is admitted that no finite class of individuals contains all individuals, it follows that there are classes of individuals having any finite number. Hence all finite cardinals exist as individual-cardinals; i.e., as the cardinal numbers of classes of individuals. It follows that there is a class of $\aleph_0$ cardinals, namely, the class of finite cardinals. Hence $\aleph_0$ exists as the cardinal of a class of classes of classes of individuals. By forming all classes of finite cardinals, we find that $2^{\aleph_0}$ exists as the cardinal of a class of classes of classes of classes of individuals; and so we can proceed indefinitely. The existence of $\aleph_n$ for every finite value of n can also be proved; but this requires the consideration of ordinals.

If, in addition to assuming that no finite class contains all individuals, we assume the multiplicative axiom (i.e., the axiom that, given a set of mutually exclusive classes, none of which are null, there is at least one class consisting of one member from each class in the set), then we can prove that there is a class of individuals containing $\aleph_0$ members, so that $\aleph_0$ will exist as an individual-cardinal. This somewhat reduces the type to which we have to go in order to prove the existence-theorem for any given cardinal, but it does not give us any existence-theorem which can not be got otherwise sooner or later.

Many elementary theorems concerning cardinals require the multiplicative axiom.* It is to be observed that this axiom is equivalent to Zermelo's,† and therefore to the assumption that

---

* Cf. Part III of a paper by the present author, 'On some Difficulties in the Theory of Transfinite Numbers and Order Types', *Proc. London Math. Soc.* Ser. II, Vol. IV, Part I.

† Cf. loc. cit. for a statement of Zermelo's axiom, and for the proof that this axiom implies the multiplicative axiom. The converse implication results as follows: Putting Prod 'k for the multiplicative class of k, consider

$$Z'\beta = \dot{R}\{(\exists x) . x\epsilon\beta . D'R = \iota'\beta . \square'R = \iota'x\} \quad \text{Df},$$

and assume

$$\gamma\epsilon \text{ Prod '}Z''cl'a . R = \hat{\hat{x}}\{(\exists S) . S\epsilon\gamma . \xi Sx\}.$$

Then R is a Zermelo-correlation. Hence if Prod 'Z'' $cl'a$ is not null, at least one Zermelo-correlation for a exists.

every class can be well ordered.* These equivalent assumptions are, apparently, all incapable of proof, though the multiplicative axiom, at least, appears highly self-evident. In the absence of proof, it seems best not to assume the multiplicative axiom, but to state it as a hypothesis on every occasion on which it is used.

X. ORDINAL NUMBERS

An ordinal number is a class of ordinally similar well-ordered series, i.e., of relations generating such series. Ordinal similarity or *likeness* is defined as follows:

$$\text{Smor} = \hat{P}\hat{Q}\{(\exists S).S\epsilon 1 \rightarrow 1 . \varPi `S = C`Q . P = S \mid Q \mid \breve{S}\} \quad \text{Df},$$

where 'Smor' is short for 'similar ordinally'.

The class of serial relations, which we will call 'Ser', is defined as follows:

$$\text{Ser} = \hat{P}\{xPy.\supset_{x,y}. \sim (x=y): xPy.yPz.\supset_{x,y,z}.xPz:$$
$$x\epsilon C`P.\supset_x.\overrightarrow{P}`x \cup \iota`x \cup \overleftarrow{P}`x = C`P\} \quad \text{Df}.$$

That is, reading P as 'precedes', a relation is serial if (1) no term precedes itself, (2) a predecessor of a predecessor is a predecessor, (3) if x is any term in the field of the relation, then the predecessors of x together with x together with the successors of x constitute the whole field of the relation.

Well ordered serial relations, which we will call Ω, are defined as follows:

$$\Omega = \hat{P}\{P\epsilon \text{Ser}:a \subset C`P.\exists!a.\supset_a.\exists!(a - \breve{P}``a)\} \quad \text{Df};$$

i.e., P generates a well ordered series if P is serial, and any class a contained in the field of P and not null has a first term. (Note that $\breve{P}``a$ are the terms coming after some term of a).

If we denote by $No`P$ the ordinal number of a well ordered relation P, and by NO the class of ordinal numbers, we shall have

$$No = \hat{a}\hat{P}\{P\epsilon\Omega.a = \overrightarrow{\text{Smor}}`P\} \quad \text{Df},$$
$$NO = No``\Omega.$$

* See Zermelo, 'Beweis, dass jede Menge wohlgeordnet werden kann'. *Math. Annalen*, Vol. LIX, pp. 514–16.

From the definition of *No* we have

$$\vdash : P \epsilon \, \Omega \, . \, \supset . \, No\,'P = \overrightarrow{\text{Smor}} \, 'P,$$
$$\vdash : \sim (P \epsilon \Omega) . \supset . \sim \text{E} \, ! \, No\,'P.$$

If we now examine our definitions with a view to their connexion with the theory of types, we see, to begin with, that the definitions of 'Ser' and Ω involve the *fields* of serial relations. Now the field is only significant when the relation is homogeneous; hence relations which are not homogeneous do not generate series. For example, the relation ι might be thought to generate series of ordinal number ω, such as

$$x, \iota\,'x, \iota\,'\iota\,'x, \ldots \iota^{n}\,'x, \ldots,$$

and we might attempt to prove in this way the existence of ω and $\aleph_0$. But x and $\iota\,'x$ are of different types, and therefore there is no such series according to the definition.

The ordinal number of a series of individuals is, by the above definition of *No*, a class of relations of individuals. It is therefore of a different type from any individual, and can not form part of any series in which individuals occur. Again, suppose all the finite ordinals exist as individual-ordinals; i.e., as the ordinals of series of individuals. Then the finite ordinals themselves form a series whose ordinal number is ω; thus ω exists as an ordinal-ordinal, i.e., as the ordinal of a series of ordinals. But the type of an ordinal-ordinal is that of classes of relations of classes of relations of individuals. Thus the existence of ω has been proved in a higher type than that of the finite ordinals. Again, the cardinal number of ordinal numbers of well ordered series that can be made out of finite ordinals is $\aleph_1$; hence $\aleph_1$ exists in the type of classes of classes of classes of relations of classes of relations of individuals. Also the ordinal numbers of well ordered series composed of finite ordinals can be arranged in order of magnitude, and the result is a well ordered series whose ordinal number is ω_1. Hence ω_1 exists as an ordinal-ordinal-ordinal. This process can be repeated any finite number of times, and thus we can establish the existence, in appropriate types, of $\aleph_n$ and ω_n for any finite value of n.

But the above process of generation no longer leads to any totality of *all* ordinals, because, if we take all the ordinals of any given type, there are always greater ordinals in higher types; and we can not add together a set of ordinals of which the type rises above any finite limit. Thus all the ordinals in any type can be arranged by order of magnitude in a well ordered series, which has an ordinal number of higher type than that of the ordinals composing the series. In the new type, this new ordinal is not the greatest. In fact, there is no greatest ordinal in any type, but in every type all ordinals are less than some ordinals of higher type. It is impossible to complete the series of ordinals, since it rises to types above every assignable finite limit; thus although every segment of the series of ordinals is well ordered, we can not say that the whole series is well ordered, because the 'whole series' is a fiction. Hence Burali-Forti's contradiction disappears.

From the last two sections it appears that, if it is allowed that the number of individuals is not finite, the existence of all Cantor's cardinal and ordinal numbers can be proved, short of $\aleph_\omega$ and ω_ω. (It is quite possible that the existence of these may also be demonstrable.) The existence of all *finite* cardinals and ordinals can be proved without assuming the existence of anything. For if the cardinal number of terms in any type is n, that of terms in the next type is 2^n. Thus if there are no individuals, there will be one class (namely, the null-class), two classes of classes (namely, that containing no class and that containing the null-class), four classes of classes of classes, and generally 2^{n-1} classes of the nth order. But we can not add together terms of different types, and thus we can not in this way prove the existence of any infinite class.

We can now sum up our whole discussion. After stating some of the paradoxes of logic, we found that all of them arise from the fact that an expression referring to *all* of some collection may itself appear to denote one of the collection; as, for example, 'all propositions are either true or false' appears to be itself a proposition. We decided that, where this appears to occur, we are dealing with a false totality, and that in fact nothing whatever can significantly be said about *all* of the supposed collection. In order to give effect to this decision, we explained a doctrine of *types* of variables, proceeding upon the principle that any expression which refers to *all* of some type must, if it denotes anything, denote something of a higher type than that to all of which it refers. Where *all* of some type is referred to, there is an *apparent variable* belonging to that type. Thus *any expression containing an apparent variable is of higher type than that variable.* This is the fundamental principle of the doctrine of types. A change in the manner in which the types are constructed, should it prove necessary, would leave the solution of contradictions untouched so long as this fundamental principle is observed. The method of constructing types explained above was shown to enable us to state all the fundamental definitions of mathematics, and at the same time to avoid all known contradictions. And it appeared that in practice the doctrine of types is never relevant except where existence-theorems are concerned, or where applications are to be made to some particular case.

The theory of types raises a number of difficult philosophical questions concerning its interpretation. Such questions are, however, essentially separable from the mathematical development of the theory, and, like all philosophical questions, introduce elements of uncertainty which do not belong to the theory itself. It seemed better, therefore, to state the theory without reference to philosophical questions, leaving these to be dealt with independently.

On the Relations of Universals and Particulars

In this essay we find Russell moving toward the logical atomism of 1918 but with his ideas still in a state of transition. Read as the Presidential Address to the Aristotelian Society (of London) in the autumn of 1911, it was published for the members at the time and later appeared in the PROCEEDINGS *for 1911–12. As the appended note of 1955 indicates, Russell no longer accepts the argument for the existence of particulars given here, although he rejects it on the basis of parsimony rather than the fact that it can be proved wrong. (It cannot be proved either way.) The question of universals and particulars is a fundamental one in philosophy, and Russell's treatment is cogent and clear, so that in spite of his later views on the validity of this argument for particulars, I recommend this paper to students of contemporary philosophy.*

Shortly after reading this paper Russell began his first period of association with Ludwig Wittgenstein, whose views were to exert a degree of influence on Russell's thinking for about seven years (i.e. until Russell became a neutral monist in late 1918 or early 1919). The comparison of this paper with those of 1914, 1918, and 1919 following will thus provide some index to Wittgenstein's effect on Russell's work.

ON THE RELATIONS OF UNIVERSALS AND PARTICULARS*

THE purpose of the following paper is to consider whether there is a fundamental division of the objects with which metaphysics is concerned into two classes, universals and particulars, or whether there is any method of overcoming this dualism. My own opinion is that the dualism is ultimate; on the other hand, many men with whom, in the main, I am in close agreement, hold that it is not ultimate. I do not feel the grounds in favour of its ultimate nature to be very conclusive, and in what follows I should lay stress rather on the distinctions and considerations introduced during the argument than on the conclusion at which the argument arrives.

It is impossible to begin our discussion with sharp definitions of universals and particulars, though we may hope to reach such definitions in the end. At the beginning, we can only roughly indicate the kind of facts that we wish to analyse and the kind of distinctions that we wish to examine. There are several cognate distinctions which produce confusion by intermingling, and which it is important to disentangle before advancing into the heart of our problem.

The first distinction that concerns us is the distinction between percepts and concepts, i.e., between objects of acts of perception and objects of acts of conception. If there is a distinction between particulars and universals, percepts will be among particulars, while concepts will be among universals. Opponents of universals, such as Berkeley and Hume, will maintain that concepts are derivable from percepts, as faint copies, or in some other way. Oppo-

---

* The thesis of the present paper is closely similar to that of Mr. Moore's paper 'Identity', read before this Society in 1900–1901. My chief reason for thinking that the question demands a fresh discussion is that the statement of the grounds for the thesis appears to require some examination of the nature of sensible space as opposed to physical space.

nents of particulars will maintain that the apparent particularity of percepts is illusory, and that, though the act of perception may differ from the act of conception, yet its objects differ only by their greater complexity, and are really composed of constituents which are, or might be, concepts.

But the distinction of percepts and concepts is too psychological for an ultimate metaphysical distinction. Percepts and concepts are respectively the relata of two different relations, perception and conception, and there is nothing in their definitions to show whether, or how, they differ. Moreover, the distinction of percepts and concepts, in itself, is incapable of being extended to entities which are not objects of cognitive acts. Hence we require some other distinction expressing the intrinsic difference which we seem to feel between percepts and concepts.

A cognate distinction, which effects part at least of what we want, is the distinction between things which exist in time and things which do not. In order to avoid any question as to whether time is relative or absolute, we may say that an entity x 'exists in time' provided x is not itself a moment or part of time, and some such proposition as 'x is before y or simultaneous with y or after y' is true of x. (It is not to be assumed that *before*, *simultaneous*, and *after* are mutually exclusive: if x has duration, they will not be so.) Prima facie, a percept exists in time, in the above sense, while a concept does not. The object of perception is simultaneous with the act of perception, while the object of conception seems indifferent to the time of conceiving and to all time. Thus, prima facie, we have here the non-psychological distinction of which we were in search. But the same controversies will break out as in the case of percepts and concepts. The man who reduces concepts to percepts will say that nothing is really out of time, and that the appearance of this in the case of concepts is illusory. The man who reduces percepts to concepts may either, like most idealists, deny that anything is in time, or, like some realists, maintain that concepts can and do exist in time.

In addition to the above distinction as regards time, there is a distinction as regards space which, as we shall find, is very important in connexion with our present question. Put as vaguely as possible, this is a distinction which divides entities into three classes: (*a*) those which are not in any place, (*b*) those which are in one place at one time, but never in more than one, (c) those which are in many places at once. To make this threefold division precise, we should have to discuss what we mean by a place, what we mean by 'in', and how the different kinds of space—visual, tactile, physical—produce different forms of this threefold division. For the present I will merely illustrate what I mean by examples. Relations, obviously, do not exist anywhere in space. Our bodies, we think, exist in one place at a time, but not in more than one. General qualities, such as whiteness, on the contrary, may be said to be in many places at once: we may say, in a sense, that whiteness is in every place where there is a white thing. This division of entities will be discussed later; for the present I merely wish to indicate that it requires examination.

In addition to the above psychological and metaphysical distinctions, there are two logical distinctions which are relevant in the present enquiry. In the first place, there is the distinction between relations and entities which are not relations. It has been customary for philosophers to ignore or reject relations, and speak as if all entities were either subjects or predicates. But this custom is on the decline, and I shall assume without further argument that there are such entities as relations. Philosophy has, so far as I know, no common name for all entities which are not relations. Among such entities are included not only all the things that would naturally be called particulars, but also all the universals that philosophers are in the habit of considering when they discuss the relation of particulars to universals, for universals are generally conceived as common properties of particulars, in fact, as predicates. For our purpose it is hardly worth while to invent a technical term *ad hoc*; I shall therefore speak of entities which are not relations simply as *non-relations*.

The second logical distinction which we require is one which may or may not be identical in extension with that between relations and non-relations, but is certainly not identical in intention. It may be expressed as the distinction between verbs and substantives, or, more correctly, between the objects denoted by verbs and the objects denoted by substantives.* (Since this more correct

* This is the distinction which I formerly spoke of as the distinction between *things* and *concepts*, but these terms no longer seem to me appropriate. Cf. *Principles of Mathematics*, § 48.

expression is long and cumbrous, I shall generally use the shorter phrase to mean the same thing. Thus, when I speak of verbs, I mean the objects denoted by verbs, and similarly for substantives.) The nature of this distinction emerges from the analysis of complexes. In most complexes, if not in all, a certain number of different entities are combined into a single entity by means of a relation. '*A*'s hatred for *B*', for example, is a complex in which *hatred* combines *A* and *B* into one whole; '*C*'s belief that *A* hates *B*' is a complex in which *belief* combines *A* and *B* and *C* and hatred into one whole, and so on. A relation is distinguished as dual, triple, quadruple, etc., or dyadic, triadic, tetradic, etc., according to the number of terms which it unites in the simplest complexes in which it occurs. Thus in the above examples, hatred is a dual relation and belief is a quadruple relation. The capacity for combining terms into a single complex is the defining characteristic of what I call *verbs*. The question now arises: Are there complexes which consist of a single term and a verb? '*A* exists' might serve as an example of what is possibly such a complex. It is the possibility that there may be complexes of this kind which makes it impossible to decide off-hand that verbs are the same as relations. There may be verbs which are philosophically as well as grammatically intransitive. Such verbs, if they exist, may be called *predicates*, and the propositions in which they are attributed may be called subject-predicate propositions.

If there are no such verbs as those whose possibility we have been considering, i.e., if all verbs are relations, it will follow that subject-predicate propositions, if there are any, will express a *relation* of subject to predicate. Such propositions will then be definable as those that involve a certain relation called *predication*. Even if there are subject-predicate propositions in which the predicate is the verb, there will still be equivalent propositions in which the predicate is related to the subject; thus '*A* exists', for example, will be equivalent to '*A* has existence'. Hence the question whether predicates are verbs or not becomes unimportant. The more important question is whether there is a specific relation of predication, or whether what are grammatically subject-predicate propositions are really of many different kinds, no one of which has the characteristics one naturally associates with subject-predicate propositions. This question is one to which we shall return at a later stage.

The above logical distinctions are relevant to our enquiry because it is natural to regard particulars as entities which can only be subjects or terms of relations, and cannot be predicates or relations. A particular is naturally conceived as a *this* or something intrinsically analogous to a *this*; and such an entity seems incapable of being a predicate or a relation. A universal, on this view, will be anything that is a predicate or a relation. But if there is no specific relation of predication, so that there is no class of entities which can properly be called predicates, then the above method of distinguishing particulars and universals fails. The question whether philosophy must recognize two ultimately distinct kinds of entities, particulars and universals, turns, as we shall see more fully later on, on the question whether non-relations are of two kinds, subjects and predicates, or rather terms which can only be subjects and terms which may be either subjects or predicates. And this question turns on whether there is an ultimate simple asymmetrical relation which may be called predication, or whether all apparent subject-predicate propositions are to be analysed into propositions of other forms, which do not require a radical difference of nature between the apparent subject and the apparent predicate.

The decision of the question whether there is a simple relation of predication ought perhaps to be possible by inspection, but for my part I am unable to come to any decision in this way. I think, however, that it can be decided in favour of predication by the analysis of *things* and by considerations as to spatio-temporal diversity. This analysis and these considerations will also show the way in which our purely logical question is bound up with the other questions as to particulars and universals which I raised at the beginning of this paper.

The common-sense notion of things and their qualities is, I suppose, the source of the conception of subject and predicate, and the reason why language is so largely based on this conception. But the thing, like other common-sense notions, is a piece of half-hearted metaphysics, which neither gives crude data nor gives a tenable hypothesis as to a reality behind the data. A thing, of the everyday sort, is constituted by a bundle of sensible qualities belonging to various senses, but supposed all to coexist in one continuous portion of space. But the common space which should contain both visual and tactile qualities is not the space of either visual or tactile perception: it is a constructed 'real' space, belief in which has, I suppose, been generated by association. And in crude fact, the visual and tactile qualities of which I am sensible are not in a common space, but each in its own space. Hence if the thing is to be impartial as between sight and touch, it must cease to have the actual qualities of which we are sensible, and become their common cause or origin or whatever vaguer word can be found. Thus the road is opened to the metaphysical theories of science and to the metaphysical theories of philosophy: the thing may be a number of electric charges in rapid motion, or an idea in the mind of God, but it is certainly not what the senses perceive.

The argument against things is trite, and I need not labour it. I introduce it here only in order to illustrate a consequence which is sometimes overlooked. Realists who reject particulars are apt to regard a thing as reducible to a number of qualities coexisting in one place. But, apart from other objections to this view, it is doubtful whether the different qualities in question ever do coexist in one place. If the qualities are sensible, the place must be in a sensible space; but this makes it necessary that the qualities should belong to only one sense, and it is not clear that genuinely different qualities belonging to one sense ever coexist in a single place in a perceptual space. If, on the other hand, we consider what may be called 'real' space, i.e. the inferred space containing the 'real' objects which we suppose to be the causes of our perceptions, then we no longer know what is the nature of the qualities, if any, which exist in this 'real' space, and it is natural to replace the bundle of qualities by a collection of pieces of matter having whatever characteristics the science of the moment may prescribe. Thus in any case the bundle of coexisting qualities in the same place is not an admissible substitute for the thing.

For our purposes, the 'real' object by which science or philosophy replaces the thing is not important. We have rather to consider the relations of sensible objects in a single sensible space, say that of sight.

The theory of sensible qualities which dispenses with particulars will say, if the same shade of colour is found in two different places, that what exists is the shade of colour itself, and that what exists in the one place is identical with what exists in the other. The theory which admits particulars will say, on the contrary, that two numerically different *instances* of the shade of colour exist in the two places: in this view, the shade of colour itself is a universal and a predicate of both the instances, but the universal does not exist in space and time. Of the above two views, the first, which does not introduce particulars, dispenses altogether with predication as a fundamental relation: according to this view, when we say 'this thing is white', the fundamental fact is that whiteness exists here. According to the other view, which admits particulars, what exists here is something of which whiteness is a predicate—not, as for common sense, the thing with many other qualities, but an instance of whiteness, a particular of which whiteness is the only predicate except shape and brightness and whatever else is necessarily connected with whiteness.

Of the above two theories, one admits only what would naturally be called universals, while the other admits both universals and particulars. Before examining them, it may be as well to examine and dismiss the theory which admits only particulars, and dispenses altogether with universals. This is the theory advocated by Berkeley and Hume in their polemic against 'abstract ideas'. Without tying ourselves down to their statements, let us see what can be made of this theory. The general name 'white', in this view, is defined for a given person at a given moment by a particular patch of white which he sees or imagines; another patch is called white if it has exact likeness in colour to the standard patch. In order to avoid making the colour a universal, we have to suppose that 'exact likeness' is a simple relation, not analysable into community of predicates; moreover, it is not the general relation of likeness that we require, but a more special relation, that of colour-likeness, since two patches might be exactly alike in shape or size but different in colour. Thus, in order to make the theory of Berkeley and Hume workable, we must assume an ultimate relation of colour-likeness, which holds between two patches which would commonly be said to have the same colour. Now, prima facie, this relation of colour-likeness will itself be a universal or an 'abstract idea', and thus we shall still have failed to avoid universals. But we may apply the same analysis to colour-likeness. We may take a standard particular case of colour-likeness, and say that anything else is to be called a colour-likeness if it is exactly like our standard case. It is obvious, however, that such a process leads to an endless regress:

we explain the likeness of two terms as consisting in the likeness which their likeness bears to the likeness of two other terms, and such a regress is plainly vicious. Likeness at least, therefore, must be admitted as a universal, and, having admitted one universal, we have no longer any reason to reject others. Thus the whole complicated theory, which had no motive except to avoid universals, falls to the ground. Whether or not there are particulars, there must be relations which are universals in the sense that (a) they are concepts, not percepts; (b) they do not exist in time; (c) they are verbs, not substantives.

It is true that the above argument does not prove that there are universal qualities as opposed to universal relations. On the contrary, it shows that universal qualities *can*, so far as logic can show, be replaced by exact likenesses of various kinds between particulars. This view has, so far as I know, nothing to recommend it beyond its logical possibility. But from the point of view of the problem whether there are particulars, it has no bearing on the argument. It is a view which is only possible if there are particulars, and it demands only an easy re-statement of subject-predicate propositions: instead of saying that an entity has such and such a predicate, we shall have to say that there are entities to which it has such and such a specific likeness. I shall therefore in future ignore this view, which in any case assumes our main thesis, namely, the existence of particulars. To the grounds in favour of this thesis we must now return.

When we endeavoured to state the two theories as to sensible qualities, we had occasion to consider two white patches. On the view which denies particulars, whiteness itself exists in both patches: a numerically single entity, whiteness, exists in all places that are white. Nevertheless, we speak of *two* white patches, and it is obvious that, in some sense, the patches are two, not one. It is this spatial plurality which makes the difficulty of the theory that denies particulars.

Without attempting, as yet, to introduce all the necessary explanations and distinctions, we may state the argument for particulars roughly as follows. It is logically possible for two exactly similar patches of white, of the same size and shape, to exist simultaneously in different places. Now, whatever may be the exact meaning of 'existing in different places', it is self-evident that, in such a case, there are two different patches of white. Their diversity might, if we adopted the theory of absolute position, be regarded as belonging, not to the white itself which exists in the two places, but to the complexes 'whiteness in this place' and 'whiteness in that place'. This would derive their diversity from the diversity of this place and that place; and since places cannot be supposed to differ as to qualities, this would require that the places should be particulars. But if we reject absolute position, it will become impossible to distinguish the two patches as two, unless each, instead of being the universal whiteness, is an *instance* of whiteness. It might be thought that the two might be distinguished by means of other qualities in the same place as the one but not in the same place as the other. This, however, presupposes that the two patches are already distinguished as numerically diverse, since otherwise what is in the same place as the one must be in the same place as the other. Thus the fact that it is logically possible for precisely similar things to coexist in two different places, but that things in different places at the same time cannot be numerically identical, forces us to admit that it is particulars, i.e., *instances* of universals, that exist in places, and not universals themselves.

The above is the outline of our argument. But various points in it have to be examined and expanded before it can be considered conclusive. In the first place, it is not necessary to assert that there ever are two exactly similar existents. It is only necessary to perceive that our judgment that this and that are two different existents is not necessarily based on any difference of qualities, but may be based on difference of spatial position alone; and that difference of qualities, whether or not it always in fact accompanies numerical difference, is not logically necessary in order to insure numerical difference where there is difference of spatial position.

Again, it is not easy to state exactly what sort of spatial distribution in perceived space warrants us in asserting plurality. Before we can use space as an argument for particulars, we must be clear on this point. We are accustomed to concede that a thing cannot be in two places at once, but this common-sense maxim, unless very carefully stated, will lead us into inextricable difficulties. Our first business, therefore, it to find out how to state this maxim in an unobjectionable form.

In rational dynamics, where we are concerned with matter and 'real' space, the maxim that nothing can be in two places at once is taken rigidly, and any matter occupying more than a point of space is regarded as at least theoretically divisible. Only what occupies a bare point is simple and single. This view is straightforward, and raises no difficulties as applied to 'real' space.

But as applied to perceived space, such a view is quite inadmissible. The immediate object of (say) visual perception is always of finite extent. If we suppose it to be, like the matter corresponding to it in 'real' space, composed of a collection of entities, one for each point which is not empty, we shall have to suppose two things, both of which seem incredible, namely: (1) that every immediate object of visual (or tactile) perception is infinitely complex; (2) that every such object is always composed of parts which are by their very nature imperceptible. It seems quite impossible that the immediate object of perception should have these properties. Hence we must suppose that an indivisible object of visual perception may occupy a finite extent of visual space. In short, we must, in dividing any complex object of visual perception, reach, after a finite number of steps, a *minimum sensibile*, which contains no plurality although it is of finite extent. Visual space may, in a sense, be infinitely *divisible*, for, by attention alone, or by the microscope, the immediate object of perception can be changed in a way which introduces complexity where formerly there was simplicity; and to this process no clear limit can be set. But this is a process which substitutes a new immediate object in place of the old one, and the new object, though more subdivided than the old one, will still consist of only a finite number of parts. We must therefore admit that the space of perception is not infinitely divided, and does not consist of points, but is composed of a finite though constantly varying number of surfaces or volumes, continually breaking up or joining together according to the fluctuations of attention. If there is a 'real' geometrical space corresponding to the space of perception, an infinite number of points in the geometrical space will have to correspond to a single simple entity in the perceived space.

It follows from this that, if we are to apply to the immediate objects of perception the maxim that a thing cannot be in two places at once, a 'place' must not be taken to be a point, but must be taken to be the extent occupied by a single object of perception.

A white sheet of paper, for example, may be seen as a single un-divided object, or as an object consisting of two parts, an upper and a lower or a right hand and a left hand part, or again as an object consisting of four parts, and so on. If we on this account consider that, even when the sheet appeared as an undivided object, its upper and lower halves were in different places, then we shall have to say that the undivided object was in both these places at once. But it is better to say that, when the sheet appeared as an undivided object, this object occupied only one 'place', though the place corresponded to what were afterwards two places. Thus a 'place' may be defined as the space occupied by one undivided object of perception.

With this definition, the maxim that a thing cannot be in two places at once might seem to reduce to a tautology. But this maxim, though it may need re-wording, will still have a substantial signific-ance, to be derived from the consideration of spatial relations. It is obvious that perceived spatial relations cannot hold between points, but must hold between the parts of a single complex object of perception. When the sheet of paper is perceived as consisting of two halves, an upper and a lower, these two halves are combined into a complex whole by means of a spatial relation which holds directly between the two halves, not between supposed smaller subdivisions which in fact do not exist in the immediate object of perception. Perceived spatial relations, therefore, must have a cer-tain roughness, not the neat smooth properties of geometrical relations between points. What, for example, shall we say of dis-tance? The distance between two simultaneously perceived objects will have to be defined by the perceived objects between them; in the case of two objects which touch, like the two halves of the sheet of paper, there is no distance between them. What remains definite is a certain order; by means of right and left, up and down, and so on, the parts of a complex object of perception acquire a spatial order, which is definite, though not subject to quite the same laws as geometrical order. The maxim that a thing cannot be in two places at once will then become the maxim that every spatial re-lation implies diversity of its terms, i.e., that nothing is to the right of itself, or above itself, and so on. In that case, given two white patches, one of which is to the right of the other, it will follow that there is not a single thing, whiteness, which is to the right of itself, but that there are two different things, instances of whiteness, of which one is to the right of the other. In this way our maxim will support the conclusion that there must be particulars as well as universals. But the above outline of an argument needs some amplification before it can be considered conclusive. Let us therefore examine, one by one, the steps of the argument.

Let us suppose, for the sake of definiteness, that within one field of vision we perceive two separated patches of white on a ground of black. It may then be taken as quite certain that the two patches are two and not one. The question is: Can we maintain that there are two if what exists in each is the universal whiteness?

If absolute space is admitted, we can of course say that it is the difference of place that makes the patches two; there is whiteness in this place, and whiteness in that place. From the point of view of our main problem, which is as to the existence of particulars, such a view would prove our thesis, since this place and that place would be or imply particulars consituting absolute space. But from the point of view of our immediate problem, which is concerned with plurality in perceived space, we may reject the above view on the ground that, whatever may be the case with 'real' space, perceived space is certainly not absolute, i.e., absolute positions are not among objects of perception. Thus the whiteness here and the whiteness there cannot be distinguished as complexes of which this place and that place are respectively constituents.

Of course the whitenesses may be of different shapes, say one round and one square, and then they could be distinguished by their shapes. It will be observed that, with the view adopted above as to the nature of perceived space, it is perfectly possible for a simple object of perception to have a shape: the shape will be a quality like another. Since a simple object of perception may be of finite extent, there is no reason to suppose that a shape must imply spatial divisibility in the object of perception. Hence our two patches may be respectively round and square, and yet not be spatially divisible. It is obvious, however, that this method of distinguishing the two patches is altogether inadequate. The two patches are just as easily distinguished if both are square or both are round. So long as we can see both at once, no degree of likeness between them causes the slightest difficulty in perceiving that there are two of them. Thus difference of shape, whether it exists or not, is not what makes the patches two entities instead of one.

It may be said that the two patches are distinguished by the difference in their relations to other things. For example, it may happen that a patch of red is to the right of one and to the left of the other. But this does not imply that the patches are two unless we know that one thing cannot be both to the right and to the left of another. This, it might be said, is obviously false. Suppose a surface of black with a small white space in the middle. Then the whole of the black may form only one simple object of perception, and would seem to be both to the right and to the left of the white space which it entirely surrounds. I think it would be more true to say, in this case, that the black is neither to the right nor to the left of the white. But right and left are complicated relations involving the body of the percipient. Let us take some other simpler relation, say that of surrounding, which the black surface has to the white patch in our example. Suppose we have another white patch, of exactly the same size and shape, entirely surrounded by red. Then, it may be said, the two patches of white are distinguished by difference of relation, since one is surrounded by black and the other by red. But if this ground of distinction is to be valid, we must know that it is impossible for one entity to be both wholly and immediately surrounded by black and wholly and immediately surrounded by red. I do not mean to deny that we do know this. But two things deserve notice—first, that it is not an analytic proposition; second, that it presupposes the numerical diversity of our two patches of white.

We are so accustomed to regarding such relations as 'inside' and 'outside' as incompatible that it is easy to suppose a *logical* incompatibility, although in fact the incompatibility is a characteristic of space, not a result of logic. I do not know what are the unanalysable spatial relations of objects of perception, whether visual or tactile, but whatever they are they must have the kind of characteristics which are required in order to generate an order. They, or some of them, must be asymmetrical, i.e., such that they are incompatible with their converses: for example, supposing 'inside' to be one of them, a thing which is inside another must not also be outside it. They, or some of them, must also be transitive, i.e., such that, for example, if x is inside y and y is inside z, then x is inside z—supposing, for the sake of illustration, 'inside' to be among fundamental spatial relations. Probably some further properties will be required, but these at least are essential, in view of the fact that there is such a thing as spatial order. It follows that some at least of the fundamental spatial relations must be such as no entity can have to itself. It is indeed self-evident that spatial relations fulfil these conditions. But these conditions are not demonstrable by purely logical considerations: they are synthetic properties of perceived spatial relations.

It is in virtue of these self-evident properties that the numerical diversity of the two patches of white is self-evident. They have the relation of being outside each other, and this requires that they should be two, not one. They may or may not have intrinsic differences—of shape, or size, or brightness, or any other quality— but whether they have or not they are two, and it is obviously logically possible that they should have no intrinsic differences whatever. It follows from this that the terms of spatial relations cannot be universals or collections of universals, but must be particulars capable of being exactly alike and yet numerically diverse.

It is very desirable, in such discussions as that on which we are at present engaged, to be able to talk of 'places' and of things or qualities 'occupying' places, without implying absolute position. It must be understood that, on the view which adopts relative position, a 'place' is not a precise notion. But its usefulness arises as follows: Suppose a set of objects, such as the walls and furniture of a room, to retain their spatial relations unchanged for a certain length of time, while a succession of other objects, say people who successively sit in a certain chair, have successively a given set of spatial relations to the relatively fixed objects. Then the people have, one after the other, a given set of properties, consisting in spatial relations to the walls and furniture. Whatever has this given set of properties at a given moment is said to 'occupy' a certain place, the 'place' itself being merely a fixed set of spatial relations to certain objects whose spatial relations to each other do not change appreciably during the time considered. Thus when we say that one thing can only be in one place at one time, we mean that it can only have one set of spatial relations to a given set of objects at one time.

It might be argued that, since we have admitted that a simple object of perception may be of finite extent, we have admitted that it may be in many places at once, and therefore may be outside itself. This, however, would be a misunderstanding. In perceived space, the finite extent occupied by a simple object of perception is not divided into many places. It is a single place occupied by a single thing. There are two different ways in which this place may 'correspond' to many places. First, if there is such a thing as 'real' space with geometrical properties, the one place in perceived space will correspond to an infinite number of points in 'real' space, and the single entity which is the object of perception will correspond to many physical entities in 'real' space. Secondly, there is a more or less partial correspondence between perceived space at one time and perceived space at another. Suppose that we attend closely to our white patch, and meanwhile no other noticeable changes occur in the field of vision. Our white patch may, and often does, change as the result of attention—we may perceive differences of shade or other differentiations, or, without differences of quality, we may merely observe parts in it which make it complex and introduce diversity and spatial relations within it. We consider, naturally, that we are still looking at the same thing as before, and that what we see now was there all along. Thus we conclude that our apparently simple white patch was not really simple. But, in fact, the object of perception is not the same as it was before; what may be the same is the physical object supposed to correspond to the object of perception. This physical object is, of course, complex. And the perception which results from attention will be in one sense more correct than that which perceived a simple object, because, if attention reveals previously unnoticed differences, it may be assumed that there are corresponding differences in the 'real' object which corresponds to the object of perception. Hence the perception resulting from attention gives more information about the 'real' object than the other perception did: but the object of perception itself is no more and no less real in the one case than in the other—that is to say, in both cases it is an object which exists when perceived, but which there is no reason to believe existent except when it is perceived.

In perceived space, the spatial unit is not a point, but a simple object of perception or an ultimate constituent in a complex object of perception. This is the reason why, although two patches of white which are visibly separated from each other must be two, a continuous area of white may not be two. A continuous area, if not too large, may be a single object of perception not consisting of parts, which is impossible for two visibly separated areas. The spatial unit is variable, constantly changing its size, and subject to every fluctuation of attention, but it must occupy a continuous portion of perceived space, since otherwise it would be perceived as plural.

The argument as to numerical diversity which we have derived from perceived space may be reinforced by a similar argument as regards the contents of different minds. If two people are both believing that two and two are four, it is at least theoretically possible that the meanings they attach to the words *two* and *and* and *are* and *four* are the same, and that therefore, so far as the objects of their beliefs are concerned, there is nothing to distinguish the one from the other. Nevertheless, it seems plain that there are two entities, one the belief of the one man and the other the belief of the other. A particular belief is a complex of which something which we may call a subject is a constituent; in our case, it is the diversity of the subjects that produces the diversity of the beliefs. But these subjects cannot be mere bundles of general qualities. Suppose one of our men is characterized by benevolence, stupidity, and love of puns. It would not be correct to say: 'Benevolence, stupidity, and love of puns believe that two and two are four'. Nor would this become correct by the addition of a larger number of general qualities. Moreover, however many qualities we add, it remains possible that the other subject may also have them; hence qualities cannot be what constitutes the diversity of the subjects. The only respect in which two different subjects *must* differ is in their relations to particulars: for example, each will have to the other relations which he does not have to himself. But it is not logically impossible that everything concerning one of the subjects and otherwise only concerning universals might be true of the other subject. Hence, even when differences in regard to such propositions occur, it is not these differences that constitute the diversity of the two subjects. The subjects, therefore, must be regarded as particulars, and as radically different from any collection of those general qualities which may be predicated of them.

It will be observed that, according to the general principles which must govern any correspondence of real things with objects of perception, any principle which introduces diversity among objects of perception must introduce a corresponding diversity among real things. I am not now concerned to argue as to what grounds exist for assuming a correspondence, but, if there is such a correspondence, it must be supposed that diversity in the effects —i.e., the perceived objects—implies diversity in the causes—i.e., the real objects. Hence if I perceive two objects in the field of vision, we must suppose that at least two real objects are concerned in causing my perception.

The essential characteristic of particulars, as they appear in perceived space, is that they cannot be in two places at once. But this is an unsatisfactory way of stating the matter, owing to the doubt as to what a 'place' is. The more correct statement is that certain perceptible spatial relations imply diversity of their terms; for example, if x is above y, x and y must be different entities. So long, however, as it is understood that this is what is meant, no harm is done by the statement that a thing cannot be in two places at once.

We may now return to the question of particulars and universals with a better hope of being able to state precisely the nature of the opposition between them. It will be remembered that we began with three different oppositions: (1) that of percept and concept, (2) that of entities existing in time and entities not existing in time, (3) that of substantives and verbs. But in the course of our discussion a different opposition developed itself, namely, (4) that between entities which can be in one place, but not in more than one, at a given time, and entities which either cannot be anywhere or can be in several places at one time. What makes a particular patch of white particular, whereas whiteness is universal, is the fact that the particular patch cannot be in two places simultaneously, whereas the whiteness, if it exists at all, exists wherever there are white things. This opposition, as stated, might be held not to apply to thoughts. We might reply that a man's thoughts are in his head; but without going into this question, we may observe that there certainly is some relation between a man's thoughts and his head (or some part of it) which there is not between his thoughts and other things in space. We may extend our definition of particulars so as to cover this relation. We may say that a man's thought 'belongs to' the place where his head is. We may then define a particular in our fourth sense as an entity which cannot be in or belong to more than one place at one time, and a universal as an entity which either cannot be in or belong to any place, or can be in or belong to many places at once. This opposition has certain affinities with the three earlier oppositions, which must be examined.

(1) Owing to the admission of particulars in our fourth sense, we can make an absolute division between percepts and concepts. The universal whiteness is a concept, whereas a particular white patch is a percept. If we had not admitted particulars in our fourth sense, percepts would have been identical with certain concepts.

(2) For the same reason, we are able to say that such general qualities as whiteness never exist in time, whereas the things that do exist in time are all particulars in our fourth sense. The converse, that all particulars in our fourth sense exist in time, holds in virtue of their definition. Hence the second and fourth senses of the opposition of particulars and universals are co-extensive.

(3) The third opposition, that of substantives and verbs, presents more difficulties, owing to the doubt whether predicates are verbs or not. In order to evade this doubt, we may substitute another opposition, which will be co-extensive with substantives and verbs if predicates are verbs, but not otherwise. This other opposition puts predicates and relations on one side, and everything else on the other. What is not a predicate or relation is, according to one traditional definition, a substance. It is true that, when substance was in vogue, it was supposed that a substance must be indestructible, and this quality will not belong to our substances. For example, what a man sees when he sees a flash of lightning is a substance in our sense. But the importance of indestructibility was metaphysical, not logical. As far as logical properties are concerned, our substances will be fairly analogous to traditional substances. Thus we have the opposition of substances on the one hand and predicates and relations on the other hand. The theory which rejects particulars allows entities commonly classed as predicates— e.g. white—to exist; thus the distinction between substances and predicates is obliterated by this theory. Our theory, on the contrary, preserves the distinction. In the world we know, substances

are identical with particulars in our fourth sense, and predicates and relations with universals.

It will be seen that, according to the theory which assumes particulars, there is a specific relation of subject to predicate, unless we adopt the view—considered above in connexion with Berkeley and Hume—that common sensible qualities are really derivative from specific kinds of likeness. Assuming this view to be false, ordinary sensible qualities will be predicates of the particulars which are instances of them. The sensible qualities themselves do not exist in time in the same sense in which the instances do. Predication is a relation involving a fundamental logical difference between its two terms. Predicates may themselves have predicates, but the predicates of predicates will be radically different from the predicates of substances. The predicate, on this view, is never part of the subject, and thus no true subject-predicate proposition is analytic. Propositions of the form 'All *A* is *B*' are not really subject-predicate propositions, but express relations of predicates; such propositions may be analytic, but the traditional confusion of them with true subject-predicate propositions has been a disgrace to formal logic.

The theory which rejects particulars, and assumes that, e.g., whiteness itself exists wherever (as common sense would say) there are white things, dispenses altogether with predication as a fundamental relation. 'This is white', which, on the other view, expresses a relation between a particular and whiteness, will, when particulars are rejected, really state that whiteness is one of the qualities in this place, or has certain spatial relations to certain other qualities. Thus the question whether predication is an ultimate simple relation may be taken as distinguishing the two theories; it is ultimate if there are particulars, but not otherwise. And if predication is an ultimate relation, the best definition of particulars is that they are entities which can only be subjects of predicates or terms of relations, i.e., that they are (in the logical sense) substances. This definition is preferable to one introducing space or time, because space and time are accidental characteristics of the world with which we happen to be acquainted, and therefore are destitute of the necessary universality belonging to purely logical categories.

We have thus a division of all entities into two classes: (1)

particulars, which enter into complexes only as the subjects of predicates or the terms of relations, and, if they belong to the world of which we have experience, exist in time, and cannot occupy more than one place at one time in the space to which they belong; (2) universals, which can occur as predicates or relations in complexes, do not exist in time, and have no relation to one place which they may not simultaneously have to another. The ground for regarding such a division as unavoidable is the self-evident fact that certain spatial relations imply diversity of their terms, together with the self-evident fact that it is logically possible for entities having such spatial relations to be wholly indistinguishable as to predicates.

The argument in the above article in favour of the existence of particulars no longer seems to me valid for reasons which I have explained in *Human Knowledge: its scope and limits*. The gist of the matter arises out of the last sentence in the above article. I no longer think that there are any spatial or temporal relations which always and necessarily imply diversity. This does not prove that the theory which asserts particulars is wrong, but only that it cannot be proved to be right. The theory which asserts particulars and the theory which denies them would seem equally tenable. If so, the latter has the merit of logical parsimony. [Note added in 1955.]

On the Nature of Acquaintance

In the spring of 1914 Russell was Lecturer in Philosophy at Harvard University, and while there he delivered under the Lowell Institute the lectures which were to appear later that year as OUR KNOWLEDGE OF THE EXTERNAL WORLD. The themes which appear in those lectures and the three papers (first printed in THE MONIST) which follow here were not new in philosophy or Russell's published work. The distinction between knowledge by acquaintance and knowledge by description is found in a clear and well developed form in St. Augustine's DE MAGISTRO; Russell had given a full exposition of it in THE PROBLEMS OF PHILOSOPHY (1912). What makes these papers of interest is that they show us Russell engaged in philosophical debate with some of the leading American philosophers of the day, and they provide us with his arguments against neutral monism, a position that he later adopted in THE ANALYSIS OF MIND (1921) and gradually abandoned, apparently for reasons similar to those given here.

The months at Harvard put Russell in direct contact with James, Perry, Sheffer, and Demos of the 'new realist' school which, except for some of its pragmatic overtones, Russell could regard as a close relative of the Cambridge philosophy which was growing out of his own work. Indeed, Russell's praise for Sheffer's 'new and very powerful method in mathematical logic' caused Russell to 'recommend' to him the re-writing of the PRINCIPIA. 'since what has so far been published by him is scarcely sufficient to enable others to undertake the necessary reconstruction'.*

In 1916 President Lowell of Harvard invited Russell to return as a permanent member of the philosophical faculty, an invitation which must have been especially appealing, since he had just been dismissed from his lectureship at Trinity College, Cambridge, because of his first conviction under the Defence of the Realm Act. He was prevented

*Principia Mathematica, Introduction to the Second Edition, Vol. I, Cambridge, 1925, p. xv. Russell's praise was an important factor in Sheffer's appointment to a chair in logic at Harvard; but the reconstruction Russell wished to see never took place, and Sheffer probably published less than any other professor in the university, his total writings in the Church bibliography coming to less than twenty-one pages.

from accepting the appointment by the refusal of the Foreign Office to permit him to leave the country, a move in the campaign of systematic persecution for nonconformity in thought which led, eventually, to his imprisonment in 1918.

Might-have-beens are a dangerous pastime, but it is interesting for all that to speculate on which might have happened to American philosophy if Russell had been a part of the scene from 1916 onwards. Surely pragmatism would never have gained as much ground as it did—only to crumple, eventually, under criticism from the very type of philosophy which Russell had initiated at Cambridge; and surely Russell would have left a stronger mark on the Harvard philosophic faculty than Whitehead (who went there in 1924), whose speculative thought ceased to be influential at Harvard within a short time after his retirement and has now seemingly vanished without a trace. When Russell lectured at Harvard for a second time, in 1940, his ideas (published as AN INQUIRY INTO MEANING AND TRUTH) had a relevance to contemporary American thought which Whitehead's cosmology had never possessed.

It is therefore as a commentary on transatlantic thinking before the 1914–18 war that these relatively unknown essays are reprinted here. Russell's comments on his changes of opinion in some of these questions will be found in IV of the lectures on logical atomism immediately following.

1914

ON THE NATURE OF ACQUAINTANCE

I. PRELIMINARY DESCRIPTION OF EXPERIENCE

THE purpose of what follows is to advocate a certain analysis of the simplest and most pervading aspect of experience, namely what I call 'acquaintance'. It will be maintained that acquaintance is a dual relation between a subject and an object which need not have any community of nature. The subject is 'mental', the object is not known to be mental except in introspection. The object may be in the present, in the past, or not in time at all; it may be a sensible particular, or a universal, or an abstract logical fact. All cognitive relations—attention, sensation, memory, imagination, believing, disbelieving, etc.—presuppose acquaintance.

This theory has to be defended against three rival theories: (1) the theory of Mach and James, according to which there is no distinctive relation such as 'acquaintance', involved in all mental facts, but merely a different grouping of the same objects as those dealt with by non-psychological sciences; (2) the theory that the immediate object is mental, as well as the subject; (3) the theory that between subject and object there is a third entity, the 'content', which is mental, and is that thought or state of mind by means of which the subject apprehends the object. The first of these rivals is the most interesting and the most formidable, and can only be met by a full and detailed discussion, which will occupy a second essay. The other theories, along with my own, will be considered in a third essay, while the first essay will consist of an introductory survey of data.*

The word 'experience', like most of the words expressing fundamental ideas in philosophy, has been imported into the technical

* [The three essays to which Russell refers in this passage are here reprinted, under their respective subheads, consecutively.—R.C.M.]

vocabulary from the language of daily life, and it retains some of the grime of its outdoor existence in spite of some scrubbing and brushing by impatient philosophers. Originally, the 'philosophy of experience' was opposed to the *a priori* philosophy, and 'experience' was confined to what we learn through the senses. Gradually, however, its scope widened until it included everything of which we are in any way conscious, and became the watchword of an emaciated idealism imported from Germany. The word had, on the one hand, the reassuring associations of the 'appeal to experience', which seemed to preclude the wilder vagaries of transcendental metaphysicians; while on the other hand it held, as it were in solution, the doctrine that nothing can happen except as the 'experience' of some mind. Thus by the use of this one word the idealists cunningly forced upon their antagonists the odium of the *a priori* and the apparent necessity of maintaining the bare dogma of an unknowable reality, which must, it was thought, be either wholly arbitrary or not really unknowable.

In the revolt against idealism, the ambiguities of the word 'experience' have been perceived, with the result that realists have more and more avoided the word. It is to be feared, however, that if the word is avoided the confusions of thought with which it has been associated may persist. It seems better to persevere in the attempt to analyse and clarify the somewhat vague and muddy ideas commonly called up by the word 'experience', since it is not improbable that in this process we may come upon something of fundamental importance to the theory of knowledge.

A certain difficulty as regards the use of words is unavoidable here, as in all philosophical inquiries. The meanings of common words are vague, fluctuating and ambiguous, like the shadow thrown by a flickering street-lamp on a windy night; yet in the nucleus of this uncertain patch of meaning, we may find some precise concept for which philosophy requires a name. If we choose a new technical term, the connexion with ordinary thought is obscured and the clarifying of ordinary thought is retarded; but if we use the common word with a new precise significance, we may seem to run counter to usage, and we may confuse the reader's thoughts by irrelevant associations. It is impossible to lay down a rule for the avoidance of these opposite dangers; sometimes it will be well to introduce a new technical term, sometimes it will be better to polish the common word until it becomes suitable for technical purposes. In the case of 'experience', the latter course seems preferable, since the actual process of polishing the word is instructive, and the confusions of thought which it covers cannot well be otherwise dispelled.

In seeking the central ideal embodied in the word 'experience', we shall at the same time be performing the analysis required for a definition of 'mind' and 'mental'. Common sense divides human beings into souls and bodies, and Cartesian philosophy generalized this division by classifying everything that exists as either mind or matter. This division is so familiar, and of such respectable antiquity, that it has become part of our habits, and seems scarcely to embody a theory. Mind is what we know from within—thoughts and feelings and volitions—while matter is what is in space outside our minds. Nevertheless, almost all the great philosophers since Leibniz have challenged the dualism of mind and matter. Most of them, regarding mind as something immediately given, have assimilated to it what appeared to be 'matter', and have thus achieved the monism of the idealist. We may define an idealist as a man who believes that whatever exists may be called 'mental', in the sense of having a certain character, known to us by introspection as belonging to our own minds. In recent times, however, this theory has been criticized from various points of view. On the one hand, men who admitted that we know by introspection things having the character we call 'mental' have urged that we also know other things not having this character. On the other hand, William James and the American realists have urged that there is no specific character of 'mental' things, but that the things which are called mental are identical with the things which are called physical, the difference being merely one of context and arrangement.

We have thus three opinions to consider. There are first those who deny that there is a character called 'mental' which is revealed in introspection. These men may be called 'neutral monists', because, while rejecting the division of the world into mind and matter, they do not say 'all reality is mind', nor yet 'all reality is matter'. Next, there are 'idealistic monists', who admit a character called 'mental', and hold that everything has this character. Next, there are 'dualists', who hold that there is such a character, but that there are things which do not possess it. In order to decide among these views, it is necessary to decide whether anything is meant by the word 'mental'; and this inquiry brings us back to the meaning of 'experience'.

When we consider the world without the knowledge and the ignorance that are taught by philosophy, we seem to see that it contains a number of things and persons, and that some of the things are 'experienced' by some of the persons. A man may experience different things at different times, and different men may experience different things at the same time. Some things, such as the inside of the earth or the other side of the moon, are never experienced by anybody, but are nevertheless believed to exist. The things which a man is said to experience are the things that are given in sensation, his own thoughts and feelings (at any rate so far as he is aware of them), and perhaps (though on this point common sense might hesitate) the facts which he comes to know by thinking. At any given moment, there are certain things of which a man is 'aware', certain things which are 'before his mind'. Now although it is very difficult to define ' awareness', it is not at all difficult to say that I am aware of such and such things. If I am asked, I can reply that I am aware of this, and that, and the other, and so on through a heterogeneous collection of objects. If I describe these objects, I may of course describe them wrongly; hence I cannot with certainty communicate to another what are the things of which I am aware. But if I speak to myself, and denote them by what may be called 'proper names', rather than by descriptive words, I cannot be in error. So long as the names which I use really are names at the moment, i.e., are naming things to me, so long the things must be objects of which I am aware, since otherwise the words would be meaningless sounds, not names of things. There is thus at any given moment a certain assemblage of objects to which I could, if I chose, give proper names; these are the objects of my 'awareness', the objects 'before my mind', or the objects that are within my present 'experience'.

There is a certain unity, important to realize but hard to analyse, in 'my present experience'. If we assumed that 'I' am the same at one time and at another, we might suppose that 'my present experience' might be defined as all the experience which 'I' have 'now'. But in fact we shall find that 'I' and 'now', in the order of knowledge, must be defined in terms of 'my present experience', rather than vice versa. Moreover, we cannot define 'my present experience' as 'all experience contemporaneous with *this*' (where *this* is some actual part of what I now experience), since that would ignore the possibility of experience other than mine. Nor can we define it as 'all experience which I experience as contemporaneous with *this*', since that would exclude all that part of my experiencing of which I do not become introspectively conscious. We shall have to say, I think, that 'being experienced together' is a relation between experienced things, which can itself be experienced, for example when we become aware of two things which we are seeing together, or of a thing seen and a thing heard simultaneously. Having come to know in this way what is meant by 'being experienced together', we can define 'my present contents of experience' as 'everything experienced together with *this*', where *this* is any experienced thing selected by attention. We shall return to this topic on several subsequent occasions.

I do not propose as yet to attempt a logical analysis of 'experience'. For the present, I wish to consider its extent, its boundaries, its prolongation in time, and the reasons for regarding it as not all-embracing. These topics may be dealt with by discussing successively the following questions: (1) Are faint and peripheral sensations included in 'experience'? (2) Are all or any of our present true beliefs included in present 'experience'? (3) Do we now 'experience' past things which we remember? (4) How do we come to know that the group of things now experienced is not all-embracing? (5) Why do we regard our present and past experiences as all parts of *one* experience, namely the experience which we call 'ours'? (6) What leads us to believe that 'our' total experience is not all-embracing? Many of these questions will have to be discussed again more fully at a later stage; for the present, we are not discussing them on their own account, but in order to become familiar with the notion of experience.

1. Are faint and peripheral sensations included in 'experience'? This question may be asked, not only with regard to sensations, but also with regard to faint wishes, dim thoughts, and whatever else is not in the focus of attention; but for illustrative purposes, the case of sensation, which is the simplest, may suffice. For the sake of definiteness, let us consider the field of vision. Normally,

if we are attending to anything seen, it is to what is in the centre of the field that we attend, but we can, by an effort of will, attend to what is in the margin. It is obvious that, when we do so, what we attend to is indubitably experienced. Thus the question we have to consider is whether *attention* constitutes experience, or whether things not attended to are also experienced. It seems we must admit things to which we do not attend, for attention is a selection among objects that are 'before the mind', and therefore presupposes a larger field, constituted in some less exclusive manner, out of which attention chooses what it wants. In cases, however, where, in spite of the physical conditions which might be expected to produce a sensation, no sensation appears to exist, as for example when we fail to hear a faint sound which we should hear if our attention were called to it, it would seem that there is no corresponding 'experience'; in such cases, in spite of the physical existence of the sound-stimulus, there seems to be sometimes no answering 'mental' existent.

2. Our mental life is largely composed of beliefs, and of what we are pleased to call 'knowledge' of 'facts'. When I speak of a 'fact', I mean the kind of thing that is expressed by the phrase 'that so-and-so is the case'. A 'fact' in this sense is something different from an existing sensible thing; it is the kind of object towards which we have a *belief*, expressed in a proposition. The question I am asking now is not whether believing is experienced, for that I take to be obvious; the question is, whether the facts towards which beliefs are directed are ever experienced. It is obvious at once that most of the facts which we consider to be within our knowledge are not experienced. We do not experience that the earth goes round the sun, or that London has six million inhabitants, or that Napoleon was defeated at Waterloo. I think, however, that some facts are experienced, namely those which we see for ourselves, without relying either upon our own reasoning from previous facts, or upon the testimony of others. These 'primitive' facts, which are known to us by an immediate insight as luminous and indubitable as that of sense, must, if I am not mistaken, be included in the original matter of experience. Their importance in the theory of knowledge is very great, and we shall have occasion to consider them very fully in the sequel.

3. Do we now experience past things which we remember? We

cannot of course discuss this question adequately without a consideration of the psychology of memory. But in a brief preliminary way, something may be said to indicate an affirmative conclusion. In the first place, we must not confound true memory with present images of past things. I may call up now before my mind an image of a man I saw yesterday; the image is not in the past, and I certainly experience it now, but the image itself is not memory. The remembering refers to something known to be in the past, to what I saw yesterday, not to the image which I call up now. But even when the present image has been set aside as irrelevant, there still remains a distinction between what may be called 'intellectual' memory and what may be called 'sensational' memory. When I merely know 'that I saw Jones yesterday', this is intellectual memory; my knowledge is of one of those 'primitive facts' which we considered in the preceding paragraph. But in the immediate memory of something which has just happened, the thing itself seems to remain in experience, in spite of the fact that it is known to be no longer present. How long this sort of memory may last, I do not profess to know; but it may certainly last long enough to make us conscious of a lapse of time since the thing remembered was present. Thus it would seem that in two different ways past things may form parts of present experience.

The conclusion that past things are experienced in memory may be reinforced by considering the difference between past and future. Through scientific prediction, we may come to know, with greater or less probability, many things about the future, but all these things are *inferred*: not one of them is known immediately. We do not even know immediately what we mean by the word 'future': the future is essentially that period of time when the present will be past. 'Present' and 'past' are given in experience, and 'future' is defined in terms of them. The difference between past and future, from the standpoint of theory of knowledge, consists just in the fact that the past is in part experienced now, while the future still lies wholly outside experience.

4. How do we come to know that the group of things now experienced is not all-embracing? This question arises naturally out of what has just been said concerning the future; for our belief that there will be a future is just one of those that take us beyond present experience. It is not, however, one of the most indubitable;

we have no very good reason to feel sure that there will be a future, whereas some of the ways in which reality must transcend present experience seem as certain as any knowledge.

This question is one of great importance, since it introduces us to the whole problem of how knowledge can transcend personal experience. For the present, however, we are not concerned with the *whole* of our individual experience, but only with the experience of a given moment. At first sight, it might seem as though the experience of each moment must be a prison for the knowledge of that moment, and as though its boundaries must be the boundaries of our present world. Every word that we now understand must have a meaning which falls within our present experience; we can never point to an object and say: '*This* lies outside my present experience'. We cannot know any particular thing unless it is part of present experience; hence it might be inferred that we cannot know that there are particular things which lie outside present experience. To suppose that we can know this, it might be said, is to suppose that we can know what we do not know. On this ground, we may be urged to a modest agnosticism with regard to everything that lies outside our momentary consciousness. Such a view, it is true, is not usually advocated in this extreme form; but the principles of solipsism and of the older empirical philosophy would seem, if rigorously applied, to reduce the knowledge of each moment within the narrow area of that moment's experience.

To this theory there are two complementary replies. The one is empirical, and consists in pointing out that in fact we do know more than the theory supposes; the other is logical, and consists in pointing out a fallacy in the inference which the theory draws from the data. Let us begin with the empirical refutation.

One of the obvious empirical refutations is derived from the knowledge that we have forgotten something. When, for example, we try to recall a person's name, we may be perfectly certain that the name came into our experience in the past, but for all our efforts it will not come into our present experience. Then again, in more abstract regions we know that there are facts which are not within our present experience; we may remember that there are 144 entries in the multiplication-table, without remembering them all individually; and we may know that there are an infinite number of facts in arithmetic, of which only a finite number are now present to our minds. In both the above cases, we have certainty, but in the one case the thing forgotten did once form part of our experience, while in the other, the fact not experienced is an abstract mathematical fact, not a particular thing existing in time. If we are willing to admit any of the beliefs of daily life, such as that there will be a future, we of course have a great extension of what exists without being experienced. We know by memory that hitherto we have constantly become aware, in sensation, of new particulars not experienced before, and that therefore throughout the past our experience has not been all-embracing. If, then, the present moment is not the last moment in the life of the universe, we must suppose that the future will contain things which we do not now experience. It is no answer to say that, since these things are future, they do not yet form part of the universe; they must, at all times, be included in any complete inventory of the universe, which must enumerate what is to come just as much as what is and what has been. For the above reasons, then, it is certain that the world contains some things not in my experience, and highly probable that it contains a vast number of such things.

It remains to show the logical possibility of the knowledge that there are things which we are not now experiencing. This depends upon the fact that we may know propositions of the form: 'There are things having such-and-such a property', even when we do not know of any instance of such things. In the abstract mathematical world, it is very easy to find examples. For instance, we know that there is no greatest prime number. But of all the prime numbers that we shall have ever thought of, there certainly is a greatest. Hence there are prime numbers greater than any that we shall have ever thought of. But in more concrete realms, the same is true: it is perfectly possible to know that there are things which I have known, but have now forgotten, although it is obviously impossible to give an instance of such things. To recur to our former example, I may perfectly remember that yesterday I knew the name of the lady I was introduced to, although to-day the name is lost to me. That I was told her name, is a fact which I know, and which implies that I knew a particular thing which I no longer know; I know that there was such a particular thing, but I do not know what particular thing it was. To pursue this topic farther would require an account of 'knowledge by description', which belongs to a later stage. For the present, I am content to have pointed out that we know that there are things outside present experience and that such knowledge raises no logical difficulty.

5. Why do we regard our present and past experiences as all parts of one experience, namely the experience which we call 'ours'? This question must be considered before we can advance to the further question, whether we can know that there are things which transcend the whole of 'our' experience. But at our present stage we can only give it a brief preliminary consideration, such as will enable us to speak of one person's total experience with some realization of what we mean and of what are the difficulties involved.

It is obvious that *memory* is what makes us call past experiences 'ours'. I do not mean that only those experiences that we now remember are considered as ours, but that memory always makes the links in the chain connecting our present with our past. It is not, however, memory *per se* that does this: it is memory of a certain sort. If we merely remember some external object, the experiencing is in the present, and there is not yet any reason to assume the past experience. It would be logically possible to remember an object which we had never experienced; indeed, it is by no means certain that this does not sometimes occur. We may hear a striking clock, for instance, and become aware that it has already struck several times before we noticed it. Perhaps, in this case, we have really experienced the earlier strokes as they occurred, but we cannot remember to have done so. Thus the case serves to illustrate an important difference, namely the difference between remembering an outside event and remembering our experiencing of the event. Normally, when we remember an event, we also remember our experiencing of it, but the two are different memories, as is shown by the case of the striking clock. The memory which prolongs our personality backwards in time is the memory of our experiencing, not merely of the things which we experienced. When we can remember experiencing something, we include the remembered experiencing with our present experiencing as part of one person's experience. Thus we are led to include also whatever experience we remembered at that earlier period, and so back, hypothetically, to earliest infancy. In the same hypothetical manner, we stretch our personality forward in time to all experiences which will remember our present experiences directly or indirectly.* By this extension of the present experience into a series of experiences linked by memory, we include within our own total experience all those particulars, spoken of under our last heading, which are known to have existed, though they do not form part of present experience; and in case time should continue beyond the present moment, we include also those future experiences which will be related to our present as our present is related to our past.

6. What leads us to believe that 'our' total experience is not all-embracing? This is the question of solipsism: What reason have we for believing that anything exists or has existed or will exist except what forms part of our total experience in the sense explained in the preceding paragraph?

The logical argument by which we showed that it is *possible* to know of the existence of things that are outside *present* experience applies, without change, to the existence of things that lie outside our *total* experience. Thus the only question we have to consider is whether, as a matter of empirical fact, we know anything which proves the existence of such things. In abstract logical and mathematical regions, it is easy, by means of the very examples which we used before, to *prove* that there are facts which do not form part of our total experience. It seems certain that we shall not think of more than a finite number of arithmetical facts in the course of our lives, and we know that the total number of arithmetical facts is infinite. If this example be thought inconclusive, on the ground that perhaps we survive death and become more interested in arithmetic hereafter, the following example will be found more stubborn. The number of functions of a real variable is infinitely greater than the number of moments of time. Therefore even if we spent all eternity thinking of a new function every instant, or of any finite or small infinite number of new functions every instant, there would still be an infinite number of functions which we should not have thought of, and therefore an infinite number of facts about them which would never enter our

---

* In the language of the logic of relations, if M is the relation 'remembering', N the sum of M and its converse, and x is any moment of experience, the total experience to which x belongs is all moments of experience which have to x the relation N^*. Cf. *Principia Mathematica*, *90.

experience. It is therefore certain that there are mathematical facts which do not enter into our total experience.

With regard to existing particulars, no such cogent argument, so far as I know, can be produced. We naturally suppose that other people's bodies are inhabited by minds more or less like ours, which experience pleasures and pains, desires and aversions, of which we have no direct awareness. But although we naturally suppose this, and although no reason can be alleged for believing that our supposition is mistaken, yet it would seem also that there is no *conclusive* reason for believing it not mistaken. Exactly the same degree of doubt attaches to the inside of the earth, the other side of the moon, and the innumerable physical facts which we habitually assume without the warrant of direct experience. If there is good reason to believe in any of these things, it must be derived from induction and causality by a complicated process which we are not at present in a position to consider. For the present, let us assume as a working hypothesis the existence of other people and of unperceived physical things. From time to time we shall reconsider this hypothesis, and at the end we shall be in a position to sum up the evidence as to its truth. For the present, we must be content with the conclusions: (*a*) that there is no logical reason against it, (*b*) that in the logical world there certainly are facts which we do not experience, (*c*) that the common-sense assumption that there are particulars which we do not experience has been found thoroughly successful as a working hypothesis, and that there is no argument of any sort or kind against it.

The conclusion to which we have been led by the above discussion is that some of the things in the world, but not all, are collected together at any given moment of my conscious life into a group which may be called 'my present experience'; that this group embraces things existing now, things that existed in the past, and abstract facts; also that in my experiencing of a thing, something more than the mere thing is involved, and may be experienced in memory; that thus a total group of my experiences throughout time may be defined by means of memory, but that this group, like the momentary group, certainly does not contain all abstract facts, and appears not to contain all existent particulars, and in especial does not contain the experiencing which we believe to be associated with other people's bodies.

We have now to consider what is the analysis of 'experiencing', i.e., what is the bond which combines certain objects into the group forming a momentary experience. And here we must first consider the theory which we have called 'neutral monism', due to William James; for the questions raised by this theory are so fundamental that until they are answered, in one way or in another, no further progress can be made.

II. NEUTRAL MONISM

'Neutral Monism'—as opposed to idealistic monism and materialistic monism—is the theory that the things commonly regarded as mental and the things commonly regarded as physical do not differ in respect of any intrinsic property possessed by the one set and not by the other, but differ only in respect of arrangement and context. The theory may be illustrated by comparison with a postal directory, in which the same names come twice over, once in alphabetical and once in geographical order; we may compare the alphabetical order to the mental, and the geographical order to the physical. The affinities of a given thing are quite different in the two orders, and its causes and effects obey different laws. Two objects may be connected in the mental world by the association of ideas, and in the physical world by the law of gravitation. The whole context of an object is so different in the mental order from what it is in the physical order that the object itself is thought to be duplicated, and in the mental order it is called an 'idea', namely the idea of the same object in the physical order. But this duplication is a mistake: 'ideas' of chairs and tables are identical with chairs and tables, but are considered in their mental context, not in the context of physics.

Just as every man in the directory has two kinds of neighbours, namely alphabetical neighbours and geographical neighbours, so every object will lie at the intersection of two causal series with different laws, namely the mental series and the physical series. 'Thoughts' are not different in substance from 'things'; the stream of my thoughts is a stream of things, namely of the things which I should commonly be said to be thinking *of*; what leads to its being called a stream of *thoughts* is merely that the laws of succession are different from the physical laws. In my mind, Caesar may call up Charlemagne, whereas in the physical world the two were widely sundered. The whole duality of mind and matter, according to this theory, is a mistake; there is only one kind of *stuff* out of which the world is made, and this stuff is called mental in one arrangement, physical in the other.*

A few quotations may serve to make the position clearer.

Mach says:

'That traditional gulf between physical and psychological research, accordingly, exists only for the habitual stereotyped method of observation. A colour is a physical object so long as we consider its dependence upon its luminous source, upon other colours, upon heat, upon space, and so forth. Regarding, however, its dependence upon the retina . . . , it becomes a psychological object, a sensation. Not the subject, but the direction of our investigation, is different in the two domains.' [*op. cit.*, page 14.]

'The primary fact is not the *I*, the ego, but the elements (sensations). The elements *constitute* the *I*. I have the sensation green, signifies that the element green occurs in a given complex of other elements (sensations, memories). When *I* cease to have the sensation green, when *I* die, then the elements no longer occur in their ordinary, familiar way of association. That is all. Only an ideal mental-economical unity, not a real unity, has ceased to exist.

'If a knowledge of the connexion of the elements does not suffice us, and we ask, *Who* possesses this connexion of sensations, *Who* experiences the sensations, then we have succumbed to the habit of subsuming every element (every sensation) under some unanalysed complex' [pages 19-20].

'Bodies do not produce sensations, but complexes of sensations (complexes of elements) make up bodies. If to the physicist bodies appear the real abiding existences, while sensations are regarded merely as their evanescent transitory show, the physicist forgets, in the assumption of such a view, that all bodies are but

* For statements of this theory, see William James, *Essays in Radical Empiricism* (Longmans, 1912) especially the first of these essays, 'Does "Consciousness" Exist?' See also Mach, *Analysis of the Sensations* (Chicago, 1897; the original was published in 1886). Mach's theory seems to be substantially the same as James's; but so far as I know James does not refer to him on this subject, so that he must have reached his conclusions independently of Mach. The same theory is advocated in Perry's *Present Philosophical Tendencies* and in *The New Realism* (1912).

thought-symbols for complexes of sensations (complexes of elements)' [page 22].

'For us, therefore, the world does not consist of mysterious entities, which by their interaction with another equally mysterious entity, the ego, produce sensations which alone are accessible. For us, colours, sounds, spaces, times, . . . are the ultimate elements, whose given connexion it is our business to investigate' [page 23].

Mach arrived at his opinions through physics. James, whose opinions are essentially the same, arrived at them through psychology. In his *Psychology* they are not yet to be found, though there is a certain approach to them. The various articles containing the opinions which concern us at present are collected in the posthumous book called *Essays in Radical Empiricism*. The following quotations will, I hope, serve to make it clear what these opinions are.

' "Consciousness",' says James, 'is the name of a non-entity, and has no right to a place among first principles. Those who still cling to it are clinging to a mere echo, the faint rumour left behind by the disappearing "soul" upon the air of philosophy. For twenty years past* I have mistrusted "consciousness" as an entity; for seven or eight years part I have suggested its non-existence to my students, and tried to give them its pragmatic equivalent in realities of experience. It seem to me that the hour is ripe for it to be openly and universally discarded.

'To deny plumply that "consciousness" exists seems so absurd on the face of it—for undeniably "thoughts" do exist—that I fear some readers will follow me no farther. Let me then immediately explain that I mean only to deny that the word stands for an entity, but to insist most emphatically that it does stand for a function. There is, I mean, no aboriginal stuff or quality of being, contrasted with that of which material objects are made, out of which our thoughts of them are made; but there is a function of experience which thoughts perform, and for the performance of which this quality of being is involved. That function is *knowing*' [pages 2–4].

'My thesis is that if we start with the supposition that there is only one primal stuff or material in the world, a stuff of which everything is composed, and if we call that stuff "pure experience",

* This article was first published in 1904.

then knowing can easily be explained as a particular sort of relation towards one another into which portions of pure experience may enter. The relation itself is a part of pure experience; one of its "terms" becomes the subject or bearer of the knowledge, the knower, the other becomes the object known' [page 4].

After explaining the view, which he rejects, that experience contains an essential opposition of subject and object, he proceeds:

'Now my contention is exactly the reverse of this. *Experience, I believe, has no such inner duplicity: and the separation of it into consciousness and content comes, not by way of subtraction, but by way of addition*—the addition, to a given concrete piece of it, of other sets of experiences, in connexion with which its use or function may be of two different kinds. The paint will also serve here as an illustration. In a pot in a paint-shop, along with other paints, it serves in its entirety as so much saleable matter. Spread on a canvas, with other paints around it, it represents, on the contrary, a feature in a picture and performs a spiritual function. Just so, I maintain, does a given undivided portion of experience, taken in one context of associates, play the part of a knower, of a state of mind, of "consciousness"; while in a different context the same undivided bit of experience plays the part of a thing known, of an objective "content". In a word, in one group it figures as a thought, in another group as a thing. And, since it can figure in both groups simultaneously, we have every right to speak of it as subjective and objective both at once' [pages 9–10; the italics are in the original].

'Consciousness connotes a kind of external relation, and does not denote a special stuff or way of being. *The peculiarity of our experiences, that they not only are, but are known, which their "conscious" quality is invoked to explain, is better explained by their relations—these relations themselves being experiences—to one another*' [page 25; the italics are in the original].

James explains, a few pages later, that a vivid image of fire or water is just as truly hot or wet as physical fire or water. The distinction, he says, lies in the fact that the imagined fire and water are not causally operative like the 'real' fire and water. 'Mental fire is what won't burn real sticks; mental water is what won't necessarily (though of course it may) put out even a mental fire. Mental knives may be sharp, but they won't cut real wood' [page 33].

'The central point of the pure-experience theory is that "outer" and "inner" are names for two groups into which we sort experiences according to the way in which they act upon their neighbours. Any one "content", such as *hard*, let us say, can be assigned to either group' [page 139].

Finally he comes to the alleged introspective certainty of consciousness. But his introspective deliverance is not the usual one. In himself, he says, 'the stream of thinking (which I recognize emphatically as a phenomenon) is only a careless name for what, when scrutinized, reveals itself to consist chiefly of the stream of my breathing. The "I think" which Kant said must be able to accompany all my objects, is the "I breathe" which actually does accompany them. There are other internal facts besides breathing . . . and these increase the assets of "consciousness" so far as the latter is subject to immediate perception; but breath, which was ever the original of "spirit", breath moving outwards, between the glottis and the nostrils, is, I am persuaded, the essence out of which philosophers have constructed the entity known to them as consciousness' [page 37].

In order to understand James's theory, it is necessary to consider more in detail his account of 'knowing'. Mere seeing and hearing, and sensation generally, he does not call 'knowing'. In all the cases where those who hold a different theory would say we have *direct* knowledge, there is, in James's view, no knowledge at all, but merely the presence of the thing itself as one of the constituents of the mind which is mistakenly supposed to know the thing. Knowing, according to him, is an external relation between two bits of experience, consisting in the fact that one of them leads to the other by means of certain intermediaries. The following illustration aptly introduces his account of knowing:

'Suppose me to be sitting here in my library at Cambridge, at ten minutes' walk from "Memorial Hall", and to be thinking truly of the latter object. My mind may have before it only the name, or it may have a clear image, or it may have a very dim image of the hall, but such intrinsic differences in the image make no difference in its cognitive function. Certain *extrinsic* phenomena, special experiences of conjunction, are what impart to the image, be it what it may, its knowing office.

'For instance, if you ask me what hall I mean by my image, and

I can tell you nothing; or if I fail to point or lead you towards the Harvard Delta; or if, being led by you, I am uncertain whether the hall I see be what I had in mind or not; you would rightly deny that I had "meant" that particular hall at all, even though my mental image might to some degree have resembled it. The resemblance would count in that case as coincidental merely, for all sorts of things of a kind resemble one another in this world without being held for that reason to take cognizance of one another.

'On the other hand, if I can lead you to the hall, and tell you of its history and present uses; if in its presence I feel my idea, however imperfect it may have been, to have led hither and to be now, *terminated*; if the associates of the image and of the felt hall run parallel, so that each term of the one context corresponds serially, as I walk, with an answering term of the other; why then my soul was prophetic, and my idea must be, and by common consent would be, called cognizant of reality. That percept was what I *meant* . . .

'In this continuing and corroborating, taken in no transcendental sense, but denoting definitely felt transitions, *lies all that the knowing of a percept by an idea can possibly contain or signify*' [pages 54–56].

It will be observed that, according to the above account, he usually ceases to 'know' Memorial Hall when he reaches it; he only 'knows' it while he has ideas which lead or enable him to perceive it by taking suitable steps. It is, however, possible, apparently, to regard an experience as 'knowing' itself in certain circumstances. In an enumeration of cases, James says:

'Either the knower and the known are:

'1. the self-same piece of experience taken twice over in different contexts: or they are

'2. two pieces of *actual* experience belonging to the same subject, with definite tracts of conjunctive transitional experience between them; or

'3. the known is a *possible* experience either of that subject or another, to which the said conjunctive transitions *would* lead, if sufficiently prolonged' [page 53].

In a later illustration, he says:

'To call my present idea of my dog, for example, cognitive of the real dog means that, as the actual tissue of experience is constituted, the idea is capable of leading into a chain of other experiences on my part that go from next to next and terminate at last in vivid sense-perceptions of a jumping, barking, hairy body. Those *are* the real dog, the dog's full presence, for my common sense' [page 198].

And again: 'Should we ever reach absolutely terminal experiences, experiences in which we were all agreed, which were superseded by no revised continuations, these would not be *true*; they would be *real*, they would simply *be*. . . . Only such *other* things as led to these by satisfactory conjunctions would be "true" ' [page 204].

Before proceeding to examine the substantial truth or falsehood of James's theory, we may observe that his use of the word 'experience' is unfortunate, and points to the lingering taint of an idealistic ancestry. This word is full of ambiguity; it inevitably suggests an experiencing subject; it hints at some common quality, 'being experienced', in all the constituents of the world, whereas there is reason to believe that no such common quality is to be found. This word is abandoned by Professor Perry, whose chapters on 'A realistic theory of mind' and 'A realistic theory of knowledge'* give an admirable account of the Mach-James hypothesis. Nevertheless, even in his account, as in the whole doctrine, it seems possible to detect the unconscious influence of an idealistic habit of mind, persisting involuntarily after the opinions upon which it was based have been abandoned. But this can only be made clear by a detailed examination of the grounds for and against the whole theory of neutral monism.

In favour of the theory, we may observe, first and foremost, the very notable simplification which it introduces. That the things given in experience should be of two fundamentally different kinds, mental and physical, is far less satisfactory to our intellectual desires than that the dualism should be merely apparent and superficial. Occam's razor, '*entia non multiplicanda praeter necessitatem*',† which I should regard as the supreme methodological maxim in philosophizing, prescribes James's theory as preferable to dualism

* Chaps. XII and XIII of *Present Philosophical Tendencies*.
† [*Entities should not be multiplied beyond necessity.*—R.C.M.]

if it can possibly be made to account for the facts. Again, 'matter', which in Descartes' time was supposed to be an obvious datum, has now, under the influence of scientific hypotheses, become a remote super-sensuous construction, connected, no doubt, with sense, but only through a long chain of intermediate inferences. What is immediately present in sense, though obviously in some way presupposed in physics, is studied rather in psychology than in physics. Thus we seem to have here, in sense, a neutral ground, a watershed, from which we may pass either to 'matter' or to 'mind', according to the nature of the problems we choose to raise.*

The ambiguous status of what is present in sense is illustrated by the difficulties surrounding the notion of 'space'. I do not intend now to attempt a solution of these difficulties; I wish only to make them felt, lest it should seem as though space afforded a clear distinction between the material and the mental. It is still sometimes thought that matter may be defined as 'what is in space', but as soon as 'space' is examined, it is found to be incredibly ambiguous, shifting and uncertain. Kant's *a priori* infinite given whole, which merely expresses our natural beliefs whenever the difficult disintegrations of analysis escape from our memories, has suffered a series of shattering blows from the most diverse quarters. The mathematicians have constructed a multiplicity of possible spaces, and have shown that many logical schemes would fit the empirical facts. Logic shows that space is not '*the* subject-matter of geometry', since an infinite number of subject-matters satisfy any given kind of geometry. Psychology disentangles the contributions of various senses to the construction of space, and reveals

---

* The neutrality of sensation in orthodox philosophy may be illustrated by the following quotation from Professor Stout's *Manual of Psychology*, page 133: 'If we compare the colour *red* as a quality of a material object with the colour *red* as a quality of the corresponding sensation, we find that redness as immediately perceived is an attribute common to both. The difference lies in the different relations into which it enters in the two cases. As a quality of the thing, it is considered in relation to other qualities of the thing—its shape, texture, flavour, odour, etc. As a psychical state, it is considered as a peculiar modification of the consciousness of the percipient, in relation to the general flow of his mental life.' There seems in this passage an acceptance, as regards sensation, of the doctrines of neutral monism which Professor Stout would be far from adopting generally.

the all-embracing space of physics as the outcome of many empirically familiar correlations. Thus the space of actual experience is appropriated by psychology, the space of geometry is appropriated by logic, and the space of physics is left halting between them in the humbled garb of a working hypothesis. It is not in 'space', therefore, that we can find a criterion to distinguish the mental and the physical.

A large part of the argument in favour of neutral monism, as stated by its advocates, consists in a polemic against the view that we know the external world through the medium of 'ideas', which are mental. I shall consider this view in the next part; for the present, I wish only to say that, as against this view, I am in agreement with neutral monism. I do not think that, when an object is known to me, there is in my mind something which may be called an 'idea' of the object, the possession of which constitutes my knowledge of the object. But when this is granted, neutral monism by no means follows. On the contrary, it is just at this point that neutral monism finds itself in agreement with idealism in making an assumption which I believe to be wholly false. The assumption is that, *if anything is immediately present to me, that thing must be part of my mind.* The upholders of 'ideas', since they believe in the duality of the mental and the physical, infer from this assumption that only ideas, not physical things, can be immediately present to me. Neutral monists, perceiving (rightly, as I think) that constituents of the physical world can be immediately present to me, infer that the mental and the physical are composed of the same 'stuff', and are merely different arrangements of the same elements. But if the assumption is false, both these opposing theories may be false, as I believe they are.

Before attempting a refutation of neutral monism, we may still further narrow the issue. Non-cognitive mental facts—feeling, emotion, volition—offer prima facie difficulties to which James offers a prima facie answer. His answer might be discussed, and might prove tenable or untenable. But as we are concerned with the theory of *knowledge*, we will ignore the non-cognitive part of the problem, and consider only what is relevant to knowledge. It is in this sphere that his theory is important to us, and in this sphere that we must make up our minds as to its truth or falsehood.

Apart from objections depending upon argument, there is an

initial difficulty in the view that there is nothing cognitive in the mere presence of an object to the mind. If I see a particular patch of colour, and then immediately shut my eyes, it is at least possible to suppose that the patch of colour continues to exist while my eyes are shut; so far, James would agree. But while my eyes are open, the patch of colour is one of the contents of my momentary experience, whereas when my eyes are shut it is not. The difference between being and not being one of the contents of my momentary experience, according to James, consists in experienced relations, chiefly causal, to other contents of my experience. It is here that I feel an insuperable difficulty. I cannot think that the difference between my seeing the patch of red, and the patch of red being there unseen, consists in the presence or absence of relations between the patch of red and other objects of the same kind. It seems to me possible to imagine a mind existing for only a fraction of a second, seeing the red, and ceasing to exist before having any other experience. But such a supposition ought, on James's theory, to be not merely improbable, but meaningless. According to him, things become parts of my experience in virtue of certain relations to each other; if there were not a system of interrelated things experienced by me, there could not be one thing experienced by me. To put the same point otherwise: it seems plain that, without reference to any other content of my experience, at the moment when I see the red I am acquainted with it in some way in which I was not acquainted with it before I saw it, and in which I shall not be acquainted with it when it ceases to be itself present in memory, however much I may be able to recall various facts which would enable me to see it again if I chose. This acquaintance which I have with what is part of my momentary experience seems to deserve to be called cognitive, with a more indefeasible right than any connected ideas such as James describes in speaking of Memorial Hall.

I shall return to the above difficulty, which seems to me the main objection to neutral monism, when I come to consider how the contents of my momentary experience are to be distinguished from other things; in this connexion, the difficulty will take a more general form, and will raise questions which can be better considered after various more detailed difficulties have been dealt with.

The first difficulty which seems to require an answer is as to the nature of *judgment* or *belief*, and more particularly of erroneous belief. Belief differs from sensation in regard to the nature of what is before the mind: if I believe, for example, 'that to-day is Wednesday', not only no sensation, but no presentation of any kind, can give the same objective content as is involved in my belief. This fact, which is fairly obvious in the above instance, is obscured, I think, by the unconscious habit of dwelling upon existential beliefs. People are said to believe in God, or to disbelieve in Adam and Eve. But in such cases what is believed or disbelieved is that there is an entity answering to a certain description. This, which can be believed or disbelieved, is quite different from the actual entity (if any) which does answer to the description. Thus the matter of belief is, in all cases, different in kind from the matter of sensation or presentation, and error is in no way analogous to hallucination. A hallucination is a fact, not an error; what is erroneous is a judgment based upon it. But if I believe that to-day is Wednesday when in fact to-day is Tuesday, 'that to-day is Wednesday' is not a fact. We cannot find anywhere in the physical world any entity corresponding to this belief. What idealists have said about the creative activity of mind, about relations being due to our relating synthesis, and so on, seems to be true in the case of error; to me, at least, it is impossible to account for the occurrence of the false belief that to-day is Wednesday, except by invoking something not to be found in the physical world.

In *The New Realism** there is an essay called 'A realistic theory of truth and error', by W. P. Montague. It will serve to illustrate the argument if we examine what is said on error in the course of this essay.

'The true and the false', says Mr. Montague, 'are respectively the real and the unreal, considered as objects of a possible belief or judgment' [page 252].

There is nothing unusual in this definition, yet it suffers from a defect so simple and so fundamental that it is amazing how so many philosophers can have failed to see it. The defect is that there is no such thing as the unreal, and therefore, by the definition, there can be no such thing as the false; yet it is notorious that false beliefs do occur. It is possible, however, that Mr. Montague

* By the American Six Realists, New York and London, 1912.

might maintain that there are unreal things as well as real ones, for with him 'real' is definable. His definition is as follows:

'The real universe consists of the space-time system of existents, together with all that is presupposed by that system' [page 255].

He proceeds at once to deduce his view of the unreal:

'And as every reality can be regarded as a true identity-complex or proposition, and as each proposition has one and only one contradictory, we may say that the remainder of the realm of subsistent objects [i.e., the unreal] must consist of the false propositions or unrealities, particular and universal, which contradict the true propositions comprising reality' (*ibid*).

From the above it appears that, according to Mr. Montague, (1) every reality is a proposition; (2) false propositions subsist as well as true ones; (3) the unreal is the class of false propositions. We cannot now pursue these topics, which belong to logic. But for reasons which I have set forth elsewhere, it would appear (1) that *no* reality is a proposition, though some realities are beliefs, (2) that *true* propositions have a certain correspondence with complex facts, while false propositions have a different correspondence, (3) that the unreal is simply nothing, and is only identical with the class of false propositions in the same sense in which it is identical with the class of simoniacal unicorns, namely in the sense that both are null. It follows, if it is not otherwise obvious, that belief involves a different kind of relation to objects from any involved in sensation and presentation. The typical error to Mr. Montague, as to neutral monists generally, is the so-called 'illusion of sense', which, as I shall try to show fully on another occasion, is no more illusory or erroneous than normal sensation. The kind of error with which we are all familiar in daily life, such as mistaking the day of the week, or thinking that America was discovered in 1066, is forced into the mould of 'illusions of sense', at the expense of supposing the world to be full of such entities as 'the discovery of America in 1066'—or in any year that the ignorance of schoolboys may suppose possible.

A further difficulty, not wholly unallied to the difficulty about error, concerns the thought of non-temporal entities, or the belief in facts that are independent of time. Whatever may be the right analysis of belief, it is plain that there are times at which I am believing that two and two are four, and other times at which I am not thinking of this fact. Now if we adopt the view that there is no specifically mental element in the universe, we shall have to hold that '2 + 2 = 4' is an entity which exists at those moments of time when some one is believing it, but not at other moments. It is however very difficult to conceive of an abstract fact of this sort actually existing at certain times. No temporal particular is a constituent of this proposition; hence it seems impossible that, except through the intermediary of some extraneous temporal particular, it should acquire that special relation to certain moments which is involved in its being sometimes thought of and sometimes not. It is, of course, merely another form of the same difficulty that we shall be compelled, if we adopt neutral monism, to attribute causal efficacy to this abstract timeless fact at those moments when it is being believed. For these reasons, it seems almost inevitable to hold that my believing that 2 + 2 = 4 involves a temporal particular not involved in the object of my belief. And the same argument, word for word, applies also to presentations when their objects are not temporal particulars.

An analogous problem arises in regard to memory. If I remember now something which happened an hour ago, the present event, namely my remembering, cannot be numerically identical with the event of an hour ago. If, then, my present experience involves nothing but the object experienced, the event which I am said to remember cannot itself be the object experienced when I remember. The object experienced must be something which might be called an 'idea' of the past event. To this, however, there seem to be the same objections, if taken (as it would have to be) as applying to *all* memory, that there are to the doctrine that all contact with outside objects occurs through the medium of 'ideas' —a doctrine against which neutral monism has arisen as a protest. If the past can never be directly experienced in memory, how, we must inquire, can it ever come to be known that the object now experienced in memory is at all similar to the past object? And if this cannot be known, the whole of our supposed knowledge of the past becomes illusory, while it becomes impossible to account for the obvious difference between our knowledge as regards the past and our knowledge as regards the future.

An objection, possibly not unavoidable, applies to James's account of 'processes of leading' as constituting knowledge. His definition of the sort of 'leading' required is vague, and would include cases which obviously could not be called knowledge. Take, for example, the instance, quoted above, of James's knowledge of his dog, which consists in the fact that 'the idea is capable of leading into a chain of other experiences on my part that go from next to next and terminate at last in vivid sense-perceptions of a jumping, barking, hairy body.' Obviously a great deal is unexpressed in this account. The original idea must have somehow 'intended' the jumping, barking, hairy body: some purpose or desire must be satisfied when the dog appears. Otherwise, an idea which had led to the dog by accident would equally be cognitive of the dog. It is in this way, I suppose, that James was led to the pragmatic theory of truth. Ideas have many effects, some intended, some unintended; they will be cognitive, according to James, when they have *intended* effects, when we have the feeling 'yes, that is what I was thinking of'. At this point, the need of a neutral theory of desire becomes very urgent; but we will not dwell on this difficulty. The purely cognitive aspect of James's view offers sufficient difficulties, and we will consider them only.

The relations of cause and effect, which James supposes to intervene between the antecedent knowledge of his dog and the dog's actual presence, will require some further definition; for unintended sequences of cause and effect, even if their final outcome were what is intended, could not be said to show that the original idea was cognitive. Suppose, for example, that I wish to be with my dog, and start towards the next street in hopes of finding him there; but on the way I accidentally fall into a coal-cellar which he has also fallen into. Although I find him, it cannot be said that I knew where he was. And apart from this difficulty, the causal relation is an extremely obscure one. I do not believe the received notions on the subject of causality can possibly be defended; yet, apart from them, James's account of the cognitive relation becomes obscure. There is in James and in some of his followers a certain *naïveté* towards science, a certain uncritical acceptance of what may be called scientific common sense, which seems to me largely to destroy the value of their speculations on fundamental problems. The notion of 'a *chain* of experiences that go from next to next', if introduced in the definition of cognition, seems to me to show an insufficiently critical attitude towards the notion of causality. But

I am not at all sure that this is a *vital* objection to James's view: it is not unlikely that it could be avoided by a re-statement.

Another difficulty is that, in order to make his account of cognition fit all cases, he has to include *potential* processes of leading as well as actual ones. Of the three kinds of relation which, according to him, may subsist between knower and known, the third, we saw, is described as follows: 'The known is a *possible* experience either of that subject or another, to which the said conjunctive transitions *would* lead, if sufficiently prolonged.' It is true he says [page 54]: 'Type 3 can always formally and hypothetically be reduced to type 2', and in type 2 both experiences are actual. But by the word 'hypothetically' he re-introduces the very element of possibility which he is nominally excluding: *if* you did such-and-such things (which perhaps in fact you do not do), your idea *would* verify itself. But this is a wholly different thing from *actual* verification. And the truth of a possible or hypothetical verification involves, necessarily, considerations which must sweep away verification altogether as the *meaning* of truth. It may be laid down generally that *possibility* always marks insufficient analysis: when analysis is completed, only the *actual* can be relevant, for the simple reason that there is only the actual, and that the merely possible is nothing.

The difficulties in the way of introducing precision into the account of James's 'processes of leading' arise, if I am not mistaken, from his having omitted to notice that there must be a *logical* relation between what is believed in the earlier stages and what is experienced in the fulfilment. Let us revert to the instance of Memorial Hall. According to James, I should be said to 'know' Memorial Hall if, for example, I know that it is reached by taking the first turning on the right and the second on the left and then going on for about 200 yards. Let us analyse this instance. In the case supposed, I know, or at least I believe truly, the following proposition: 'Memorial Hall is the building which is reached by taking the first turning on the right and the second on the left, and then going on for 200 yards'. For brevity, let us call this proposition *p*. The name 'Memorial Hall', in this proposition, may be assumed to occur as a *description*, i.e. to mean 'the building called "Memorial Hall"'. It may occur as a proper name, i.e., as a name for an object directly present in experience; but in the case supposed, when it is being questioned whether I know Memorial Hall at all, it is more instructive to consider the occurrence of the name as a description. Thus p asserts that two descriptions apply to the same entity; it says nothing about this entity except that the two descriptions apply to it. A person may know p (for instance, by the help of a map) without ever having seen Memorial Hall, and without Memorial Hall having ever been directly present in his experience. But if I wish to discover whether the belief in p is true or not, two courses are open to me. I may either search for other propositions giving other descriptions of Memorial Hall, such as that it comes at such and such a point on the map; or I may proceed to discover the actual entity satisfying one of the descriptions, and then ascertain whether it satisfies the other. The order, as between the two descriptions, is theoretically irrelevant; but it happens that one of the two descriptions, namely the one telling me the way, makes it easy to find the entity described. I may therefore take the first turning on the right and the second on the left and proceed for 200 yards, and then inquire the name of the building in front of me. If the answer is 'Memorial Hall', the belief in p is verified. But it seems a misuse of terms to say that belief in p, when p is in fact true, constitutes knowledge of Memorial Hall. Belief in p is belief in a proposition of which Memorial Hall itself is not even a constituent; it may be entertained, on adequate grounds, by a person who has never experienced Memorial Hall; it may be rejected erroneously by a person who vividly remembers Memorial Hall. And when I actually see Memorial Hall, even if I do not know that that is its name, and even if I make no propositions about it, I must be said to know it in some sense more fundamental than any which can be constituted by the belief in true propositions describing it.

If what has been said is correct, certain points emerge as vital. First, that James and his followers, like many other philosophers, unduly assimilate belief to presentation, and thereby obscure the problem of error; secondly, that what they call knowledge of an object is really knowledge of a proposition in which the object itself does not occur, but is replaced by a *description* in terms of images or other constituents of actual present experience; thirdly, that what makes such a proposition true is the relations of the constituents of this actual proposition, relations which *may* be (but need not always be) established by the intermediary of the object described, but even then are not relations into which the actual object described enters as a term or constituent. Thus what James calls knowledge of objects is really knowledge of propositions in which the objects do not occur, but are replaced by descriptions; and the constituents of such propositions are contained in the present experience of the person who is believing them.

This brings us to the last objection which I have to urge against neutral monism, namely the question: How is the group of my present experiences distinguished from other things? Whatever may be meant by 'my experience', it is undeniable that, at any given moment, some of the things in the world, but not all, are somehow collected together into a bundle consisting of what now lies within my immediate experience. The question I wish to consider is: Can neutral monism give a tenable account of the bond which unites the parts of this bundle, and the difference which marks them out from the rest of the things in the world?

This problem is incidentally discussed by Professor Perry in his *Present Philosophical Tendencies*, in the chapter called 'A Realistic Theory of Mind'. He emphasizes first the fact that the same thing may enter into two different people's experience, and that therefore one mind's objects are not necessarily cut off from the direct observation of another mind. So far, I should agree. But it does not follow, unless neutral monism is assumed (if then), that one man can directly know that a certain thing is part of another man's experience. *A* and *B* may both know a certain object *O*, but it does not follow that *A* knows that *B* knows *O*. Thus the fact that two minds may know the same object does not show that they are themselves accessible to each other's direct observation, unless they *are* simply the objects which constitute the contents of their experience. In that case, of course, they must be accessible to each other's direct observation. Professor Perry regards a shrinking from this conclusion as a mere mistake, due to the fact that so many of our objects are internal bodily states which, for physical reasons, are hidden from other observers. I cannot think that he is right in this. Consider something in no way private: suppose I am thinking $3 + 3 = 6$. I can know directly that I am thinking this, but no other man can. Professor Perry says:

'If you are a psychologist, or an interpreter of dreams, I may "tell" you what is in my mind. Now it is frequently assumed by the sophisticated that when I thus verbally reveal my mind you do not *directly* know it. You are supposed directly to know only my words. But I cannot understand such a supposition, unless it means simply that you know my mind only *after* and *through* hearing my words' [page 290].

This passage appears to me to embody a logical error, namely a confusion of universals and particulars. The meanings of words, in so far as they are common to two people, are almost all universals. Perhaps the only exception is 'now'.* If I say 'this', pointing to some visible object, what another man sees is not exactly the same as what I see, because he looks from a different place. Thus if he takes the word as designating the object which he sees, it has not the same meaning to him as to me. If he attempts to correct this, he will have to replace the immediate datum of his sight by a description, such as 'the object which, from the point of view of my friend, corresponds with the object which I see'. The words, therefore, in which I try to tell my experience will omit what is particular to it, and convey only what is universal. (I do not mean that it is *logically* impossible for two men to know the same particular, but only that practically it does not occur, owing to difference of point of view.) It may be said, however, that this difficulty does not apply in the case of an abstract thought consisting wholly of universal or logical constituents. In that case, it is true, I can convey wholly the *object* of my thought; but even then, there is something which I cannot convey, namely that something which makes my thought a particular dated event. If I think, at a certain moment, that $3 + 3 = 6$, that is an event in time; if you think it at the same moment, that is a second event at the same time. There is thus something in my thought over and above the bare logical fact that $3 + 3 = 6$; and it is just this something which is partly incommunicable. When I tell you that I am thinking that $3 + 3 = 6$, I give you information even if you are not wholly ignorant of arithmetic. It is this further something, which makes the thought *my* thought, that we have to consider.

On this point, Professor Perry says:

'When I am thinking abstractions, the contents of my mind, namely the abstractions themselves, are such as you also may think.

* Even this exception is open to doubt.

They are not possessed by me in any exclusive sense. And the fact that they are my contents means that they are somehow bound up with the history of my nervous system. The contents, and the linkage which makes them mine, are alike common objects, lying in the field of general observation and study' [page 297].

The important sentence here is 'the fact that they are my contents means that they are somehow bound up with my nervous system'. The same idea is expressed elsewhere in the same chapter. 'Elements become mental content', he says, *when reacted to in the specific manner characteristic of the central nervous system* [page 299, his italics]. And again, more fully:

'A mind is a complex so organized as to act desideratively or interestedly. I mean here to indicate that character which distinguishes the living organism, having originally the instinct of self-preservation, and acquiring in the course of its development a variety of special interests. I use the term *interest* primarily in its biological rather than its physiological sense. Certain natural processes act consistently in such wise as to isolate, protect, and renew themselves' [pages 303-4].

But such an account of what makes a mind seems impossible to reconcile with obvious facts. In order to know that such and such a thing lies within my experience, it is not necessary to know anything about my nervous system: those who have never learned physiology, and are unaware that they possess nerves, are quite competent to know that this or that comes within their experience. It may be—I have no wish either to affirm or deny it—that the things which I experience have some relation to my nervous system which other things do not have; but if so, this must be a late scientific discovery, built up on masses of observation as to the connexions of the object of consciousness with the nervous system and with the physical object. The distinction between things of which I am aware—for instance, between the things I see before my eyes and the things behind my back—is not a late, elaborate, scientific distinction, nor is it one depending upon the relations of these things to each other. So much, I think, is clear to inspection; I do not know how to prove it, for I cannot think of anything more evident. But if so, then neutral monism cannot be true, for it is obliged to have recourse to extraneous considerations, such as the nervous system, in order to explain the difference between what I experience and what I do not experience, and this difference is too immediate for any explanation that neutral monism can give.

We may now sum up this long discussion, in the course of which it has been necessary to anticipate many topics to be treated more fully at a later stage. Neutral monism, we saw, maintains that there are not two sorts of entities, mental and physical, but only two sorts of relations between entities, namely those belonging to what is called the mental order and those belonging to what is called the physical order. In favour of the theory, we may admit that what is experienced may itself be part of the physical world, and often is so; that the same thing may be experienced by different minds; that the old distinction of 'mind' and 'matter', besides ignoring the abstract facts that are neither mental nor physical, errs in regarding 'matter', and the 'space' in which matter is, as something obvious, given, and unambiguous, and is in hopeless doubt as to whether the facts of sensation are to be called physical or mental. In emphasizing all this, we must acknowledge that neutral monism has performed an important service to philosophy. Nevertheless, if I am not mistaken, there are problems which this theory cannot solve, and there are facts which it cannot account for. The theory has arisen chiefly as a protest against the view that external objects are known through the medium of subjective 'ideas' or 'images', not directly. But it shares with this view the doctrine that whatever I experience must be part of my mind; and when this doctrine is rejected, much of its plausibility ceases.

The first and chief objection against the theory is based on inspection. Between (say) a colour seen and the same colour not seen, there seems to be a difference not consisting in relations to other colours, or to other objects of experience, or to the nervous system, but in some way more immediate, more intimate, more intuitively evident. If neutral monism were true, a mind which had only one experience would be a logical impossibility, since a thing is only mental in virtue of its external relations; and correspondingly, it is difficult for this philosophy to define the respect in which the whole of my experience is different from the things that lie outside my experience.

A second difficulty is derived from *belief* or *judgment*, which James and his followers unduly assimilate to sensation and presentation, with fatal results as regards the theory of error. Error is defined as 'belief in the unreal', which compels the admission that there actually are unreal things.

A third difficulty is that the thought of what is not in time, or a belief in a non-temporal fact, is an event in time with a definite date, which seems impossible unless it contains some constituent over and above the timeless thing thought of or believed. The same point arises in regard to memory; for if what is remembered actually exists in the remembering mind, its position in the time-series becomes ambiguous, and the essential pastness of the remembered object disappears.

A fourth difficulty arises in regard to the definition of knowledge offered by James, though here it is hard to say how far this definition is essential to neutral monism. James considers throughout rather knowledge of things than knowledge of truths, and he regards it as consisting in the presence of other things capable of leading to the thing which these other things are said to know. Immediate experience, which I should regard as the only real knowledge of things, he refuses to regard as knowledge at all; and it would seem that what he calls knowledge of a thing is really knowledge of a proposition of which the thing is not even a constituent.

In addition to the above difficulties, there is a fifth, more fatal, I think, than any of them, which is derived from considerations of 'this' and 'now' and 'I'. But this difficulty demands considerable discussion, and is therefore reserved for the next part.

For these reasons— some of which, it must be confessed, assume the results of future discussions—I conclude that neutral monism, though largely right in its polemic against previous theories, cannot be regarded as able to deal with all the facts, and must be replaced by a theory in which the difference between what is experienced and what is not experienced by a given subject at a given moment is made simpler and more prominent than it can be in theory which wholly denies the existence of specifically mental entities.

III. ANALYSIS OF EXPERIENCE

IN our first part, we took a preliminary survey of the objects experienced. In the second part, we considered the theory that experience is merely a certain interrelation of these objects, involving no particular existent in addition to what is experienced. Having found this theory unsatisfactory, we have now to seek out the additional constituent of experience, and to consider the nature of its relation to the objects experienced.

Before embarking upon our analysis, let us again take stock of those relevant facts which are least open to doubt. From the diversity of philosophical theories on the subject, it is evident that the true analysis, whatever it may be, cannot itself be among the facts that are evident at once, but must be reached, like a scientific hypothesis, as the theoretic residue left by the comparison of data. Here, as in philosophy generally, it is not the few logically simplest facts that form our data, but a large mass of complex everyday facts, of which the analysis offers fresh difficulties and doubts at every step. For this reason, if we wish to start with what is undeniable, we have to use words, at first, which, though familiar, stand in need of a dissection and definition only possible at a later stage.

The most obvious fact, in our present inquiry, is that, whatever may be the definition of 'experience', some objects undoubtedly fall within my present experience, and of these objects some at least did not fall within my experience at earlier times which I can still remember. What is only slightly less obvious is that remembered objects sometimes—at least in the case of the immediate past—are still experienced, so that the objects experienced are not necessarily contemporaneous with the experiencing. It is obvious also that we can think of abstract facts, such as those of logic and mathematics; but in this case some argument is needed to discover what we experience when we think of them. If it were not for the fact that neutral monism has been believed, I should have said it was obvious that we can experience our own experiencing, and that this is different from experiencing the object of our experiencing; and in spite of neutral monism, I think a place must be found for what appears as an experience of our experiencing, since it is hard to see how otherwise we should have arrived at the notion that we have experiences.

At an earlier stage, we decided that our present experience can be known not to be all-embracing. It is sometimes maintained that this cannot be known, on the ground that if a thing lies outside our experience we cannot know that there is such a thing. At the risk of repetition, it may be worth while to repeat the reasons (belonging to logic rather than to theory of knowledge) which show that this argument is fallacious. An object may be *described* by means of terms which lie within our experience, and the proposition that there is an object answering to this description is then one composed wholly of experienced constituents. It is therefore possible to know the truth of this proposition without passing outside experience. If it appears on examination that no *experienced* object answers to this description, the conclusion follows that there are objects not experienced. For example, we may know Jones and paternity and the fact that every man has a father. Then we know there is 'the father of Jones', although we may never have experienced him. To consider this case more fully would demand a discussion of knowledge by description. For the present, it is only necessary to remove a possible objection to the view, which I shall henceforth assume, that what is experienced at any moment is known not to be the sum total of the things in the world. At the same time, it is important to remember that I can never give an actual instance of a thing not now within my experience, for everything that I can mention otherwise than by a description must lie within my present experience. This is involved in the very nature of experience, and is one of the most important of the obvious facts about it.

Experiencing is only one, though perhaps the most characteristic and comprehensive, of the things that happen in the mental world. Judging, feeling, desiring, willing, though they presuppose experiencing, are themselves different from it; they may be themselves experienced, and they doubtless require that we should experience the objects with which they are concerned, but they do not themselves consist *merely* in experiencing objects.

It is important to be clear as to the extent to which the experience of one mind may overlap that of another. Neutral monists have done a service to philosophy in pointing out that the same object may be experienced by two minds. This certainly applies, as a matter of fact, to all experiencing of universals and abstracts; it applies also, though I think only as a theoretic possibility, to the things of sense. But there remain a large number of things which only one mind can experience. First and foremost, an experiencing, as opposed to the mere object experienced, seems, empirically, not as a matter of *a priori* necessity, to be only capable of being experienced by one person. I can know by immediate experience what I am seeing at this moment; but antoher person, though it is theoretically possible for him to see the same object, cannot, as a matter of empirical fact, know by immediate experience that I am seeing it. Exactly the same is true of other mental facts, such as judging, feeling, desiring, willing. All these can only be experienced by one person.

Thus when an object O is experienced by two different persons A and B, the experiencing of O by A is one fact, and the experiencing of O by B is another. The experiencing of O by A may be experienced by A, and the experiencing of O by B may be experienced by B, but neither can experience the other's experiencing. A can experience his experiencing of O without logically requiring any other experience; hence the fact that he experiences O cannot consist in a relation to other objects of experience, as neutral monism supposes. From these characteristics of experience, it seems an unavoidable inference that A's experiencing of O is different from O, and is in fact a complex, of which A himself, or some simpler entity bound up with A, is a constituent as well as O. Hence experiencing must be a relation, in which one term is the object experienced, while the other term is that which experiences. We might continue to call this relation 'experience', but we have employed the word 'experience' hitherto because it is a non-committal word, which seemed not to prejudge the issue of our analysis. Now, since we have decided that experience is constituted by a relation, it will be better to employ a less neutral word; we shall employ synonymously the two words 'acquaintance' and 'awareness', generally the former. Thus when A experiences an object O, we shall say that A is acquainted with O.

We will define a 'subject' as any entity which is acquainted with something, i.e., 'subjects' are the domain of the relation 'acquaintance'. Conversely, any entity with which something is acquainted will be called an 'object', i.e., 'objects' are the converse domain of the relation 'acquaintance'. An entity with which nothing is acquainted will not be called an object. A fact will be called 'mental' if it contains either acquaintance or some relation presupposing acquaintance as a component. Thus any instance of acquaintance is mental, since it is a complex in which a subject and an object are united by the relation of acquaintance. The object by itself need not be mental. We will call a fact 'physical' when some particular, but no relation presupposing acquaintance, is a constituent of if. The reason for defining mental *facts* rather than mental *entities* is that we reach subjects only by description, and cannot know whether they are among objects or not.

It is to be observed that we do not identify a mind with a subject. A mind is something which persists through a certain period of time, but it must not be assumed that the subject persists. So far as our arguments have hitherto carried us, they give no evidence as to whether the subject of one experience is the same as the subject of another experience or not. For the present, nothing is to be assumed as to the identity of the subjects of different experiences belonging to the same person.

The strongest objection which can be urged against the above analysis of experience into a dual relation of subject and object is derived from the elusiveness of the subject in introspection. We can easily become aware of our own experiences, but we seem never to become aware of the subject itself. This argument tends, of course, to support neutral monism. It is a serious argument, and deserves careful consideration. We may attempt to meet it in either of two ways, namely by maintaining that we do have acquaintance with the subject, or by maintaining that there is no reason why, even if the theory is true, we should have acquaintance with the subject.

Let us consider first the theory that we have acquaintance with the subject.* It is obvious that the question is bound up with that of the meaning of the word 'I'. This is a question in which confusions are very hard to avoid, but very fatal if they are not avoided. In the first place, the meaning of the word 'I' must not be confused with the meaning of 'the ego'. 'The ego' has a meaning which is a universal: it does not mean one person more than another, but rather that general characteristic, whatever it is, which makes each one of us call himself 'I'. But 'I' itself is not a universal: on each occasion of its use, there is only one person who is I, though this person differs according to the speaker. It is more nearly correct

---

* In a former discussion of this point, I maintained tentatively that we have such acquaintance. Cf. "Knowledge by Acquaintance and Knowledge by Description" *Arist. Soc. Proc.*, 1910-11, esp. pp. 110, 127.

to describe 'I' as an ambiguous proper name than to describe it as a universal. But when used, 'I' is not in the least ambiguous: it means the person using it, and no one else. In order, however, to obtain a clear statement of our problem, it is necessary to pare away from 'I' a great deal that is usually included—not only the body, but also the past and future in so far as they may possibly not belong to the subject of the present experience. It is obvious that all these are obtained by an extension from the present subject, and that the essential problem is concerned with our consciousness of the present subject. Let it therefore be assumed, in this discussion, that 'I' means the subject of the experience which I am now having (the vicious circle here is important to observe), and that we have to ask ourselves whether 'I' in this sense is something with which we are acquainted.

On this question, it must be confessed that introspection does not give a favourable answer. Hume's inability to perceive himself was not peculiar, and I think most unprejudiced observers would agree with him. Even if by great exertion some rare person could catch a glimpse of himself, this would not suffice; for 'I' is a term which we all know how to use, and which must therefore have some easily accessible meaning. It follows that the word 'I', as commonly employed, must stand for a description; it cannot be a true proper name in the logical sense, since true proper names can only be conferred on objects with which we are acquainted.

We are thus forced to investigate the second answer suggested above, and to ask ourselves whether our theory of acquaintance in any way implies a direct consciousness of the bare subject. If it does, it would seem that it must be false; but I think we can show that it does not. Our theory maintains that the datum when we are aware of experiencing an object O is the fact 'something is acquainted with O'. The subject appears here, not in its individual capacity, but as an 'apparent variable'; thus such a fact may be a datum in spite of incapacity for acquaintance with the subject.

If it is true, as it seems to be, that subjects are not given in acquaintance, it follows that nothing can be known as to their intrinsic nature. We cannot know, for example, that they differ from matter, nor yet that they do not differ. They are known merely as referents for the relation of acquaintance, and for those other psychical relations—judging, desiring, etc.—which imply acquaintance. It follows that psychical data—at any rate those that are cognitive—consist not of particulars, but of certain *facts* (i.e., of *what certain propositions assert*), and of *relations*, namely acquaintance and certain others which presuppose acquaintance. We may distinguish sensation from perception by saying that the former gives *particulars* while the latter gives *facts*; in this case, introspection consists wholly of perceptions, not of sensations.

The definition of what is 'mental' as what involves subjects is inadmissible, in view of the fact that we do not know what subjects are. We may define a 'mental fact as one involving acquaintance or one of those other relations—judging, desiring, etc.—which presuppose acquaintance. It *may* be that subjects are constituents of other facts of the kind we should call physical, and therefore a fact which involves a subject may not be always a mental fact.

When two objects O and O' are given as parts of one experience, we perceive the fact 'something is acquainted with both O and O''. Thus two instances of acquaintance can be given as having a common subject, even when the subject is not given. It is in this way, I think, that 'I' comes to be popularly intelligible. When we have recognized that an experience is constituted by the relation of acquaintance, we may define 'I' as the subject of the present experience, and we can see that, so defined, it denotes the same entity as is denoted by our former more popular definition. But in neither form does it require us to assume that we are ever acquainted with the bare subject of an acquaintance.

One very interesting and important point, however, remains to be investigated in the above definition of 'I', and that is, what is meant by the 'present' experience. If 'I' is to be defined as we have suggested, it seems evident that the 'present' experience must be known by acquaintance. There are here several points to be brought out. First, it is necessary to consider the connexion (if any) between psychological presence and the present time. Secondly, it is necessary to consider what is psychologically involved in our acquaintance with the present experience. Thirdly, it is necessary to consider the logical difficulty of the vicious circle in which any definition of the present experience appears to be entangled.

1. Whatever I experience is, in one sense, 'present' to me at the time when I experience it, but in the temporal sense it need not

be present—for example, if it is something remembered, or something abstract which is not in time at all. The sense in which everything experienced is 'present' may be disregarded, the rather as we already have three words—experience, acquaintance, and awareness—to describe what is meant by this sense. There is, however, another sense in which objects given in *sensation* are 'present'. As we shall find later, there is reason to suppose that there are several species of the general relation 'acquaintance', and it would seem that one of these species is 'presence' in the sense in which objects are present in sensation and perception but not in memory. The relation of 'presence' in this sense is, I think, one of the ultimate constituents out of which our knowledge of time is built, and the 'present' time may be defined as the time of those things which have to me the relation of 'presence'. But remembering what has been said about 'I', we see that, when we speak of things which have the relation of presence to 'me', we mean things which have the relation of presence to the subject of the present experience. Thus 'the present experience' is a more fundamental notion than 'the present time': the latter can be defined in terms of the former, but not vice versa.

2. What is psychologically involved in our acquaintance with the present experience? The least that is possible is obviously that there should be an experience of an object O, and another experience of experiencing O. This second experience must involve presence in the sense in which objects of sensation and perception are present and objects of memory are not present. Let us call this sense P. Then it is necessary that a subject should have the relation P to an object which is itself an experience, which we may symbolize by $S-A-O$. Thus we require an experience which might be symbolized by

$$S'-P-(S-A-O).*$$

When such an experience occurs, we may say that we have an instance of 'self-consciousness', or 'experience of a present experience'. It is to be observed that there is no good reason why the two subjects S and S' should be numerically the same: the one 'self' or 'mind' which embraces both may be a construction, and need not, so far as the logical necessities of our problem are concerned,

---

* or rather, $S' - P - [(\exists S) . (S - A - O)]$.

involve any identity of the two subjects. Thus 'present experiences' are those experiences that have the relation of presence to the subject using the phrase.

3. But there remains a logical difficulty, of which the solution is both interesting and important. In order to know a present experience, it is not necessary that I should perceive the fact

$$S'-P-(S-A-O),$$

and it must be possible to pick out an experience as present without having perception of this fact. If it were necessary to perceive this fact, it is fairly evident that we should be embarked upon an endless regress. It is in fact obvious that 'the present experience', or 'the present object', or some phrase fulfilling a similar purpose, must be capable of being used as a proper name; all manner of objects are present on different occasions to different subjects, and we have already seen that the subject concerned in presence to 'me' must be defined by means of presence.

The main consideration is undoubtedly to be derived from remembering what 'presence' actually is. When an object is in my present experience, then I am acquainted with it; it is not necessary for me to reflect upon my experience, or to observe that the object has the property of belonging to my experience, in order to be acquainted with it, but, on the contrary, the object itself is known to me without the need of any reflection on my part as to its properties or relations. This point may perhaps be made clearer by an illustrative hypothesis. Suppose I were occupied, like Adam, in bestowing names upon various objects. The objects upon which I should bestow names would all be objects with which I was acquainted, but it would not be necessary for me to reflect that I was acquainted with them, or to realize that they all shared a certain relation to myself. What distinguishes the objects to which I can give names from other things is the fact that these objects are within my experience, that I am acquainted with them, but it is only subsequent reflection that proves that they all have this distinguishing characteristic; during the process of naming they appear merely as this, that, and the other.

Further consideration of the word 'this' will help to make the point clear. The word 'this' is always a proper name, in the sense that it applies directly to just one object, and does not in any way *describe* the object to which it applies. But on different occasions it applies to different objects. For the purposes of our present problem, we may say that 'this' is the name of the object attended to at the moment by the person using the word. The relation of attention, here introduced, is of course different from that of acquaintance, and one point in which it differs is that a subject can only attend to one object, or at least a very small number, at a time. (This may of course be disputed, but for our purposes it may be assumed.) Thus we may speak of '*the* object of attention of a given subject at a given moment'. The object so described is the object which that subject at that moment will call 'this'. But it would be an error to suppose that 'this' *means* 'the object to which I am now attending'. 'This' is a proper name applied to the object to which I am now attending. If it be asked how I come to select this object, the answer is that, by hypothesis, I am selecting it, since it is the object of my attention. 'This' is not waiting to be defined by the property of being given, but is given; first it is actually given, and then reflection shows that it is 'that which is given'.

We may now retrace our steps in the opposite order. At any moment of my conscious life, there is one object (or at most some very small number of objects) to which I am attending. All knowledge of particulars radiates out from this object. This object is not intrinsically distinguishable from other objects—it just happens (owing to causes which do not concern us) that I am attending to it. Since I am attending to it, I can name it; I may give it any name I choose, but when inventiveness gives out, I am apt to name it 'this'. By the help of reflection and special experiences, it becomes evident that there is such a relation as 'attention', and that there is always a subject attending to the object called 'this'. The subject attending to 'this' is called 'I', and the time of the things which have to 'I' the relation of presence is called the present time. 'This' is the point from which the whole process starts, and 'this' itself is not defined, but simply given. The confusions and difficulties arise from regarding 'this' as *defined by the fact of being given*, rather than simply as given.

The objection to our theory of acquaintance which was derived from the absence of acquaintance with the subject is thus capable of being answered, while admitting that the objectors are in the right in maintaining that we are not acquainted with the subject. Having answered the objection, we can now retort on neutral monism with the demand that it should produce an account of 'this' and 'I' and 'now'. I do not mean merely that it should produce an account of particularity and selfhood and moments of time; all this it might accomplish without in any way touching the problem. What I demand is an account of that principle of selection which, to a given person at a given moment, makes one object, one subject and one time intimate and near and immediate, as no other object or subject or time can be to that subject at that time, though the same intimacy and nearness and immediacy will belong to these others in relation to other subjects and other times. In a world where there were no specifically mental facts, is it not plain that there would be a complete impartiality, an evenly diffused light, not the central illumination fading away into outer darkness, which is characteristic of objects in relation to a mind? It may be that some answer can be found to these queries without admitting specifically mental facts; but to me it seems obvious that such 'emphatic particulars' as 'this' and 'I' and 'now' would be impossible without the selectiveness of mind. I conclude, therefore, that the consideration of emphatic particulars affords a new refutation, and the most conclusive one, of neutral monism.

Before leaving the analysis of experience, we must take account of a widely held theory according to which our acquaintance with objects involves not only subject and object, but also what is called 'content'. The distinction between content and object is set forth very explicitly by Meinong, for instance in his article 'Über Gegenstände höherer Ordnung und deren Verhältniss zur inneren Wahrnehmung'.* The following quotations from this article may serve to make the theory plain.

'That it is essential to everything psychical to have an object, will presumably be admitted without reserve at least in regard to that psychical material which will here exclusively concern us. For no one doubts that one cannot have a presentation† without having a presentation of *something*, and also that one cannot judge

---

* *Zeitschrift für Psychologie und Physiologie der Sinnesorgane*, Vol. XXI (1899), pp. 182f.

† I think the relation of subject and object in presentation may be identified with the relation which I call 'acquaintance.'

without judging about *something*. People will probably also concede just as willingly that there is no presentation or judgment
without content; but for not a few this readiness comes from the
assumption that content and object are pretty much the same thing.
I also long believed that the two expressions could be used in-
differently, and that therefore one of them could be dispensed with.
To-day I regard this as a mistake' [p. 185]. He proceeds at once to
give his grounds. The chief ground, he says, is that we may have a
presentation or judgment whose object is non-existent, whether
because it is self-contradictory, like the round square, or because,
like the golden mountain, there happens to be no such thing, or
because, like the difference between red and green, it is not the
kind of thing which can exist, although it may 'subsist', or because,
though now presented, its existence belongs to the past or the
future. He concludes: 'Thus the presentation exists: but who,
except in the interests of a theoretical preconception, will be willing to assume that the presentation exists, but not its content?'
[p. 186]. Thus the first difference between object and content is
that the object may be something non-existent, but the content
must exist when the presentation exists. A second difference is
that the object may be not psychical, whereas the content must be
psychical. The object may be blue or warm or heavy, but the content cannot have attributes of this kind [pp. 187–8]. All presentations, however different their objects, have in common, he says,
just what makes them presentations, namely 'das Vorstellen oder
den Vorstellungsact'; but two presentations of different objects
cannot be completely similar to each other, and therefore the
difference in the objects must point to some difference in the
presentations. Now that in which two presentations may differ in
spite of the identity of the 'act' is what is to be called the 'content'.
This exists now and is psychical, even when the object does not
exist, or is past or future, or is not psychical [p. 188].

Before deciding whether in fact there are 'contents' as well as
objects of presentations, let us examine Meinong's arguments in
the above. The instances of non-existent objects quoted by Meinong are largely disposed of by the theory of incomplete symbols—
the round square and the golden mountain, at any rate, are not
objects. (I do *not* mean that they are objects which do not exist.)
The other instances are less intractable. The difference between

red and green, for example, has the kind of subsistence appropriate to objects of this kind; and future things are not presented,
although they may be known by description. Nevertheless, it remains the case that we can have a presentation of an abstract
(which has no position in time), or of a remembered object which
exists no longer. The case of memory suffices to illustrate Meinong's difficulty in the supposition that a presentation can exist
when its content does not exist. We should say that we remember
now, and in popular language we should say that we are in a different 'state of mind' when we remember from that in which we
should be if we were not remembering. Meinong's 'content' is in
fact what would commonly be called a 'state of mind'. Thus the
question is: Are there 'states of mind', as opposed to objects cog-
nized in various ways? We are told that it is impossible the presentation should exist now, if its content does not exist now. But if
presentation consists wholly and solely, as we have contended, in
a relation of subject and object, then a memory-presentation is a
complex of which one constituent is present while the other is past.
It is not clear that such a complex has any definite position in the
time-series: the fact that the remembering subject is in the present
is no sufficient reason for regarding the whole complex as present.
And similar remarks apply to the case of presentations whose objects are not in time at all. Thus the question 'who will be willing
to assume that the presentation exists but not its content?' loses
its force: the word 'exist' is very ambiguous, but if it means 'being
at some part of the time-series', then it is not at all clear that the
presentation does exist; and if it means any other legitimate meaning, it is not clear that the object does not exist.

The arguments that the content but not the object must be
psychical, and that the object but not the content may have such
attributes as blue or warm or heavy, may be passed by, since they
do not afford any independent ground for believing that there are
such things as contents.

The argument which has probably done most to produce a belief
in 'contents' as opposed to objects is the last of those adduced by
Meinong, namely that there must be some difference between a
presentation of one object and a presentation of another, and this
difference is not to be found in the 'act' of presentation. At first
sight, it seems obvious that my mind is in different 'states' when

I am thinking of one thing and when I am thinking of another. But in fact the difference of object supplies all the difference required. There seems to be, in the hypothesis of 'states' of mind, an operation (generally unconscious) of the 'internal' theory of relations: it is thought that some intrinsic difference in the subject must correspond to the difference in the objects to which it has the relation of presentation. I have argued this question at length elsewhere, and shall therefore now assume the 'external' theory of relations, according to which difference of relations affords no evidence for difference of intrinsic predicates. It follows that, from the fact that the complex 'my awareness of A' is different from the complex 'my awareness of B', it does not follow that when I am aware of A I have some intrinsic quality which I do not have when I am aware of B but not of A. There is therefore no reason for assuming a difference in the subject corresponding to the difference between two presented objects.

It remains to inquire whether there are any other reasons for assuming 'contents'. I think perhaps belief in them has been encouraged by a careless use of such words as 'image' and 'idea'. It may be thought that, when a given physical object is seen from many different points of view, the physical object itself is the object of many presentations, and that the different images are the different contents. Meinong himself is far from any such confusion, but language tends to encourage it. In fact, of course, the one physical object which is supposed to be seen from different points of view is a theoretical construction, and is not the object of any presentation. The objects of the various presentations concerned are the immediate visual data from the different points of view. The change in the visual data, combined with the belief that the physical object is unchanged, tends to generate the belief that the visual data are 'subjective modifications', and thus to obscure their character as objects. I shall not enlarge on this subject now, as I have dealt with it at length in an article in *Scientia* for July 1914.*

It may be urged that different people can know the same object, but cannot have the same presentation, and that this points to something other than the object as a constituent of a presentation. As against neutral monism, the argument is valid if its premise is

* [Reprinted as Chapter VIII of *Mysticism and Logic*—R.C.M.]

granted; but in our theory, the difference between the subjects suffices to distinguish the two presentations, and therefore no problem arises.

The chief argument *against* contents is the difficulty of discovering them introspectively. It may be said that this difficulty—which is admitted—applies equally to the subject in our theory of acquaintance. This is true; but our theory is based on inference from the nature of experience, not on any supposed introspective perception of the subject. If the arguments by which Meinong supports his belief in contents had appeared to us valid, we should have admitted contents; but in the absence of valid arguments introspective evidence alone could lead us to admit contents. Since such evidence is lacking, we may therefore conclude that there is no reason to admit contents.

The belief in 'contents' as subjective modifications is often held in a more extreme form than that advocated by Meinong. It is thought that whatever can be immediately known must be 'in the mind', and that it can only be by inference that we arrive at a knowledge of anything external to ourselves. This view may be combated in many ways. It would be well to know, first of all, what is meant by 'my mind', and what really is being debated when it is asked whether this or that is 'in my mind'. We might next point out that abstract facts and universals may be known to many people, and that therefore, if they are 'in my mind', the same thing may be in two minds at once. But I think the main source of subjective theories has always been the supposed illusions of sense. The sun, as it appears in astronomical theory, is not immediately given: what is immediately given is a certain visible bright patch, which according to physics depends upon the intervening medium and our sense-organs. Hence if we suppose that the astronomer's sun is the object when we 'see the sun', then what is actually given has to be degraded to the level of something subjective. But in fact, the physical object which the astronomer deals with is an inference, and the bright patch that we see, in spite of its variability, is only thought to be illusory as the result of fallacious arguments.

To sum up: The obvious characteristics of experience seem to show that experiencing is a two-term relation; we call the relation *acquaintance*, and we give the name *subject* to anything which has acquaintance with objects. The subject itself appears to be not acquainted with itself; but this does not prevent our theory from explaining the meaning of the word 'I' by the help of the meaning of the word 'this', which is the proper name of the object of attention. In this respect, especially, we found our theory superior to neutral monism, which seems unable to explain the selectiveness of experience. Finally we considered and rejected the opinion that experience involves mental modifications called 'contents', having a diversity which reproduces that of objects—an opinion which appeared to rest upon the internal theory of relations; and along with this opinion we rejected—though partly by arguments which await amplification on another occasion—the doctrine that all immediate knowledge is confined to knowledge of ourselves.

The Philosophy of Logical Atomism

Ludwig Wittgenstein came to England (from the Technische Hochschule, Berlin) at the age of nineteen and began studies in aeronautics as a research student in the Engineering Laboratory of the University of Manchester. While there he read THE PRINCIPLES OF MATHEMATICS, *and in January of* 1912 *he went to Cambridge as an 'Advanced Student', presumably a candidate for the B.A. 'for research' since Cambridge did not offer the Ph.D. until* 1920. *He stayed five terms, working for the most part with Russell, who was in contact with him during the fourteen months between his departure from Cambridge in the summer of* 1913 *and the outbreak of war the following year. Very little remains to tell us what occupied their conversations. In the preface to his Harvard lectures of* 1914 *Russell speaks of the 'vitally important discoveries, not yet published' of 'my friend, Mr. Ludwig Wittgenstein' [p. 9], a phrase that suggests a quite different relationship than that one would expect between a student of twenty-four and his distinguished supervisor of forty-one (but not at all surprising in the light of Russell's character).**

Russell's lectures on logical atomism of 1918 *are probably the best record of his development of the ideas which he had discussed with Wittgenstein in the period* 1912–14. *It is not to be inferred that Wittgenstein would have approved of the manner in which Russell treated this material; indeed, Wittgenstein is known to have taken exception to Russell's introduction to the English edition of the* TRACTATUS. *It is a common failing of great philosophers that they think their own thoughts well and do not fully appreciate the thought of others (second-rate minds, with few ideas of their own, can often do*

---

*Russell was chiefly responsible for the publication (in 1922) of Wittgenstein's *Tractatus Logico-Philosophicus*. When Wittgenstein returned to Cambridge in 1929 he was still a degreeless 'student' and only after he had kept two further terms was he able to proceed (at the age of forty) to the Ph.D., submitting the *Tractatus* as a thesis and undergoing examination at the hands of Russell and Moore. Russell was also instrumental in Wittgenstein's appointment to a research fellowship at Trinity College; but apart from these things, there was no resumption of their previous relationship, as Russell was then removed from the precincts of Cambridge and involved in other philosophical problems than those of his earlier period.

this much better). We see the ideas of the young Wittgenstein, therefore, only in the form in which they have been assimilated into the thought of the mature Russell, but for all that, the view is an interesting one.

These lectures provide an extended and systematic account of Russell's thought in a critical period in the development of his philosophy. It is strange that in the nearly forty years since they were given they have never been reprinted in an authorized form. One thing they do is show that 'one of the greatest merits of modern logic is that it has allowed us to give precision to [several types of philosophical] problems while definitely abandoning any pretensions of solving them.' The author of that statement (it could be either Russell or P. E. B. Jourdain) was a wiser man than the sceptic he appears to be.

1918

THE PHILOSOPHY OF LOGICAL ATOMISM

The following [is the text] of a course of eight lectures delivered in [Gordon Square] London, in the first months of 1918, [which] are very largely concerned with explaining certain ideas which I learnt from my friend and former pupil Ludwig Wittgenstein. I have had no opportunity of knowing his views since August, 1914, and I do not even know whether he is alive or dead.* He has therefore no responsibility for what is said in these lectures beyond that of having originally supplied many of the theories contained in them.

CONTENTS

I	Facts and Propositions	178
II	Particulars, Predicates, and Relations	189
III	Atomic and Molecular Propositions	203
IV	Propositions and Facts with more than one Verb; Beliefs, etc.	216
V	General Propositions and Existence	228
VI	Descriptions and Incomplete Symbols	241
VII	The Theory of Types and Symbolism; Classes	254
VIII	Excursus into Metaphysics: What There Is	269

* [This was written in 1918 as a preface to publication in three consecutive issues of *The Monist*. I have made four trivial editorial changes for the present reprinting in an entirely different format.—R.C.M.]

I. FACTS AND PROPOSITIONS

THIS course of lectures which I am now beginning I have called the Philosophy of Logical Atomism. Perhaps I had better begin by saying a word or two as to what I understand by that title. The kind of philosophy that I wish to advocate, which I call Logical Atomism, is one which has forced itself upon me in the course of thinking about the philosophy of mathematics, although I should find it hard to say exactly how far there is a definite logical connexion between the two. The things I am going to say in these lectures are mainly my own personal opinions and I do not claim that they are more than that.

As I have attempted to prove in *The Principles of Mathematics*, when we analyse mathematics we bring it all back to logic. It all comes back to logic in the strictest and most formal sense. In the present lectures, I shall try to set forth in a sort of outline, rather briefly and rather unsatisfactorily, a kind of logical doctrine which seems to me to result from the philosophy of mathematics—not exactly logically, but as what emerges as one reflects: a certain kind of logical doctrine, and on the basis of this a certain kind of metaphysic. The logic which I shall advocate is atomistic, as opposed to the monistic logic of the people who more or less follow Hegel. When I say that my logic is atomistic, I mean that I share the common-sense belief that there are many separate things; I do not regard the apparent multiplicity of the world as consisting merely in phases and unreal divisions of a single indivisible Reality. It results from that, that a considerable part of what one would have to do to justify the sort of philosophy I wish to advocate would consist in justifying the process of analysis. One is often told that the process of analysis is falsification, that when you analyse any given concrete whole you falsify it and that the results of analysis are not true. I do not think that is a right view. I do not mean to say, of course, and nobody would maintain, that when you have analysed you keep everything that you had before you analysed. If you did, you would never attain anything in analysing. I do not propose to meet the views that I disagree with by controversy, by arguing against those views, but rather by positively setting forth what I believe to be the truth about the matter, and endeavouring all the way through to make the views that I advocate result inevitably from absolutely undeniable data. When I talk of 'undeniable data' that is not to be regarded as synonymous with 'true data', because 'undeniable' is a psychological term and 'true' is not. When I say that something is 'undeniable', I mean that it is not the sort of thing that anybody is going to deny; it does not follow from that that it is true, though it does follow that we shall all think it true—and that is as near to truth as we seem able to get. When you are considering any sort of theory of knowledge, you are more or less tied to a certain unavoidable subjectivity, because you are not concerned simply with the question what is true of the world, but 'What can I know of the world?' You always have to start any kind of argument from something which appears to you to be true; if it appears to you to be true, there is no more to be done. You cannot go outside yourself and consider abstractly whether the things that appear to you to be true are true; you may do this in a particular case, where one of your beliefs is changed in consequence of others among your beliefs.

The reason that I call my doctrine *logical* atomism is because the atoms that I wish to arrive at as the sort of last residue in analysis are logical atoms and not physical atoms. Some of them will be what I call 'particulars'—such things as little patches of colour or sounds, momentary things—and some of them will be predicates or relations and so on. The point is that the atom I wish to arrive at is the atom of logical analysis, not the atom of physical analysis.

It is a rather curious fact in philosophy that the data which are undeniable to start with are always rather vague and ambiguous. You can, for instance, say: 'There are a number of people in this room at this moment.' That is obviously in some sense undeniable. But when you come to try and define what this room is, and what it is for a person to be in a room, and how you are going to distinguish one person from another, and so forth, you find that what you have said is most fearfully vague and that you really do not know what you meant. That is a rather singular fact, that everything you are really sure of, right off is something that you do not know the meaning of, and the moment you get a precise statement you will not be sure whether it is true or false, at least right off. The process of sound philosophizing, to my mind, consists mainly in passing from those obvious, vague, ambiguous things, that we feel quite sure of, to something precise, clear, definite, which by reflection and analysis we find is involved in the vague thing that we start from, and is, so to speak, the real truth of which that vague thing is a sort of shadow. I should like, if time were longer and if I knew more than I do, to spend a whole lecture on the conception of vagueness. I think vagueness is very much more important in the theory of knowledge than you would judge it to be from the writings of most people. Everything is vague to a degree you do not realize till you have tried to make it precise, and everything precise is so remote from everything that we normally think, that you cannot for a moment suppose that is what we really mean when we say what we think.

When you pass from the vague to the precise by the method of analysis and reflection that I am speaking of, you always run a certain risk of error. If I start with the statement that there are so and so many people in this room, and then set to work to make that statement precise, I shall run a great many risks and it will be extremely likely that any precise statement I make will be something not true at all. So you cannot very easily or simply get from these vague undeniable things to precise things which are going to retain the undeniability of the starting-point. The precise propositions that you arrive at may be *logically* premisses to the system that you build up upon the basis of them, but they are not premisses for the theory of knowledge. It is important to realize the difference between that from which your knowledge is, in fact, derived, and that from which, if you already had complete knowledge, you would deduce it. Those are quite different things. The sort of premiss that a logician will take for a science will not be the sort of thing which is first known or easiest known: it will be a proposition having great deductive power, great cogency and exactitude, quite a different thing from the actual premiss that your knowledge started from. When you are talking of the premiss for theory of knowledge, you are not talking of anything objective, but of something that will vary from man to man, because the premisses of one man's theory of knowledge will not be the same as those of another man's. There is a great tendency among a very large school to suppose that when you are trying to philosophize about what you know, you ought to carry back your premisses further and further into the region of the inexact and vague, beyond the point where you yourself are, right back to the child or monkey, and that anything whatsoever that *you* seem to know—but that the psychologist recognizes as being the product of previous thought and analysis and reflection on your part—cannot really be taken as a premiss in your own knowledge. That, I say, is a theory which is very widely held and which is used against that kind of analytic outlook which I wish to urge. It seems to me that when your object is, not simply to study the history or development of mind, but to ascertain the nature of the world, you do not want to go any further back than you are already yourself. You do not want to go back to the vagueness of the child or monkey, because you will find that quite sufficient difficulty is raised by your own vagueness. But there one is confronted by one of those difficulties that occur constantly in philosophy, where you have two ultimate prejudices conflicting and where argument ceases. There is the type of mind which considers that what is called primitive experience must be a better guide to wisdom than the experience of reflective persons, and there is the type of mind which takes exactly the opposite view. On that point I cannot see any argument whatsoever. It is quite clear that a highly educated person sees, hears, feels, does everything in a very different way from a young child or animal, and that this whole manner of experiencing the world and of thinking about the world is very much more analytic than that of a more primitive experience. The things we have got to take as premisses in any kind of work of analysis are the things which appear to *us* undeniable—to us here and now, as we are— and I think on the whole that the sort of method adopted by Descartes is right: that you should set to work to doubt things and retain only what you cannot doubt because of its clearness and distinctness, not because you are sure not to be induced into error, for there does not exist a method which will safeguard you against the possibility of error. The wish for perfect security is one of those snares we are always falling into, and is just as untenable in the realm of knowledge as in everything else. Nevertheless, granting all this, I think that Descartes's method is on the whole a sound one for the starting-point.

I propose, therefore, always to begin any argument that I have to make by appealing to data which will be quite ludicrously obvious. Any philosophical skill that is required will consist in the selection of those which are capable of yielding a good deal of reflection and analysis, and in the reflection and analysis themselves.

What I have said so far is by way of introduction.

The first truism to which I wish to draw your attention—and I hope you will agree with me that these things that I call truisms are so obvious that it is almost laughable to mention them—is that the world contains *facts*, which are what they are whatever we may choose to think about them, and that there are also *beliefs*, which have reference to facts, and by reference to facts are either true or false. I will try first of all to give you a preliminary explanation of what I mean by a 'fact'. When I speak of a fact—I do not propose to attempt an exact definition, but an explanation, so that you will know what I am talking about—I mean the kind of thing that makes a proposition true or false. If I say 'It is raining', what I say is true in a certain condition of weather and is false in other conditions of weather. The condition of weather that makes my statement true (or false as the case may be), is what I should call a 'fact'. If I say 'Socrates is dead', my statement will be true owing to a certain physiological occurrence which happened in Athens long ago. If I say, 'Gravitation varies inversely as the square of the distance', my statement is rendered true by astronomical fact. If I say, 'Two and two are four', it is arithmetical fact that makes my statement true. On the other hand, if I say 'Socrates is alive', or 'Gravitation varies directly as the distance', or 'Two and two are five', the very same facts which made my previous statements true show that these new statements are false.

I want you to realize that when I speak of a fact I do not mean a particular existing thing, such as Socrates or the rain or the sun. Socrates himself does not render any statement true or false. You might be inclined to suppose that all by himself he would give truth to the statement 'Socrates existed', but as a matter of fact that is a mistake. It is due to a confusion which I shall try to explain in the sixth lecture of this course, when I come to deal with the notion of existence. Socrates* himself, or any particular thing just by itself, does not make any proposition true or false. 'Socrates is dead' and 'Socrates is alive' are both of them statements about Socrates. One is true and the other false. What I call a fact is the sort of

---

* I am here for the moment treating Socrates as a 'particular'. But we shall see shortly that this view requires modification.

thing that is expressed by a whole sentence, not by a single name like 'Socrates'. When a single word does come to express a fact, like 'fire' or 'wolf', it is always due to an unexpressed context, and the full expression of a fact will always involve a sentence. We express a fact, for example, when we say that a certain thing has a certain property, or that it has a certain relation to another thing; but the thing which has the property or the relation is not what I call a 'fact'.

It is important to observe that facts belong to the objective world. They are not created by our thoughts or beliefs except in special cases. That is one of the sort of things which I should set up as an obvious truism, but, of course, one is aware, the moment one has read any philosophy at all, how very much there is to be said before such a statement as that can become the kind of position that you want. The first thing I want to emphasize is that the outer world—the world, so to speak, which knowledge is aiming at knowing—is not completely described by a lot of 'particulars', but that you must also take account of these things that I call facts, which are the sort of things that you express by a sentence, and that these, just as much as particular chairs and tables, are part of the real world. Except in psychology, most of our statements are not intended merely to express our condition of mind, though that is often all that they succeed in doing. They are intended to express facts, which (except when they are psychological facts) will be about the outer world. There are such facts involved, equally when we speak truly and when we speak falsely. When we speak falsely it is an objective fact that makes what we say false, and it is an objective fact which makes what we say true when we speak truly.

There are a great many different kinds of facts, and we shall be concerned in later lectures with a certain amount of classification of facts. I will just point out a few kinds of facts to begin with, so that you may not imagine that facts are all very much alike. There are *particular facts*, such as 'This is white'; then there are *general facts*, such as 'All men are mortal'. Of course, the distinction between particular and general facts is one of the most important. There again it would be a very great mistake to suppose that you could describe the world completely by means of particular facts alone. Suppose that you had succeeded in chronicling every single particular fact throughout the universe, and that there did not exist a single particular fact of any sort anywhere that you had not chronicled, you still would not have got a complete description of the universe unless you also added: 'These that I have chronicled are all the particular facts there are'. <u>So you cannot hope to describe the world completely without having general facts as well as particular facts</u>. Another distinction, which is perhaps a little more difficult to make, is between positive facts and negative facts, such as 'Socrates was alive'—a positive fact—and 'Socrates is not alive'—you might say a negative fact.* But the distinction is difficult to make precise. Then there are facts concerning particular things or particular qualities or relations, and, apart from them, the completely general facts of the sort that you have in logic, where there is no mention of any constituent whatever of the actual world, no mention of any particular thing or particular quality or particular relation, indeed strictly you may say no mention of anything. That is one of the characteristics of logical propositions, that they mention nothing. Such a proposition is: 'If one class is part of another, a term which is a member of the one is also a member of the other'. All those words that come in the statement of a pure logical proposition are words really belonging to syntax. They are words merely expressing form or connexion, not mentioning any particular constituent of the proposition in which they occur. This is, of course, a thing that wants to be proved; I am not laying it down as self-evident. Then there are facts about the properties of single things; and facts about the relations between two things, three things, and so on; and any number of different classifications of some of the facts in the world, which are important for different purposes.

It is obvious that there is not a dualism of true and false facts; there are only just facts. It would be a mistake, of course, to say that all facts are true. That would be a mistake because true and false are correlatives, and you would only say of a thing that it was true if it was the sort of thing that *might* be false. A fact cannot be either true or false. That brings us on to the question of statements or propositions or judgments, all those things that do have the duality of truth and falsehood. For the purposes of logic, though not, I think, for the purposes of theory of knowledge, it is natural to concentrate upon the proposition as the thing which is going

* Negative facts are further discussed in a later lecture.

to be our typical vehicle on the duality of truth and falsehood. A proposition, one may say, is a sentence in the indicative, a sentence asserting something, not questioning or commanding or wishing. It may also be a sentence of that sort preceded by the word 'that'. For example, 'That Socrates is alive', 'That two and two are four', 'That two and two are five', anything of that sort will be a proposition.

A proposition is just a symbol. It is a complex symbol in the sense that it has parts which are also symbols: a symbol may be defined as complex when it has parts that are symbols. In a sentence containing several words, the several words are each symbols, and the sentence composing them is therefore a complex symbol in that sense. There is a good deal of importance to philosophy in the theory of symbolism, a good deal more than at one time I thought. I think the importance is almost entirely negative, i.e., the importance lies in the fact that unless you are fairly self-conscious about symbols, unless you are fairly aware of the relation of the symbol to what it symbolizes, you will find yourself attributing to the thing properties which only belong to the symbol. That, of course, is especially likely in very abstract studies such as philosophical logic, because the subject-matter that you are supposed to be thinking of is so exceedingly difficult and elusive that any person who has ever tried to think about it knows you do not think about it except perhaps once in six months for half a minute. The rest of the time you think about the symbols, because they are tangible, but the thing you are supposed to be thinking about is fearfully difficult and one does not often manage to think about it. The really good philosopher is the one who does once in six months think about it for a minute. Bad philosophers never do. That is why the theory of symbolism has a certain importance, because otherwise you are so certain to mistake the properties of the symbolism for the properties of the thing. It has other interesting sides to it too. There are different kinds of symbols, different kinds of relation between symbol and what is symbolized, and very important fallacies arise from not realizing this. The sort of contradictions about which I shall be speaking in connexion with types in a later lecture all arise from mistakes in symbolism, from putting one sort of symbol in the place where another sort of symbol ought to be. Some of the notions that have been thought absolutely fundamental in philosophy have arisen, I believe, entirely through mistakes as to symbolism—e.g., the notion of existence, or, if you like, reality. Those two words stand for a great deal that has been discussed in philosophy. There has been the theory about every proposition being really a description of reality as a whole and so on, and altogether these notions of reality and existence have played a very prominent part in philosophy. Now my own belief is that as they have occurred in philosophy, they have been entirely the outcome of a muddle about symbolism, and that when you have cleared up that muddle, you find that practically everything that has been said about existence is sheer and simple mistake, and that is all you can say about it. I shall go into that in a later lecture, but it is an example of the way in which symbolism is important.

Perhaps I ought to say a word or two about what I am understanding by symbolism, because I think some people think you only mean mathematical symbols when you talk about symbolism. I am using it in a sense to include all language of every sort and kind, so that every word is a symbol, and every sentence, and so forth. When I speak of a symbol I simply mean something that 'means' something else, and as to what I mean by 'meaning' I am not prepared to tell you. I will in the course of time enumerate a strictly infinite number of different things that 'meaning' may mean but I shall not consider that I have exhausted the discussion by doing that. I think that the notion of meaning is always more or less psychological, and that it is not possible to get a pure logical theory of meaning, nor therefore of symbolism. I think that it is of the very essence of the explanation of what you mean by a symbol to take account of such things as knowing, of cognitive relations, and probably also of association. At any rate I am pretty clear that the theory of symbolism and the use of symbolism is not a thing that can be explained in pure logic without taking account of the various cognitive relations that you may have to things.

As to what one means by 'meaning', I will give a few illustrations. For instance, the word 'Socrates', you will say, means a certain man; the word 'mortal' means a certain quality; and the sentence 'Socrates is mortal' means a certain fact. But these three sorts of meaning are entirely distinct, and you will get into the most hopeless contradictions if you think the word 'meaning' has the same meaning in each of these three cases. It is very important not to suppose that there is just one thing which is meant by 'meaning', and that therefore there is just one sort of relation of the symbol to what is symbolized. A name would be a proper symbol to use for a person; a sentence (or a proposition) is the proper symbol for a fact.

A belief or a statement has duality of truth and falsehood, which the fact does not have. A belief or a statement always involves a proposition. You say that a man believes that so and so is the case. A man believes that Socrates is dead. What he believes is a proposition on the face of it, and for formal purposes it is convenient to take the proposition as the essential thing having the duality of truth and falsehood. It is very important to realize such things, for instance, as that *propositions are not names for facts*. It is quite obvious as soon as it is pointed out to you, but as a matter of fact I never had realized it until it was pointed out to me by a former pupil of mine, Wittgenstein. It is perfectly evident as soon as you think of it, that a proposition is not a name for a fact, from the mere circumstance that there are *two* propositions corresponding to each fact. Suppose it is a fact that Socrates is dead. You have two propositions: 'Socrates is dead' and 'Socrates is not dead'. And those two propositions corresponding to the same fact, there is one fact in the world which makes one true and one false. That is not accidental, and illustrates how the relation of proposition to fact is a totally different one from the relation of name to the thing named. For each fact there are two propositions, one true and one false, and there is nothing in the nature of the symbol to show us which is the true one and which is the false one. If there were, you could ascertain the truth about the world by examining propositions without looking around you.

There are two different relations, as you see, that a proposition may have to a fact: the one the relation that you may call being true to the fact, and the other being false to the fact. Both are equally essentially logical relations which may subsist between the two, whereas in the case of a name, there is only one relation that it can have to what it names. A name can just name a particular, or, if it does not, it is not a name at all, it is a noise. It cannot be a name without having just that one particular relation of naming a certain thing, whereas a proposition does not cease to be a proposition if it is false. It has these two ways, of being true and being false, which together correspond to the property of being a name. Just as a word may be a name or be not a name but just a meaningless noise, so a phrase which is apparently a proposition may be either true or false, or may be meaningless, but the true and false belong together as against the meaningless. That shows, of course, that the formal logical characteristics of propositions are quite different from those of names, and that the relations they have to facts are quite different, and therefore propositions are not names for facts. You must not run away with the idea that you can name facts in any other way; you cannot. You cannot name them at all. You cannot properly name a fact. The only thing you can do is to assert it, or deny it, or desire it, or will it, or wish it, or question it, but all those are things involving the whole proposition. You can never put the sort of thing that makes a proposition to be true or false in the position of a logical subject. You can only have it there as something to be asserted or denied or something of that sort, but not something to be named.

Discussion

Question: Do you take your starting-point 'That there are many things' as a postulate which is to be carried along all through, or has to be proved afterward?

Mr. Russell: No, neither the one nor the other. I do not take it as a postulate that 'There are many things'. I should take it that, in so far as it can be proved, the proof is empirical, and that the disproofs that have been offered are *a priori*. The empirical person would naturally say, there are many things. The monistic philosopher attempts to show that there are not. I should propose to refute his *a priori* arguments. I do not consider there is any *logical* necessity for there to be many things, nor for there not to be many things.

Question: I mean in making a start, whether you start with the empirical or the *a priori* philosophy, do you make your statement just at the beginning and come back to prove it, or do you never come back to the proof of it?

Mr. Russell: No, you never come back. It is like the acorn to the oak. You never get back to the acorn in the oak. I should like a statement which would be rough and vague and have that sort of obviousness that belongs to things of which you never know what they mean, but I should never get back to that statement. I should say, here is a thing. We seem somehow convinced that there is truth buried in this thing somewhere. We will look at it inside and out until we have extracted something and can say, now that is true. It will not really be the same as the thing we started from because it will be so much more analytic and precise.

Question: Does it not look as though you could name a fact by a date?

Mr. Russell: You can apparently name facts, but I do not think you can really: you always find that if you set out the whole thing fully, it was not so. Suppose you say 'The death of Socrates'. You might say, that is a name for the fact that Socrates died. But it obviously is not. You can see that the moment you take account of truth and falsehood. Supposing he had not died, the phrase would still be just as significant although there could not be then anything you could name. But supposing he had never lived, the sound 'Socrates' would not be a name at all. You can see it in another way. You can say 'The death of Socrates is a fiction'. Suppose you had read in the paper that the Kaiser had been assassinated, and it turned out to be not true. You could then say, 'The death of the Kaiser is a fiction'. It is clear that there is no such thing in the world as a fiction, and yet that statement is a perfectly sound statement. From this it follows that 'The death of the Kaiser' is not a name.

II. PARTICULARS, PREDICATES, AND RELATIONS

I propose to begin to-day the analysis of facts and propositions, for in a way the chief thesis that I have to maintain is the legitimacy of analysis, because if one goes into what I call Logical Atomism that means that one does believe the world can be analysed into a number of separate things with relations and so forth, and that the sort of arguments that many philosophers use against analysis are not justifiable.

In a philosophy of logical atomism one might suppose that the first thing to do would be to discover the kinds of atoms out of which logical structures are composed. But I do not think that is quite the first thing; it is one of the early things, but not quite the first. There are two other questions that one has to consider, and one of these at least is prior. You have to consider:

1. Are the things that look like logically complex entities really complex?
2. Are they really entities?

The second question we can put off; in fact, I shall not deal with it fully until my last lecture. The first question, whether they are really complex, is one that you have to consider at the start. Neither of these questions is, as it stands, a very precise question. I do not pretend to start with precise questions. I do not think you can start with anything precise. You have to achieve such precision as you can, as you go along. Each of these two questions, however, is *capable* of a precise meaning, and each is really important.

There is another question which comes still earlier, namely: what shall we take as prima facie examples of logically complex entities? That really is the first question of all to start with. What sort of things shall we regard as prima facie complex?

Of course, all the ordinary objects of daily life are apparently complex entities: such things as tables and chairs, loaves and fishes, persons and principalities and powers—they are all on the face of it complex entities. All the kinds of things to which we habitually give proper names are on the face of them complex entities: Socrates, Piccadilly, Rumania, Twelfth Night or anything you like to think of, to which you give a proper name, they are all apparently complex entities. They seem to be complex systems bound together into some kind of a unity, that sort of a unity that leads to the bestowal of a single appellation. I think it is the contemplation of this sort of apparent unity which has very largely led to the philosophy of monism, and to the suggestion that the universe as a whole is a single complex entity more or less in the sense in which these things are that I have been talking about.

For my part, I do not believe in complex entities of this kind, and it is not such things as these that I am going to take as the prima facie examples of complex entities. My reasons will appear more and more plainly as I go on. I cannot give them all to-day, but I can more or less explain what I mean in a preliminary way. Suppose, for example, that you were to analyse what appears to be a fact about Piccadilly. Suppose you made any statement about Piccadilly, such as: 'Piccadilly is a pleasant street'. If you analyse a statement of that sort correctly, I believe you will find that the fact corresponding to your statement does not contain any constituent corresponding to the word 'Piccadilly'. The word 'Piccadilly' will form part of many significant propositions, but the facts corresponding to these propositions do not contain any single constituent, whether simple or complex, corresponding to the word 'Piccadilly'. That is to say, if you take language as a guide in your analysis of the fact expressed, you will be led astray in a statement of that sort. The reasons for that I shall give at length in Lecture VI, and partly also in Lecture VII, but I could say in a preliminary way certain things that would make you understand what I mean. 'Piccadilly', on the face of it, is the name for a certain portion of the earth's surface, and I suppose, if you wanted to define it, you would have to define it as a series of classes of material entities, namely those which, at varying times, occupy that portion of the earth's surface. So that you would find that the logical status of Piccadilly is bound up with the logical status of series and classes, and if you are going to hold Piccadilly as real, you must hold that series of classes are real, and whatever sort of metaphysical status you assign to them, you must assign to it. As you know, I believe that series and classes are of the nature of logical fictions: therefore that thesis, if it can be maintained, will dissolve Piccadilly into a fiction. Exactly similar remarks will apply to other instances: Rumania, Twelfth Night, and Socrates. Socrates, perhaps, raises some special questions, because the question what constitutes a person has special difficulties in it. But, for the sake of argument, one might identify Socrates with the series of his experiences. He would be really a series of classes, because one has many experiences simultaneously. Therefore he comes to be very like Piccadilly.

Considerations of that sort seem to take us away from such prima facie complex entities as we started with to others as being more stubborn and more deserving of analytic attention, namely facts. I explained last time what I meant by a fact, namely, that sort of thing that makes a proposition true or false, the sort of thing which is the case when your statement is true and is not the case when your statement is false. Facts are, as I said last time, plainly something you have to take account of if you are going to give a complete account of the world. You cannot do that by merely enumerating the particular things that are in it: you must also mention the relations of these things, and their properties, and so forth, all of which are facts, so that facts certainly belong to an account of the objective world, and facts do seem much more clearly complex and much more not capable of being explained away than things like Socrates and Rumania. However you may explain away the meaning of the word 'Socrates', you will still be left with the truth that the proposition 'Socrates is mortal' expresses a fact. You may not know exactly what Socrates means, but it is quite clear that 'Socrates is mortal' does express a fact. There is clearly some valid meaning in saying that the fact expressed by 'Socrates is mortal' is *complex*. The things in the world have various properties, and stand in various relations to each other. That they have these properties and relations are *facts*, and the things and their qualities or relations are quite clearly in some sense or other components of the facts that have those qualities or relations. The analysis of apparently complex *things* such as we started with can be reduced by various means, to the analysis of facts which are apparently about those things. Therefore it is with the analysis of *facts* that one's consideration of the problem of complexity must begin, not by the analysis of apparently complex things.

The complexity of a fact is evidenced, to begin with, by the circumstance that the proposition which asserts a fact consists of several words, each of which may occur in other contexts. Of course, sometimes you get a proposition expressed by a single word but if it is expressed fully it is bound to contain several words. The proposition 'Socrates is mortal' may be replaced by 'Plato is mortal' or by 'Socrates is human'; in the first case we alter the subject, in the second the predicate. It is clear that all the propositions in which the word 'Socrates' occurs have something in common, and again all the propositions in which the word 'mortal' occurs have something in common, something which they do not have in common with all propositions, but only with those which are about Socrates or mortality. It is clear, I think, that the facts corresponding to propositions in which the word 'Socrates' occurs have something in common corresponding to the common word 'Socrates' which occurs in the propositions, so that you have that sense of complexity to begin with, that in a fact you can get something which it may have in common with other facts, just as you may have 'Socrates is human' and 'Socrates is mortal', both of them facts, and both having to do with Socrates, although Socrates does not constitute the whole of either of these facts. It is quite clear that in that sense there is a possibility of cutting up a fact into component parts, of which one component may be altered without altering the others, and one component may occur in certain other facts though not in all other facts. I want to make it clear, to begin with, that there is a sense in which facts can be analysed. I am not concerned with all the difficulties of any analysis, but only with meeting the prima facie objections of philosophers who think you really cannot analyse at all.

I am trying as far as possible again this time, as I did last time, to start with perfectly plain truisms. My desire and wish is that the things I start with should be so obvious that you wonder why I spend my time stating them. That is what I aim at, because the point of philosophy is to start with something so simple as not to seem worth stating, and to end with something so paradoxical that no one will believe it.

One prima facie mark of complexity in propositions is the fact that they are expressed by several words. I come now to another point, which applies primarily to propositions and thence derivatively to facts. You can understand a proposition when you understand the words of which it is composed even though you never heard the proposition before. That seems a very humble property, but it is a property which marks it as complex and distinguishes it from words whose meaning is simple. When you know the vocabulary, grammar, and syntax of a language, you can understand a proposition in that language even though you never saw it before. In reading a newspaper, for example, you become aware of a number of statements which are new to you, and they are intelligible to you immediately, in spite of the fact that they are new, because you understand the words of which they are composed. This characteristic, that you can understand a proposition through the understanding of its component words, is absent from the component words when those words express something simple. Take the word 'red', for example, and suppose—as one always has to do—that 'red' stands for a particular shade of colour. You will pardon that assumption, but one never can get on otherwise. You cannot understand the meaning of the word 'red' except through seeing red things. There is no other way in which it can be done. It is no use to learn languages, or to look up dictionaries. None of these things will help you to understand the meaning of the word 'red'. In that way it is quite different from the meaning of a proposition. Of course, you can give a definition of the word 'red', and here it is very important to distinguish between a definition and an analysis. [All analysis is only possible in regard to what is complex, and it always depends, in the last analysis, upon direct acquaintance with the objects which are the meanings of certain simple symbols.] It is hardly necessary to observe that one does not define a thing but a symbol. (A 'simple' symbol is a symbol whose parts are not symbols.) A simple symbol is quite a different thing from a simple thing. Those objects which it is impossible to symbolize otherwise than by simple symbols may be called 'simple', while those which can be symbolized by a combination of symbols may be called 'complex'. This is, of course, a preliminary definition, and perhaps somewhat circular, but that doesn't much matter at this stage.

I have said that 'red' could not be understood except by seeing red things. You might object to that on the ground that you can define red, for example, as 'The colour with the greatest wavelength'. That, you might say, is a definition of 'red' and a person could understand that definition even if he had seen nothing red, provided he understood the physical theory of colour. But that does not really constitute the meaning of the word 'red' in the very slightest. If you take such a proposition as 'This is red' and substitute for it 'This has the colour with the greatest wave-length', you have a different proposition altogether. You can see that at once, because a person who knows nothing of the physical theory of colour can understand the proposition 'This is red', and can know that it is true, but cannot know that 'This has the colour which has the greatest wave-length'. Conversely, you might have a hypothetical person who could not see red, but who understood the physical theory of colour and could apprehend the proposition 'This has the colour with the greatest wave-length', but who would not be able to understand the proposition 'This is red' as understood by the normal uneducated person. Therefore it is clear that if you define 'red' as 'The colour with the greatest wave-length', you are not giving the actual meaning of the word at all; you are simply giving a true description, which is quite a different thing, and the propositions which result are different propositions from those in which the word 'red' occurs. In that sense the word 'red' cannot be defined, though in the sense in which a correct description constitutes a definition it can be defined. In the sense of analysis you cannot define 'red'. That is how it is that dictionaries are able to get on, because a dictionary professes to define all words in the language by means of words in the language, and therefore it is clear that a dictionary must be guilty of a vicious circle somewhere, but it manages it by means of correct descriptions.

I have made it clear, then, in what sense I should say that the word 'red' is a simple symbol and the phrase 'This is red' a complex symbol. The word 'red' can only be understood through acquaintance with the object, whereas the phrase 'Roses are red' can be understood if you know what 'red' is and what 'roses' are, without ever having heard the phrase before. That is a clear mark of what is complex. It is the mark of a complex symbol, and also the mark of the object symbolized by the complex symbol. That is to say, propositions are complex symbols, and the facts they stand for are complex.

The whole question of the meaning of words is very full of complexities and ambiguities in ordinary language. When one person uses a word, he does not mean by it the same thing as another person means by it. I have often heard it said that that is a misfortune. That is a mistake. It would be absolutely fatal if people meant the same things by their words. It would make all intercourse impossible, and language the most hopeless and useless thing imaginable, because the meaning you attach to your words must depend on the nature of the objects you are acquainted with, and since different people are acquainted with different objects, they would not be able to talk to each other unless they attached quite different meanings to their words. We should have to talk only about logic—a not wholly undesirable result. Take, for example, the word 'Piccadilly'. We, who are acquainted with Piccadilly, attach quite a different meaning to that word from any which could be attached to it by a person who had never been in London: and, supposing that you travel in foreign parts and expatiate on Piccadilly, you will convey to your hearers entirely different propositions from those in your mind. They will know Piccadilly as an important street in London; they may know a lot about it, but they will not know just the things one knows when one is walking along it. If you were to insist on language which was unambiguous, you would be unable to tell people at home what you had seen in foreign parts. It would be altogether incredibly inconvenient to have an unambiguous language, and therefore mercifully we have not got one.

Analysis is not the same thing as definition. You can define a term by means of a correct description, but that does not constitute an analysis. It is analysis, not definition, that we are concerned with at the present moment, so I will come back to the question of analysis.

We may lay down the following provisional definitions:

That the components of a proposition are the symbols we must understand in order to understand the proposition;

That the components of the fact which makes a proposition true or false, as the case may be, are the *meanings* of the symbols which we must understand in order to understand the proposition.

That is not absolutely correct, but it will enable you to understand my meaning. One reason why it fails of correctness is that it does not apply to words which, like 'or' and 'not', are parts of propositions without corresponding to any part of the corresponding facts. This is a topic for Lecture III.

I call these definitions *preliminary* because they start from the complexity of the proposition, which they define psychologically, and proceed to the complexity of the fact, whereas it is quite clear that in an orderly, proper procedure it is the complexity of the fact that you would start from. It is also clear that the complexity of the fact cannot be something merely psychological. If in astronomical fact the earth moves round the sun, that is genuinely complex. It is not that you think it complex, it is a sort of genuine objective complexity, and therefore one ought in a proper, orderly procedure to start from the complexity of the world and arrive at the complexity of the proposition. The only reason for going the other way round is that in all abstract matters symbols are easier to grasp. I doubt, however, whether complexity, in that fundamental objective sense in which one starts from complexity of a fact, is definable at all. You cannot analyse what you mean by complexity in that sense. You must just apprehend it—at least so I am inclined to think. There is nothing one could say about it, beyond giving criteria such as I have been giving. Therefore, when you cannot get a real proper analysis of a thing, it is generally best to talk round it without professing that you have given an exact definition.

It might be suggested that complexity is essentially to do with symbols, or that it is essentially psychological. I do not think it would be possible seriously to maintain either of these views, but they are the sort of views that will occur to one, the sort of thing that one would try, to see whether it would work. I do not think they will do at all. When we come to the principles of symbolism which I shall deal with in Lecture VII, I shall try to persuade you that in a logically correct symbolism there will always be a certain fundamental identity of structure between a fact and the symbol for it; and that the complexity of the symbol corresponds very closely with the complexity of the facts symbolized by it. Also, as I said before, it is quite directly evident to inspection that the fact, for example, that two things stand in a certain relation to one another—e.g., that this is to the left of that—is itself objectively complex, and not merely that the apprehension of it is complex. The fact that two things stand in a certain relation to each other, or any statement of that sort, has a complexity all of its own. I shall therefore in future assume that there is an objective complexity in the world, and that it is mirrored by the complexity of propositions.

A moment ago I was speaking about the great advantages that we derive from the logical imperfections of language, from the fact that our words are all ambiguous. I propose now to consider what sort of language a logically perfect language would be. In a logically perfect language the words in a proposition would correspond one by one with the components of the corresponding fact, with the exception of such words as 'or', 'not', 'if', 'then', which have a different function. In a logically perfect language, there will be one word and no more for every simple object, and everything that is not simple will be expressed by a combination of words, by a combination derived, of course, from the words for

the simple things that enter in, one word for each simple component. A language of that sort will be completely analytic, and will
show at a glance the logical structure of the facts asserted or denied.
The language which is set forth in *Principia Mathematica* is intended to be a language of that sort. It is a language which has only
syntax and no vocabulary whatsoever. Barring the omission of a
vocabulary I maintain that it is quite a nice language. It aims at
being that sort of a language that, if you add a vocabulary, would
be a logically perfect language. Actual languages are not logically
perfect in this sense, and they cannot possibly be, if they are to
serve the purposes of daily life. A logically perfect language, if it
could be constructed, would not only be intolerably prolix, but,
as regards its vocabulary, would be very largely private to one
speaker. That is to say, all the names that it would use would be
private to that speaker and could not enter into the language of
another speaker. It could not use proper names for Socrates or
Piccadilly or Rumania for the reasons which I went into earlier
in the lecture. Altogether you would find that it would be a very
inconvenient language indeed. That is one reason why logic is so
very backward as a science, because the needs of logic are so extraordinarily different from the needs of daily life. One wants a
language in both, and unfortunately it is logic that has to give way,
not daily life. I shall, however, assume that we have constructed
a logically perfect language, and that we are going on State occasions to use it, and I will now come back to the question which I
intended to start with, namely, the analysis of facts.

The simplest imaginable facts are those which consist in the
possession of a quality by some particular thing. Such facts, say,
as 'This is white'. They have to be taken in a very sophisticated
sense. I do not want you to think about the piece of chalk I am
holding, but of what you see when you look at the chalk. If one
says, 'This is white' it will do for about as simple a fact as you can
get hold of. The next simplest would be those in which you have a
relation between two facts, such as: 'This is to the left of that'.
Next you come to those where you have a triadic relation between
three particulars. (An instance which Royce gives is '*A* gives *B* to
C'.) So you get relations which require as their minimum three
terms, those we call triadic relations; and those which require
four terms, which we call tetradic, and so on. There you have a

whole infinite hierarchy of facts—facts in which you have a thing and a quality, two things and a relation, three things and a relation, four things and a relation, and so on. That whole hierarchy constitutes what I call *atomic* facts, and they are the simplest sort of fact. You can distinguish among them some simpler than others, because the ones containing a quality are simpler than those in which you have, say, a pentadic relation, and so on. The whole lot of them, taken together, are as facts go very simple, and are what I call atomic facts. The propositions expressing them are what I call *atomic propositions*.

In every atomic fact there is one component which is naturally expressed by a verb (or, in the case of quality, it may be expressed by a predicate, by an adjective). This one component is a quality or dyadic or triadic or tetradic . . . relation. It would be very convenient, for purposes of talking about these matters, to call a quality a 'monadic relation' and I shall do so; it saves a great deal of circumlocution.

In that case you can say that all atomic propositions assert relations of varying orders. Atomic facts contain, besides the relation, the terms of the relation—one term if it is a monadic relation, two if it is dyadic, and so on. These 'terms' which come into atomic facts I define as 'particulars'.

Particulars = terms of relations in atomic facts.   Df.

That is the definition of particulars, and I want to emphasize it because the definition of a particular is something purely logical. The question whether this or that is a particular, is a question to be decided in terms of that logical definition. In order to understand the definition it is not necessary to know beforehand 'This is a particular' or 'That is a particular'. It remains to be investigated what particulars you can find in the world, if any. The whole question of what particulars you actually find in the real world is a purely empirical one which does not interest the logician as such. The logician as such never gives instances, because it is one of the tests of a logical proposition that you need not know anything whatsoever about the real world in order to understand it.

Passing from atomic facts to atomic propositions, the word expressing a monadic relation or quality is called a 'predicate', and the word expressing a relation of any higher order would generally be a verb, sometimes a single verb, sometimes a whole phrase. At any rate the verb gives the essential nerve, as it were, of the relation. The other words that occur in the atomic propositions, the words that are not the predicate or verb, may be called the subjects of the proposition. There will be one subject in a monadic proposition, two in a dyadic one, and so on. The subjects in a proposition will be the words expressing the terms of the relation which is expressed by the proposition.

The only kind of word that is theoretically capable of standing for a particular is a *proper name*, and the whole matter of proper names is rather curious.

Proper names = words for particulars.   Df.

I have put that down although, as far as common language goes, it is obviously false. It is true that if you try to think how you are to talk about particulars, you will see that you cannot ever talk about a particular particular except by means of a proper name. You cannot use general words except by way of description. How are you to express in words an atomic proposition? An atomic proposition is one which does mention actual particulars, not merely describe them but actually name them, and you can only name them by means of names. You can see at once for yourself, therefore, that every other part of speech except proper names is obviously quite incapable of standing for a particular. Yet it does seem a little odd if, having made a dot on the blackboard, I call it 'John'. You would be surprised, and yet how are you to know otherwise what it is that I am speaking of. If I say, 'The dot that is on the right-hand side is white' that is a proposition. If I say 'This is white' that is quite a different proposition. 'This' will do very well while we are all here and can see it, but if I wanted to talk about it to-morrow it would be convenient to have christened it and called it 'John'. There is no other way in which you can mention it. You cannot really mention *it* itself except by means of a name.

What pass for names in language, like 'Socrates', 'Plato', and so forth, were originally intended to fulfil this function of standing for particulars, and we do accept, in ordinary daily life, as particulars all sorts of things that really are not so. The names that we commonly use, like 'Socrates', are really abbreviations for descriptions; not only that, but what they describe are not particulars but complicated systems of classes or series. A name, in the narrow logical sense of a word whose meaning is a particular, can only be applied to a particular with which the speaker is acquainted, because you cannot name anything you are not acquainted with. You remember, when Adam named the beasts, they came before him one by one, and he became acquainted with them and named them. We are not acquainted with Socrates, and therefore cannot name him. When we use the word 'Socrates', we are really using a description. Our thought may be rendered by some such phrase as, 'The Master of Plato', or 'The philosopher who drank the hemlock', or 'The person whom logicians assert to be mortal', but we certainly do not use the name as a name in the proper sense of the word.

That makes it very difficult to get any instance of a name at all in the proper strict logical sense of the word. The only words one does use as names in the logical sense are words like 'this' or 'that'. One can use 'this' as a name to stand for a particular with which one is acquainted at the moment. We say 'This is white'. If you agree that 'This is white', meaning the 'this' that you see, you are using 'this' as a proper name. But if you try to apprehend the proposition that I am expressing when I say 'This is white', you cannot do it. If you mean this piece of chalk as a physical object, then you are not using a proper name. It is only when you use 'this' quite strictly, to stand for an actual object of sense, that it is really a proper name. And in that it has a very odd property for a proper name, namely that it seldom means the same thing two moments running and does not mean the same thing to the speaker and to the hearer. It is an *ambiguous* proper name, but it is really a proper name all the same, and it is almost the only thing I can think of that is used properly and logically in the sense that I was talking of for a proper name. The importance of proper names, in the sense of which I am talking, is in the sense of logic, not of daily life. You can see why it is that in the logical language set forth in *Principia Mathematica* there are not any names, because there we are not interested in particular particulars but only in general particulars, if I may be allowed such a phrase.

Particulars have this peculiarity, among the sort of objects that you have to take account of in an inventory of the world, that each of them stands entirely alone and is completely self-subsistent. It has that sort of self-subsistence that used to belong to substance, except that it usually only persists through a very short time, so far as our experience goes. That is to say, each particular that there is in the world does not in any way logically depend upon any other particular. Each one might happen to be the whole universe; it is a merely empirical fact that this is not the case. There is no reason why you should not have a universe consisting of one particular and nothing else. That is a peculiarity of particulars. In the same way, in order to understand a name for a particular, the only thing necessary is to be acquainted with that particular. When you are acquainted with that particular, you have a full, adequate, and complete understanding of the name, and no further information is required. No further information as to the facts that are true of that particular would enable you to have a fuller understanding of the meaning of the name.

Discussion

Mr. Carr: You think there are simple facts that are not complex. Are complexes all composed of simples? Are not the simples that go into complexes themselves complex?

Mr. Russell: No facts are simple. As to your second question, that is, of course, a question that might be argued—whether when a thing is complex it is necessary that it should in analysis have constituents that are simple. I think it is perfectly possible to suppose that complex things are capable of analysis *ad infinitum*, and that you never reach the simple. I do not think it is true, but it is a thing that one might argue, certainly. I do myself think that complexes—I do not like to talk of complexes—are composed of simples, but I admit that that is a difficult argument, and it might be that analysis could go on forever.

Mr. Carr: You do not mean that in calling the thing complex, you have asserted that there really are simples?

Mr. Russell: No, I do not think that is *necessarily* implied.

Mr. Neville: I do not feel clear that the proposition 'This is white' is in any case a simpler proposition than the proposition 'This and that have the same colour'.

Mr. Russell: That is one of the things I have not had time for. It may be the same as the proposition 'This and that have the same colour'. It may be that white is defined as the colour of 'this',

or rather that the proposition 'This is white' means 'This is identical in colour with that', the colour of 'that' being, so to speak, the definition of white. That may be, but there is no special reason to think that it is.

Mr. Neville: Are there any monadic relations which would be better examples?

Mr. Russell: I think not. It is perfectly obvious *a priori* that you can get rid of all monadic relations by that trick. One of the things I was going to say if I had had time was that you can get rid of dyadic and reduce to triadic, and so on. But there is no particular reason to suppose that that is the way the world begins, that it begins with relations of order *n* instead of relations of order 1. You cannot reduce them downward, but you can reduce them upward.

Question: If the proper name of a thing, a 'this', varies from instant to instant, how is it possible to make any argument?

Mr. Russell: You can keep 'this' going for about a minute or two. I made that dot and talked about it for some little time. I mean it varies often. If you argue quickly, you can get some little way before it is finished. I think things last for a finite time, a matter of some seconds or minutes or whatever it may happen to be.

Question: You do not think that air is acting on that and changing it?

Mr. Russell: It does not matter about that if it does not alter its appearance enough for you to have a different sense-datum.

III. ATOMIC AND MOLECULAR PROPOSITIONS

I did not quite finish last time the syllabus that I intended for Lecture II, so I must first do that.

I had been speaking at the end of my last lecture on the subject of the self-subsistence of particulars, how each particular has its being independently of any other and does not depend upon anything else for the logical possibility of its existence. I compared particulars with the old conception of substance, that is to say, they have the quality of self-subsistence that used to belong to substance, but not the quality of persistence through time. A particular, as a rule, is apt to last for a very short time indeed, not an instant but a very short time. In that respect particulars differ from the old substances but in their logical position they do not. There is, as you know, a logical theory which is quite opposed to that view, a logical theory according to which, if you really understood any one thing, you would understand everything. I think that rests upon a certain confusion of ideas. When you have acquaintance with a particular, you understand that particular itself quite fully, independently of the fact that there are a great many propositions about it that you do not know, but propositions concerning the particular are not necessary to be known in order that you may know what the particular itself is. It is rather the other way round. In order to understand a proposition in which the name of a particular occurs, you must already be acquainted with that particular. The acquaintance with the simpler is presupposed in the understanding of the more complex, but the logic that I should wish to combat maintains that in order thoroughly to know any one thing, you must know all its relations and all its qualities, all the propositions in fact in which that thing is mentioned; and you deduce of course from that that the world is an interdependent whole. It is on a basis of that sort that the logic of monism develops. Generally one supports this theory by talking about the 'nature' of a thing, assuming that a thing has something which you call its 'nature' which is generally elaborately confounded and distinguished from the thing, so that you can get a comfortable see-saw which enables you to deduce whichever results suit the moment. The 'nature' of the thing would come to mean all the true propositions in which the thing is mentioned. Of course it is clear that since everything has relations to everything else, you cannot know all the facts of which a thing is a constituent without having some knowledge of everything in the universe. When you realize that what one calls 'knowing a particular' merely means acquaintance with that particular and is presupposed in the understanding of any proposition in which that particular is mentioned. I think you also realize that you cannot take the view that the understanding of the name of the particular presupposes knowledge of all the propositions concerning that particular.

I should like to say about understanding, that that phrase is often used mistakenly. People speak of 'understanding the universe' and so on. But, of course, the only thing you can really understand (in the strict sense of the word) is a symbol, and to understand a symbol is to know what it stands for.

I pass on from particulars to predicates and relations and what we mean by understanding the words that we use for predicates and relations. A very great deal of what I am saying in this course of lectures consists of ideas which I derived from my friend Wittgenstein. But I have had no opportunity of knowing how far his ideas have changed since August 1914, nor whether he is alive or dead, so I cannot make any one but myself responsible for them.

Understanding a predicate is quite a different thing from understanding a name. By a predicate, as you know, I mean the word that is used to designate a quality such as red, white, square, round, and the understanding of a word like that involves a different kind of act of mind from that which is involved in understanding a name. To understand a name you must be acquainted with the particular of which it is a name, and you must know that it is the name of that particular. You do not, that is to say, have any suggestion of the form of a proposition, whereas in understanding a predicate you do. To understand 'red', for instance, is to understand what is meant by saying that a thing is red. You have to bring in the form of a proposition. You do not have to know, concerning any particular 'this', that 'This is red' but you have to know what is the meaning of saying that anything is red. You have to understand what one would call 'being red'. The importance of that is in connection with the theory of types, which I shall come to later on. It is in the fact that a predicate can never occur except as a predicate. When it seems to occur as a subject, the phrase wants amplifying and explaining, unless, of course, you are talking about the word itself. You may say " 'Red' is a predicate", but then you must have 'red' in inverted commas because you are talking about the word 'red'. When you understand 'red' it means that you understand propositions of the form that 'x is red'. So that the understanding of a predicate is something a little more complicated than the understanding of a name, just because of that. Exactly the same applies to relations, and in fact all those things that are not particulars. Take, e.g., 'before' in 'x is before y': you understand 'before' when you understand what that would mean if x and y were given. I do not mean you know whether it is true, but you understand the proposition. Here again the same thing applies. A relation can never occur except as a relation, never as a subject. You will always have to put in hypothetical terms, if not real ones, such as 'If I say that x is before y, I assert a relation between x and y'. It is in this way that you will have to expand such a statement as ' "Before" is a relation' in order to get its meaning.

The different sorts of words, in fact, have different sorts of uses and must be kept always to the right use and not to the wrong use, and it is fallacies arising from putting symbols to wrong uses that lead to the contradictions concerned with types.

There is just one more point before I leave the subjects I meant to have dealt with last time, and that is a point which came up in discussion at the conclusion of the last lecture, namely, that if you like you can get a formal reduction of (say) monadic relations to dyadic, or of dyadic to triadic, or of all the relations below a certain order to all above that order, but the converse reduction is not possible. Suppose one takes, for example, 'red'. One says, 'This is red', 'That is red', and so forth. Now, if anyone is of opinion that there is reason to try to get on without subject-predicate propositions, all that is necessary is to take some standard red thing and have a relation which one might call 'colour-like-ness', sameness of colour, which would be a direct relation, not consisting in having a certain colour. You can then define the things which are red, as all the things that have colour-likeness to this standard thing. That is practically the treatment that Berkeley and Hume recommended, except that they did not recognize that they were reducing qualities to relations, but thought they were getting rid of 'abstract ideas' altogether. You can perfectly well do in that way a formal reduction of predicates to relations. There is no objection to that either empirically or logically. If you think it is worth while you can proceed in exactly the same way with dyadic relations, which you can reduce to triadic. Royce used to have a great affection for that process. For some reason he always liked triadic relations better than dyadic ones; he illustrated his preference in his contributions to mathematical logic and the principles of geometry.

All that is possible. I do not myself see any particular point in doing it as soon as you have realized that it is possible. I see no particular reason to suppose that the simplest relations that occur in the world are (say) of order n, but there is no *a priori* reason against it. The converse reduction, on the other hand, is quite impossible except in certain special cases where the relation has some special properties. For example, dyadic relations can be reduced to sameness of predicate when they are symmetrical and transitive. Thus, e.g., the relation of colour-likeness will have the property that if A has exact colour-likeness with B and B with C, then A has exact colour-likeness with C; and if A has it with B, B has it with A. But the case is otherwise with asymmetrical relations.

Take for example 'A is greater than B'. It is obvious that 'A is greater than B' does not consist in A and B having a common predicate, for if it did it would require that B should also be greater than A. It is also obvious that it does not consist merely in their having different predicates, because if A has a different predicate from B, B has a different predicate from A, so that in either case, whether of sameness or difference of predicate, you get a symmetrical relation. For instance, if A is of a different colour from B, B is of a different colour from A. Therefore when you get symmetrical relations, you have relations which it is formally possible to reduce to either sameness of predicate or difference of predicate, but when you come to asymmetrical relations there is no such possibility. This impossibility of reducing dyadic relations to sameness or difference of predicate is a matter of a good deal of importance in connection with traditional philosophy, because a great deal of traditional philosophy depends upon the assumption that every proposition really is of the subject-predicate form, and that is certainly not the case. That theory dominates a great part of traditional metaphysics and the old idea of substance and a good deal of the theory of the Absolute, so that that sort of logical outlook which had its imagination dominated by the theory that you could always express a proposition in a subject-predicate form has had a very great deal of influence upon traditional metaphysics.

That is the end of what I ought to have said last time, and I come on now to the proper topic of to-day's lecture, that is *molecular* propositions. I call them molecular propositions because they contain other propositions which you may call their atoms, and by molecular propositions I mean propositions having such words as 'or', 'if', 'and', and so forth. If I say, 'Either to-day is Tuesday, or we have all made a mistake in being here', that is the sort of proposition that I mean that is molecular. Or if I say, 'If it rains, I shall bring my umbrella', that again is a molecular proposition because it contains the two parts 'It rains' and 'I shall being my umbrella'. If I say, 'It did rain and I did bring my umbrella', that again is a molecular proposition. Or if I say, 'The supposition of its raining is incompatible with the supposition of my not bringing my umbrella', that again is a molecular proposition. There are various propositions of that sort, which you can complicate *ad infinitum*. They are built up out of propositions related by such words as 'or', 'if', 'and', and so on. You remember that I defined an atomic proposition as one which contains a single verb. Now there are two different lines of complication in proceeding from these to more complex propositions. There is the line that I have just been talking about, where you proceed to molecular propositions, and there is another line which I shall come to in a later lecture, where you have not two related propositions, but one proposition containing two or more verbs. Examples are got from believing, wishing, and so forth. 'I believe Socrates is mortal.' You have there two verbs, 'believe' and 'is'. Or 'I wish I were immortal'. Anything like that where you have a wish or a belief or a doubt involves two verbs. A lot of psychological attitudes involve two verbs, not, as it were, crystallized out, but two verbs within the one unitary proposition. But I am talking to-day about molecular propositions and you will understand that you can make propositions with 'or' and 'and' and so forth, where the constituent propositions are not atomic, but for the moment we can confine ourselves to the case where the constituent propositions are atomic. When you take an atomic proposition, or one of these propositions like 'believing', when you take any proposition of that sort, there is just one fact which is pointed to by the proposition, pointed to either truly or falsely. The essence of a proposition is that it can correspond in two ways with a fact, in what one may call the true way or the false way. You might illustrate it in a picture like this:

$$\text{True:} \quad \overrightarrow{\text{Prop.} \quad \text{Fact}}$$
$$\text{False:} \quad \text{Fact} \overrightarrow{\quad \text{Prop.}}$$

Supposing you have the proposition 'Socrates is mortal', either there would be the fact that Socrates is mortal or there would be the fact that Socrates is not mortal. In the one case it corresponds in a way that makes the proposition true, in the other case in a way that makes the proposition false. That is one way in which a proposition differs from a name.

There are, of course, two propositions corresponding to every fact, one true and one false. There are no false facts, so you cannot get one fact for every proposition but only for every pair of propositions. All that applies to atomic propositions. But when you take such a proposition as 'p or q', 'Socrates is mortal or Socrates is living still', there you will have two different facts involved in the truth or the falsehood of your proposition 'p or q'. There will be the fact that corresponds to p and there will be the fact that corresponds to q, and both of those facts are relevant in discovering the truth or falsehood of 'p or q'. I do not suppose there is in the world a single disjunctive fact corresponding to 'p or q'. It does not look plausible that in the actual objective world there are facts going about which you could describe as 'p or q', but I would not lay too much stress on what strikes one as plausible: it is not a thing you can rely on altogether. For the present I do not think any difficulties will arise from the supposition that the truth or falsehood of this proposition 'p or q' does not depend upon a single objective fact which is disjunctive but depends on the two facts one of which corresponds to p and the other to q: p will have a fact corresponding to it and q will have a fact corresponding to it. That is to say, the truth or falsehood of this proposition 'p or q' depends upon two facts and not upon one, as p does and as q does. Generally speaking, as regards these things that you make up out of two propositions, the whole of what is necessary in order to know their meaning is to know under what circumstances they are true, given the truth or falsehood of p and the truth or falsehood of q. That is perfectly obvious. You have as a schema, for 'p or q',
using 'TT' for 'p and q both true'
    'TF' for 'p true and q false', etc.,

TT	TF	FT	FF
T	T	T	F

where the bottom line states the truth or the falsehood of 'p or q'. You must not look about the real world for an object which you can call 'or', and say, 'Now, look at this. This is "or".' There is no such thing, and if you try to analyse 'p or q' in that way you will get into trouble. But the meaning of disjunction will be entirely explained by the above schema.

I call these things truth-functions of propositions, when the truth or falsehood of the molecular proposition depends only on the truth or falsehood of the propositions that enter into it. The same applies to 'p and q' and 'if p then q' and 'p is incompatible with q'. When I say 'p is incompatible with q' I simply mean to say that they are not both true. I do not mean any more. Those sorts of things are called truth-functions, and these molecular propositions that we are dealing with to-day are instances of truth-functions. If p is a proposition, the statement that 'I believe p' does not depend for its truth or falsehood, simply upon the truth or falsehood of p, since I believe some but not all true propositions and some but not all false propositions.

I just want to give you a little talk about the way these truth-functions are built up. You can build up all these different sorts of truth-functions out of one source, namely 'p is incompatible with q', meaning by that that they are not both true, that one at least of them is false.

We will denote 'p is incompatible with q' by p/q.

Take for instance p/p, i.e., 'p is incompatible with itself'. In that case clearly p will be false, so that you can take 'p/p' as meaning 'p is false', i.e., $p/p = $ not p. The meaning of molecular propositions is entirely determined by their truth-schema and there is nothing more in it than that, so that when you have got two things of the same truth-schema you can identify them.

Suppose you want 'if p then q', that simply means that you cannot have p without having q, so that p is incompatible with the falsehood of q. Thus,

$$\text{'If } p \text{ then } q\text{'} = p/(q/q).$$

When you have that, it follows of course at once that if p is true, q is true, because you cannot have p true and q false.

Suppose you want 'p or q', that means that the falsehood of p is incompatible with the falsehood of q. If p is false, q is not false, and vice versa. That will be

$$(p/p)/(q/q).$$

Suppose you want 'p and q are both true'. That will mean that p is not incompatible with q. When p and q are both true, it is not the case that at least one of them is false. Thus,

$$\text{'}p \text{ and } q \text{ are both true'} = (p/q)/(p/q).$$

The whole of the logic of deduction is concerned simply with complications and developments of this idea. This idea of incompatibility was first shown to be sufficient for the purpose by Mr. Sheffer, and there was a good deal of work done subsequently by M. Nicod. It is a good deal simpler when it is done this way than when it is done in the way of *Principia Mathematica*, where there are two primitive ideas to start with, namely 'or' and 'not'. Here you can get on with only a single premise for deduction. I will not develop this subject further because it takes you right into mathematical logic.

I do not see any reason to suppose that there is a complexity in the facts corresponding to these molecular propositions, because, as I was saying, the correspondence of a molecular proposition with facts is of a different sort from the correspondence of an atomic proposition with a fact. There is one special point that has to be gone into in connexion with this, that is the question: Are there negative facts? Are there such facts as you might call the fact that 'Socrates is not alive'? I have assumed in all that I have said hitherto that there are negative facts, that for example if you say 'Socrates is alive', there is corresponding to that proposition in the real world the fact that Socrates is not alive. One has a certain repugnance to negative facts, the same sort of feeling that makes you wish not to have a fact 'p or q' going about the world. You have a feeling that there are only positive facts, and that negative propositions have somehow or other got to be expressions of positive facts. When I was lecturing on this subject at Harvard* I argued that there were negative facts, and it nearly produced a riot: the class would not hear of there being negative facts at all. I am still inclined to think that there are. However, one of the men to whom I was lecturing at Harvard, Mr. Demos, subsequently wrote an article in *Mind* to explain why there are no negative facts. It is in *Mind* for April, 1917. I think he makes

* [In 1914—R.C.M.]

as good a case as can be made for the view that there are no negative facts. It is a difficult question. I really only ask that you should not dogmatize. I do not say positively that there are, but there may be.

There are certain things you can notice about negative propositions. Mr. Demos points out, *first* of all, that a negative proposition is not in any way dependent on a cognitive subject for its definition. To this I agree. Suppose you say, when I say 'Socrates is not alive', I am merely expressing disbelief in the proposition that Socrates is alive. You have got to find something or other in the real world to make this disbelief true, and the only question is what. That is his *first* point.

His *second* is that a negative proposition must not be taken at its face value. You cannot, he says, regard the statement 'Socrates is not alive' as being an expression of a fact in the same sort of direct way in which 'Socrates is human' would be an expression of a fact. His argument for that is solely that he cannot believe that there are negative facts in the world. He maintains that there cannot be in the real world such facts as 'Socrates is not alive', taken, i.e., as simple facts, and that therefore you have got to find some explanation of negative propositions, some interpretation, and that they cannot be just as simple as positive propositions. I shall come back to that point, but on this I do not feel inclined to agree.

His *third* point I do not entirely agree with: that when the word 'not' occurs, it cannot be taken as a qualification of the predicate. For instance, if you say that 'This is not red', you might attempt to say that 'not-red' is a predicate, but that of course won't do; in the first place because a great many propositions are not expressions of predicates; in the second place because the word 'not' applies to the whole proposition. The proper expression would be 'not: this is red'; the 'not' applies to the whole proposition 'this is red', and of course in many cases you can see that quite clearly. If you take a case I took in discussing descriptions: 'The present king of France is not bald', and if you take 'not-bald' as a predicate, that would have to be judged false on the ground that there is not a present king of France. But it is clear that the proposition 'The present king of France is bald' is a false proposition, and therefore the negative of that will have to be a true proposition, and that could not be the case if you take 'not-bald' as a predicate, so that in all cases where a 'not' comes in, the 'not' has to be taken to apply to the whole proposition. 'Not-p' is the proper formula.

We have come now to the question, how are we really to interpret 'not-p', and the suggestion offered by Mr. Demos is that when we assert 'not-p' we are really asserting that there is some proposition q which is true and is incompatible with p ('an opposite of p' is his phrase, but I think the meaning is the same). That is his suggested definition:

> 'not-p' means 'There is a proposition q which is
> true and is incompatible with p.'

As, e.g., if I say 'This chalk is not red', I shall be meaning to assert that there is some proposition, which in this case would be the proposition 'This chalk is white', which is inconsistent with the proposition 'It is red', and that you use these general negative forms because you do not happen to know what the actual proposition is that is true and is incompatible with p. Or, of course, you may possibly know what the actual proposition is, but you may be more interested in the fact that p is false than you are in the particular example which makes it false. As, for instance, you might be anxious to prove that someone is a liar, and you might be very much interested in the falsehood of some proposition which he had asserted. You might also be more interested in the general proposition than in the particular case, so that if someone had asserted that that chalk was red, you might be more interested in the fact that it was not red than in the fact that it was white.

I find it very difficult to believe that theory of falsehood. You will observe that in the first place there is this objection, that it makes incompatibility fundamental and an objective fact, which is not so very much simpler than allowing negative facts. You have got to have here 'That p is incompatible with q' in order to reduce 'not' to incompatibility, because this has got to be the corresponding fact. It is perfectly clear, whatever may be the interpretation of 'not', that there is *some* interpretation which will give you a fact. If I say 'There is not a hippopotamus in this room', it is quite clear there is some way of interpreting that statement according to which there is a corresponding fact, and the fact cannot be merely that every part of this room is filled up with something that is not a hippopotamus. You would come back to the necessity for some kind or other of fact of the sort that we have been trying to avoid. We have been trying to avoid both negative facts and molecular facts, and all that this succeeds in doing is to substitute molecular facts for negative facts, and I do not consider that that is very successful as a means of avoiding paradox, especially when you consider this, that even if incompatibility is to be taken as a sort of fundamental expression of fact, incompatibility is not between facts but between propositions. If I say '*p* is incompatible with *q*', one at least of *p* and *q* has got to be false. It is clear that no two *facts* are incompatible. The incompatibility holds *between the propositions*, between the *p* and the *q*, and therefore if you are going to take incompatibility as a fundamental fact, you have got, in explaining negatives, to take as your fundamental fact something involving propositions as opposed to facts. It is quite clear that propositions are not what you might call 'real'. If you were making an inventory of the world, propositions would not come in. Facts would, beliefs, wishes, wills would, but propositions would not. They do not have being independently, so that this incompatibility of propositions taken as an ultimate fact of the real world will want a great deal of treatment, a lot of dressing up before it will do. Therefore as a simplification to avoid negative facts, I do not think it really is very successful. I think you will find that it is simpler to take negative facts as facts, to assume that 'Socrates is not alive' is really an objective fact in the same sense in which 'Socrates is human' is a fact. This theory of Mr. Demos's that I have been setting forth here is a development of the one one hits upon at once when one tries to get round negative facts, but for the reasons that I have given, I do not think it really answers to take things that way, and I think you will find that it is better to take negative facts as ultimate. Otherwise you will find it so difficult to say what it is that corresponds to a proposition. When, e.g., you have a false positive proposition, say 'Socrates is alive', it is false because of a fact in the real world. A thing cannot be false except because of a fact, so that you find it extremely difficult to say what exactly happens when you make a positive assertion that is false, unless you are going to admit negative facts. I think all those questions are difficult and there are arguments always to be adduced both ways, but on the whole I do incline to believe that there are negative facts and that there are not disjunctive facts. But the denial of disjunctive facts leads to certain difficulties which we shall have to consider in connexion with general propositions in a later lecture.

Discussion

Question: Do you consider that the proposition 'Socrates is dead' is a positive or a negative fact?

Mr. Russell: It is partly a negative fact. To say that a person is dead is complicated. It is two statements rolled into one: 'Socrates was alive' and 'Socrates is not alive'.

Question: Does putting the 'not' into it give it a formal character of negative and vice versa?

Mr. Russell: No, I think you must go into the meaning of words.

Question: I should have thought there was a great difference between saying that 'Socrates is alive' and saying that 'Socrates is not a living man'. I think it is possible to have what one might call a negative existence and that things exist of which we cannot take cognizance. Socrates undoubtedly did live but he is no longer in the condition of living as a man.

Mr. Russell: I was not going into the question of existence after death but simply taking words in their everyday signification.

Question: What is precisely your test as to whether you have got a positive or negative proposition before you?

Mr. Russell: There is no formal test.

Question: If you had a formal test, would it not follow that you would know whether there were negative facts or not?

Mr. Russell: No, I think not. In the perfect logical language that I sketched in theory, it would always be obvious at once whether a proposition was positive or negative. But it would not bear upon how you are going to interpret negative propositions.

Question: Would the existence of negative facts ever be anything more than a mere definition?

Mr. Russell: Yes, I think it would. It seems to me that the business of metaphysics is to describe the world, and it is in my opinion a real definite question whether in a complete description of the world you would have to mention negative facts or not.

Question: How do you define a negative fact?

Mr. Russell: You could not give a general definition if it is right that negativeness is an ultimate.

IV. PROPOSITIONS AND FACTS WITH MORE THAN ONE VERB; BELIEFS, ETC.

You will remember that after speaking about atomic proposi- itons I pointed out two more complicated forms of propositions which arise immediately on proceeding further than that: the *first*, which I call molecular propositions, which I dealt with last time, involving such words as 'or', 'and', 'if', and the *second* in- volving two or more verbs such as believing, wishing, willing, and so forth. In the case of molecular propositions it was not clear that we had to deal with any new form of fact, but only with a new form of proposition, i.e., if you have a disjunctive proposition such as '*p* or *q*' it does not seem very plausible to say there there is in the world a disjunctive fact corresponding to '*p* or *q*' but merely that there is a fact corresponding to *p* and a fact corresponding to *q*, and the disjunctive proposition derives its truth or falsehood from those two separate facts. Therefore in that case one was dealing only with a new form of proposition and not with a new form of fact. To-day we have to deal with a new form of fact.

I think one might describe philosophical logic, the philosophical portion of logic which is the portion that I am concerned with in these lectures since Christmas (1917), as an inventory, or if you like a more humble word, a 'zoo' containing all the different forms that facts may have. I should prefer to say 'forms of facts' rather than 'forms of propositions'. To apply that to the case of molecular propositions which I dealt with last time, if one were pursuing this analysis of the forms of facts, it would be *belief in* a molecular proposition that one would deal with rather than the molecular proposition itself. In accordance with the sort of realistic bias that I should put into all study of metaphysics, I should always wish to be engaged in the investigation of some actual fact or set of facts, and it seems to me that that is so in logic just as much as it is in zoology. In logic you are concerned with the forms of facts, with getting hold of the different sorts of facts, different *logical* sorts of facts, that there are in the world. Now I want to point out to-day that the facts that occur when one believes or wishes or wills have a different logical form from the atomic facts containing a single verb which I dealt with in my second lecture. (There are, of course, a good many forms that facts may have, a strictly infinite number, and I do not wish you to suppose that I pretend to deal with all of them.) Suppose you take any actual occurrence of a belief. I want you to understand that I am not talking about beliefs in the sort of way in which judgment is spoken of in theory of knowledge, in which you would say there is *the* judgment that two and two are four. I am talking of the actual occurrence of a belief in a particular person's mind at a particular moment, and discussing what sort of a fact that is. If I say 'What day of the week is this?' and you say 'Tuesday', there occurs in your mind at that moment the belief that this is Tuesday. The thing I want to deal with to-day is the question. What is the form of the fact which occurs when a person has a belief. Of course you see that the sort of obvious first notion that one would naturally arrive at would be that a belief is a relation to the proposition. 'I believe the proposition *p*'. 'I believe that to-day is Tuesday'. 'I believe that two and two are four'. Something like that. It seems on the face of it as if you had there a relation of the believing subject to a proposition. That view won't do for various reasons which I shall go into. But you have therefore got to have a theory of belief which is not exactly that. Take any sort of proposition, say 'I believe Socrates is mortal'. Suppose that that belief does actually occur. The statement that it occurs is a statement of fact. You have there two verbs. You may have more than two verbs, you may have any number greater than one. I may believe that Jones is of the opinion that Socrates is mortal. There you have more than two verbs. You may have any number, but you cannot have less than two. You will perceive that it is not only the proposition that has the two verbs, but also the fact, which is expressed by the proposition, has two constituents corresponding to verbs. I shall call those constituents verbs for the sake of shortness, as it is very difficult to find any word to describe all those objects which one denotes by verbs. Of course, that is strictly using the word 'verb' in two different senses, but I do not think it can lead to any confusion if you understand that it is being so used. This fact (the belief) is one fact. It is not like what you had in molecular propositions where you had (say) '*p* or *q*'. It is just one single fact that you have a belief. That is obvious from the fact that you can believe a falsehood. It is obvious from the fact of false belief that you cannot cut off one part: you cannot have

I believe/Socrates is mortal.

There are certain questions that arise about such facts, and the first that arises is, Are they undeniable facts or can you reduce them in some way to relations of other facts? Is it really necessary to suppose that there are irreducible facts, of which that sort of thing is a verbal expression? On that question until fairly lately I should certainly not have supposed that any doubt could arise. It had not really seemed to me until fairly lately that that was a debatable point. I still believe that there are facts of that form, but I see that it is a substantial question that needs to be discussed.

1. *Are beliefs, etc., irreducible facts?*

'Etc.' covers understanding a proposition; it covers desiring, willing, any other attitude of that sort that you may think of that involves a proposition. It seems natural to say one believes a proposition and unnatural to say one desires a proposition, but as a matter of fact that is only a prejudice. What you believe and what you desire are of exactly the same nature. You may desire to get some sugar to-morrow and of course you may possibly believe that you will. I am not sure that the logical form is the same in the case of will. I am inclined to think that the case of will is more analogous to that of perception, in going direct to facts, and excluding the possibility of falsehood. In any case desire and belief are of exactly the same form logically.

Pragmatists and some of the American realists, the school whom one calls neutral monists, deny altogether that there is such a phenomenon as belief in the sense I am dealing with. They do not deny it in words, they do not use the same sort of language that I am using, and that makes it difficult to compare their views with the views I am speaking about. One has really to translate what they say into language more or less analogous to ours before one can make out where the points of contact or difference are.

If you take the works of James in his *Essays in Radical Empiricism* or Dewey in his *Essays in Experimental Logic* you will find that they are denying altogether that there is such a phenomenon as belief in the sense I am talking of. They use the word 'believe' but they mean something different. You come to the view called 'behaviourism', according to which you mean, if you say a person believes a thing, that he behaves in a certain fashion; and that hangs together with James's pragmatism. James and Dewey would say: when I believe a proposition, that *means* that I act in a certain fashion, that my behaviour has certain characteristics, and my belief is a true one if the behaviour leads to the desired result and is a false one if it does not. That, if it is true, makes their pragmatism a perfectly rational account of truth and falsehood, if you do accept their view that belief as an isolated phenomenon does not occur. That is therefore the first thing one has to consider. It would take me too far from logic to consider that subject as it deserves to be considered, because it is a subject belonging to psychology, and it is only relevant to logic in this one way that it raises a doubt whether there are any facts having the logical form that I am speaking of. In the question of this logical form that involves two or more verbs you have a curious interlacing of logic with empirical studies, and of course that may occur elsewhere, in this way, that an empirical study gives you an example of a thing having a certain logical form, and you cannot really be sure that there are things having a given logical form except by finding an example, and the finding of an example is itself empirical. Therefore in that way empirical facts are relevant to logic at certain points. I think theoretically one might know that there were those forms without knowing any instance of them, but practically, situated as we are, that does not seem to occur. Practically, unless you can find an example of the form you won't know that there is that form. If I cannot find an example containing two or more verbs, you will not have reason to believe in the theory that such a form occurs.

When you read the works of people like James and Dewey on the subject of belief, one thing that strikes you at once is that the sort of thing they are thinking of as the object of belief is quite different from the sort of thing I am thinking of. They think of it always as a thing. They think you believe in God or Homer: you believe in an object. That is the picture they have in their minds. It is common enough, in common parlance, to talk that way, and they would say, the first crude approximation that they would suggest would be that you believe truly when there is such an object and that you believe falsely when there is not. I do not mean they would say that exactly, but that would be the crude view from which they would start. They do not seem to have grasped the fact that the objective side in belief is better expressed by a proposition than by a single word, and that, I think, has a great deal to do with their whole outlook on the matter of what belief consists of. The object of belief in their view is generally, not relations between things, or things having qualities, or what not, but just single things which may or may not exist. That view seems to me radically and absolutely mistaken. In the *first* place there are a great many judgments you cannot possibly fit into that scheme, and in the *second* place it cannot possibly give any explanation to false beliefs, because when you believe that a thing exists and it does not exist, the thing is not there, it is nothing, and it cannot be the right analysis of a false belief to regard it as a relation to what is really nothing. This is an objection to supposing that belief consists simply in relation to the object. It is obvious that if you say 'I believe in Homer' and there was no such person as Homer, your belief cannot be a relation to Homer, since there is no 'Homer'. Every fact that occurs in the world must be composed entirely of constituents that there are, and not of constituents that there are not. Therefore when you say 'I believe in Homer' it cannot be the right analysis of the thing to put it like that. What the right analysis is I shall come on to in the theory of descriptions. I come back now to the theory of behaviourism which I spoke of a moment ago. Suppose, e.g., that you are said to believe that there is a train at 10.25. This means, we are told, that you start for the station at a certain time. When you reach the station you see it is 10.24 and you run. That behaviour constitutes your belief that there is a train at that time. If you catch your train by running, your belief was true. If the train went at 10.23, you miss it, and your belief was false. That is the sort of thing that they would say constitutes belief. There is not a single state of mind which consists in contemplating this eternal verity, that the train starts at 10.25. They would apply that even to the most abstract things. I do not myself feel that that view of things is tenable. It is a difficult one to refute because it goes very deep and one has the feeling that perhaps, if one thought it out long enough and became sufficiently aware of all its implications, one might find after all that it was a feasible view; but yet I do not *feel* it feasible. It hangs together, of course, with the theory of neutral monism, with the theory that the material constituting the mental is the same as the material constituting the physical, just like the Post Office directory which gives you people arranged geographically and alphabetically. This whole theory hangs together with that. I do not mean necessarily that all the people that profess the one profess the other, but that the two do essentially belong together. If you are going to take that view, you have to explain away belief and desire, because things of that sort do seem to be mental phenomena. They do seem rather far removed from the sort of thing that happens in the physical world. Therefore people will set to work to explain away such things as belief, and reduce them to bodily behaviour; and your belief in a certain proposition will consist in the behaviour of your body. In the crudest terms that is what that view amounts to. It does enable you to get on very well without mind. Truth and falsehood in that case consist in the relation of your bodily behaviour to a certain fact, the sort of distant fact which is the purpose of your behaviour, as it were, and when your behaviour is satisfactory in regard to that fact your belief is true, and when your behaviour is unsatisfactory in regard to that fact your belief is false. The logical essence, in that view, will be a relation between two facts having the same sort of form as a causal relation, i.e., on the one hand there will be your bodily behaviour which is one fact, and on the other hand the fact that the train starts at such and such a time, which is another fact, and out of a relation of those two the whole phenomenon is constituted. The thing you will get will be logically of the same form as you have in cause, where you have 'This fact causes that fact'. It is quite a different logical form from the facts containing two verbs that I am talking of to-day.

I have naturally a bias in favour of the theory of neutral monism because it exemplifies Occam's razor. I always wish to get on in philosophy with the smallest possible apparatus, partly because it diminishes the risk of error, because it is not necessary to deny the entities you do not assert, and therefore you run less risk of error the fewer entities you assume. The other reason—perhaps a somewhat frivolous one—is that every diminution in the number of entities increases the amount of work for mathematical logic to do in building up things that look like the entities you used to assume. Therefore the whole theory of neutral monism is pleasing to me, but I do find so far very great difficulty in believing it. You will find a discussion of the whole question in some articles I wrote in *The Monist*,* especially in July 1914, and in the two previous numbers also. I should really want to rewrite them rather because I think some of the arguments I used against neutral monism are not valid. I place most reliance on the argument about 'emphatic particulars', 'this', 'I', all that class of words, that pick out certain particulars from the universe by their relation to oneself, and I think by the fact that they, or particulars related to them, are present to you at the moment of speaking. 'This', of course, is what I call an 'emphatic particular'. It is simply a proper name for the present object of attention, a proper name, meaning nothing. It is ambiguous, because, of course, the object of attention is always changing from moment to moment and from person to person. I think it is extremely difficult, if you get rid of consciousness altogether, to explain what you mean by such a word as 'this', what it is that makes the absence of impartiality. You would say that in a purely physical world there would be a complete impartiality. All parts of time and all regions of space would seem equally emphatic. But what really happens is that we pick out certain facts, past and future and all that sort of thing; they all radiate out from 'this', and I have not myself seen how one can deal with the notion of 'this' on the basis of neutral monism. I do not lay that down dogmatically, only I do not see how it can be done. I shall assume for the rest of this lecture that there are such facts as beliefs and wishes and so forth. It would take me really the whole of my course to go into the question fully. Thus we come back to more purely logical questions from this excursion into psychology, for which I apologize.

2. *What is the status of* p *in 'I believe* p'?

You cannot say that you believe *facts*, because your beliefs are

*[The three parts of this essay are the fifth paper in this collection.—R.C.M.]

sometimes wrong. You can say that you *perceive* facts, because perceiving is not liable to error. Wherever it is facts alone that are involved, error is impossible. Therefore you cannot say you believe facts. You have to say that you believe propositions. The awkwardness of that is that obviously propositions are nothing. Therefore that cannot be the true account of the matter. When I say 'Obviously propositions are nothing' it is not perhaps quite ✝ obvious. Time was when I thought there were propositions, but it does not seem to me very plausible to say that in addition to facts there are also these curious shadowy things going about such as 'That to-day is Wednesday' when in fact it is Tuesday. I cannot believe they go about the real world. It is more than one can manage to believe, and I do think no person with a vivid sense of reality can imagine it. One of the difficulties of the study of logic is that it is an exceedingly abstract study dealing with the most abstract things imaginable, and yet you cannot pursue it properly unless you have a vivid instinct as to what is real. You must have that instinct rather well developed in logic. I think otherwise you will get into fantastic things. I think Meinong is rather deficient in just that instinct for reality. Meinong maintains that there is such an object as the round square only it does not exist, and it does not even subsist, but nevertheless there is such an object, and when you say 'The round square is a fiction', he takes it that there is an object 'the round square' and there is a predicate 'fiction'. No one with a sense of reality would so analyse that proposition. He would see that the proposition wants analysing in such a way that you won't have to regard the round square as a constituent of that proposition. To suppose that in the actual world of nature there is a whole set of false propositions going about is to my mind monstrous. I cannot bring myself to suppose it. I cannot believe that they are there in the sense in which facts are there. There seems to me something about the fact that 'To-day is Tuesday' on a different level of reality from the supposition 'That to-day is Wednesday'. When I speak of the proposition 'That to-day is Wednesday' I do not mean the occurrence in future of a state of mind in which you think it is Wednesday, but I am talking about the theory that there is something quite logical, something not involving mind in any way; and such a thing as that I do not think you can take a false proposition to be. I think a false proposition must, wherever it occurs, be subject to analyses, be taken to pieces, pulled to bits, and shown to be simply separate pieces of one fact in which the false proposition has been analysed away. I say that simply on the ground of what I should call an instinct of reality. I ought to say a word or two about 'reality'. It is a vague word, and most of its uses are improper. When I talk about reality as I am now doing, I can explain best what I mean by saying that I mean everything you would have to mention in a complete description of the world; that will convey to you what I mean. Now I do *not* think that false propositions would have to be mentioned in a complete description of the world. False beliefs would, of course, false suppositions would, and desires for what does not come to pass, but not false propositions all alone, and therefore when you, as one says, believe a false proposition, that cannot be an accurate account of what occurs. It is not accurate to say 'I believe the proposition p' and regard the occurrence as a twofold relation between me and p. The logical form is just the same whether you believe a false or a true proposition. Therefore in all cases you are not to regard belief as a two-term relation between yourself and a proposition, and you have to analyse up the proposition and treat your belief differently. Therefore the belief does not really contain a proposition as a constituent but only contains the constituents of the proposition as constituents. You cannot say when you believe, 'What is it that you believe?' There is no answer to that question, i.e., there is not a single thing that you are believing. 'I believe that to-day is Tuesday.' You must not suppose that 'That to-day is Tuesday' is a single object which I am believing. That would be an error. That is not the right way to analyse the occurrence, although that analysis is linguistically convenient, and one may keep it provided one knows that it is not the truth.

3. *How shall we describe the logical form of a belief?*

I want to try to get an account of the way that a belief is made up. That is not an easy question at all. You cannot make what I should call a map-in-space of a belief. You can make a map of an atomic fact but not of a belief, for the simple reason that space-relations always are of the atomic sort or complications of the atomic sort. I will try to illustrate what I mean. The point is in connexion with there being two verbs in the judgment and with the fact that both verbs have got to occur as verbs, because if a thing is a verb it cannot occur otherwise than as a verb. Suppose I take '*A* believes that *B* loves *C*'. 'Othello believes that Desdemona loves Cassio.' There you have a false belief. You have this odd state of affairs that the verb 'loves' occurs in that proposition and seems to occur as relating Desdemona to Cassio whereas in fact it does not do so, but yet it does occur as a verb, it does occur in the sort of way that a verb should do. I mean that when *A* believes that *B* loves *C*, you have to have a verb in the place where 'loves' occurs. You cannot put a substantive in its place. Therefore it is clear that the subordinate verb (i.e., the verb other than believing) is functioning as a verb, and seems to be relating two terms, but as a matter of fact does not when a judgment happens to be false. That is what constitutes the puzzle about the nature of belief. You will notice that wherever one gets to really close quarters with the theory of error one has the puzzle of how to deal with error without assuming the existence of the non-existent. I mean that every theory of error sooner or later wrecks itself by assuming the existence of the non-existent. As when I say 'Desdemona loves Cassio', it seems as if you have a non-existent love between Desdemona and Cassio, but that is just as wrong as a non-existent unicorn. So you have to explain the whole theory of judgment in some other way. I come now to this question of a map. Suppose you try such a map as this:

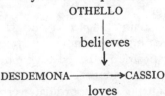

This question of making a map is not so strange as you might suppose because it is part of the whole theory of symbolism. It is important to realize where and how a symbolism of that sort would be wrong: where and how it is wrong is that in the symbol you have this relationship relating these two things and in the fact it doesn't really relate them. You cannot get in space any occurrence which is logically of the same form as belief. When I say 'logically of the same form' I mean that one can be obtained from the other by replacing the constituents of the one by the new terms. If I say 'Desdemona loves Cassio' that is of the same form as '*A* is to the right of *B*'. Those are of the same form, and I say that nothing that occurs in space is of the same form as belief. I have got on here to a new sort of thing, a new beast for our zoo, not another member of our former species but a new species. The discovery of this fact is due to Mr. Wittgenstein.

There is a great deal that is odd about belief from a logical point of view. One of the things that are odd is that you can believe propositions of all sorts of forms. I can believe that 'This is white' and that 'Two and two are four'. They are quite different forms, yet one can believe both. The actual occurrence can hardly be of exactly the same logical form in those two cases because of the great difference in the forms of the propositions believed. Therefore it would seem that belief cannot strictly be logically one in all different cases but must be distinguished according to the nature of the proposition that you believe. If you have 'I believe p' and 'I believe q' those two facts, if p and q are not of the same logical form, are not of the same logical form in the sense I was speaking of a moment ago, that is in the sense that from 'I believe p' you can derive 'I believe q' by replacing the constituents of one by the constituents of the other. [That means that belief itself cannot be treated as being a proper sort of single term. Belief will really have to have different logical forms according to the nature of what is believed. So that the apparent sameness of believing in different cases is more or less illusory.]

There are really two main things that one wants to notice in this matter that I am treating of just now. The *first* is the impossibility of treating the proposition believed as an independent entity, entering as a unit into the occurrence of the belief, and the *other* is the impossibility of putting the subordinate verb on a level with its terms as an object term in the belief. That is a point in which I think that the theory of judgment which I set forth once in print some years ago was a little unduly simple, because I did then treat the object verb as if one could put it as just an object like the terms, as if one could put 'loves' on a level with Desdemona and Cassio as a term for the relation 'believe'. That is why I have been laying such an emphasis in this lecture to-day on the fact that there are two verbs at least. I hope you will forgive the fact that so much of what I say to-day is tentative and consists of pointing out difficulties. The subject is not very easy and it has not been much dealt with or discussed. Practically nobody has until quite lately begun to consider the problem of the nature of belief with anything like a proper logical apparatus and therefore one has very little to help one in any discussion and so one has to be content on many points at present with pointing out difficulties rather than laying down quite clear solutions.

4. *The question of nomenclature.*

What sort of name shall we give to verbs like 'believe' and 'wish' and so forth? I should be inclined to call them 'propositional verbs'. This is merely a suggested name for convenience, because they are verbs which have the *form* of relating an object to a proposition. As I have been explaining, that is not what they really do, but it is convenient to call them propositional verbs. Of course you might call them 'attitudes', but I should not like that because it is a psychological term, and although all the instances in our experience are psychological, there is no reason to suppose that all the verbs I am talking of are psychological. There is never any reason to suppose that sort of thing. One should always remember Spinoza's infinite attributes of Deity. It is quite likely that there are in the world the analogues of his infinite attributes. We have no acquaintance with them, but there is no reason to suppose that the mental and the physical exhaust the whole universe, so one can never say that all the instances of any logical sort of thing are of such and such a nature which is not a logical nature: you do not know enough about the world for that. Therefore I should not suggest that all the verbs that have the form exemplified by believing and willing are psychological. I can only say all I know are.

I notice that in my syllabus I said I was going to deal with truth and falsehood to-day, but there is not much to say about them specifically as they are coming in all the time. The thing one first thinks of as true or false is a proposition, and a proposition is nothing. But a belief is true or false in the same way as a proposition is, so that you do have facts in the world that are true or false. I said a while back that there was no distinction of true and false among facts, but as regards that special class of facts that we call 'beliefs', there is, in that sense that a belief which occurs may be true or false, though it is equally a fact in either case. One *might* call wishes false in the same sense when one wishes something that does not happen. The truth or falsehood depends upon the proposition that enters in. I am inclined to think that perception, as opposed to belief, does go straight to the fact and not through the proposition. When you perceive the fact you do not, of course, have error coming in, because the moment it is a fact that is your object error is excluded. I think that verification in the last resort would always reduce itself to the perception of facts. Therefore the logical form of perception will be different from the logical form of believing, just because of that circumstance that it is a *fact* that comes in. That raises also a number of logical difficulties which I do not propose to go into, but I think you can see for yourself that perceiving would also involve two verbs just as believing does. I am inclined to think that volition differs from desire logically, in a way strictly analogous to that in which perception differs from belief. But it would take us too far from logic to discuss this view.

V. GENERAL PROPOSITIONS AND EXISTENCE

I am going to speak to-day about general propositions and existence. The two subjects really belong together; they are the same topic, although it might not have seemed so at the first glance. The propositions and facts that I have been talking about hitherto have all been such as involved only perfectly definite particulars, or relations, or qualities, or things of that sort, never involved the sort of indefinite things one alludes to by such words as 'all', 'some', 'a', 'any', and it is propositions and facts of that sort that I am coming on to to-day.

Really all the propositions of the sort that I mean to talk of to-day collect themselves into two groups—the *first* that are about 'all', and the *second* that are about 'some'. These two sorts belong together; they are each other's negations. If you say, for instance, 'All men are mortal', that is the negative of 'Some men are not mortal'. In regard to general propositions, the distinction of affirmative and negative is arbitrary. Whether you are going to regard the propositions about 'all' as the affirmative ones and the propositions about 'some' as the negative ones, or vice versa, is purely a matter of taste. For example, if I say 'I met no one as I came along', that, on the face of it, you would think is a negative proposition. Of course, that is really a proposition about 'all', i.e., 'All men are among those whom I did not meet'. If, on the other hand, I say 'I met a man as I came along', that would strike you as affirmative, whereas it is the negative of 'All men are among those I did not meet as I came along'. If you consider such propositions as 'All men are mortal' and 'Some men are not mortal', you might say it was more natural to take the general propositions as the affirmative and the existence-propositions as the negative, but, simply because it is quite arbitrary which one is to choose, it is better to forget these words and to speak only of general propositions and pro-positions asserting existence. All general propositions deny the existence of something or other. If you say 'All men are mortal', that denies the existence of an immortal man, and so on.

I want to say emphatically that general propositions are to be interpreted as not involving existence. When I say, for instance, 'All Greeks are men', I do not want you to suppose that that im-plies that there are Greeks. It is to be considered emphatically as not implying that. That would have to be added as a separate pro-position. If you want to interpret it in that sense, you will have to add the further statement 'and there are Greeks'. That is for pur-poses of practical convenience. If you include the fact that there are Greeks, you are rolling two propositions into one, and it causes unnecessary confusion in your logic, because the sorts of pro-positions that you want are those that do assert the existence of something and general propositions which do not assert existence. If it happened that there were no Greeks, both the proposition that 'All Greeks are men' and the proposition that 'No Greeks are men' would be true. The proposition 'No Greeks are men' is, of course, the proposition 'All Greeks are not-men'. Both propositions will be true simultaneously if it happens that there are no Greeks. All statements about all the members of a class that has no mem-bers are true, because the contradictory of any general statement does assert existence and is therefore false in this case. This notion, of course, of general propositions not involving existence is one which is not in the traditional doctrine of the syllogism. In the traditional doctrine of the syllogism, it was assumed that when you have such a statement as 'All Greeks are men', that implies that there are Greeks, and this produced fallacies. For instance, 'All chimeras are animals, and all chimeras breathe flame, therefore some animals breathe flame.' This is a syllogism in Darapti, but that mood of the syllogism is fallacious, as this instance shows. That was a point, by the way, which had a certain historical interest, because it impeded Leibniz in his attempts to construct a mathematical logic. He was always engaged in trying to construct such a mathematical logic as we have now, or rather such a one as Boole constructed, and he was always failing because of his respect for Aristotle. Whenever he invented a really good system, as he did several times, it always brought out that such moods as Darapti are fallacious. If you say 'All A is B and all A is C, therefore some B is C'—if you say this you incur a fallacy, but he could not bring himself to believe that it was fallacious, so he began again. That shows you that you should not have too much respect for distinguished men.*

Now when you come to ask what really is asserted in a general proposition, such as 'All Greeks are men' for instance, you find that what is asserted is the truth of all values of what I call a propositional function. A *propositional function* is simply *any expression containing an undetermined constituent, or several undetermined constituents, and becoming a proposition as soon as the undetermined constituents are determined.* If I say 'x is a man' or 'n is a number', that is a propositional function; so is any formula of algebra, say $(x+y)(x-y)=x^2-y^2$. A propositional function is nothing, but, like most of the things one wants to talk about in logic, it does not lose its importance through that fact. The only thing really that you can do with a propositional function is to assert either that it is always true, or that it is sometimes true, or that it is never true. If you take:

'If x is a man, x is mortal',

that is always true (just as much when x is not a man as when x is a man); if you take:

'x is a man',

that is sometimes true; if you take:

'x is a unicorn',

that is never true.

* Cf. Couturat, *La logique de Leibniz*.

One may call a propositional function

> *necessary*, when it is always true;
> *possible*, when it is sometimes true;
> *impossible*, when it is never true.

Much false philosophy has arisen out of confusing propositional functions and propositions. There is a great deal in ordinary traditional philosophy which consists simply in attributing to propositions the predicates which only apply to propositional functions, and, still worse, sometimes in attributing to individuals predicates which merely apply to propositional functions. This case of *necessary, possible, impossible*, is a case in point. In all traditional philosophy there comes a heading of 'modality', which discusses *necessary, possible*, and *impossible* as properties of propositions, whereas in fact they are properties of propositional functions. Propositions are only true or false.

If you take '*x* is *x*', that is a propositional function which is true whatever '*x*' may be, i.e., a necessary propositional function. If you take '*x* is a man', that is a possible one. If you take '*x* is a unicorn', that is an impossible one.

Propositions can only be true or false, but propositional functions have these three possibilities. It is important, I think, to realize that the whole doctrine of modality only applies to propositional functions, not to propositions.

Propositional functions are involved in ordinary language in a great many cases where one does not usually realize them. In such a statement as 'I met a man', you can understand my statement perfectly well without knowing whom I met, and the actual person is not a constituent of the proposition. You are really asserting there that a certain propositional function is sometimes true, namely the propositional function 'I met *x* and *x* is human'. There is at least one value of *x* for which that is true, and that therefore is a possible propositional function. Whenever you get such words as 'a', 'some', 'all', 'every', it is always a mark of the presence of a propositional function, so that these things are not, so to speak, remote or recondite: they are obvious and familiar.

A propositional function comes in again in such a statement as 'Socrates is mortal', because 'to be mortal' means 'to die at some time or other'. You mean there is a time at which Socrates dies, and that again involves a propositional function, namely, that 't is a time, and Socrates dies at t' is possible. If you say 'Socrates is immortal', that also will involve a propositional function. That means that 'If t is any time whatever, Socrates is alive at time t', if we take immortality as involving existence throughout the whole of the past as well as throughout the whole of the future. But if we take immortality as only involving existence throughout the whole of the future, the interpretation of 'Socrates is immortal' becomes more complete, viz., 'There is a time t, such that if t' is any time later than t, Socrates is alive at t'.' Thus when you come to write out properly what one means by a great many ordinary statements, it turns out a little complicated. 'Socrates is mortal' and 'Socrates is immortal' are not each other's contradictories, because they both imply that Socrates exists in time, otherwise he would not be either mortal or immortal. One says, 'There is a time at which he dies', and the other says, 'Whatever time you take, he is alive at that time', whereas the contradictory of 'Socrates is mortal' would be true if there is not a time at which he lives.

An undetermined constituent in a propositional function is called a *variable*.

Existence. When you take any propositional function and assert of it that it is possible, that it is sometimes true, that gives you the fundamental meaning of 'existence'. You may express it by saying that there is at least one value of x for which that propositional function is true. Take 'x is a man', there is at least one value of x for which this is true. That is what one means by saying that 'There are men', or that 'Men exist'. Existence is essentially a property of a propositional function. It means that that propositional function is true in at least one instance. If you say 'There are unicorns', that will mean that 'There is an x, such that x is a unicorn'. That is written in phrasing which is unduly approximated to ordinary language, but the proper way to put it would be '(x is a unicorn) is possible'. We have got to have some idea that we do not define, and one takes the idea of 'always true', or of 'sometimes true', as one's undefined idea in this matter, and then you can define the other one as the negative of that. In some ways it is better to take them both as undefined, for reasons which I shall not go into at present. It will be out of this notion of *sometimes*, which is the same as the notion of *possible*, that we get the notion of existence. To say that unicorns exist is simply to say that '(x is a unicorn) is possible'.

It is perfectly clear that when you say 'Unicorns exist', you are not saying anything that would apply to any unicorns there might happen to be, because as a matter of fact there are not any, and therefore if what you say had any application to the actual individuals, it could not possibly be significant unless it were true. You can consider the proposition 'Unicorns exist' and can see that it is false. It is not nonsense. Of course, if the proposition went through the general conception of the unicorn to the individual, it could not be even significant unless there were unicorns. Therefore when you say 'Unicorns exist', you are not saying anything about any individual things, and the same applies when you say 'Men exist'. If you say that 'Men exist, and Socrates is a man, therefore Socrates exists', that is exactly the same sort of fallacy as it would be if you said 'Men are numerous, Socrates is a man, therefore Socrates is numerous', because existence is a predicate of a propositional function, or derivatively of a class. When you say of a propositional function that it is numerous, you will mean that there are several values of x that will satisfy it, that there are more than one; or, if you like to take 'numerous' in a larger sense, more than ten, more than twenty, or whatever number you think fitting. If x, y, and z all satisfy a propositional function, you may say that that proposition is numerous, but x, y, and z severally are not numerous. Exactly the same applies to existence, that is to say that the actual things that there are in the world do not exist, or, at least, that is putting it too strongly, because that is utter nonsense. To say that they do not exist is strictly nonsense, but to say that they do exist is also strictly nonsense.

It is of propositional functions that you can assert or deny existence. You must not run away with the idea that this entails consequences that it does not entail. If I say 'The things that there are in the world exist', that is a perfectly correct statement, because I am there saying something about a certain class of things; I say it in the same sense in which I say 'Men exist'. But I must not go on to 'This is a thing in the world, and therefore this exists'. It is there the fallacy comes in, and it is simply, as you see, a fallacy of transferring to the individual that satisfies a propositional function a predicate which only applies to a propositional function.

You can see this in various ways. For instance, you sometimes know the truth of an existence-proposition without knowing any instance of it. You know that there are people in Timbuctoo, but I doubt if any of you could give me an instance of one. Therefore you clearly can know existence-propositions without knowing any individual that makes them true. Existence-propositions do not say anything about the actual individual but only about the class or function.

It is exceedingly difficult to make this point clear as long as one adheres to ordinary language, because ordinary language is rooted in a certain feeling about logic, a certain feeling that our primeval ancestors had, and as long as you keep to ordinary language you find it very difficult to get away from the bias which is imposed upon you by language. When I say, e.g., 'There is a x such that x is a man', that is not the sort of phrase one would like to use. 'There is an x' is meaningless. What is 'an x' anyhow? There is not such a thing. The only way you can really state it correctly is by inventing a new language *ad hoc*, and making the statement apply straight off to 'x is a man', as when one says '(x is a man) is possible', or invent a special symbol for the statement that 'x is a man' is sometimes true.

I have dwelt on this point because it really is of very fundamental importance. I shall come back to existence in my next lecture: existence as it applies to descriptions, which is a slightly more complicated case than I am discussing here. I think an almost unbelievable amount of false philosophy has arisen through not realizing what 'existence' means.

As I was saying a moment ago, a propositional function in itself is nothing: it is merely a schema. Therefore in the inventory of the world, which is what I am trying to get at, one comes to the question: What is there really in the world that corresponds with these things? Of course, it is clear that we have general *propositions*, in the same sense in which we have atomic propositions. For the moment I will include existence-propositions with general propositions. We have such propositions as 'All men are mortal' and 'Some men are Greeks'. But you have not only such *propositions*; you have also such *facts*, and that, of course, is where you get back to the inventory of the world: that, in addition to particular facts, which I have been talking about in previous lectures, there are also general facts and existence-facts, that is to say, there are not merely *propositions* of that sort but also *facts* of that sort. That is rather an important point to realize. You cannot ever arrive at a general fact by inference from particular facts, however numerous. The old plan of complete induction, which used to occur in books, which was always supposed to be quite safe and easy as opposed to ordinary induction, that plan of complete induction, unless it is accompanied by at least one general proposition, will not yield you the result that you want. Suppose, for example, that you wish to prove in that way that 'All men are mortal', you are supposed to proceed by complete induction, and say 'A is a man that is mortal', 'B is a man that is mortal', 'C is a man that is mortal', and so on until you finish. You will not be able, in that way, to arrive at the proposition 'All men are mortal' unless you know when you have finished. That is to say that, in order to arrive by this road at the general proposition 'All men are mortal', you must already have the general proposition 'All men are among those I have enumerated'. You never can arrive at a general proposition by inference from particular propositions alone. You will always have to have at least one general proposition in your premises. That illustrates, I think, various points. One, which is epistemological, is that if there is, as there seems to be, knowledge of general propositions, then there must be *primitive* knowledge of general propositions (I mean by that, knowledge of general propositions which is not obtained by inference), because if you can never infer a general proposition except from premises of which one at least is general, it is clear that you can never have knowledge of such propositions by inference unless there is knowledge of some general propositions which is not by inference. I think that the sort of way such knowledge—or rather the belief that we have such knowledge—comes into ordinary life is probably very odd. I mean to say that we do habitually assume general propositions which are exceedingly doubtful; as, for instance, one might, if one were counting up the people in this room, assume that one could see all of them, which is a general proposition, and very doubtful as there may be people under the tables. But, apart from that sort of thing, you do have in any empirical verification of general propositions some kind of assumption that amounts to this, that what you do not see is not there. Of course, you would not put it so strongly as that, but you would assume that, with certain limitations and certain qualifications, if a thing does not appear to your senses, it is not there. That is a general proposition, and it is only through such propositions that you arrive at the ordinary empirical results that one obtains in ordinary ways. If you take a census of the country, for instance, you assume that the people you do not see are not there, provided you search properly and carefully, otherwise your census might be wrong. It is some assumption of that sort which would underlie what seems purely empirical. You could not prove empirically that what you do not perceive is not there, because an empirical proof would consist in perceiving, and by hypothesis you do not perceive it, so that any proposition of that sort, if it is accepted, has to be accepted on its own evidence. I only take that as an illustration. There are many other illustrations one could take of the sort of propositions that are commonly assumed, many of them with very little justification.

I come now to a question which concerns logic more nearly, namely, the reasons for supposing that there are general facts as well as general propositions. When we were discussing molecular propositions I threw doubt upon the supposition that there are molecular facts, but I do not think one can doubt that there are general facts. It is perfectly clear, I think, that when you have enumerated all the atomic facts in the world, it is a further fact about the world that those are all the atomic facts there are about the world, and that is just as much an objective fact about the world as any of them are. It is clear, I think, that you must admit general facts as distinct from and over and above particular facts. The same thing applies to 'All men are mortal'. When you have taken all the particular men that there are, and found each one of them severally to be mortal, it is definitely a new fact that all men are mortal; how new a fact, appears from what I said a moment ago, that it could not be inferred from the mortality of the several men that there are in the world. Of course, it is not so difficult to admit what I might call existence-facts—such facts as 'There are men', 'There are sheep', and so on. Those, I think, you will readily admit as separate and distinct facts over and above the atomic facts I spoke of before. Those facts have got to come into the inventory of the world, and in that way propositional functions come in as involved in the study of general facts. I do not profess to know what the right analysis of general facts is. It is an exceedingly difficult question, and one which I should very much like to see studied. I am sure that, although the convenient technical treatment is by means of propositional functions, that is not the whole of the right analysis. Beyond that I cannot go.

There is one point about whether there are molecular facts. I think I mentioned, when I was saying that I did not think there were disjunctive facts, that a certain difficulty does arise in regard to general facts. Take 'All men are mortal'. That means:

> ' "x is a man" implies
> "x is a mortal" whatever
> x may be.'

You can see at once that it is a hypothetical proposition. It does not imply that there are any men, nor who are men, and who are not; it simply says that if you have anything which is a man, that thing is mortal. As Mr. Bradley has pointed out in the second chapter of his *Principles of Logic*, 'Trespassers will be prosecuted' may be true even if no one trespasses, since it means merely that, *if* any one trespasses, he will be prosecuted. It comes down to this that

> ' "x is a man" implies "x is a mortal" is always true',

is a fact. It is perhaps a little difficult to see how that can be true if one is going to say that ' "Socrates is a man" implies "Socrates is a mortal" ' is not itself a fact, which is what I suggested when I was discussing disjunctive facts. I do not feel sure that you could not get round that difficulty. I only suggest it as a point which should be considered when one is denying that there are molecular facts, since, if it cannot be got round, we shall have to admit molecular facts.

Now I want to come to the subject of *completely general* propositions and propositional functions. By those I mean propositions and propositional functions that contain only variables and nothing else at all. This covers the whole of logic. Every logical proposition consists wholly and solely of variables, though it is not true that every proposition consisting wholly and solely of variables is logical. You can consider stages of generalizations as, e.g.,

'Socrates loves Plato'
'x loves Plato'
'x loves y'
'$x\,R\,y$.'

There you have been going through a process of successive generalization. When you have got to xRy, you have got a schema consisting only of variables, containing no constants at all, the pure schema of dual relations, and it is clear that any proposition which expresses a dual relation can be derived from $x\!Ry$ by assigning values to x and R and y. So that that is, as you might say, the pure form of all those propositions. I mean by the form of a proposition that which you get when for every single one of its constituents you substitute a variable. If you want a different definition of the form of a proposition, you might be inclined to define it as the class of all those propositions that you can obtain from a given one by substituting other constituents for one or more of the constituents the proposition contains. E.g., in 'Socrates loves Plato', you can substitute somebody else for Socrates, somebody else for Plato, and some other verb for 'loves'. In that way there are a certain number of propositions which you can derive from the proposition 'Socrates loves Plato', by replacing the constituents of that proposition by other constituents, so that you have there a certain class of propositions, and those propositions all have a certain form, and one can, if one likes, say that the form they all have is the class consisting of all of them. That is rather a provisional definition, because as a matter of fact, the idea of form is more fundamental than the idea of class. I should not suggest that as a really good definition, but it will do provisionally to explain the sort of thing one means by the form of a proposition. The form of a proposition is that which is in common between any two propositions of which the one can be obtained from the other by substituting other constituents for the original ones. When you have got down to those formulas that contain only variables, like xRy, you are on the way to the sort of thing that you can assert in logic.

To give an illustration, you know what I mean by the domain of a relation: I mean all the terms that have that relation to something. Suppose I say: 'xRy implies that x belongs to the domain of R', that would be a proposition of logic and is one that contains only variables. You might think it contains such words as 'belong' and 'domain', but that is an error. It is only the habit of using ordinary language that makes those words appear. They are not really there. That is a proposition of pure logic. It does not mention any particular thing at all. This is to be understood as being asserted whatever x and R and y may be. All the statements of logic are of that sort.

It is not a very easy thing to see what are the constituents of a logical proposition. When one takes 'Socrates loves Plato', 'Socrates' is a constituent, 'loves' is a constituent, and 'Plato' is a constituent. Then you turn 'Socrates' into x, 'loves' into R, and 'Plato' into y. x and R and y are nothing, and they are not constituents, so it seems as though all the propositions of logic were entirely devoid of constituents. I do not think that can quite be true. But then the only other thing you can seem to say is that the *form* is a constituent, that propositions of a certain form are always true: that *may* be the right analysis, though I very much doubt whether it is.

There is, however, just this to observe, viz., that the form of a proposition is never a constituent of that proposition itself. If you assert that 'Socrates loves Plato', the form of that proposition is the form of the dual relation, but this is not a constituent of the proposition. If it were you would have to have that constituent related to the other constituents. You will make the form much too substantial if you think of it as really one of the things that have that form, so that the form of a proposition is certainly not a constituent of the proposition itself. Nevertheless it may possibly be a constituent of general statements about propositions that have that form, so I think it is *possible that* logical propositions might be interpreted as being about forms.

I can only say, in conclusion, as regards the constituents of logical propositions, that it is a problem which is rather new. There has not been much opportunity to consider it. I do not think any literature exists at all which deals with it in any way whatever, and it is an interesting problem.

I just want now to give you a few illustrations of propositions which can be expressed in the language of pure variables but are not propositions of logic. Among the propositions that are propositions of logic are included all the propositions of pure mathematics, all of which cannot only be expressed in logical terms but can also be deduced from the premises of logic, and therefore they are logical propositions. Apart from them there are many that can be expressed in logical terms, but cannot be proved from logic, and are certainly not propositions that form part of logic. Suppose you take such a proposition as: 'There is at least one thing in the world'. That is a proposition that you can express in logical terms. It will mean, if you like, that the propositional function '$x = x$' is a possible one. That is a proposition, therefore, that you can express in logical terms; but you cannot know from logic whether it is true or false. So far as you do know it, you know it empirically, because there might happen not to be a universe, and then it would not be true. It is merely an accident, so to speak, that there is a universe. The proposition that there are exactly 30,000 things in the world can also be expressed in purely logical terms, and is certainly not a proposition of logic but an empirical proposition (true or false), because a world containing more than 30,000 things and a world containing fewer than 30,000 things are both possible, so that if it happens that there are exactly 30,000 things, that is what one might call an accident and is not a proposition of logic. There are again two propositions that one is used to in mathematical logic, namely, the multiplicative axiom and the axiom of infinity. These also can be expressed in logical terms, but cannot be proved or disproved by logic. In regard to the axiom of infinity, the impossibility of logical proof or disproof may be taken as certain, but in the case of the multiplicative axiom, it is perhaps still open to some degree to doubt. Everything that is a proposition of logic has got to be in some sense or other like a tautology. It has got to be something that has some peculiar quality, which I do not know how to define, that belongs to logical propositions and not to others. Examples of typical logical propositions are:

'If p implies q and q implies r, then p implies r.'
'If all a's are b's and all b's are c's, then all a's are c's.'
'If all a's are b's, and x is an a, then x is a b.'

Those are propositions of logic. They have a certain peculiar quality which marks them out from other propositions and enables us to know them *a priori*. But what exactly that characteristic is, I am not able to tell you. Although it is a necessary characteristic of logical propositions that they should consist solely of variables, i.e., that they should assert the universal truth, or the sometimes-truth, of a propositional function consisting wholly of variables—although that is a necessary characteristic, it is not a sufficient one. I am sorry that I have had to leave so many problems unsolved. I always have to make this apology, but the world really is rather puzzling and I cannot help it.

Discussion

Question: Is there any word you would substitute for 'existence' which would give existence to individuals? Are you applying the word 'existence' to two ideas, or do you deny that there are two ideas?

Mr. Russell: No, there is not an idea that will apply to individuals. As regards the actual things there are in the world, there is nothing at all you can say about them that in any way corresponds to this notion of existence. It is a sheer mistake to say that there is anything analogous to existence that you can say about them. You get into confusion through language, because it is a perfectly correct thing to say 'All the things in the world exist', and it is so easy to pass from this to 'This exists because it is a thing in the world'. There is no sort of point in a predicate which could not conceivably be false. I mean, it is perfectly clear that, if there were such a thing as this existence of individuals that we talk of, it would be absolutely impossible for it not to apply, and that is the characteristic of a mistake.

VI. DESCRIPTIONS AND INCOMPLETE SYMBOLS

I am proposing to deal this time with the subject of descriptions, and what I call 'incomplete symbols', and the existence of described individuals. You will remember that last time I dealt with the existence of *kinds* of things, what you mean by saying 'There are men' or 'There are Greeks' or phrases of that sort, where you have an existence which may be plural. I am going to deal to-day with an existence which is asserted to be singular, such as 'The man with the iron mask existed' or some phrase of that sort, where you have some object described by the phrase 'The so-and-so' in the singular, and I want to discuss the analysis of propositions in which phrases of that kind occur.

There are, of course, a great many propositions very familiar in metaphysics which are of that sort: 'I exist' or 'God exists' or 'Homer existed', and other such statements are always occurring in metaphysical discussions, and are, I think, treated in ordinary metaphysics in a way which embodies a simple logical mistake that we shall be concerned with to-day, the same sort of mistake that I spoke of last week in connexion with the existence of kinds of things. One way of examining a proposition of that sort is to ask yourself what would happen if it were false. If you take such a proposition as 'Romulus existed', probably most of us think that Romulus did not exist. It is obviously a perfectly significant statement, whether true or false, to say that Romulus existed. If Romulus himself entered into our statement, it would be plain that the statement that he did not exist would be nonsense, because you cannot have a constituent of a proposition which is nothing at all. Every constituent has got to be there as one of the things in the world, and therefore if Romulus himself entered into the propositions that he existed or that he did not exist, both these propositions could not only not be true, but could not be even significant, unless he existed. That is obviously not the case, and the first conclusion one draws is that, although it *looks* as if Romulus were a constituent of that proposition, that is really a mistake. Romulus does not occur in the proposition 'Romulus did not exist'.

Suppose you try to make out what you do mean by that proposition. You can take, say, all the things that Livy has to say about Romulus, all the properties he ascribes to him, including the only one probably that most of us remember, namely, the fact that he was called 'Romulus'. You can put all this together, and make a propositional function saying 'x has such-and-such properties', the properties being those you find enumerated in Livy. There you have a propositional function, and when you say that Romulus did not exist you are simply saying that that propositional function is never true, that it is impossible in the sense I was explaining last time, i.e., that there is no value of x that makes it true. That reduces the non-existence of Romulus to the sort of non-existence I spoke of last time, where we had the non-existence of unicorns. But it is not a *complete* account of this kind of existence or non-existence, because there is one other way in which a described individual can fail to exist, and that is where the description applies to more than one person. You cannot, e.g., speak of 'The inhabitant of London', not because there are none, but because there are so many.

You see, therefore, that this proposition 'Romulus existed' or 'Romulus did not exist' does introduce a propositional function, because the name 'Romulus' is not really a name but a sort of truncated description. It stands for a person who did such-and-such things, who killed Remus, and founded Rome, and so on. It is short for that description; if you like, it is short for 'the person who was called "Romulus".' If it were really a name, the question of existence could not arise, because a name has got to name something or it is not a name, and if there is no such person as Romulus there cannot be a name for that person who is not there, so that this single word 'Romulus' is really a sort of truncated or telescoped description, and if you think of it as a name you will get into logical errors. When you realize that it is a description, you realize therefore that any proposition about Romulus really introduces the propositional function embodying the description, as (say) 'x was called "Romulus".' That introduces you at once to a propositional function, and when you say 'Romulus did not exist', you mean that this propositional function is not true for one value of x.

There are two sorts of descriptions, what one may call 'ambiguous descriptions', when we speak of 'a so-and-so', and what one may call 'definite descriptions', when we speak of 'the so-and-so' (in the singular). Instances are:

Ambiguous: A man, a dog, a pig, a Cabinet Minister.
Definite: The man with the iron mask.
　　　　　The last person who came into this room.
　　　　　The only Englishman who ever occupied the Papal See.
　　　　　The number of the inhabitants of London.
　　　　　The sum of 43 and 34.

(It is not necessary for a description that it should describe an individual: it may describe a predicate or a relation or anything else.)

It is phrases of that sort, definite descriptions, that I want to talk about to-day. I do not want to talk about ambiguous descriptions, as what there was to say about them was said last time.

I want you to realize that the question whether a phrase is a definite description turns only upon its form, not upon the question whether there is a definite individual so described. For instance, I should call 'The inhabitant of London' a definite description, although it does not in fact describe any definite individual.

The first thing to realize about a definite description is that it is not a name. We will take 'The author of *Waverley*'. That is a definite description, and it is easy to see that it is not a name. A name is a simple symbol (i.e., a symbol which does not have any parts that are symbols), a simple symbol used to designate a certain particular or by extension an object which is not a particular but is treated for the moment as if it were, or is falsely believed to be a particular, such as a person. This sort of phrase, 'The author of *Waverley*', is not a name because it is a complex symbol. It contains parts which *are* symbols. It contains four words, and the meanings of those four words are already fixed and they have fixed the meaning of 'The author of *Waverley*' in the only sense in which that phrase does have any meaning. In that sense, its meaning is already determinate, i.e., there is nothing arbitrary or conventional about the meaning of that whole phrase, when the meanings of 'the', 'author', 'of', and '*Waverley*' have already been fixed. In that respect, it differs from 'Scott', because when you have fixed the meaning of all the other words in the language, you have done nothing toward fixing the meaning of the name 'Scott'. That is to say, if you understand the English language, you would understand the meaning of the phrase 'The author of *Waverley*' if you had never heard it before, whereas you would not understand the meaning of 'Scott' if you had never heard the word before because to know the meaning of a name is to know who it is applied to.

You sometimes find people speaking as if descriptive phrases were names, and you will find it suggested, e.g., that such a proposition as 'Scott is the author of *Waverley*' really asserts that 'Scott' and the 'the author of *Waverley*' are two names for the same person. That is an entire delusion; first of all, because 'the author of *Waverley*' is not a name, and, secondly, because, as you can perfectly well see, if that were what is meant, the proposition would be one like 'Scott is Sir Walter', and would not depend upon any fact except that the person in question was so called, because a name is what a man is called. As a matter of fact, Scott was the author of *Waverley* at a time when no one called him so, when no one knew whether he was or not, and the fact that he was the author was a physical fact, the fact that he sat down and wrote it with his own hand, which does not have anything to do with what he was called. It is in no way arbitrary. You cannot settle by any choice of nomenclature whether he is or is not to be the author of *Waverley*, because in actual fact he chose to write it and you cannot help yourself. That illustrates how 'the author of *Waverley*' is quite a different thing from a name. You can prove this point very clearly by formal arguments. In 'Scott is the author of *Waverley*' the 'is', of course, expresses identity, i.e., the entity whose name is Scott is identical with the author of *Waverley*. But, when I say 'Scott is mortal' this 'is', is the 'is' of predication, which is quite different from the 'is' of identity. It is a mistake to interpret 'Scott is mortal' as meaning 'Scott is identical with one among mortals', because (among other reasons) you will not be able to say what 'mortals' are except by means of the propositional function '*x* is mortal', which brings back the 'is' of predication. You cannot reduce the 'is' of predication to the other 'is'. But the 'is' in 'Scott is the author of *Waverley*' is the 'is' of identity and not of predication.*

If you were to try to substitute for 'the author of *Waverley*' in that proposition any name whatever, say '*c*', so that the proposition becomes 'Scott is *c*', then if '*c*' is a name for anybody who is not Scott, that proposition would become false, while if, on the other hand, '*c*' is a name for Scott, then the proposition will become simply a tautology. It is at once obvious that if '*c*' were 'Scott' itself, 'Scott is Scott' is just a tautology. But if you take any other name which is just a name for Scott, then if the name is being used *as* a name and not as a description, the proposition will still be a tautology. For the name itself is merely a means of pointing to the thing, and does not occur in what you are asserting, so that if one thing has two names, you make exactly the same assertion whichever of the two names you use, provided they are really names and not truncated descriptions.

So there are only two alternatives. If '*c*' is a name, the proposition 'Scott is *c*' is either false or tautologous. But the proposition

---

* The confusion of these two meanings of 'is' is essential to the Hegelian conception of identity-in-difference.

'Scott is the author of *Waverley*' is neither, and therefore is not the same as any proposition of the form 'Scott is *c*', where '*c*' is a name. That is another way of illustrating the fact that a description is quite a different thing from a name.

I should like to make clear what I was saying just now, that if you substitute another name in place of 'Scott' which is also a name of the same individual, say, 'Scott is Sir Walter', then 'Scott' and 'Sir Walter' are being used as names and not as descriptions, your proposition is strictly a tautology. If one asserts 'Scott is Sir Walter', the way one would mean it would be that one was using the names as descriptions. One would mean that the person called 'Scott' is the person called 'Sir Walter', and 'the person called "Scott" ' is a description, and so is 'the person called "Sir Walter".' So that would not be a tautology. It would mean that the person called 'Scott' is identical with the person called 'Sir Walter'. But if you are using both as names, the matter is quite different. You must observe that the name does not occur in that which you assert when you use the name. The name is merely that which is a means of expressing what it is you are tryng to assert, and when I say 'Scott wrote *Waverley*', the name 'Scott' does not occur in the thing I am asserting. The thing I am asserting is about the person, not about the name. So if I say 'Scott is Sir Walter', using these two names *as* names, neither 'Scott' nor 'Sir Walter' occurs in what I am asserting, but only the person who has these names, and thus what I am asserting is a pure tautology.

It is rather important to realize this about the two different uses of names or of any other symbols: the one when you are talking about the symbol and the other when you are using it *as* a symbol, as a means of talking about something else. Normally, if you talk about your dinner, you are not talking about the word 'dinner' but about what you are going to eat, and that is a different thing altogether. The ordinary use of words is as a means of getting through to things, and when you are using words in that way the statement 'Scott is Sir Walter' is a pure tautology, exactly on the same level as 'Scott is Scott'.

That brings me back to the point that when you take 'Scott is the author of *Waverley*' and you substitute for 'the author of *Waverley*' a name in the place of a description, you get necessarily either a tautology or a falsehood—a tautology if you substitute 'Scott' or some other name for the same person, and a falsehood if you substitute anything else. But the proposition itself is neither a tautology nor a falsehood, and that shows you that the proposition 'Scott is the author of *Waverley*' is a different proposition from any that can be obtained if you substitute a name in the place of 'the author of *Waverley*'. That conclusion is equally true of any other proposition in which the phrase 'the author of *Waverley*' occurs. If you take any proposition in which that phrase occurs and substitute for that phrase a proper name, whether that name be 'Scott' or any other, you will get a different proposition. Generally speaking, if the name that you substitute is 'Scott', your proposition, if it was true before will remain true, and if it was false before will remain false. But it is a *different* proposition. It is not *always* true that it will remain true or false, as may be seen by the example: 'George IV wished to know if Scott was the author of *Waverley*'. It is not true that George IV wished to know if Scott was Scott. So it is even the case that the truth or the falsehood of a proposition is sometimes changed when you substitute a name of an object for a description of the same object. But in any case it is always a different proposition when you substitute a name for a description.

Identity is a rather puzzling thing at first sight. When you say 'Scott is the author of *Waverley*', you are half-tempted to think there are two people, one of whom is Scott and the other the author of *Waverley*, and they happen to be the same. That is obviously absurd, but that is the sort of way one is always tempted to deal with identity.

When I say 'Scott is the author of *Waverley*' and that 'is' expresses identity, the reason that identity can be asserted there truly and without tautology is just the fact that the one is a name and the other a description. Or they might both be descriptions. If I say 'The author of *Waverley* is the author of *Marmion*', that, of course, asserts identity between two descriptions.

Now the next point that I want to make clear is that when a description (when I say 'description' I mean, for the future, a *definite* description) occurs in a proposition, there is no constituent of that proposition corresponding to that description as a whole. In the true analysis of the proposition, the description is broken up and disappears. That is to say, when I say 'Scott is the author of *Waverley*' it is a wrong analysis of that to suppose that you have there three constituents, 'Scott', 'is', and 'the author of *Waverley*'. That, of course, is the sort of way you might think of analysing. You might admit that 'the author of *Waverley*' was complex and could be further cut up, but you might think the proposition could be split into those three bits to begin with. That is an entire mistake. 'The author of *Waverley*' is not a constituent of the proposition at all. There is no constituent really there corresponding to the descriptive phrase. I will try to prove that to you now.

The first and most obvious reason is that you can have significant propositions denying the existence of 'the so-and-so'. 'The unicorn does not exist.' 'The greatest finite number does not exist.' Propositions of that sort are perfectly significant, are perfectly sober, true, decent propositions, and that could not possibly be the case if the unicorn were a constituent of the proposition, because plainly it could not be a constituent as long as there were not any unicorns. Because the constituents of propositions, of course, are the same as the constituents of the corresponding facts, and since it is a fact that the unicorn does not exist, it is perfectly clear that the unicorn is not a constituent of that fact, because if there were any fact of which the unicorn was a constituent, there would be a unicorn, and it would not be true that it did not exist. That applies in this case of descriptions particularly. Now since it is possible for 'the so-and-so' not to exist and yet for propositions in which 'the so-and-so' occurs to be significant and even true, we must try to see what is meant by saying that the so-and-so does exist.

The occurrence of tense in verbs is an exceedingly annoying vulgarity due to our preoccupation with practical affairs. It would be much more agreeable if they had no tense, as I believe is the case in Chinese, but I do not know Chinese. You ought to be able to say 'Socrates exists in the past', 'Socrates exists in the present' or 'Socrates exists in the future', or simply 'Socrates exists', without any implication of tense, but language does not allow that, unfortunately. Nevertheless, I am going to use language in this tenseless way: when I say 'The so-and-so exists', I am not going to mean that it exists in the present or in the past or in the future, but simply that it exists, without implying anything involving tense.

'The author of *Waverley* exists': there are two things required for that. First of all, what is 'the author of *Waverley*'? It is the person who wrote *Waverley*, i.e., we are coming now to this, that you have a propositional function involved, viz., '*x* writes *Waverley*', and the author of *Waverley* is the person who writes *Waverley*, and in order that the person who writes *Waverley* may exist, it is necessary that this propositional function should have two properties:

1. It must be true for *at least* one *x*.
2. It must be true for *at most* one *x*.

If nobody had ever written *Waverley* the author could not exist, and if two people had written it, *the* author could not exist. So that you want these two properties, the one that it is true for at least one *x*, and the other that it is true for at most one *x*, both of which are required for existence.

The property of being true for at least one *x* is the one we dealt with last time: what I expressed by saying that the propositional function is *possible*. Then we come on to the second condition, that it is true for at most one *x*, and that you can express in this way: 'If *x* and *y* wrote *Waverley*, then *x* is identical with *y*, whatever *x* and *y* may be'. That says that at most one wrote it. It does not say that anybody wrote *Waverley* at all, because if nobody had written it, that statement would still be true. It only says that at most one person wrote it.

The first of these conditions for existence fails in the case of the unicorn, and the second in the case of the inhabitant of London.

We can put these two conditions together and get a portmanteau expression including the meaning of both. You can reduce them both down to this, that: '("*x* wrote *Waverley*" is equivalent to "*x* is *c*" whatever *x* may be) is possible in respect of *c*.' That is as simple, I think, as you can make the statement.

You see that means to say that there is some entity *c*, we may not know what it is, which is such that when *x* is *c*, it is true that *x* wrote *Waverley*, and when *x* is not *c*, it is not true that *x* wrote *Waverley*, which amounts to saying that *c* is the only person who wrote *Waverley*; and I say there is a value of *c* which makes that true. So that this whole expression, which is a propositional function about *c*, is *possible* in respect of *c* (in the sense explained last time).

That is what I mean when I say that the author of *Waverley* exists. When I say 'the author of *Waverley* exists', I mean that there is an entity c such that 'x wrote *Waverley*' is true when x is c, and is false when x is not c. 'The author of *Waverley*' as a constituent has quite disappeared there, so that when I say 'The author of *Waverley* exists' I am not saying anything about the author of *Waverley*. You have instead this elaborate to-do with propositional functions, and 'the author of *Waverley*' has disappeared. That is why it is possible to say significantly 'The author of *Waverley* did not exist'. It would not be possible if 'the author of *Waverley*' were a constituent of propositions in whose verbal expression this descriptive phrase occurs.

The fact that you can discuss the proposition 'God exists' is a proof that 'God', as used in that proposition, is a description and not a name. If 'God' were a name, no question as to existence could arise.

I have now defined what I mean by saying that a thing described exists. I have still to explain what I mean by saying that a thing described has a certain property. Supposing you want to say 'The author of *Waverley* was human', that will be represented thus: '("x wrote *Waverley*" is equivalent to "x is c" whatever x may be, and c is human) is possible with respect to c'.

You will observe that what we gave before as the meaning of 'The author of *Waverley* exists' is part of this proposition. It is part of any proposition in which 'the author of *Waverley*' has what I call a 'primary occurrence'. When I speak of a 'primary occurrence' I mean that you are not having a proposition about the author of *Waverley* occurring as a part of some larger proposition, such as 'I believe that the author of *Waverley* was human' or 'I believe that the author of *Waverley* exists'. When it is a primary occurrence, i.e., when the proposition concerning it is not just part of a larger proposition, the phrase which we defined as the meaning of 'The author of *Waverley* exists' will be part of that proposition. If I say the author of *Waverley* was human, or a poet, or a Scotsman, or whatever I say about the author of *Waverley* in the way of a primary occurrence, always this statement of his existence is part of the proposition. In that sense all these propositions that I make about the author of *Waverley* imply that the author of *Waverley* exists. So that any statement in which a description has a primary occurrence implies that the object described exists. If I say 'The present King of France is bald', that implies that the present King of France exists. If I say, 'The present King of France has a fine head of hair', that also implies that the present King of France exists. Therefore unless you understand how a proposition containing a description is to be denied, you will come to the conclusion that it is not true either that the present King of France is bald or that he is not bald, because if you were to enumerate all the things that are bald you would not find him there, and if you were to enumerate all the things that are not bald, you would not find him there either. The only suggestion I have found for dealing with that on conventional lines is to suppose that he wears a wig. You can only avoid the hypothesis that he wears a wig by observing that the denial of the proposition 'The present King of France is bald' will not be 'The present King of France is not bald', if you mean by that 'There is such a person as the King of France and that person is not bald'. The reason of this is that when you state that the present King of France is bald you say 'There is a *c* such that *c* is now King of France and *c* is bald' and the denial is not 'There is a *c* such that *c* is now King of France and *c* is not bald'. It is more complicated. It is: 'Either there is not a *c* such that *c* is now King of France, or, if there is such a *c*, then *c* is not bald.' Therefore you see that, if you want to deny the proposition 'The present King of France is bald', you can do it by denying that he exists, instead of by denying that he is bald. In order to deny this statement that the present King of France is bald, which is a statement consisting of two parts, you can proceed by denying either part. You can deny the one part, which would lead you to suppose that the present King of France exists but is not bald, or the other part, which will lead you to the denial that the present King of France exists; and either of those two denials will lead you to the falsehood of the proposition 'The present King of France is bald'. When you say 'Scott is human' there is no possibility of a double denial. The only way you can deny 'Scott is human' is by saying 'Scott is not human'. But where a descriptive phrase occurs, you do have the double possibility of denial.

It is of the utmost importance to realize that 'the so-and-so' does not occur in the analysis of propositions in whose verbal expression it occurs, that when I say 'The author of *Waverley* is human', 'the author of *Waverley*' is not the subject of that proposition, in the sort of way that Scott would be if I said 'Scott is human', using 'Scott' as a name. I cannot emphasize sufficiently how important this point is, and how much error you get into metaphysics if you do not realize that when I say 'The author of *Waverley* is human' that is not a proposition of the same form as 'Scott is human'. It does not contain a constituent 'the author of *Waverley*'. The importance of that is very great for many reasons, and one of them is this question of existence. As I pointed out to you last time, there is a vast amount of philosophy that rests upon the notion that existence is, so to speak, a property that you can attribute to things, and that the things that exist have the property of existence and the things that do not exist do not. That is rubbish, whether you take kinds of things, or individual things described. When I say, e.g., 'Homer existed', I am meaning by 'Homer' some description, say 'the author of the Homeric poems', and I am asserting that those poems were written by one man, which is a very doubtful proposition; but if you could get hold of the actual person who did actually write those poems (supposing there was such a person), to say of him that he existed would be uttering nonsense, not a falsehood but nonsense, because it is only of persons described that it can be significantly said that they exist. Last time I pointed out the fallacy in saying 'Men exist, Socrates is a man, therefore Socrates exists'. When I say 'Homer exists, this is Homer, therefore this exists', that is a fallacy of the same sort. It is an entire mistake to argue: 'This is the author of the Homeric poems and the author of the Homeric poems exists, therefore this exists'. It is only where a prepositional function comes in that existence may be significantly asserted. You can assert 'The so-and-so exists', meaning that there is just one c which has those properties, but when you get hold of a c that has them, you cannot say of this c that it exists, because that is nonsense: it is not false, but it has no meaning at all.

So the individuals that there are in the world do not exist, or rather it is nonsense to say that they exist and nonsense to say that they do not exist. It is not a thing you can say when you have named them, but only when you have described them. When you say 'Homer exists', you mean 'Homer' is a description which applies to something. A description when it is fully stated is always of the form 'the so-and-so'.

The sort of things that are like these descriptions in that they occur in words in a proposition, but are not in actual fact constituents of the proposition rightly analysed, things of that sort I call 'incomplete symbols'. There are a great many sorts of incomplete symbols in logic, and they are sources of a great deal of confusion and false philosophy, because people get misled by grammar. You think that the proposition 'Scott is mortal' and the proposition 'The author of *Waverley* is mortal' are of the same form. You think that they are both simple propositions attributing a predicate to a subject. That is an entire delusion: one of them is (or rather might be) and one of them is not. These things, like 'the author of *Waverley*', which I call incomplete symbols, are things that have absolutely no meaning whatsoever in isolation but merely acquire a meaning in a context. 'Scott' taken as a name has a meaning all by itself. It stands for a certain person, and there it is. But 'the author of *Waverley*' is not a name, and does not all by itself mean anything at all, because when it is rightly used in propositions, those propositions do not contain any constituent corresponding to it.

There are a great many other sorts of incomplete symbols besides descriptions. These are classes, which I shall speak of next time, and relations taken in extension, and so on. Such aggregations of symbols are really the same thing as what I call 'logical fictions', and they embrace practically all the familiar objects of daily life: tables, chairs, Piccadilly, Socrates, and so on. Most of them are either classes, or series, or series of classes. In any case they are all incomplete symbols, i.e., they are aggregations that only have a meaning in use and do not have any meaning in themselves.

It is important, if you want to understand the analysis of the world, or the analysis of facts, or if you want to have any idea what there really is in the world, to realize how much of what there is in phraseology is of the nature of incomplete symbols. You can see that very easily in the case of 'the author of *Waverley*' because 'the author of *Waverley*' does not stand simply for Scott, nor for anything else. If it stood for Scott, 'Scott is the author of *Waverley*' would be the same proposition as 'Scott is Scott', which it is not, since George IV wished to know the truth of the one and did **not** wish to know the truth of the other. If 'the author of *Waverley*' stood for anything other than Scott, 'Scott is the author of *Waverley*' would be false, which it is not. Hence you have to conclude that 'the author of *Waverley*' does not, in isolation, really stand for anything at all; and that is the characteristic of incomplete symbols.

VII. THE THEORY OF TYPES AND SYMBOLISM: CLASSES

Before I begin to-day the main subject of my lecture, I should like to make a few remarks in explanation and amplification of what I have said about existence in my previous two lectures. This is chiefly on account of a letter I have received from a member of the class, raising many points which, I think, were present in other minds too.

The *first* point I wish to clear up is this: I did not mean to say that when one says a thing exists, one means the same as when one says it is possible. What I meant was, that the fundamental logical idea, the primitive idea, out of which both those are derived is the same. That is not quite the same thing as to say that the statement that a thing exists is the same as the statement that it is possible, which I do not hold. I used the word 'possible' in perhaps a somewhat strange sense, because I wanted some word for a fundamental logical idea for which no word exists in ordinary language, and therefore if one is to try to express in ordinary language the idea in question, one has to take some word and make it convey the sense that I was giving to the word 'possible', which is by no means the only sense that it has but is a sense that was convenient for my purpose. We say of a propositional function that it is possible, where there are cases in which it is true. That is not exactly the same thing as what one ordinarily means, for instance, when one says that it is possible it may rain to-morrow. But what I contend is, that the ordinary uses of the word 'possible' are derived from this notion by a process. E.g., normally when you say of a proposition that it is possible, you mean something like this: first of all it is implied that you do not know whether it is true or false; and I think it is implied, secondly, that it is one of a class of propositions, some of which are known to be true. When

I say, e.g., 'It is possible that it may rain to-morrow'—'It will rain to-morrow' is one of the class of propositions 'It rains at time t', where t is different times. We mean partly that we do not know whether it will rain or whether it will not, but also that we do know that that is the sort of proposition that is quite apt to be true, that it is a value of a propositional function of which we know some value to be true. Many of the ordinary uses of 'possible' come under that head, I think you will find. That is to say, that if you say of a proposition that it is possible, what you have is this: 'There is in this proposition some constituent, which, if you turn it into a variable, will give you a propositional function that is sometimes true.' You ought not therefore to say of a proposition simply that it is possible, but rather that it is possible in respect of such-and-such a constituent. That would be a more full expression.

When I say, for instance, that 'Lions exist', I do not mean the same as if I said that lions were possible; because when you say 'Lions exist', that means that the propositional function 'x is a lion' is a possible one in the sense that there are lions, while when you say 'Lions are possible' that is a different sort of statement altogether, not meaning that a casual individual animal may be a lion, but rather that a *sort* of animal may be the *sort* that we call 'lions'. If you say 'Unicorns are possible', e.g., you would mean that you do not know any reason why there should not be unicorns, which is quite a different proposition from 'Unicorns exist'. As to what you would mean by saying that unicorns are possible, it would always come down to the same thing as 'It is possible it may rain to-morrow'. You would mean, the proposition 'There are unicorns' is one of a certain set of propositions some of which are known to be true, and that the description of the unicorn does not contain in it anything that *shows* there could not be such beasts.

When I say a propositional function is possible, meaning there are cases in which it is true, I am consciously using the word 'possible' in an unusual sense, because I want a single word for my fundamental idea, and cannot find any word in ordinary language that expresses what I mean.

Secondly, it is suggested that when one says a thing exists, it means that it is in time, or in time and space, at any rate in time. That is a very common suggestion, but I do not think that really there is much to be said for that use of the words; in the first place, because if that were all you meant, there would be no need for a separate word. In the second place, because after all in the sense, whatever that sense may be, in which the things are said to exist that one ordinarily regards as existing, one may very well wish to discuss the question whether there are things that exist without being in time. Orthodox metaphysics holds that whatever is really real is not in time, that to be in time is to be more or less unreal, and that what really exists is not in time at all. And orthodox theology holds that God is not in time. I see no reason why you should frame your definition of existence in such a way as to preclude that notion of existence. I am inclined to think that there are things that are not in time, and I should be sorry to use the word existence in that sense when you have already the phrase 'being in time' which quite sufficiently expresses what you mean.

Another objection to that definition is, that it does not in the least fit the sort of use of 'existence' which was underlying my discussion, which is the common one in mathematics. When you take existence-theorems, for instance, as when you say 'An even prime exists', you do not mean that the number two is in time but that you can find a number of which you can say 'This is even and prime'. One does ordinarily in mathematics speak of propositions of that sort as existence-theorems, i.e., you establish that there is an object of such-and-such a sort, that object being, of course, in mathematics a logical object, not a particular, not a thing like a lion or a unicorn, but an object like a function or a number, something which plainly does not have the property of being in time at all, and it is that sort of sense of existence-theorems that is relevant in discussing the meaning of existence as I was doing in the last two lectures. I do, of course, hold that that sense of existence can be carried on to cover the more ordinary uses of existence, and does in fact give the key to what is underlying those ordinary uses, as when one says that 'Homer existed' or 'Romulus did not exist', or whatever we may say of that kind.

I come now to a *third* suggestion about existence, which is also a not uncommon one, that of a given particular 'this' you can say 'This exists' in the sense that it is not a phantom or an image or a universal. Now I think that use of existence involves confusions which it is exceedingly important to get out of one's mind, really rather dangerous mistakes. In the first place, we must separate phantoms and images from universals; they are on a different level. Phantoms and images do undoubtedly exist in that sense, whatever it is, in which ordinary objects exist. I mean, if you shut your eyes and imagine some visual scene, the images that are before your mind while you are imagining are undoubtedly there. They are images, something is happening, and what is happening is that the images are before your mind, and these images are just as much part of the world as tables and chairs and anything else. They are perfectly decent objects, and you only call them unreal (if you call them so), or treat them as non-existent, because they do not have the usual sort of relations to other objects. If you shut your eyes and imagine a visual scene and you stretch out your hand to touch what is imaged, you won't get a tactile sensation, or even necessarily a tactile image. You will not get the usual correlation of sight and touch. If you imagine a heavy oak table, you can remove it without any muscular effort, which is not the case with oak tables that you actually see. The general correlations of your images are quite different from the correlations of what one chooses to call 'real' objects. But that is not to say images are unreal. It is only to say they are not part of physics. Of course, I know that this belief in the physical world has established a sort of reign of terror. You have got to treat with disrespect whatever does not fit into the physical world. But that is really very unfair to the things that do not fit in. They are just as much there as the things that do. The physical world is a sort of governing aristocracy, which has somehow managed to cause everything else to be treated with disrespect. That sort of attitude is unworthy of a philosopher. We should treat with exactly equal respect the things that do not fit in with the physical world, and images are among them.

'Phantoms', I suppose, are intended to differ from 'images' by being of the nature of hallucinations, things that are not merely imagined but that go with belief. They again are perfectly real; the only odd thing about them is their correlations. Macbeth sees a dagger. If he tried to touch it, he would not get any tactile sensation, but that does not imply that he was not *seeing* a dagger, it only implies that he was not *touching* it. It does not in any way imply that the visual sensation was not there. It only means to say that the sort of correlation between sight and touch that we are used to is the normal rule but not a universal one. In order to pretend that it is universal, we say that a thing is unreal when it does not fit in. You say 'Any man who is a man will do such-and-such a thing.' You then find a man who will not, and you say, he is not a man. That is just the same sort of thing as with these daggers that you cannot touch.

I have explained elsewhere the sense in which phantoms are unreal.* When you see a 'real' man, the immediate object that you see is one of a whole system of particulars, all of which belong together and make up collectively the various 'appearances' of the man to himself and others. On the other hand, when you see a phantom of a man, that is an isolated particular, not fitting into a system as does a particular which one calls an appearance of the 'real' man. The phantom is in itself just as much part of the world as the normal sense-datum, but it lacks the usual correlation and therefore gives rise to false inferences and becomes deceptive.

As to universals, when I say of a particular that it exists, I certainly do not mean the same thing as if I were to say that it is not a universal. The statement concerning any particular that it is not a universal is quite strictly nonsense—not false, but strictly and exactly nonsense. You never can place a particular in the sort of place where a universal ought to be, and vice versa. If I say 'a is not b', or if I say 'a is b', that implies that a and b are of the same logical type. When I say of a universal that it exists, I should be meaning it in a different sense from that in which one says that particulars exist. E.g., you might say 'Colours exist in the spectrum between blue and yellow.' That would be a perfectly respectable statement, the colours being taken as universals. You mean simply that the propositional function 'x is a colour between blue and yellow' is one which is capable of truth. But the x which occurs there is not a particular, it is a universal. So that you arrive at the fact that the ultimate important notion involved in existence is the notion that I developed in the lecture before last, the notion of a propositional function being sometimes true, or being, in other words, possible. The distinction between what some people would call real existence, and existence in people's imagination or in my subjective activity, that distinction, as we have just seen, is entirely one of correlation. I mean that anything which appears to you,

* See *Our Knowledge of the External World*, Chap. III. Also Section XII of 'Sense-Data and Physics' in *Mysticism and Logic*.

you will be mistakenly inclined to say has some more glorified form of existence if it is associated with those other things I was talking of in the way that the appearance of Socrates to you would be associated with his appearance to other people. You would say he was only in your imagination if there were not those other correlated appearances that you would naturally expect. But that does not mean that the appearance to you is not exactly as much a part of the world as if there were other correlated appearances. It will be exactly as much a part of the real world, only it will fail to have the correlations that you expect. That applies to the question of sensation and imagination. Things imagined do not have the same sort of correlations as things sensated. If you care to see more about this question, I wrote a discussion in *The Monist* for January, 1915, and if any of you are interested, you will find the discussion there.

I come now to the proper subject of my lecture, but shall have to deal with it rather hastily. It was to explain the theory of types and the definition of classes. Now first of all, as I suppose most of you are aware, if you proceed carelessly with formal logic, you can very easily get into contradictions. Many of them have been known for a long time, some even since the time of the Greeks, but it is only fairly recently that it has been discovered that they bear upon mathematics, and that the ordinary mathematician is liable to fall into them when he approaches the realms of logic, unless he is very cautious. Unfortunately the mathematical ones are more difficult to expound, and the ones easy to expound strike one as mere puzzles or tricks.

You can start with the question whether or not there is a greatest cardinal number. Every class of things that you can choose to mention has some cardinal number. That follows very easily from the definition of cardinal numbers as classes of similar classes, and you would be inclined to suppose that the class of all things there are in the world would have about as many members as a class could be reasonably expected to have. The plain man would suppose you could not get a larger class than the class of all the things there are in the world. On the other hand, it is very easy to prove that if you take selections of some of the members of a class, making those selections in every conceivable way that you can, the number of different selections that you can make is greater than the original number of terms. That is easy to see with small numbers. Suppose you have a class with just three numbers, *a,b,c*. The first selection that you can make is the selection of no terms. The next of *a* alone, *b* alone, *c* alone. Then *bc*, *ca*, *ab*, *abc*, which makes in all 8 (i.e., 2^3) selections. Generally speaking, if you have *n* terms, you can make 2^n selections. It is very easy to prove that 2^n is always greater than *n*, whether *n* happens to be finite or not. So you find that the total number of things in the world is not so great as the number of classes that can be made up out of those things. I am asking you to take all these propositions for granted, because there is not time to go into the proofs, but they are all in Cantor's work. Therefore you will find that the total number of things in the world is by no means the greatest number. On the contrary, there is a heirarchy of numbers greater than that. That, on the face of it, seems to land you in a contradiction. You have, in fact, a perfectly precise arithmetical proof that there are *fewer* things in heaven or earth than are dreamt of in *our* philosophy. That shows how philosophy advances.

You are met with the necessity, therefore, of distinguishing between classes and particulars. You are met with the necessity of saying that a class consisting of two particulars is not itself in turn a fresh particular, and that has to be expanded in all sorts of ways; i.e., you will have to say that in the sense in which there are particulars, in that sense it is not true to say there are classes. The sense in which there are classes is a different one from the sense in which there are particulars, because if the senses of the two were exactly the same, a world in which there are three particulars and therefore eight classes, would be a world in which there are at least eleven things. As the Chinese philosopher pointed out long ago, a dun cow and a bay horse makes three things: separately they are each one, and taken together they are another, and therefore three.

I pass now to the contradiction about classes that are not members of themselves. You would say generally that you would not expect a class to be a member of itself. For instance, if you take the class of all the teaspoons in the world, that is not in itself a teaspoon. Or if you take all the human beings in the world, the whole class of them is not in turn a human being. Normally you would say you cannot expect a whole class of things to be itself a member of that class. But there are apparent exceptions. If you take, e.g., all the things in the world that are not teaspoons and make up a class of them, that class obviously (you would say) will not be a teaspoon. And so generally with negative classes. And not only with negative classes, either, for if you think for a moment that classes are things in the same sense in which things are things, you will then have to say that the class consisting of all the things in the world is itself a thing in the world, and that therefore this class is a member of itself. Certainly you would have thought that it was clear that the class consisting of all the classes in the world is itself a class. That I think most people would feel inclined to suppose, and therefore you would get there a case of a class which is a member of itself. If there is any sense in asking whether a class is a member of itself or not, then certainly in all the cases of the ordinary classes of everyday life you find that a class is not a member of itself. Accordingly, that being so, you could go on to make up the class of all those classes that are not members of themselves, and you can ask yourself, when you have done that, is that class a member of itself or is it not?

Let us first suppose that it is a member of itself. In that case it is one of those classes that are not members of themselves, i.e., it is not a member of itself. Let us then suppose that it is not a member of itself. In that case it is not one of those classes that are not members of themselves, i.e., it is one of those classes that are members of themselves, i.e., it is a member of itself. Hence either hypothesis, that it is or that it is not a member of itself, leads to its contradiction. If it is a member of itself, it is not, and if it is not, it is.

That contradiction is extremely interesting. You can modify its form; some forms of modification are valid and some are not. I once had a form suggested to me which was not valid, namely the question whether the barber shaves himself or not. You can define the barber as 'one who shaves all those, and those only, who do not shave themselves'. The question is, does the barber shave himself? In this form the contradiction is not very difficult to solve. But in our previous form I think it is clear that you can only get around it by observing that the whole question whether a class is or is not a member of itself is nonsense, i.e., that no class either is or is not a member of itself, and that it is not even true to say that, because the whole form of words is just a noise without meaning. That has to do with the fact that classes, as I shall be coming on to show, are incomplete symbols in the same sense in which the descriptions are that I was talking of last time; you are talking nonsense when you ask yourself whether a class is or is not a member of itself, because in any full statement of what is meant by a proposition which seems to be about a class, you will find that the class is not mentioned at all and that there is nothing about a class in that statement. It is absolutely necessary, if a statement about a class is to be significant and not pure nonsense, that it should be capable of being translated into a form in which it does not mention the class at all. This sort of statement, 'Such-and-such a class is or is not a member of itself', will not be capable of that kind of translation. It is analogous to what I was saying about descriptions: the symbol for a class is an incomplete symbol; it does not really stand for part of the propositions in which symbolically it occurs, but in the right analysis of those propositions that symbol has been broken up and disappeared.

There is one other of these contradictions that I may as well mention, the most ancient, the saying of Epimenides that 'All Cretans are liars'. Epimenides was a man who slept for sixty years without stopping, and I believe that it was at the end of that nap that he made the remark that all Cretans were liars. It can be put more simply in the form: if a man makes the statement 'I am lying', is he lying or not? If he is, that is what he said he was doing, so he is speaking the truth and not lying. If, on the other hand, he is not lying, then plainly he is speaking the truth in saying that he is lying, and therefore he is lying, since he says truly that that is what he is doing. It is an ancient puzzle, and nobody treated that sort of thing as anything but a joke until it was found that it had to do with such important and practical problems as whether there is a greatest cardinal or ordinal number. Then at last these contradictions were treated seriously. The man who says 'I am lying' is really asserting 'There is a proposition which I am asserting and which is false'. That is presumably what you mean by lying. In order to get out the contradiction you have to take that whole assertion of his as one of the propositions to which his assertion applies; i.e., when he says 'There is a proposition which I am asserting and which is false', the word 'proposition' has to be interpreted as to include among propositions his statement to the effect that he is asserting a false proposition. Therefore you have to suppose that you have a certain totality, viz., that of propositions, but that that totality contains members which can only be defined in terms of itself. Because when you say 'There is a proposition which I am asserting and which is false', that is a statement whose meaning can only be got by reference to the totality of propositions. You are not saying which among all the propositions there are in the world it is that you are asserting and that is false. Therefore it presupposes that the totality of proposition is spread out before you and that some one, though you do not say which, is being asserted falsely. It is quite clear that you get into a vicious circle if you first suppose that this totality of propositions is spread out before you, so that you can without picking any definite one say 'Some one out of this totality is being asserted falsely', and that yet, when you have gone on to say 'Some one out of this totality is being asserted falsely', that assertion is itself one of the totality you were to pick out from. That is exactly the situation you have in the paradox of the liar. You are supposed to be given first of all a set of propositions, and you assert that some one of these is being asserted falsely, then that assertion itself turns out to be one of the set, so that it is obviously fallacious to suppose the set already there in its entirety. If you are going to say anything about 'all propositions', you will have to define propositions, first of all, in some such way as to exclude those that refer to all the propositions of the sort already defined. It follows that the word 'proposition', in the sense in which we ordinarily try to use it, is a meaningless one, and that we have got to divide propositions up into sets and can make statements about all propositions in a given set, but those propositions will not themselves be members of the set. For instance, I may say 'All atomic propositions are either true or false', but that itself will not be an atomic proposition. If you try to say 'All propositions are either true or false', without qualification, you are uttering nonsense, because if it were not nonsense it would have to be itself a proposition and one of those included in its own scope, and therefore the law of excluded middle as enunciated just now is a meaningless noise. You have to cut propositions up into different types, and you can start with atomic propositions or, if you like, you can start with those propositions that do not refer to sets of propositions at all. Then you will take next those that refer to sets of propositions of that sort that you had first. Those that refer to sets of propositions of the first type, you may call the second type, and so on.

If you apply that to the person who says 'I am lying', you will find that the contradiction has disappeared, because he will have to say what type of liar he is. If he says 'I am asserting a false proposition of the first type', as a matter of fact that statement, since it refers to the totality of propositions of the first type, is of the second type. Hence it is not true that he is asserting a false proposition of the first type, and he remains a liar. Similarly, if he said he was asserting a false proposition of the 30,000th type, that would be a statement of the 30,001st type, so he would still be a liar. And the counter-argument to prove that he was also not a liar has collapsed.

You can lay it down that a totality of any sort cannot be a member of itself. That applies to what we are saying about classes. For instance, the totality of classes in the world cannot be a class in the same sense in which they are. So we shall have to distinguish a hierarchy of classes. We will start with the classes that are composed entirely of particulars: that will be the first type of classes. Then we will go on to classes whose members are classes of the first type: that will be the second type. Then we will go on to classes whose members are classes of the second type: that will be the third type, and so on. Never is it possible for a class of one type either to be or not to be identical with a class of another type. That applies to the question I was discussing a moment ago, as to how many things there are in the world. Supposing there are three particulars in the world. There are then, as I was explaining, 8 classes of particulars. There will be 2^8 (i.e., 256) classes of classes of particulars, and 2^{256} classes of classes of classes of particulars, and so on. You do not get any contradiction arising out of that, and when you ask yourself the question: 'Is there, or is there not a greatest cardinal number?' the answer depends entirely upon whether you are confining yourself within some one type, or whether you are not. Within any given type there is a greatest cardinal number, namely, the number of objects of that type, but you will always be able to get a larger number by going up to the next type. Therefore, there is no number so great but what you can get a greater number in a sufficiently high type. There you have the two sides of the argument: the one side when the type is given, the other side when the type is not given.

I have been talking, for brevity's sake, as if there really were all these different sorts of things. Of course, that is nonsense. There are particulars, but when one comes on to classes, and classes of classes, and classes of classes of classes, one is talking of logical fictions. When I say there are no such things, that again is not correct. It is not significant to say 'There are such things', in the same sense of the words 'there are' in which you can say 'There are particulars'. If I say 'There are particulars' and 'There are classes', the two phrases 'there are' will have to have different meanings in those two propositions, and if they have suitable different meanings, both propositions may be true. If, on the other hand, the words 'there are' are used in the same sense in both, then one at least of those statements must be nonsense, not false but nonsense. The question then arises, what is the sense in which one can say 'There are classes', or in other words, what do you mean by a statement in which a class appears to come in? First of all, what are the sort of things you would like to say about classes? They are just the same as the sort of things you want to say about propositional functions. You want to say of a propositional function that it is sometimes true. That is the same thing as saying of a class that it has members. You want to say that is it true for exactly 100 values of the variables. That is the same as saying of a class that it has a hundred members. All the things you want to say about classes are the same as the things you want to say about propositional functions excepting for accidental and irrelevant linguistic forms, with, however, a certain proviso which must now be explained.

Take, e.g., two propositional functions such as 'x is a man', 'x is a featherless biped'. Those two are formally equivalent, i.e., when one is true so is the other, and vice versa. Some of the things that you can say about a propositional function will not necessarily remain true if you substitute another formally equivalent propositional function in its place. For instance, the propositional function 'x is a man' is one which has to do with the concept of humanity. That will not be true of 'x is a featherless biped'. Or if you say, 'so-and-so asserts that such-and-such is a man' the propositional function 'x is a man' comes in there, but 'x is a featherless biped' does not. There are a certain number of things which you can say about a propositional function which would be not true if you substitute another formally equivalent propositional function. On the other hand, any statement about a propositional function which will remain true or remain false, as the case may be, when you substitute for it another formally equivalent propositional function, may be regarded as being about the class which is associated with the propositional function. I want you to take the words *may be regarded* strictly. I am using them instead of *is*, because *is* would be untrue. 'Extensional' statements about functions are those that remain true when you substitute any other formally equivalent function, and these are the ones that may be regarded as being about the class. If you have any statement about a function which is not extensional, you can always derive from it a somewhat similar statement which is extensional, viz., there is a function formally equivalent to the one in question about which the statement in question is true. This statement, which is manufactured out of the one you started with, will be extensional. It will always be equally true or equally false of any two formally equivalent functions, and this derived extensional statement may be regarded as being the corresponding statement about the associated class. So, when I say that 'The class of men has so-and-so many members', that is to say 'There are so-and-so many men in the world', that will be derived from the statement that 'x is human' is satisfied by so-and-so many values of x, and in order to get it into the extensional form, one will put it in this way, that 'There is a function formally equivalent to "x is human", which is true for so-and-so many values of x'. That I should define as what I mean by saying 'The class of men has so-and-so many members'. In that way you find that all the formal properties that you desire of classes, all their formal uses in mathematics, can be obtained without supposing for a moment that there are such things as classes, without supposing, that is to say, that a proposition in which symbolically a class occurs, does in fact contain a constituent corresponding to that symbol, and when rightly analysed that symbol will disappear, in the same sort of way as descriptions disappear when the propositions are rightly analysed in which they occur.

There are certain difficulties in the more usual view of classes, in addition to those we have already mentioned, that are solved by our theory. One of these concerns the null-class, i.e., the class consisting of no members, which is difficult to deal with on a purely extensional basis. Another is concerned with unit-classes. With the ordinary view of classes you would say that a class that has only one member was the same as that one member. That will land you in terrible difficulties, because in that case that one member is a member of that class, namely, itself. Take, e.g., the class of 'Lecture audiences in Gordon Square'.* That is obviously a class of classes, and probably it is a class that has only one member, and that one member itself (so far) has more than one member. Therefore if you were to identify the class of lecture audiences in Gordon Square with the only lecture audience that there is in Gordon Square, you would have to say both that it has one member and that it has twenty members, and you will be landed in contradictions, because this audience has more than one member, but the class of audiences in Gordon Square has only one member. Generally speaking, if you have any collection of many objects forming a class, you can make a class of which that class is the only member, and the class of which that class is the only member will have only one member, though this only member will have many members. This is one reason why you must distinguish a unit-class from its only member. Another is that, if you do not, you will find that the class is a member of itself, which is objectionable, as we saw earlier in this lecture. I have omitted a subtlety connected with the fact that two formally equivalent functions may be of different types. For the way of treating this point, see *Principia Mathematica*, page 20, and Introduction, Chapter III.

I have not said quite all that I ought to have said on this subject. I meant to have gone a little more into the theory of types. The theory of types is really a theory of symbols, not of things. In a proper logical language it would be perfectly obvious. The trouble that there is arises from our inveterate habit of trying to name what cannot be named. If we had a proper logical language, we should not be tempted to do that. Strictly speaking, only particulars can be named. In that sense in which there are particulars,

* [These lectures were given 'in Dr. Williams's library in Gordon Square,' Russell informs me, on eight consecutive Tuesdays. Although University College London, stands nearby, this was probably the only lecture audience in Gordon Square proper.—R.C.M.]

you cannot say either truly or falsely that there is anything else. The word 'there is' is a word having 'systematic ambiguity', i.e., having a strictly infinite number of different meanings which it is important to distinguish.

Discussion

Question: Could you lump all those classes, and classes of classes, and so on, together?

Mr. Russell: All are fictions, but they are different fictions in each case. When you say 'There are classes of particulars', the statement 'there are' wants expanding and explaining away, and when you have put down what you really do mean, or ought to mean, you will find that it is something quite different from what you thought. That process of expanding and writing down fully what you mean, will be different if you go on to 'there are classes of classes of particulars'. There are infinite numbers of meanings to 'there are'. The first only is fundamental, so far as the hierarchy of classes is concerned.

Question: I was wondering whether it was rather analogous to spaces, where the first three dimensions are actual, and the higher ones are merely symbolic. I see there is a difference, there are higher dimensions, but you can lump those together.

Mr. Russell: There is only one fundamental one, which is the first one, the one about particulars, but when you have gone to classes, you have travelled already just as much away from what there is as if you have gone to classes of classes. There are no classes really in the physical world. The particulars are there, but not classes. If you say 'There is a universe' that meaning of 'there is' will be quite different from the meaning in which you say 'There is a particular', which means that 'the propositional function "x is a particular" is sometimes true'.

All those statements are about symbols. They are never about the things themselves, and they have to do with 'types.' This is really important and I ought not to have forgotten to say it, that the relation of the symbol to what it means is different in different types. I am not now talking about this hierarchy of classes and so on, but the relation of a predicate to what it means is different from the relation of a name to what it means. There is not one single concept of 'meaning' as one ordinarily thinks there is, so that you can say in a uniform sense 'All symbols have meaning', but there are infinite numbers of different ways of meaning, i.e., different sorts of relation of the symbol to the symbolized, which are absolutely distinct. The relation, e.g., of a proposition to a fact, is quite different from the relation of a name to a particular, as you can see from the fact that there are two propositions always related to one given fact, and that is not so with names. That shows you that the relation that the proposition has to the fact is quite different from the relation of a name to a particular. You must not suppose that there is, over and above that, another way in which you could get at facts by naming them. You can always only get at the thing you are aiming at by the proper sort of symbol, which approaches it in the appropriate way. That is the real philosophical truth that is at the bottom of all this theory of types.

VIII. EXCURSUS INTO METAPHYSICS: WHAT THERE IS

I come now to the last lecture of this course, and I propose briefly to point to a few of the morals that are to be gathered from what has gone before, in the way of suggesting the bearing of the doctrines that I have been advocating upon various problems of metaphysics. I have dealt hitherto upon what one may call philosophical grammar, and I am afraid I have had to take you through a good many very dry and dusty regions in the course of that investigation, but I think the importance of philosophical grammar is very much greater than it is generally thought to be. I think that practically all traditional metaphysics is filled with mistakes due to bad grammar, and that almost all the traditional problems of metaphysics and traditional results—supposed results—of metaphysics are due to a failure to make the kind of distinctions in what we may call philosophical grammar with which we have been concerned in these previous lectures.

Take, as a very simple example, the philosophy of arithmetic. If you think that 1, 2, 3, and 4, and the rest of the numbers, are in any sense entities, if you think that there are objects, having those names, in the realm of being, you have at once a very considerable apparatus for your metaphysics to deal with, and you have offered to you a certain kind of analysis of arithmetical propositions. When you say, e.g., that 2 and 2 are 4, you suppose in that case that you are making a proposition of which the number 2 and the number 4 are constituents, and that has all sorts of consequences, all sorts of bearings upon your general metaphysical outlook. If there has been any truth in the doctrines that we have been considering, all numbers are what I call logical fictions. Numbers are classes of classes, and classes are logical fictions, so that numbers are, as it were, fictions at two removes, fictions of fictions. Therefore you do not have, as part of the ultimate constituents of your world, these queer entities that you are inclined to call numbers. The same applies in many other directions.

One purpose that has run through all that I have said, has been the justification of analysis, i.e., the justification of logical atomism, of the view that you can get down in theory, if not in practice, to ultimate simples, out of which the world is built, and that those simples have a kind of reality not belonging to anything else. Simples, as I tried to explain, are of an infinite number of sorts. There are particulars and qualities and relations of various orders, a whole hierarchy of different sorts of simples, but all of them, if we were right, have in their various ways some kind of reality that does not belong to anything else. The only other sort of object you come across in the world is what we call *facts*, and facts are the sort of things that are asserted or denied by propositions, and are not properly entities at all in the same sense in which their constituents are. That is shown in the fact that you cannot name them. You can only deny, or assert, or consider them, but you cannot name them because they are not there to be named, although in another sense it is true that you cannot know the world unless you know the facts that make up the truths of the world; but the knowing of facts is a different sort of thing from the knowing of simples.

Another purpose which runs through all that I have been saying is the purpose embodied in the maxim called Occam's Razor. That maxim comes in, in practice, in this way: take some science, say physics. You have there a given body of doctrine, a set of propositions expressed in symbols—I am including words among symbols —and you think that you have reason to believe that on the whole those propositions, rightly interpreted, are fairly true, but you do not know what is the actual meaning of the symbols that you are using. The meaning they have *in use* would have to be explained in some pragmatic way: they have a certain kind of practical or emotional significance to you which is a datum, but the logical significance is not a datum, but a thing to be sought, and you go through, if you are analysing a science like physics, these propositions with a view to finding out what is the smallest empirical apparatus—or the smallest apparatus, not necessarily wholly empirical—out of which you can build up these propositions. What is the smallest number of simple undefined things at the start, and the smallest number of undemonstrated premises, out of which you can define the things that need to be defined and prove the things that need to be proved? That problem, in any case that you like to take, is by no means a simple one, but on the contrary an extremely difficult one. It is one which requires a very great amount of logical technique; and the sort of thing that I have been talking about in these lectures is the preliminaries and first steps in that logical technique. You cannot possibly get at the solution of such a problem as I am talking about if you go at it in a straightforward fashion with just the ordinary acumen that one accumulates in the course of reading or in the study of traditional philosophy. You do need this apparatus of symbolical logic that I have been talking about. (The description of the subject as symbolical logic is an inadequate one. I should like to describe it simply as logic, on the ground that nothing else really is logic, but that would sound so arrogant that I hesitate to do so.)

Let us consider further the example of physics for a moment. You find, if you read the works of physicists, that they reduce matter down to certain elements—atoms, ions, corpuscles, or what not. But in any case the sort of thing that you are aiming at in the physical analysis of matter is to get down to very little bits of matter that still are just like matter in the fact that they persist through time, and that they travel about in space. They have in fact all the ordinary everyday properties of physical matter, not the matter that one has in ordinary life—they do not taste or smell or appear to the naked eye—but they have the properties that you very soon get to when you travel toward physics from ordinary life. Things of that sort, I say, are not the ultimate consituents of matter in any metaphysical sense. Those things are all of them, as I think a very little reflection shows, logical fictions in the sense that I was speaking of. At least, when I say they are, I speak somewhat too dogmatically. It is possible that there may be all these things that the physicist talks about in actual reality, but it is impossible that we should ever have any reason whatsoever for supposing that there are. That is the situation that you arrive at generally in such analyses. You find that a certain thing which has been set up as a metaphysical entity can either be assumed dogmatically to be real, and then you will have no possible argument either for its reality or against its reality; or, instead of doing that, you can construct a logical fiction having the same formal properties, or rather having formally analogous formal properties to those of the supposed metaphysical entity and itself composed of empirically given things, and that logical fiction can be substituted for your supposed metaphysical entity and will fulfil all the scientific purposes that anybody can desire. With atoms and the rest it is so, with all the metaphysical entities whether of science or of metaphysics. By metaphysical entities I mean those things which are supposed to be part of the ultimate constituents of the world, but not to be the kind of thing that is ever empirically given—I do not say merely not being itself empirically given, but not being the *kind* of thing that is empirically given. In the case of matter, you can start from what is empirically given, what one sees and hears and smells and so forth, all the ordinary data of sense, or you can start with some definite ordinary object, say this desk, and you can ask yourselves, 'What do I mean by saying that this desk that I am looking at now is the same as the one I was looking at a week ago?' The first simple ordinary answer would be that it *is* the same desk, it is actually identical, there is a perfect identity of substance, or whatever you like to call it. But when that apparently simple answer is suggested, it is important to observe that you cannot have an empirical reason for such a view as that, and if you hold it, you hold it simply because you like it and for no other reason whatever. All that you really know is such facts as that what you see now, when you look at the desk, bears a very close similarity to what you saw a week ago when you looked at it. Rather more than that one fact of similarity I admit you know, or you may know. You might have paid some one to watch the desk continuously throughout the week, and might then have discovered that it was presenting appearances of the same sort all through that period, assuming that the light was kept on all through the night. In that way you could have established continuity. You have not in fact done so. You do not in fact know that that desk has gone on looking the same all the time, but we will assume that. Now the essential point is this: What is the empirical reason that makes you call a number of appearances, appearances of the same desk? What makes you say on successive occasions, I am seeing the same desk? The first thing to notice is this, that it does not matter what is the answer, so long as you have realized that the answer consists in something empirical and not in a recognized metaphysical identity of substance. There is something given in experience which makes you call it the same desk, and having once grasped that fact, you can go on and say, it is that something (whatever it is) that makes you call it the same desk which shall be *defined* as *constituting* it the same desk, and there shall be no assumption of a metaphysical substance which is identical throughout. It is a little easier to the untrained mind to conceive of an identity than it is to conceive of a system of correlated particulars, hung one to another by relations of similarity and continuous change and so on. That idea is apparently more complicated, but that is what is empirically given in the real world, and substance, in the sense of something which is continuously identical in the same desk, is not given to you. Therefore in all cases where you seem to have a continuous entity persisting through changes, what you have to do is to ask yourself what makes you consider the successive appearances as belonging to one thing. When you have found out what makes you take the view that they belong to the same thing, you will then see that that which has made you say so, is all that is *certainly* there in the way of unity. Anything that there may be over and above that, I shall recognize as something I cannot know. What I can know is that there are a certain series of appearances linked together, and the series of those appearances I shall define as being a desk. In that way the desk is reduced to being a logical fiction, because a series is a logical fiction. In that way all the ordinary objects of daily life are extruded from the world of what there is, and in their place as what there is you find a number of passing particulars of the kind that one is immediately conscious of in sense. I want to make clear that I am not *denying* the existence of anything; I am only refusing to affirm it. I refuse to affirm the existence of anything for which there is no evidence, but I equally refuse to deny the existence of anything against which there is no evidence. Therefore I neither affirm nor deny it, but merely say, that is not in the realm of the knowable and is certainly not a part of physics; and physics, if it is to be interpreted, must be interpreted in terms of the sort of thing that can be empirical. If your atom is going to serve purposes in physics, as it undoubtedly does, your atom has got to turn out to be a construction, and your atom will in fact turn out to be a series of classes of particulars. The same process which one applies to physics, one will also apply elsewhere. The application to physics I explained briefly in my book on the *External World*, Chapters III and IV.

I have talked so far about the unreality of the things we think real. I want to speak with equal emphasis about the reality of things we think unreal, such as phantoms and hallucinations. Phantoms and hallucinations, considered in themselves, are, as I explained in the preceding lectures, on exactly the same level as ordinary sense-data. They differ from ordinary sense-data only in the fact that they do not have the usual correlations with other things. In themselves they have the same reality as ordinary sense-data. They have the most complete and absolute and perfect reality that anything can have. They are part of the ultimate constituents of the world, just as the fleeting sense-data are. Speaking of the fleeting sense-data, I think it is very important to remove out of one's instincts any disposition to believe that the real is the permanent. There has been a metaphysical prejudice always that if a thing is really real, it has to last either forever or for a fairly decent length of time. That is to my mind an entire mistake. The things that are really real last a very short time. Again I am not denying that there *may* be things that last forever, or for thousands of years; I only say that those are not within our experience, and that the real things that we know by experience last for a very short time, one tenth or half a second, or whatever it may be. Phantoms and hallucinations are among those, among the ultimate constituents of the world. The things that we call real, like tables and chairs, are systems, series of classes of particulars, and the particulars are the real things, the particulars being sense-data when they happen to be given to you. A table or chair will be a series of classes of particulars, and therefore a logical fiction. Those particulars will be on the same level of reality as a hallucination or a phantom. I ought to explain in what sense a chair is a series of classes. A chair presents at each moment a number of different appearances. All the appearances that it is presenting at a given moment make up a certain class. All those sets of appearances vary from time to time. If I take a chair and smash it, it will present a whole set of different appearances from what it did before, and without going as far as that, it will always be changing as the light changes, and so on. So you get a series in time of different sets of appearances, and that is what I mean by saying that a chair is a series of classes. That explanation is too crude, but I leave out the niceties, as that is not the actual topic I am dealing with. Now each single particular which is part of this whole system is linked up with the others in the system. Supposing, e.g., I take as my particular the appearance which that chair is presenting to me at this moment. That is linked up first of all with the appearance which the same chair is presenting to any one of you at the same moment, and with the appearance which it is going to present to me at later moments. There you get at once two journeys that you can take away from that particular, and that particular will be correlated in certain definite ways with the other particulars which also belong to that chair. That is what you mean by saying—or what you ought to mean by saying—that what I see before me is a real thing as opposed to a phantom. It means that it has a whole set of correlations of different kinds. It means that that particular, which is the appearance of the chair to me at this moment, is not isolated but is connected in a certain well-known familiar fashion with others, in the sort of way that makes it answer one's expectations. And so, when you go and buy a chair, you buy not only the appearance which it presents to you at that moment, but also those other appearances that it is going to present when it gets home. If it were a phantom chair, it would not present any appearances when it got home, and would not be the sort of thing you would want to buy. The sort one calls real is one of a whole correlated system, whereas the sort you call hallucinations are not. The respectable particulars in the world are all of them linked up with other particulars in respectable, conventional ways. Then sometimes you get a wild particular, like a merely visual chair that you cannot sit on, and say it is a phantom, a hallucination, you exhaust all the vocabulary of abuse upon it. That is what one means by calling it unreal, because 'unreal' applied in that way is a term of abuse and never would be applied to a thing that *was* unreal because you would not be so angry with it.

I will pass on to some other illustrations. Take a person. What is it that makes you say, when you meet your friend Jones, 'Why, this is Jones'? It is clearly not the persistence of a metaphysical entity inside Jones somewhere, because even if there be such an entity, it certainly is not what you see when you see Jones coming along the street; it certainly is something that you are not acquainted with, not an empirical datum. Therefore plainly there is something in the empirical appearances which he presents to you, something in their relations one to another, which enables you to collect all these together and say, 'These are what I call the appearances of one person', and that something that makes you collect them together is not the persistence of a metaphysical subject, because that, whether there be such a persistent subject or not, is certainly not a datum, and that which makes you say 'Why, it is Jones' is a datum. Therefore Jones is not constituted as he is known by a sort of pin-point ego that is underlying his appearances, and you have got to find some correlations among the appearances which are of the sort that make you put all those appearances together and say, they are the appearances of one person. Those are different when it is other people and when it is yourself. When it is yourself, you have more to go by. You have not only what you look like, you have also your thoughts and memories and all your organic sensations, so that you have a much richer material and are therefore much less likely to be mistaken as to your own identity than as to some one else's. It happens, of course, that there are mistakes even as to one's own identity, in cases of multiple personality and so forth, but as a rule you will know that it is you because you have more to go by than other people have, and you would know it is you, not by a consciousness of the ego at all but by all sorts of things, by memory, by the way you feel and the way you look and a host of things. But all those are empirical data, and those enable you to say that the person to whom something happened yesterday was yourself. So you can collect a whole set of experiences into one string as all belonging to you, and similarly other people's experiences can be collected together as all belonging to them by relations that actually are observable and without assuming the existence of the persistent ego. It does not matter in the least to what we are concerned with, what exactly is the given empirical relation between two experiences that makes us say, 'These are two experiences of the same person'. It does not matter precisely what that relation is, because the logical formula for the construction of the person is the same whatever that relation may be, and because the mere fact that you can know that two experiences belong to the same person proves that there is such an empirical relation to be ascertained by analysis. Let us call the relation R. We shall say that when two experiences have to each other the relation R, then they are said to be experiences of the same person. That is a definition of what I mean by 'experiences of the same person'. We proceed here just in the same way as when we are defining numbers. We first define what is meant by saying that two classes 'have the same number', and then define what a number is. The person who has a given experience x will be the class of all those experiences which are 'experiences of the same person' as the one who experiences x. You can say that two events are co-personal when there is between them a certain relation R, namely that relation which makes us say that they are experiences of the same person. You can define the person who has a certain experience as being those experiences that are co-personal with that experience, and it will be better perhaps to take them as a series than as a class, because you want to know which is the beginning of a man's life and which is the end. Therefore we shall say that a person is a certain series of experiences. We shall not deny that there may be a metaphysical ego. We shall merely say that it is a question that does not concern us in any way, because it is a matter about which we know nothing and can know nothing, and therefore it obviously cannot be a thing that comes into science in any way. What we know is this string of experiences that makes up a person, and that is put together by means of certain empirically given relations, such, e.g., as memory.

I will take another illustration, a kind of problem that our method is useful in helping to deal with. You all know the American theory of neutral monism, which derives really from William James and is also suggested in the work of Mach, but in a rather less developed form. The theory of neutral monism maintains that the distinction between the mental and the physical is entirely an affair of arrangement, that the actual material arranged is exactly the same in the case of the mental as it is in the case of the physical, but they differ merely in the fact that when you take a thing as belonging in the same context with certain other things, it will belong to psychology, while when you take it in a certain other context with other things, it will belong to physics, and the difference is as to what you consider to be its context, just the same sort of difference as there is between arranging the people in London alphabetically or geographically. So, according to William James, the actual material of the world can be arranged in two different ways, one of which gives you physics and the other psychology. It is just like rows or columns: in an arrangement of rows and columns, you can take an item as either a member of a certain row or a member of a certain column; the item is the same in the two cases, but its context is different.

If you will allow me a little undue simplicity I can go on to say rather more about neutral monism, but you must understand that I am talking more simply than I ought to do because there is not time to put in all the shadings and qualifications. I was talking a moment ago about the appearances that a chair presents. If we take any one of these chairs, we can all look at it, and it presents a different appearance to each of us. Taken all together, taking all the different appearances that that chair is presenting to all of us at this moment, you get something that belongs to physics. So that, if one takes sense-data and arranges together all those sense-data that appear to different people at a given moment and are such as we should ordinarily say are appearances of the same physical object, then that class of sense-data will give you something that belongs to physics, namely, the chair at this moment. On the other hand, if instead of taking all the appearances that that chair presents to all of us at this moment, I take all the appearances that the different chairs in this room present to me at this moment, I get quite another group of particulars. All the different appearances that different chairs present to me now will give you something belonging to psychology, because that will give you my experiences at the present moment. Broadly speaking, according to what one may take as an expansion of William James, that should be the definition of the difference between physics and psychology.

We commonly assume that there is a phenomenon which we call

seeing the chair, but what I call my seeing the chair according to neutral monism is merely the existence of a certain particular, namely the particular which is the sense-datum of that chair at that moment. And I and the chair are both logical fictions, both being in fact a series of classes of particulars, of which one will be that particular which we call my seeing the chair. That actual appearance that the chair is presenting to me now is a member of me and a member of the chair, I and the chair being logical fictions. That will be at any rate a view that you can consider if you are engaged in vindicating neutral monism. There is no simple entity that you can point to and say: this entity is physical and not mental. According to William James and neutral monists that will not be the case with any simple entity that you may take. Any such entity will be a member of physical series and a member of mental series. Now I want to say that if you wish to test such a theory as that of neutral monism, if you wish to discover whether it is true or false, you cannot hope to get any distance with your problem unless you have at your fingers' ends the theory of logic that I have been talking of. You never can tell otherwise what can be done with a given material, whether you can concoct out of a given material the sort of logical fictions that will have the properties you want in psychology and in physics. That sort of thing is by no means easy to decide. You can only decide it if you really have a very considerable technical facility in these matters. Having said that, I ought to proceed to tell you that I have discovered whether neutral monism is true or not, because otherwise you may not believe that logic is any use in the matter. But I do not profess to know whether it is true or not. I feel more and more inclined to think that it may be true. I feel more and more that the difficulties that occur in regard to it are all of the sort that may be solved by ingenuity. But nevertheless there *are* a number of difficulties; there are a number of problems, some of which I have spoken about in the course of these lectures. One is the question of belief and the other sorts of facts involving two verbs. If there are such facts as this, that, I think, may make neutral monism rather difficult, but as I was pointing out, there is the theory that one calls behaviourism, which belongs logically with neutral monism, and that theory would altogether dispense with those facts containing two verbs, and would therefore dispose of that argument against neutral monism. There is, on the other hand, the argument from emphatic particulars, such as 'this' and 'now' and 'here' and such words as that, which are not very easy to reconcile, to my mind, with the view which does not distinguish between a particular and experiencing that particular. But the argument about emphatic particulars is so delicate and so subtle that I cannot feel quite sure whether it is a valid one or not, and I think the longer one pursues philosophy, the more conscious one becomes how extremely often one has been taken in by fallacies, and the less willing one is to be quite sure that an argument is valid if there is anything about it that is at all subtle or elusive, at all difficult to grasp. That makes me a little cautious and doubtful about all these arguments, and therefore although I am quite sure that the question of the truth or falsehood of neutral monism is not to be solved except by these means, yet I do not profess to know whether neutral monism is true or is not. I am not without hopes of finding out in the course of time, but I do not profess to know yet.

As I said earlier in this lecture, one thing that our techinique does, is to give us a means of constructing a given body of symbolic propositions with the minimum of apparatus, and every diminution in apparatus diminishes the risk of error. Suppose, e.g., that you have constructed your physics with a certain number of entities and a certain number of premises; suppose you discover that by a little ingenuity you can dispense with half of those entities and half of those premises, you clearly have diminished the risk of error, because if you had before 10 entities and 10 premises, then the 5 you have now would be all right, but it is not true conversely that if the 5 you have now are all right, the 10 must have been. Therefore you diminish the risk of error with every diminution of entities and premises. When I spoke about the desk and said I was not going to assume the existence of a persistent substance underlying its appearances, it is an example of the case in point. You have anyhow the successive appearances, and if you can get on without assuming the metaphysical and constant desk, you have a smaller risk of error than you had before. You would not necessarily have a smaller risk of error if you were tied down to *denying* the metaphysical desk. That is the advantage of Occam's Razor, that it diminishes your risk of error. Considered in that way you may say that the whole of our problem belongs rather to science than to philosophy. I think perhaps that is true, but I believe the only difference between science and philosophy is, that science is what you more or less know and philosophy is what you do not know. Philosophy is that part of science which at present people choose to have opinions about, but which they have no knowledge about. Therefore every advance in knowledge robs philosophy of some problems which formerly it had, and if there is any truth, if there is any value in the kind of procedure of mathematical logic, it will follow that a number of problems which had belonged to philosophy will have ceased to belong to philosophy and will belong to science. And of course the moment they become soluble, they become to a large class of philosophical minds uninteresting, because to many of the people who like philosophy, the charm of it consists in the speculative freedom, in the fact that you can play with hypotheses. You can think out this or that which *may* be true, which is a very valuable exercise until you discover what *is* true; but when you discover what is true the whole fruitful play of fancy in that region is curtailed, and you will abandon that region and pass on. Just as there are families in America who from the time of the Pilgrim Fathers onward had always migrated westward, toward the backwoods, because they did not like civilized life, so the philosopher has an adventurous disposition and likes to dwell in the region where there are still uncertainties. It is true that the transferring of a region from philosophy into science will make it distasteful to a very important and useful type of mind. I think that is true of a good deal of the applications of mathematical logic in the directions that I have been indicating. It makes it dry, precise, methodical, and in that way robs it of a certain quality that it had when you could play with it more freely. I do not feel that it is my place to apologize for that, because if it is true, it is true. If it is not true, of course, I do owe you an apology; but if it is, it is not my fault, and therefore I do not feel I owe any apology for any sort of dryness or dulness in the world. I would say this too, that for those who have any taste for mathematics, for those who like symbolic constructions, that sort of world is a very delightful one, and if you do not find it otherwise attractive, all that is necessary to do is to acquire a taste for mathematics, and then you will have a very agreeable world, and with that conclusion I will bring this course of lectures to an end.

On Propositions: what they are and how they mean

Russell has never had any hesitation about saying that he has changed his mind, a characteristic that runs contrary to two common occupational disorders of philosophers: the illusion of infallibility (or the necessity to suggest the same), and hesitation about airing one's views (based on the fear that in time one may find them to be faulty). Both of these tendencies Russell deplores and feels to be lingering influences of the days in which philosophy was closely united with theology. A theologian cannot change his mind on major issues of doctrine, for the consequence of this is heresy. A scientist, however, can change his theories if further investigations reveal his earlier formulations to be wrong. It is Russell's hope that as philosophy comes closer to a scientific point of view, the right of the philosopher to alter his opinions in the light of his later thoughts will be accepted as a matter of course.

This essay, composed a year after the lectures on logical atomism, shows the development of Russell's theory as to the nature of propositions. Essentially what is involved is the further assimilation of the views of Wittgenstein, whose influence upon the 1918 series was far more clearly marked. There is no doubt about the theory given here being Russell's characteristic work. For one thing, it introduces considerations of behaviourism which are typical of Russell's thought of the twenties and lie apart from his conversations with Wittgenstein before 1914. It is reprinted here to show the manner in which Russell modified his views immediately after the publication of the 1918 lectures and to show the steps that led from his earlier thought (to which the lectures of 1918 can be taken as a sort of cap-stone and summation) to his later views. It is this later Russell that historians of contemporary philosophy frequently neglect or misrepresent.

ON PROPOSITIONS: WHAT THEY ARE
AND HOW THEY MEAN*

A PROPOSITION may be defined as: *What we believe when we believe truly or falsely*. This definition is so framed as to avoid the assumption that, whenever we believe, our belief is true or false. In order to arrive, from the definition, at an account of what a proposition is, we must decide what belief is, what is the sort of thing that can be believed, and what constitutes truth or falsehood in a belief. I take it as evident that the truth or falsehood of a belief depends upon a *fact* to which the belief 'refers'. Therefore it is well to begin our inquiry by examining the nature of facts.

I. STRUCTURE OF FACTS

I mean by a 'fact' anything complex. If the world contains no simples, then whatever it contains is a fact; if it contains any simples, then facts are whatever it contains except simples. When it is raining, that is a fact; when the sun is shining, that is a fact. The distance from London to Edinburgh is a fact. That all men die is probably a fact. That the planets move round the sun approximately in ellipses is a fact. In speaking of these as facts, I am not alluding to the phrases in which we assert them, or to our frame of mind while we make the assertions, but to those features in the constitution of the world which make our assertions true (if they are true) or false (if they are false).

---

* In what follows, the first section, on the structure of facts, contains nothing essentially novel, and is only included for the convenience of the reader. I have defended its doctrines elsewhere, and have therefore here set them down dogmatically. On the other hand, later sections contain views which I have not hitherto advocated, resulting chiefly from an attempt to define what constitutes 'meaning' and to dispense with the 'subject' except as a logical construction.

To say that facts are complex is the same thing as to say that they have *constituents*. That Socrates was Greek, that he married Xantippe, that he died of drinking the hemlock, are facts that all have something in common, namely, that they are 'about' Socrates, who is accordingly said to be a constituent of each of them.

Every constituent of a fact has a *position* (or several positions) in the fact. For example, 'Socrates loves Plato' and 'Plato loves Socrates' have the same constituents, but are different facts, because the constituents do not have the same positions in the two facts. 'Socrates loves Socrates' (if it is a fact) contains Socrates in two positions. 'Two and two are four' contains *two* in two positions. '$2 + 2 = 2^2$' contains 2 in four positions.

Two facts are said to have the same 'form' when they differ only as regards their constituents. In this case, we may suppose the one to result from the other by *substitution* of different constituents. For example, 'Napoleon hates Wellington' results from 'Socrates loves Plato' by substituting Napoleon for Socrates, Wellington for Plato, and *hates* for *loves*. It is obvious that some, but not all, facts can be thus derived from 'Socrates loves Plato'. Thus some facts have the same form as this, and some have not. We can represent the form of a fact by the use of variables: thus '$x R y$' may be used to represent the form of the fact that Socrates loves Plato. But the use of such expressions, as well as of ordinary language, is liable to lead to mistakes unless care is taken to avoid them.

There are an infinite number of forms of facts. It will conduce to simplicity to confine ourselves, for the moment, to facts having only three constituents, namely, two terms and a dual (or dyadic) relation. In a fact which has three constituents, two can be distinguished from the third by the circumstance that, if these two are interchanged, we still have a fact, or, at worst, we obtain a fact by taking the contradictory of what results from the interchange, whereas the third constituent (the relation) cannot ever be interchanged with either of the others. Thus if there is such a fact as 'Socrates loves Plato', there is either 'Plato loves Socrates' or 'Plato does not love Socrates', but neither Socrates nor Plato can replace *loves*. (For purposes of illustration, I am for the moment neglecting the fact that Socrates and Plato are themselves complex.) The essentially non-interchangeable constituent of a fact containing three constituents is called a *dual* (or dyadic) *relation*; the other two constituents are called the *terms* of that relation in that fact. The terms of dual relations are called *particulars*.*

Facts containing three constituents are not all of the same form. There are two forms that they may have, which are each other's opposites. 'Socrates loves Plato' and 'Napoleon does not love Wellington' are facts which have opposite forms. We will call the form of 'Socrates loves Plato' *positive*, and the form of 'Napoleon does not love Wellington' *negative*. So long as we confine ourselves to atomic facts, i.e., to such as contain only one verb and neither generality nor its denial, the distinction between positive and negative facts is easily made. In more complicated cases there are still two kinds of facts, though it is less clear which is positive and which negative.

Thus the forms of facts divide into pairs, such that, given appropriate constituents, there is always a fact of one of the two correlated forms but not of the other. Given any two particulars of a dual relation, say x and y and R, there will be either a fact '$x R y$', or a fact 'not - $x R y$'. Let us suppose, for the sake of illustration, that x has the relation R to y, and z does not have the relation S to w. Each of these facts contains only three constituents, a relation and two terms; but the two facts do not have the same form. In the one, R relates x and y; in the other, S does not relate z and w. It must not be supposed that the negative fact contains a constituent corresponding to the word 'not'. It contains no more constituents than a positive fact of the correlative positive form. The difference between the two forms is ultimate and irreducible. We will call this characteristic of a form its *quality*. Thus facts, and forms of facts, have two opposite qualities, positive and negative.

There is implanted in the human breast an almost unquenchable desire to find some way of avoiding the admission that negative facts are as ultimate as those that are positive. The 'infinite negative' has been endlessly abused and interpreted. Usually it is said that, when we deny something, we are really asserting something else which is incompatible with what we deny. If we say 'roses are

---

* The above discussion might be replaced by that of subject-predicate facts or of facts containing triadic, tetradic . . . relations. But it is possible to doubt whether there are subject-predicate facts, and the others are more complicated than those containing three constituents. Hence these are best for purposes of illustration.

not blue', we mean 'roses are white or red or yellow'. But such a view will not bear a moment's scrutiny. It is only plausible when the positive quality by which our denial is supposed to be replaced is incapable of existing together with the quality denied. 'The table is square' may be denied by 'the table is round', but not by 'the table is wooden'. The only reason we can deny 'the table is square' by 'the table is round' is that what is round is *not* square. And this has to be a *fact*, though just as negative as the fact that this table is not square. Thus it is plain that incompatibility cannot exist without negative facts.

There might be an attempt to substitute for a negative fact the mere absence of a fact. If A loves B, it may be said, that is a good substantial fact; while if A does not love B, that merely expresses the absence of a fact composed of A and loving and B, and by no means involves the actual existence of a negative fact. But the absence of a fact is itself a negative fact; it is the fact that there is *not* such a fact as A loving B. Thus, we cannot escape from negative facts in this way.

Of the many attempts that have been made to dispense with negative facts, the best known to me is that of Mr. Demos.* His view is as follows: There is among propositions an ultimate relation of *opposition*; this relation is indefinable, but has the characteristic that when two propositions are opposites they cannot both be true, though they may both be false. Thus 'John is in' and 'John is gone to Semipalatinsk' are opposites. When we deny a proposition, what we are really doing is to assert: 'Some opposite of this proposition is true'. The difficulty of this theory is to state the very important fact that two opposites cannot both be true. 'The relation of opposition,' says Mr. Demos, 'is such that, if p opposes q, p and q are not both true (at least one of them is false). This must not be taken as a definition, for it makes use of the notion "not" which, I said, is equivalent to the notion "opposite". In fact, opposition seems epistemologically to be a primitive notion' (page 191). Now if we take Mr. Demos's statement that 'p and q are not both true' and apply his definition to it, it becomes 'an opposite of "p and q are both true" is true'. But this does not yield what we want. Suppose some obstinate person were to say: 'I believe p,

* 'A Discussion of a Certain Type of Negative Proposition', *Mind*, N.S., No. 102 (April, 1917), pp. 188–96.

and I believe q, and I also believe that an opposite of "p and q are both true" is true'. What could Mr. Demos reply to such a person? He would presumably reply; 'Don't you see that that is impossible? It cannot be the case that p and q are both true, and also that an opposite of "p and q are both true" is true'. But an opponent would retort by asking him to state his negation in his own language, in which case all that Mr. Demos could say would be: 'Let us give the name P to the proposition "p and q are both true". Then the proposition that you assert and that I deny is "P is true, and also some opposite of P is true". Calling this proposition Q, and applying my definition of negation, what I am asserting is that some opposite of Q is true.' This also the obstinate person would admit. He would go on for ever admitting opposites, but refusing to make any denials. To such an attitude, so far as I can see, there would be no reply except to change the subject. It is, in fact, necessary to admit that two opposites cannot both be true, and not to regard this as a statement to which the suggested definition of negation is to be applied. And the reason is that we must be able to say that a proposition is not true without having to refer to any other proposition.

The above discussion has prematurely introduced propositions, in order to follow Mr. Demos's argument. We shall see later, when we have defined propositions, that all propositions *are* positive facts, even when they assert negative facts. This is, I believe, the source of our unwillingness to admit negative facts as ultimate. The subject of negative facts might be argued at great length, but as I wish to reach the proper topic of my paper, I will say no more about it, and will merely observe that a not dissimilar set of considerations shows the necessity of admitting *general* facts, i.e., facts about all or some of a collection.

II. MEANING OF IMAGES AND WORDS

The questions which arise concerning propositions are so many and various that it is not easy to know where to begin. One very important question is as to whether propositions are what I call 'incomplete symbols' or not. Another question is as to whether the word 'proposition' can stand for anything except a form of words. A third question is as to the manner in which a proposition refers to the fact that makes it true or false. I am not suggesting that these are the only important questions, but they are, at any rate, questions which any theory of propositions should be able to answer.

Let us begin with the most tangible thing: the proposition as a form of words. Take again 'Socrates loves Plato'. This is a complex symbol, composed of three symbols, namely 'Socrates' and 'loves' and 'Plato'. Whatever may be the meaning of the complex symbol, it is clear that it depends upon the meanings of the separate words. Thus before we can hope to understand the meaning of a proposition as a form of words, we must understand what constitutes the meaning of single words.

Logicians, so far as I know, have done very little towards explaining the nature of the relation called 'meaning', nor are they to blame in this, since the problem is essentially one for psychology. But before we tackle the question of the meaning of a word, there is one important observation to be made as to what a word *is*.

If we confine ourselves to spoken words in one language, a word is a class of closely similar noises produced by breath combined with movements of the throat and tongue and lips. This is not a *definition* of 'words', since some noises are meaningless, and meaning is part of the definition of 'words'. It is important, however, to realize at the outset that what we call one word is not a single entity, but a class of entities: there are instances of the word 'dog' just as there are instances of dogs. And when we hear a noise, we may be doubtful whether it is the word 'dog' badly pronounced or not: the noises that are instances of a word shade off into other noises by continuous gradations, just as dogs themselves may shade off into wolves according to the evolutionary hypothesis. And, of course, exactly the same remarks apply to written words.

It is obvious to begin with that, if we take some such word as 'Socrates' or 'dog', the meaning of the word consists in some relation to an object or set of objects. The first question to be asked is: Can the relation called 'meaning' be a direct relation between the word as a physical occurrence and the object itself, or must the relation pass through a 'mental' intermediary, which could be called the 'idea' of the object?

If we take the view that no 'mental' intermediary is required, we shall have to regard the 'meaning' of a word as consisting in what James would call 'processes of leading'. That is to say, the causes and effects of the occurrence of a word will be connected, in some way to be further defined, with the object which is its meaning. To take an unusually crude instance: You see John, and you say, 'Hullo, John'—this gives the *cause* of the word; you call 'John', and John appears at the door—this gives the *effect* of the word. Thus, in this case, John is both cause and effect of the word 'John'. When we say of a dog that he 'knows' his name, it is only such causal correlations that are indubitable: we cannot be sure that there is any 'mental' occurrence in the dog when we call him and he comes. Is it possible that all use and understanding of language consists merely in the fact that certain events cause it, and it, in turn, causes certain events?

This view of language has been advocated, more or less tentatively, by Professor Watson in his book on *Behaviour*.* The behaviourist view, as I understand it, maintains that 'mental' phenomena, though they may exist, are not amenable to scientific treatment, because each of them can only be observed by one observer—in fact, it is highly doubtful whether even one observer can be aware of anything not reducible to some bodily occurrence. Behaviourism is not a metaphysic, but a principle of method. Since language is an observable phenomenon, and since language has a property which we call 'meaning', it is essential to behaviourism to give an account of 'meaning' which introduces nothing known only through introspection. Professor Watson recognizes this obligation and sets to work to fulfil it. Nor is it to be lightly *assumed* that he cannot do so, though I incline to the belief that a theory of language which takes no account of images is incomplete in a vital point. But let us first see what is to be said in favour of the behaviourist theory of language.

Professor Watson denies altogether the occurrence of images, which he replaces by faint kinaesthetic sensations, especially those belonging to the pronunciation of words *sotto voce*. He defines 'implicit behaviour' as 'involving only the speech mechanisms (or the larger musculature in a minimal way; e.g., bodily attitudes or sets)' (page 19). He adds: 'It is implied in these words that there exists, or ought to exist, a method of observing implicit behaviour.

* *Behavior: An Introduction to Comparative Psychology* (New York, 1914), by John B. Watson, Professor of Psychology in the Johns Hopkins University. See especially pp. 321–34.

There is none at present. The larynx and tongue, we believe, are the loci of most of the phenomena' (page 20). He repeats these views in greater detail in a later chapter. The way in which the intelligent use of words is learnt is thus set forth:

'The stimulus (object) to which the child often responds, a box, e.g., by movements such as opening and closing and putting objects into it, may serve to illustrate our argument. The nurse, observing that the child reacts with his hands, feet, etc., to the box, begins to say "*box*" when the child is handed the box, "*open box*" when the child opens it, "*close box*" when he closes it, and "*put doll in box*" when that act is executed. This is repeated over and over again. In the process of time it comes about that without any other stimulus than that of the box which originally called out only the bodily habits, he begins to say "*box*" when he sees it, "*open box*" when he opens it, etc. The visible box now becomes a stimulus capable of releasing either the bodily habits or the word-habit, i.e., development has brought about two things: (1) a series of functional connexions among arcs which run from visual receptor to muscles of throat, and (2) a series of already earlier connected arcs which run from the same receptor to the bodily muscles. . . . The object meets the child's vision. He runs to it and tries to reach it and says "*box*". . . . Finally the word is uttered without the movement of going towards the box being executed. . . . Habits are formed of going to the box when the arms are full of toys. The child has been taught to deposit them there. When his arms are laden with toys and no box is there, the word-habit arises and he calls "*box*"; it is handed to him and he opens it and deposits the toys therein. This roughly marks what we would call the genesis of a true language habit' (pages 329–30).

A few pages earlier, he says: 'We say nothing of reasoning since we do not admit this as a genuine type of human behavior except as a special form of language habit' (page 319).

The questions raised by the above theory of language are of great importance, since the possibility of what may be called a materialistic psychology turns on them. If a person talks and writes intelligently, he gives us as much evidence as we can ever hope to have of his possessing a mind. If his intelligent speech and writing can be explained on Professor Watson's lines, there seems to remain nothing he can do to persuade us that he is not merely physical.

There is, I think, a valid objection to the behaviouristic view of language on the basis of fact and an invalid one of theory. The objection of fact is that the denial of images appears empirically indefensible. The objection of theory (which, in spite of its apparent force, I do not believe to be unanswerable) is that it is difficult, on the basis of the above quotations, to account for the occurrence of the word when the object is merely desired, not actually present. Let us take these in succession.

(1) *Existence of Images.*—Professor Watson, one must conclude, does not possess the faculty of visualizing, and is unwilling to believe that others do. Kinaesthetic images can be explained away, as being really small sensations of the same kind as those that would belong to actual movements. Inner speech, in particular, in so far as it is not accompanied by auditory images, may, I think, really consist of such small sensations, and be accompanied by small movements of the tongue or throat such as behaviourism requires. Tactile images might possibly be similarly explained. But visual and auditory images cannot be so explained, because, if taken as sensations, they actually contradict the laws of physics. The chair opposite to you is empty; you shut your eyes and visualize your friend as sitting in it. This is an event in you, not in the outer world. It *may* be a *physiological* event, but even so it must be radically distinguished from a visual sensation, since it affords no part of the data upon which our knowledge of the physical world outside our own body is built. If you try to persuade an ordinary uneducated person that she cannot call up a visual picture of a friend sitting in a chair, but can only use words describing what such an occurrence would be like, she will conclude that you are mad. (This statement is based upon experiment.) I see no reason whatever to reject the conclusion originally suggested by Galton's investigations, namely, that the habit of abstract pursuits makes learned men much inferior to the average in the power of visualizing, and much more exclusively occupied with words in their 'thinking'. When Professor Watson says: 'I should throw out imagery altogether and attempt to show that practically all natural thought goes on in terms of sensori-motor processes in the larynx (but not in terms of imageless thought)' (*Psychological Review*, 1913, page 174n), he is, it seems to me, mistaking a personal peculiarity for a universal human characteristic.

The rejection of images by behaviourists is, of course, part of their rejection of introspection as a source of knowledge. It will be well, therefore, to consider for a moment the grounds in favour of this rejection.

The arguments of those who oppose introspection as a scientific method seem to me to rest upon two quite distinct grounds, of which one is much more explicit in their writings than the other. The ground which is the more explicit is that data obtained by introspection are private and only verifiable by one observer, and cannot therefore have that degree of public certainty which science demands. The other, less explicit, ground is that physical science has constructed a spatio-temporal cosmos obeying certain laws, and it is irritating to have to admit that there are things in the world which do not obey these laws. It is worth while to observe that the definition of introspection is different according as we take the one or the other of these grounds of objection.

If privacy is the main objection to introspective data, we shall have to include among such data all bodily sensations. A toothache, for example, is essentially private. The dentist may see that your tooth is in a condition in which it is likely to ache, but he does not feel your ache, and only knows what you mean by an ache through his own experience of similar occurrences. The correlation of cavities with toothaches has been established by a number of observations, each of which was private, in exactly the sense which is considered objectionable. And yet one would not call a person introspective because he was conscious of toothache, and it is not very difficult to find a place for toothache in the physical world. I shall not insist upon the fact that, in the last analysis, all our sensations are private, and the public world of physics is built on similarities, not on identities. But it is worth while to insist upon the privacy of the sensations which gives us knowledge of our own body over and above the knowledge we have of other bodies. This is important, because no one regards as scientifically negligible the knowledge of our own body which is obtained through these private data.

This brings us to the second ground of objection to introspection, namely, that its data do not obey the laws of physics. This, though less emphasized, is, I think, the objection which is really felt the more strongly of the two. And this objection leads to a definition of introspection which is much more in harmony with usage than that which results from making privacy the essential characteristic of its data. For example, Knight Dunlap, a vigorous opponent of introspection, contends that images are really muscular contractions,* and evidently regards our awareness of muscular contractions as not coming under the head of introspection. I think it will be found that the essential characteristic of introspective data is concerned with *localization*: either they are not localized at all, or they are localized in a place already physically occupied by something which would be inconsistent with them if they were regarded as part of the physical world. In either case, introspective data have to be regarded as not obeying the laws of physics, and this is, I think, the fundamental reason why an attempt is made to reject them.

The question of the publicity of data and the question of their physical status are not wholly unconnected. We may distinguish a gradually diminishing degree of publicity in various data. Those of sight and hearing are the most public; smell somewhat less so; touch still less; visceral sensations hardly at all. The question turns on the degree and frequency of similarity of sensations in neighbours at the same time. If we hear a clap of thunder when no one else does, we think we are mad; if we feel a stomach-ache when no one else does, we are in no way surprised. We say, therefore, that the stomach-ache is *mine*, while the thunder is not. But what is mine includes what belongs to the body, and it is here that the stomach-ache belongs. The stomach-ache is *localized*: it has a position near the surface of the stomach, which is visible and palpable. (How the localization is effected need not concern us in this connexion.) Now, when we consider the localization of images, we find a difference according to the nature of the images. Images of private sensations can be localized where the private sensations would be, without causing any gross or obvious violation of physical laws. Images of words in the mouth can be located in the

* *Psychological Review* (1916), 'Thought-Content and Feeling', p. 59. See also his articles in an earlier volume of the same review, 'The Case against Introspection', (1912), pp. 404–13, and 'The Nature of Perceived Relations', *ibid.*, pp. 415–46. In this last article he states 'that "introspection", divested of its mythological suggestion of the observing of consciousness, is really the observation of bodily sensations (sensibles) and feelings (feelables)' (p. 427*n*).

mouth. For this reason, there is no prima facie objection to regarding them, as Watson does, as small sensations: this view may or may not be true, but it is not capable of being rejected without more ado. In regard to all private sensations, the distinction between image and sensation is not sharp and definite. But visual and auditory images are in quite a different position, since the physical event to which they would point if they were sensations is not taking place.

Thus the crucial phenomena as regards introspection are images of public sensations, i.e., especially visual and auditory images. On grounds of observation, in spite of Watson, it seems impossible to deny that such images occur. But they are not public, and, if taken as sensations, contradict the laws of physics. Reverting to the case of visualizing a friend in a chair which, in fact, is empty, you cannot locate the image in the body because it is visual, nor (as a physical phenomenon) in the chair, because the chair, as a physical object, is empty. Thus it seems that the physical world does not include all that we are aware of, and that introspection must be admitted as a source of knowledge distinct from sensation.

I do not, of course, mean to suggest that visual and auditory images are our only non-physical data. I have taken them as affording the strongest case for the argument; but when they are admitted, there is no longer any reason to reject other images.

Our criticism of fact, as against Watson, has led us to the conclusion that it is impossible to escape the admission of images as something radically distinct from sensations, particularly as being not amenable to the laws of physics. It remains to consider a possible criticism of theory, namely, that it is difficult, on his view, to account for the occurrence of a word when an absent object is desired. I do not think this criticism valid, but I think the considerations which it suggests are important.

(2) *Words in the Absence of their Objects.*— In the account given by Watson of the child learning to use the word 'box', attention is almost wholly concentrated on the way the word comes to occur in the presence of the box. There is only a brief reference to the use of the word when the object is absent but desired: 'Habits are formed of going to the box when the arms are full of toys. The child has been taught to deposit them there. When his arms are laden with toys and no box is there, the word-habit arises and he

calls "*box*".' The difficulty—I think not insuperable—which arises in regard to this account is that there seems no adequate stimulus for the word-habit in the circumstances supposed. We are assuming that the habit has been formed of saying 'box' when the box is present; but how can such a habit lead to the use of the same word when the box is absent? The believer in images will say that, in the absence of the box, an image of it will occur in the child, and this image will have the same associations as the box has, including the association with the word 'box'. In this way the use of the word is accounted for; but in Watson's account it remains mysterious. Let us see what this objection amounts to.

The phenomenon called 'thinking', however it may be analysed, has certain characteristics which cannot be denied. One of the most obvious of these is that it enables us to act with reference to absent objects, and not only with reference to those that are sensibly present. The tendency of the behaviourist school is to subordinate cognition to action, and to regard action as physically explicable. Now I do not wish to deny that much action, perhaps most, is physically explicable, but nevertheless it seems impossible to account for *all* action without taking account of 'ideas', i.e., images of absent objects. If this view is rejected, it will be necessary to explain away all desire. Desire is not dealt with by Watson*: it and kindred words are absent from the index to his book. In the absence of such a phenomenon as desire, it is difficult to see what is happening when the child with his arms full of toys says 'box'. One would naturally say that an image of the box occurs, combined with the feeling we call 'desire', and that the image is associated with the word just as the object would be, because the image resembles the object. But Watson requires that the arms full of toys should cause the word 'box' without any intermediary. And it is not at first sight obvious how this is to be brought about.

To this objection there seem two possible replies: one, that the occurrence of the image on the usual theory is just as mysterious as the occurrence of the word on Watson's theory; the other, that the passage from full arms to the word 'box' is a telescoped process,

* The only discussion of desire by Watson, as far as I know, is in connexion with psycho-analysis in his article, 'The Psychology of Wish Fulfilment', *Scientific Monthly* (November, 1916).

derived from the habit of the transition from full arms to the box and thence to the word 'box'. The objection to the second of these replies seems to be that the transition to the word 'box' in the absence of the box feels quite unlike the transition to the word through the actual box: in the latter there is satisfaction, in the former dissatisfaction. Telescoped processes give similar feelings to complete processes; in so far as they differ, they give more satisfaction as involving less effort. The word 'box' is not the terminus of the child's efforts, but a stage towards their success. It seems difficult, therefore, to assimilate the occurrence of a word in desire to a telescoped process. The retort to the first reply, namely, that the occurrence of the image is as mysterious as the occurrence of the word, is that, if images are admitted, we can admit psychological causal laws which are different from those of the physical world, whereas on Watson's view we shall have to admit physiological laws which are different from those of physics. In the physical world, if A often causes B, and B often causes C, it does not happen that, in those cases where A fails to cause B, it nevertheless causes C by a telescoped process. I go often to a certain restaurant (A), eat there (B), and find my hunger satisfied (C). But, however often this has happened, if, on a certain occasion, the restaurant is closed, so that B fails, I cannot arrive at C. If I could, economy in wartime would be easier than it is. Now, the process Watson assumes is strictly analogous to this. In his theory we have a frequent transition from arms-full (A) to the box (B) and thence to the word 'box' (C). Then one day the transition from A to B fails, but nevertheless the transition from A to C takes place. This demands other causal laws than those of physics— at least prima facie. If images are admitted, it is easy to see that the laws of their occurrence and effects are different from those of physics, and therefore the above difficulty does not exist in regard to them; but if they are denied, a difference of causal laws is required within the realm of matter.

This argument, however, is by no means conclusive. The behaviour of living matter is obviously in some respects different from that of dead matter, but this does not prove that the difference is ultimate. Gases and solids behave differently, yet both obey ultimate physical laws. The chief peculiarities in the behaviour of animals are those due to habit and association, all of which, I believe, may be summarized in the one law: 'When A and B have often existed in close temporal contiguity, either tends to cause the other'. This law will only apply to occurrences within the body of a single animal. But I think it suffices to account for telescoped processes, and for the use of words in the absence of their objects. Thus in Watson's instance, the child has frequently experienced the sequence: arms-full, box, the word 'box'. Thus arms-full and the word 'box' have frequently existed in close temporal contiguity, and hence arms-full can come to cause the word 'box'. They cannot cause the box itself, because this is governed by physical laws independent of the child's body; but they can cause the word. (The above law, however, may be explained on orthodox physical lines by the properties of nervous tissue, and does not demand a *fundamental* distinction between physiology and physics.) If, therefore, images were not empirically undeniable, I should not consider them theoretically necessary in order to account for the occurrence of words in the absence of their objects.

William James, in his *Essays in Radical Empiricism*, developed the view that the mental and the physical are not distinguished by the stuff of which they are made, but only by their causal laws. This view is very attractive, and I have made great endeavours to believe it. I think James is right in making the distinction between the causal laws the essential thing. There do seem to be psychological and physical causal laws which are distinct from each other.* We may define psychology as the study of the one sort of laws, and physics as the study of the other. But when we come to consider the stuff of the two sciences, it would seem that there are some particulars which obey only physical laws (namely, unperceived material things), some which obey only psychological laws (namely, images, at least), and some which obey both (namely, sensations). Thus sensations will be both physical and mental, while images will be purely mental. The use of words actually pronounced or written is part of the physical world, but in so far as words obtain their meaning through images, it is impossible to deal adequately with words without introducing psychology and taking account of data obtained by introspection. If this conclusion is valid, the

* I do not pretend to know whether the distinction is ultimate and irreducible. I say only that it is to be accepted practically in the present condition of science.

behaviourist theory of language is inadequate, in spite of the fact that it suggests much that is true and important.

I shall henceforth assume the existence of images, and shall proceed, on this assumption, to define the 'meaning' of words and images.

In considering the meaning of either a word or an image, we have to distinguish:

(1) The causes of the word or image,
(2) Its effects,
(3) What is the relation that constitutes meaning.

It is fairly clear that 'meaning' is a relation involving causal laws, but it involves also something else which is less easy to define.

The meaning of words differs, as a rule, from that of images by depending upon association, not upon similarity.

To 'think' of the meaning of a word is to call up images of what it means. Normally, grown-up people speaking their own language use words without thinking of their meaning. A person 'understands' a word when (a) suitable circumstances make him use it, (b) the hearing of it causes suitable behaviour in him. We may call these two active and passive understanding respectively. Dogs often have passive understanding of some words, but not active understanding.

It is not necessary to 'understanding' a word that a person should 'know what it means', in the sense of being able to say 'this word means so-and-so'. A word has a meaning, more or less vague; but the meaning is only to be discovered by observing its use: the use comes first, and the meaning is distilled out of it. The relation of a word to its meaning is, in fact, of the nature of a causal law, and there is no more reason why a person using a word correctly should be conscious of its meaning than there is for a planet which is moving correctly to be conscious of Kepler's laws.

To illustrate what is meant by 'understanding' words and sentences, let us suppose that you are walking in London with an absent-minded friend. You say 'look out, there's a motor coming'. He will glance round and jump aside without the need of any 'mental' intermediary. There need be no 'ideas', but only a stiffening of the muscles, followed quickly by action. He 'understands' the words, because he does the right thing. Such 'understanding' may be regarded as belonging to the nerves and brain, being habits which they have acquired while the language was being learnt. Thus understanding in this sense may be reduced to mere physiological causal laws.

If you say the same thing to a Frenchman with a slight knowledge of English, he will go through some inner speech which may be represented by 'Que dit-il? Ah oui, une automobile'. After this, the rest follows as with the Englishman. Watson would contend that the inner speech must be actually incipiently pronounced; we should argue that it might be merely imagined. But this point need not detain us at present.

If you say the same thing to a child who does not yet know the word 'motor', but does know the other words you are using, you produce a feeling of anxiety and doubt: you will have to point and say 'there, that's a motor'. After that, the child will roughly understand the word 'motor', though he may include trains and steamrollers. If this is the first time the child has heard the word 'motor', he may, for a long time, continue to recall this scene when he hears the word.

So far we have found four ways of understanding words:

(1) On suitable occasions you use the word properly.

(2) When you hear it, you act appropriately.

(3) You associate the word with another word (say in a different language) which has the appropriate effect on behaviour.

(4) When the word is being first learnt, you associate it with an object, which is what it 'means'; thus the word acquires some of the same causal efficacy as the object. The word 'motor!' can make you leap aside, just as the motor can, but it cannot break your bones.

So far, everything can be accounted for by behaviour. But so far we have only considered what may be called the 'demonstrative' use of language to point out a feature in the present environment; we have not considered what we may call its 'narrative' use, of which we may take as an instance the telling of some remembered event.

Let us take again the case of the child hearing the word 'motor' for the first time. On some later occasion, we will suppose, the child remembers the incident and relates it to someone else. In this case, both the active and passive understanding of words is different from what it is when words are used demonstratively. The child is not seeing a motor, but only remembering one; the hearer does not look round in expectation of seeing a motor coming, but 'understands' that a motor came at some earlier time. The whole of this occurrence is much more difficult to account for on behaviourist lines—indeed, it does not call for any particular behaviour. It is clear that, in so far as the child is genuinely remembering, he has a picture of the past occurrence, and his words are chosen so as to describe the picture; and in so far as the hearer is genuinely apprehending what is said, the hearer is acquiring a picture more or less like that of the child. It is true that this process may be telescoped through the operation of the word-habit. The child may not genuinely remember the incident, but only have the habit of the appropriate words, as in the case of a poem which we know by heart though we cannot remember learning it. And the hearer also may only pay attention to the words, and not call up any corresponding picture. But it is nevertheless the possibility of a memory-image in the child and an imagination-image in the hearer that makes the essence of the 'meaning' of the words. In so far as this is absent, the words are mere counters, capable of meaning, but not at the moment possessing it. We may say that, while words used demonstratively describe and are intended to cause sensations, the same words used in narrative describe and are intended to cause images.

We have thus two other ways in which words can mean (perhaps not fundamentally distinct), namely, the way of memory and the way of imagination. That is to say:

(5) Words may be used to describe or recall a memory-image: to describe it when it already exists, or to recall it where the words exist as a habit and are known to be descriptive of some past experience.

(6) Words may be used to describe or create an imagination-image: to describe it, for example, in the case of a poet or novelist, or to create it in the ordinary case of giving information—though in the latter case, it is intended that the imagination-image, when created, shall be accompanied by belief that something of the sort has occurred.

These two ways of using words may be spoken of together as the use of words in 'thinking'. This way of using words, since it depends upon images, cannot be fully dealt with on behaviourist lines. And this is really the most essential function of words: that, primarily through their connexion with images, they bring us into touch with what is remote in time or space. When they operate without the medium of images, this seems to be a telescoped process. Thus the problem of the meaning of words is reduced to the problem of the meaning of images.

The 'meaning' of images is the simplest kind of meaning, because images resemble what they mean, whereas words, as a rule, do not. Images are said to be 'copies' of sensations. It is true that this assumption is liable to sceptical criticism, but I shall assume it to be true. It appears to common sense to be verified by such experiences as, e.g., recalling a familiar room, and then going into the room and finding it as it was remembered. If our memory was wrong, we must suppose that the room and our image of it have undergone similar changes, which does not seem a plausible hypothesis. Thus for practical purposes we are justified in assuming that, in this case, our image resembled what the room was when we previously saw it. We may then say that our image 'means' the room.

The question what a given image 'means' is partly within the control of our will. The image of a printed word may mean, not the word, but what the word means. The image of a triangle may mean one particular triangle, or triangles in general. In thinking of dogs in general, we may use a vague image of a dog, which means the species, not any individual. Similarly in recalling a friend's face we usually do not recall any one special occasion when we have seen it, but a compromise image of many occasions.

While some images mean particulars and others mean universals (in early stages of thought meaning is too vague to be either definitely particular or definitely universal), all images *are* particulars, but what they mean depends upon the nature of their causal efficacy. An image means a universal if its effects depend only upon its prototype being an instance of that universal. Thus, if I call up an image of a dog with a view to a general statement about dogs, I only *use* those characteristics of my image which it shares with all images of dogs. We can, to some extent, use or ignore the particular features of an image as we choose. In using *words*, we always ignore all that is peculiar to the instance of the word, except in elocution and calligraphy. Two instances of the word 'dog' are more alike than two dogs; this is one reason why words help in dealing with universals.

If we accept Hume's principle that simple ideas are derived from impressions, we shall hold that at any rate the simple sensible qualities that enter into an image are 'copies' of sensible qualities that have been given in sensation. Complex images are often, but not always, copies of complex sensations; their constituents, if Hume is right, are always copies of something given in sensation. That of which an image is a copy is called its 'prototype'; and this, or its parts, by Hume's principle, is always an indispensable part of the cause either of the image, or of its constituents (in the case of a complex imagination-image).

The effects of an image tend to resemble those of its prototype, or to produce desire or aversion for it. This is one link between an image and its meaning. The thought of a drink has effects on a thirsty man which are similar to those of a sight of the foaming glass. This similarity belongs also to words, primarily, no doubt, through their power of calling up images, but afterwards directly.

The way in which an image resembles its prototype is peculiar. Images as a class have (with rare exceptions) characteristic differences from sensations as a class, but individual images, subject to these differences, resemble individual sensations. Images, however, are of various degrees of vagueness, and the vaguer they are the more different objects can be accepted as their prototypes. The nearest approach that I can make to a definition of the relation of image and prototype is this: If an object O is the prototype (or a prototype, in the case of vagueness) of an image, then, in the presence of O, we can recognize it as what we had an image 'of'. We may then say that O is the 'meaning' (or a meaning, in the case of vagueness) of the image. But, as we saw, meaning is to some extent subject to the will: a 'generic' image, for example, is simply one intended to be generic.

III. PROPOSITIONS AND BELIEF

In regard to belief, there are three elements to be considered, namely: (1) the content which is believed, (2) the relation of the content to its 'objective', i.e., to the fact which makes it true or false, (3) the element which *is* belief, as opposed to consideration of the same content, or doubt concerning it, or desire for it, etc. The second of these questions I propose to postpone until the next section; for the present, therefore, we are not concerned with the question what makes a belief true or false, though it is important to remember that the property of being true or false is what specially characterizes beliefs. The other two questions we will consider in this section.

(1) *The Content of a Belief.*—The view to be taken on this question depends, to some extent, upon the view we take of 'ideas' or 'presentations'. We have here a great variety of theories urged by different authors. Many analytic psychologists—Meinong, for example—distinguish three elements in a presentation, namely, the act (or subject), the content, and the object. Realists such as Dr. Moore and myself have been in the habit of rejecting the content, while retaining the act and the object. American realists, on the other hand, have rejected both the act and the content, and have kept only the object; while idealists, in effect if not in words, have rejected the object and kept the content.

Is there any way of deciding amid this bewildering variety of hypotheses?

I have to confess that the theory which analyses a presentation into act and object no longer satisfies me. The act, or subject, is schematically convenient, but not empirically discoverable. It seems to serve the same sort of purpose as is served by points and instants, by numbers and particles and the rest of the apparatus of mathematics. All these things have to be *constructed*, not postulated: they are not of the stuff of the world, but assemblages which it is convenient to be able to designate as if they were single things. The same seems to be true of the subject, and I am at a loss to discover any actual phenomenon which could be called an 'act' and could be regarded as a constituent of a presentation. The logical analogies which have led me to this conclusion have been reinforced by the arguments of James and the American realists. It seems to me imperative, therefore, to construct a theory of presentation and belief which makes no use of the 'subject', or of an 'act' as a constituent of a presentation. Not that it is certain that there is no such thing as a 'subject', any more than it is certain that there are no points and instants. Such things *may* exist, but we have no reason to suppose that they do, and therefore our theories ought to avoid assuming either that they exist or that they do not exist. The *practical* effect of this is the same as if we assumed that they did not exist, but the theoretical attitude is different.

The first effect of the rejection of the subject is to render necessary a less relational theory of mental occurrences. Brentano's view, for example, that mental phenomena are characterized by 'objective reference', cannot be accepted in its obvious sense. A sensation in particular can no longer be regarded as a relation of a subject to a sense-datum; accordingly the distinction between sensation and sense-datum lapses, and it becomes impossible to regard a sensation as in any sense cognitive. *Per contra*, a sensation becomes equally part of the subject-matter of physics and of psychology: it is simultaneously part of the mind of the person who 'has' the sensation, and part of the body which is 'perceived' by means of the sensation.* This topic demands amplification, but not here, since it is not very relevant to our present theme.

Apart from sensations, 'presentations' appear, as a matter of observation, to be composed of images. Images, in accordance with what has just been said, are not to be regarded as relational in their own nature; nevertheless, at least in the case of memory-images, they are felt to point beyond themselves to something which they 'mean'. We have already dealt with the meaning of images as far as was possible without introducing belief; but it is clear that, when we remember by means of images, the images are accompanied by a belief, a belief which may be expressed (though with undue explicitness) by saying that they are felt to be copies of something that existed previously. And, without memory, images could hardly acquire meaning. Thus the analysis of belief is essential even to a full account of the meaning of words and images —for the meaning of words, we found, depends on that of images, which in turn depends on memory, which is itself a form of belief.

We have thus, so far, two sorts of mental 'stuff', namely, (*a*) sensations, which are also physical, and (*b*) images, which are purely mental. Sensations do not 'mean', but images often do, through the medium of belief.

The theory of belief which I formerly advocated, namely, that

---

* Assuming the theory of bodies developed in my *Our Knowledge of the External World*.

it consisted in a multiple relation of the subject to the objects constituting the 'objective', i.e., the fact that makes the belief true or false, is rendered impossible by the rejection of the subject. The constituents of the belief cannot, when the subject is rejected, be the same as the constituents of its 'objective'. This has both advantages and disadvantages. The disadvantages are those resulting from the gulf between the content and the objective, which seem to make it doubtful in what sense we can be said to 'know' the objective.* The advantages are those derived from the rehabilitation of the content, making it possible to admit propositions as actual complex occurrences, and doing away with the difficulty of answering the question: what do we believe when we believe falsely? The theory I wish to advocate, however, is not to be recommended by these advantages, or rejected on account of these disadvantages: it is presented for acceptance on the ground that it accords with what can be empirically observed, and that it rejects everything mythological or merely schematic. Whether it is epistemologically convenient or inconvenient is a question which has no bearing upon its truth or falsehood, and which I do not propose to consider further.

Are sensations and images, suitably related, a sufficient stuff out of which to compose beliefs? I think they are. But this question has to be asked twice over, once as regards the content, i.e., what is believed, and then again as regards the believing. For the present, we are concerned with the content.

That what is believed must always be the sort of thing which we express by a proposition, is a view which I am not concerned either to assert or to deny. It may be that a single simple image may be believed. For our purposes, however, the important beliefs, even if they be not the only ones, are those which, if rendered into explicit words, take the form of a proposition, i.e., that *A* is *B*, or that *x* has the relation *R* to *y*, or that all men are mortal, or that something like *this* existed before, or any other such sentence. But the psychological classification of the contents of beliefs is very

---

* An important part of 'knowing' will consist in the fact that, by means of 'ideas', we are able to act in a way which is appropriate to an absent object, and are not dependent upon the stimulus of present sensation. I have not developed this order of ideas in the present paper, but I do not wish to minimize its importance.

different from the logical classification, and at present it is psychological questions that concern us. Psychologically, some of the simplest beliefs that occur seem to be among memories and expectations. When you recall some recent event, you are believing something. When you go to a familiar place, you may be expecting to find things much as usual: you may have an image of your host saying how-do-you-do, and you may believe that this will happen. In such cases, the belief is probably not put into words, but if it were, it would take the form of a proposition.

For the present I shall define a 'proposition' as *the content of a belief*, except when, if ever, the content is simple. But since we have not yet defined 'belief', this definition cannot be regarded as yet as a very valuable one.

The content of a belief *may* consist only of words, but if it does, this is a telescoped process. The primary phenomenon of belief consists of belief in images, of which, perhaps, memory is the most elementary example. But, it may be urged, a memory-belief does not consist *only* of the memory-image, together with bare believing: it is clear that the images may be the same for a memory and an expectation, which are nevertheless different beliefs. I incline to the view that the difference, in this case, is not in the content of what is believed, but in the believing; 'believing' seems to be a generic term, covering different kinds of occurrences, of which memory and expectation are two. If this is so, difference of tense, in its psychologically earliest form, is no part of what is believed, but only of the way of believing it; the putting of the tense into the content is a result of later reflection. We may accordingly continue to regard images as giving the whole content of what is believed, when this is not expressed in words.

I shall distinguish a proposition expressed in words as a 'word-proposition', and one consisting of images as an 'image-proposition'. As a general rule, a word-proposition 'means' an image-proposition; this is the case with false propositions as well as with true ones, since image-propositions are as capable of falsehood as word-propositions.* I shall not speak of the fact which makes a

---

* There are, however, limitations of parallelism due to the fact that words often express also what belongs to the nature of the believing, as well as what belongs to the content. We have just had an instance of this in the case of tense; another will be considered later as regards negation.

proposition true or false as its 'meaning', because this usage would be confusing in the case of falsehood. I shall speak of the relation of the proposition to the fact which makes it true or false as its 'objective reference', or simply its 'reference'. But this will not occupy us till the next section.

The correspondence of word-propositions and image-propositions is, as a rule, by no means exact or simple. A form of words, unless artificially constructed, usually expresses not only the content of a proposition, but also what may be called a 'propositional attitude'—memory, expectation, desire, etc. These attitudes do not form part of the proposition, i.e., of the content of what is believed when we believe, or desired when we desire.

Let us illustrate the content of a belief by an example. Suppose I am believing, but not in words, that 'it will rain'. What is happening? (1) Images, say, of the visual appearance of rain, the feeling of wetness, the patter of drops, interrelated, roughly, as the sensations would be if it were raining, i.e., there is a complex *fact composed of images*, having a structure analogous to that of the objective fact which would make the belief true. (2) There is *expectation*, i.e., that form of belief which refers to the future; we shall examine this shortly. (3) There is a relation between (1) and (2), making us say that (1) is 'what is expected'. This relation also demands investigation.

The most important thing about a proposition is that, whether it consists of images or of words, it is, whenever it occurs, an actual fact, having a certain analogy of structure—to be further investigated—with the fact which makes it true or false. A word-proposition, apart from niceties, 'means' the corresponding image-proposition, and an image-proposition has an objective reference dependent upon the meanings of its constituent images.

(2) *Believing*.—We come now to the question what actually constitutes believing, as opposed to the question of the content believed.

'Everyone', says William James, 'knows the difference between imagining a thing and believing in its existence, between supposing a proposition and acquiescing in its truth. . . . *In its inner nature, belief, or the sense of reality, is a sort of feeling more allied to the emotions than to anything else.*'*

* *Psychology*, Vol. II, Chap. XXI, p. 283. James's italics.

In the main, this view seems inevitable. When we believe a proposition, we have a certain feeling which is related to the content of the proposition in the way described as 'believing that proposition'. But I think various different feelings are collected together under the one word 'belief', and that there is not any one feeling which pre-eminently *is* belief.

Before we can begin the analysis of belief, however, it is necessary to consider a theory which, whether explicitly advocated or not, seems implicit in pragmatism, and capable, if true, of affording a strong argument in favour of that philosophy. According to this theory—for which I cannot make any author responsible—there is no single occurrence which can be described as 'believing a proposition', but belief simply consists in causal efficacy. Some ideas move us to action, others do not; those that do so move us are said to be 'believed'. A behaviourist who denies images will have to go even further, and deny image-propositions altogether. For him, I suppose, a belief will be, like a force in physics, an imagined fictitious cause of a series of actions. An animal, desiring A (in whatever may be the behaviouristic sense of 'desire'), proceeds to try to realize B; we then say that the animal 'believes' that B is a means to A. This is merely a way of collecting together a certain set of acts; it does not represent any single occurrence in the animal. But this view, whatever may be said in its favour where animals are concerned, is condemned as regards human beings by the admission of images. These being admitted, it becomes impossible to deny that image-propositions occur in people, and it is clear that belief has specially to do with propositions, given that propositions occur. And, this being admitted, we cannot make the differentia between a proposition believed and a proposition merely considered consist *only* in the presence or absence of causal efficacy. If we adhere to the maxim 'same cause, same effect', we must hold that, if a proposition believed has different effects from those of the same proposition merely considered, there must be some *intrinsic* difference between believing and considering. The fact that believing moves us as considering does not, is evidence of some intrinsic difference between the two phenomena, even when the proposition concerned is the same in both cases.* This objection

* Cf. Brentano, *Psychologie vom empirischen Standpunkte* (Leipzig, 1874), p. 268 (criticizing Bain, *The Emotions and the Will*).

seems fatal to the causal-efficacy view as above stated, though I think some things that are true are *suggested* by the view.

It seems to me that there are various feelings that may attach to a proposition, any one of which constitutes belief. Of these I would instance memory, expectation, and bare non-temporal assent. Whether there are others, I do not know. Memory requires for its truth that the objective of the proposition should be in the past, expectation that it should be in the future, while bare assent does not necessitate any special time-relation of the belief to the objective. Possibly disjunctions and implications may involve other kinds of belief-feelings. The chief importance of these different feelings, from our point of view, lies in the difficulty they create in translating the phenomena of belief into words. Tense puts the time-relation, apparently, into the content of what is believed, whereas, if the above theory is correct, tense is primarily embodied in the nature of the belief-feeling. However this may be, we can simplify our discussion by confining ourselves to bare assent, since it is undoubtedly possible to assent to a proposition concerning the past or the future, as opposed to remembering or expecting it.

When a belief, not expressed in words, is occurring in a person, and is constituted by the feeling of assent, what is actually happening, if we are right, is as follows: (*a*) we have a proposition, consisting of interrelated images, and possibly partly of sensations; (*b*) we have the feeling of assent; (*c*) we have a relation, actually subsisting, between the feeling of assent and the proposition, such as is expressed by saying that that is the proposition assented to. For other forms of belief, we have only to substitute other feelings in place of assent.

It might be urged, as against the above theory, that belief is not a positive phenomenon, though doubt and disbelief are so. It might be contended that what we call belief involves only the existence of the appropriate images, which will have the effects that are characteristic of belief unless some other simultaneous force operates against them. It is possible to develop a behaviouristic logic, starting with the definition that two propositions are logically incompatible when they prompt bodily movements which are physically incompatible. E.g., if one were a fish, one could not at the same time believe the two propositions 'this worm is good to eat' and 'this worm is on a hook'. For beliefs (in this view) would be embodied in behaviour: the one belief, in eating the worm; the other, in avoiding it—always assuming (as behaviourists invariably do) that the fish in question is not tired of life. Without going so far as this, we might nevertheless agree with the passage which James (*loc. cit.*, page 288) quotes (inaccurately) from Spinoza:

'Let us conceive a boy imagining to himself a horse, and taking note of nothing else. As this imagination involves the existence of the horse, *and the boy has no perception which annuls its existence* [James's italics], he will necessarily contemplate the horse as present, nor will he be able to doubt of its existence, however little certain of it he may be. I deny that a man in so far as he imagines [*percipit*] affirms nothing. For what is it to imagine a winged horse but to affirm that the horse [that horse, namely] has wings? For if the mind had nothing before it but the winged horse it would contemplate the same as present, would have no cause to doubt of its existence, nor any power of dissenting from its existence, unless the imagination of the winged horse were joined to an idea which contradicted [*tollit*] its existence.' (*Ethics*, II, 49, Scholium.)

To this doctrine James entirely assents, adding in italics:

'*Any object which remains uncontradicted is ipso facto believed and posited as absolute reality.*'

Now if this view is correct, it would seem to follow (though James does not draw this inference) that there is no need of any specific feeling of belief, and that the mere existence of images yields all that is required. The state of mind in which we merely consider a proposition, without believing or disbelieving it, will then appear as a sophisticated product, the result of some rival force adding to the image-proposition a positive feeling which may be called suspense or non-belief—a feeling which may be compared to that of a man about to run a race, waiting for the signal. Such a man, though not moving, is in a very different condition from that of a man quietly at rest. And so the man who is considering a proposition without believing it will be in a state of tension, restraining the natural tendency to act upon the proposition which he would display if nothing interfered. In this view, belief primarily consists merely in the existence of the appropriate images without any counteracting forces.

What most recommends the above view, to my mind, is the way in which it accords with mental development. Doubt, suspense of judgment, and disbelief all seem later and more complex than a wholly unreflecting assent. Belief as a positive phenomenon, if it exists, seems to be a product of doubt, a decision after debate, an acceptance, not merely of *this*, but of *this-rather-than-that*. It is not difficult to suppose that a dog has images (possibly olfactory) of his absent master, or of the rabbit that he dreams of hunting. But it is very difficult to suppose that he can entertain mere imagination-images to which no assent is given. (When we speak of 'assent' we mean for the moment merely that influence upon action which might naturally be expected to accompany belief.) The influence of hallucinatory images also fits well with this theory. Such images, it would seem, often become gradually more and more vivid, until at last they exclude the contrary images which would prevent them from influencing action.

I think it may be conceded that a mere image, without the addition of any positive feeling that could be called 'belief', is apt to have a certain dynamic power, and in this sense an uncombated image has the force of a belief. But although this may be true, it does not account for any but the simplest phenomena in the region of belief. It will not, for example, explain either memory or expectation, in both of which, though they differ widely in their effects on action, the image is a sign, something pointing beyond itself to a different event. Nor can it explain the beliefs which do not issue in any proximate action, such as those of mathematics. I conclude, therefore, that there are belief-feelings of the same order as those of doubt or desire or disbelief, although phenomena closely analogous to those of belief can be produced by mere uncontradicted images.

Instances like that of the boy imagining a winged horse are liable to produce a certain confusion. The image of the winged horse of course exists, and if the boy took this to be real, he would not be in error. But images accompanied by belief are normally taken as signs: the belief is not in the image, but in something else that is indicated (or, in logical language 'described') by the image. This is especially obvious in such a case as memory. When we remember an event by means of present images, we are not believing in the present existence of the images, but in the past existence of something resembling them. It is almost impossible to translate what is occurring into words without great distortion. The view which I am advocating is that, in such a case, we have a specific feeling, called remembering, which has a certain relation to the memory-image. The memory-image constitutes the image-proposition, but the translation of our belief into words is 'something like this *was*', not 'something like this *is*', as it would be in assent not of the nature of memory or expectation. And even this translation is hardly accurate, for words point not only to images, but beyond images to what these mean. Therefore, when we use a word as if it meant the image, we need an unnatural duplication of words in order to reach what the image stands for. This produces the appearance of unexpected complication, leading to an undue lack of plausibility. But the whole question of adapting language to psychology, after all the ages during which it has been adapted to bad logic, is so difficult that I can hardly do more than indicate some of its problems.

IV. TRUTH AND FALSEHOOD

We come now to the question which we left on one side at the beginning of our third section, namely: What is the relation of the content of a belief to its 'objective', i.e., to the fact which makes it true or false?

In an earlier paper before the Aristotelian Society,* in criticism of Mr. Joachim, I have given my reasons for holding that truth consists in correspondence rather than in internal consistency. I do not propose to repeat those arguments at present, but shall assume, without more ado, that the truth or falsehood of a belief depends upon its relation to a fact other than itself. This fact I call its 'objective'. In so doing, I am not following exactly the same usage as Meinong, who holds that there are false objectives as well as true ones, and who, therefore, does not identify his objectives with the facts that make propositions true or false. I cannot call the fact the 'meaning' of the proposition, since that is confusing when the proposition is false: if on a fine day I say 'it is raining', we cannot say that the meaning of my statement is the fact that the sun is shining. Nor can I use the word 'denotation', since that

* 'On the Nature of Truth', *Proc. Arist. Soc.*, (1907). Reprinted, with some alterations, in *Philosophical Essays*, under the title, 'The Monistic Theory of Truth'.

assimilates propositions too much to names and descriptions. But I shall say that a proposition 'refers to' its objective. Thus, when we are concerned with image-propositions, 'referring to' takes the place of 'meaning'. Word-propositions, on the other hand, while also 'referring to' objectives, may, in simple cases, be legitimately spoken of as 'meaning' image-propositions.

According to the theory of propositions suggested in the previous section, it would be a mistake to regard truth and falsehood as relations of the 'ideal' to the 'real'. Propositions are facts in exactly the same sense in which their objectives are facts. The relation of a proposition to its objective is not a relation of something imagined to something actual: it is a relation between two equally solid and equally actual facts. One of these, the proposition, is composed of images, with a possible admixture of sensations; the other may be composed of anything.

Whether an image which is too simple to be called a proposition can be in any sense true or false, is a question which I shall not discuss. It is propositions, and *their* truth and falsehood, that I am concerned with; whether there is any other truth or falsehood may be left an open question.

There are two different questions in regard to truth and falsehood, of which one may be called formal, the other material. The formal question concerns the relations between the form of a proposition and the form of its objective in the respective cases of truth and falsehood; the material question, which has been specially emphasized by pragmatists, concerns the nature of the effects of true and false beliefs respectively. In so far as people wish to believe truly (which I am told is sometimes the case), it is because true beliefs are supposed to be, as a rule, a better means to the realization of desires than false ones. Unless the material question is remembered, the schematic treatment of the formal question may appear very barren and scholastic. Nevertheless, it is to the formal question that I propose to address myself.

The simplest possible schema of correspondence between proposition and objective is afforded by such cases as visual memory-images. I call up a picture of a room that I know, and in my picture the window is to the left of the fire. I give to this picture that sort of belief which we call 'memory'. When the room was present to sense, the window was, in fact, to the left of the fire. In this case,

I have a complex image, which we may analyse, for our purposes, into (a) the image of the window, (b) the image of the fire, (c) the relation that (a) is to the left of (b). The objective consists of the window and the fire with the very same relation between them. In such a case, the objective of a proposition consists of the meanings of its constituent images related (or not related, as the case may be) by the same relation as that which holds between the constituent images in the proposition. When the objective is that the same relation holds, the proposition is true; when the objective is that the same relation does not hold, the proposition is false. According to what was said about negative facts in Section I, there is always one or other of these two possible objectives, and the proposition is therefore always either true or false.

But such idyllic simplicity of correspondence is rare. It is already absent in the word-propositions which mean such simple visual image-propositions. In the phrase '*A* is to the left of *B*', even if we treat 'is-to-the-left-of' as one word, we have a fact consisting of *three* terms with a *triadic* relation, not two terms with a dyadic relation. The linguistic symbol for a relation is not itself a relation, but a term as solid as the other words of the sentence. Language might have been so constructed that this should not have been always the case: a few specially important relations might have been symbolized by relations between words. For instance, '*AB*' might have meant '*A* is to the left of *B*'. It might have been the practice that pronouncing *A* on a high note and *B* on a low note meant that *A* was *B*'s social superior. But the practical possibilities of this method of symbolizing relations are obviously very limited, and in actual language relations are symbolized by words (verbs and prepositions chiefly) or parts of words (inflections).* Hence the linguistic statement of a fact is a more complex fact than that which it asserts, and the correspondence of a word-proposition with its objective is never so simple as the simplest correspondence in the case of image-propositions.

Again, the case of negative facts and negative propositions is full of complexities. Propositions, whether of images or words, are

---

* This is not wholly true of very primitive languages. But they are so vague and ambiguous that often they cannot be said to have any way of expressing one relation rather than a number of others that might equally be meant by the phrase which is used.

always themselves *positive* facts. In the case of word-propositions, there are different positive facts (phrases), of which one is true when the objective is positive, the other when it is negative: the phrases '*A* loves *B*' and '*A* does not love *B*' are both themselves positive facts. We cannot symbolize the assertion that *A* does not love *B* by merely having the words '*A*' and '*B*' without the word 'loves' between them, since we cannot practically distinguish the fact that the word 'loves' does not occur between them from the fact that, e.g., the word 'hates' does not occur between them. Words and phrases, being intended for communication, have to be sensible; and sensible facts are always positive. Thus there is no identity between the distinction of positive and negative facts and the distinction of positive and negative word-propositions: the latter are themselves both positive facts, though differing by the absence or presence of the word 'not'.

In the case of image-propositions, there is again a lack of parallelism with negative facts, but of a different kind. Not only are image-propositions always positive, but there are not even two kinds of positive image-propositions as there are of word-propositions. There is no 'not' in an image-proposition; the 'not' belongs to the feeling, not to the content of the proposition. An image-proposition may be believed or disbelieved; these are different feelings towards the same content, not the same feeling towards different contents. There is no way of visualizing '*A*-not-to-the-left-of-*B*'. When we attempt it, we find ourselves visualizing '*A*-to-the-right-of-*B*' or something of the sort. This is one strong reason for the reluctance to admit negative facts.

We have thus, as regards the opposition of positive and negative, the following different sorts of duality:

(1) Positive and negative facts.

(2) Image propositions, which may be believed or disbelieved but do not allow any duality of content corresponding to positive and negative facts.

(3) Word-propositions, which are always positive facts, but are of two kinds, one verified by a positive objective, the other by a negative objective.

Thus the simpler kinds of parallelism between proposition and fact are only to be looked for in the case of positive facts and

propositions. Where the fact is negative, the correspondence necessarily becomes more complicated. It is partly the failure to realize
the lack of parallelism between negative facts and negative word-
propositions that has made a correct theory of negative facts so
difficult either to discover or to believe.

Let us now return to positive facts and beliefs in image-propositions. In the case of spatial relations, we found that it is possible for the relation of the constituent images to be the same as
the relation of the constituents of the objective. In my visualizing
of A to the left of B, my image of A is to the left of my image
of B. Does this identity of relation, as between the image-proposition and its objective, ever occur except in the case of spatial
relations?

The case which it is natural to consider next is that of temporal
relations. Suppose I believe that A precedes B. Can this belief
have for its content an image of A preceding an image of B? At
first sight, most people would unhesitatingly reject such an hypothesis. We have been told so often that an idea of succession is not
a succession of ideas, that we almost automatically regard the
apprehension of a sequence as something in which the earlier and
later parts of the sequence must be simultaneously presented. It
seems rash to challenge a view so generally regarded as unquestionable, and yet I cannot resist grave doubts as to its truth. Of course
it is a fact that we often have successive images without the belief
that their prototypes have the same time-order. But that proves
nothing, since in any case belief is something which has to be
added to an image-proposition. Is it certain that we cannot have
an image of A followed by an image of B, and proceed to *believe*
this sequence? And cannot this *be* the belief that A precedes B?
I see no reason why this should not be the case. When, for example,
I imagine a person speaking a sentence, or when, for that matter,
I actually hear him speak it, there does not seem, as a question of
empirical fact, to be any moment at which the whole sentence is
present to imagination or sense, and yet, in whatever may be the
usual meaning of the phrase, I can 'apprehend the sentence as a
whole'. I hear the words in order, but never the whole sentence
at once; yet I apprehend the sentence as a whole, in the sense that
it produces upon me the intended effect, whatever that may be.
You come to me and say: 'Your roof has fallen in, and the rain is

pouring down into the rooms, ruining all your furniture'. I understand what you say, since I express consternation, ring up the land-
lord, write to the insurance company, and order a van to remove
my belongings. Yet it by no means follows that the whole sentence
was imaginatively present to me at any one moment. My belief in
your statement is a causal unit, and it is therefore supposed to be
a unitary occurrence. But in mental affairs the causal unit may well
be several events at different times. This is part of Bergson's point
about repetition; it is also suggested by the law of habit. It may
well turn out to be one of the fundamental differences between
physics and psychology. Thus, there seems no good reason why,
when we believe in a succession, there should be any one moment
within which the whole content of the belief is existing. The belief
in a succession may quite well be itself a succession. If so, temporal
relations, like spatial ones, allow the simplest type of correspondence, in which the relation in the image-proposition is identical
with that in the objective. But I only wish to suggest this view as a
possible one: I do not feel prepared to say with any conviction
that it is in fact true.

The correspondence of proposition and fact grows increasingly
complicated as we pass to more complicated types of propositions:
existence-propositions, general propositions, disjunctive and hypothetical propositions, and so on. The subject is important, and
capable, I believe, of throwing much new light on logic; but I shall
not pursue it here.

The general nature of the formal correspondence which makes
truth or falsehood can be seen from the simplest case: the case of a
dyadic relation which is the same in the fact and in the image-proposition. You have an image of A which is to the left of your image
of B: this occurrence is an image-proposition. If A is to the left
of B, the proposition is true; if A is not to the left of B, it is false.
The *phrase* 'A is to the left of B' means the image-proposition, and
is true when this is true, false when this is false; on the other hand,
the phrase 'A is not to the left of B' is true when the image-
proposition is false, and false when it is true. Thus for this simplest
case we have obtained a formal definition of truth and falsehood,
both for image-propositions and for word-propositions. It is easy
to see that the same *kind* of definition can be extended to more
complicated cases.

It will be observed that truth and falsehood, in their formal sense, are primarily properties of propositions rather than of beliefs. Derivatively, we call a belief true when it is belief in a true proposition, and a disbelief true when it is disbelief in a false proposition; but it is to propositions that the *primary* formal meanings of 'truth' and 'falsehood' apply.

But when we come to what gives importance to truth and falsehood, as opposed to what constitutes their formal definition, it is beliefs, not propositions, that are important. Beliefs influence action, and the effects of true beliefs, I am told, are more agreeable than those of false beliefs. The attempt to *define* truth in this way seems to me a mistake. But so long as we confine ourselves to the formal definition of truth, it is difficult to see why any one should take an interest in it. It is therefore important to remember the connexion of beliefs with action. But I do not think either that the pleasant effects of a belief are alone a sufficient verification of it, or that verification can be used to *define* truth. There are true propositions, for example, about past matters of fact, which cannot be verified. The formal definition of truth by correspondence of a proposition with its objective seems the only one which is theoretically adequate. The further inquiry whether, if our definition of truth is correct, there is anything that can be known, is one that I cannot now undertake; but if the result of such an inquiry should prove adverse, I should not regard that as affording any theoretical objection to the proposed definition.

Logical Atomism

One of the things that philosophy finally is learning is how to state problems in such a manner that they are not, on the face of them, nonsensical, insoluble, or muddled. This is an achievem entthat does not appear to be impressive, but, in fact, represents the culmination of constructive philosophic tendencies that began with Socrates. A result of this general desire for clarification has been that a considerable amount of philosophical writing that, in time, is not very old, has come to be regarded as belonging to a remote period before the force of scientific criticism became generally felt.

In 1924–25 when Professor J. H. Muirhead issued the two series of essays entitled CONTEMPORARY BRITISH PHILOSOPHY the dominant figure among the thinkers of the day was F. H. Bradley, whose idealism was a statement of the 'position' which most of the contributors defended in one way or another. This viewpoint reflected the conviction that the humanist had access to Truth in a higher and nobler form than any group of 'uncultured button-pushers and knob-twiddlers' (the phrase, as one might expect, comes from the Oxford Holy of Holies, All Souls', but is of 1956 rather than 1920 vintage), from which it followed that the speculative philosopher could make statements about what was ultimately the case, could 'interpret' the findings of empirical investigations to meet his personal ends, and could reserve the right to speak of real reality to those who had pondered over Hegel and mastered Greek.

Russell's essay in this volume shows him, philosophically, mid-way between THE ANALYSIS OF MIND (1921) and THE ANALYSIS OF MATTER (1927). He still feels some influence from Wittgenstein, but Wittgenstein's views are now wholly assimilated into his own and have taken a form which we know Wittgenstein would not have approved. He is, however, still somewhat on the defensive, and his philosophy, which now is (I feel) generally seen to represent the most important tendencies of the period, was then by no means so well regarded and most certainly lacked the high prestige of the work of the leading idealists. Mr. Bradley probably thought he was writing for the ages, and it is interesting to speculate on how he would have reacted if some unusually competent soothsayer had given him a glimpse of his eventual reputation. 'Bad philosophy has always been an Oxford specialty,' says BR, 'and bad philosophy is still philosopy!' In the idealist period the primary objective of Oxford philosophy, Russell has told me, 'was to give the place a moral tone'. The objectives of some recent capers of Oxford philosophers are hardly so clear and may even suggest the idea that, philosophically anyway, after establishing itself as the traditional home of lost causes, Oxford has finally become a lost cause itself.*

Extracted, then, from a setting not greatly different or more relevant to current thought than that in which ON DENOTING first appeared nineteen years earlier, here is an essay in which Russell provides a succinct and eloquent summation of his point of view of some thirty years ago.

*As a once fully matriculated member of that university, I think I can make this remark without being charged with expressing mere Cambridge prejudices.

LOGICAL ATOMISM

THE PHILOSOPHY which I advocate is generally regarded as a species of realism, and accused of inconsistency because of the elements in it which seem contrary to that doctrine. For my part, I do not regard the issue between realists and their opponents as a fundamental one; I could alter my view on this issue without changing my mind as to any of the doctrines upon which I wish to lay stress. I hold that logic is what is fundamental in philosophy, and that schools should be characterized rather by their logic than by their metaphysic. My own logic is atomic, and it is this aspect upon which I should wish to lay stess. Therefore I prefer to describe my philosophy as 'logical atomism', rather than as 'realism', whether with or without some prefixed adjective.

A few words as to historical development may be useful by way of preface. I came to philosophy through mathematics, or rather through the wish to find some reason to believe in the truth of mathematics. From early youth, I had an ardent desire to believe that there can be such a thing as knowledge, combined with a great difficulty in accepting much that passes as knowledge. It seemed clear that the best chance of finding indubitable truth would be in pure mathematics, yet some of Euclid's axioms were obviously doubtful, and the infinitesimal calculus, as I was taught it, was a mass of sophisms, which I could not bring myself to regard as anything else. I saw no reason to doubt the truth of arithmetic, but I did not then know that arithmetic can be made to embrace all traditional pure mathematics. At the age of eighteen I read Mill's *Logic*, but was profoundly dissatisfied with his reasons for accepting arithmetic and geometry. I had not read Hume, but it seemed to me that pure empiricism (which I was disposed to accept) must lead to scepticism rather than to Mill's support of received scientific doctrines. At Cambridge I read Kant and Hegel, as well as Mr. Bradley's *Logic*, which influenced me profoundly. For some years I was a disciple of Mr. Bradley, but about 1898 I changed my views, largely as a result of arguments with G. E. Moore. I could no longer believe that knowing makes any difference to what is known. Also I found myself driven to pluralism. Analysis of mathematical propositions persuaded me that they could not be explained as even partial truths unless one admitted pluralism and the reality of relations. An accident led me at this time to study Leibniz, and I came to the conclusion (subsequently confirmed by Couturat's masterly researches) that many of his most characteristic opinions were due to the purely logical doctrine that every proposition has a subject and a predicate. This doctrine is one which Leibniz shares with Spinoza, Hegel, and Mr. Bradley; it seemed to me that, if it is rejected, the whole foundation for the metaphysics of all these philosophers is shattered. I therefore returned to the problem which had originally led me to philosophy, namely, the foundations of mathematics, applying to it a new logic derived largely from Peano and Frege, which proved (at least, so I believe) far more fruitful than that of traditional philosophy.

In the first place, I found that many of the stock philosophical arguments about mathematics (derived in the main from Kant) had been rendered invalid by the progress of mathematics in the meanwhile. Non-Euclidean geometry had undermined the argument of the transcendental aesthetic. Weierstrass had shown that the differential and integral calculus do not require the conception of the infinitesimal, and that, therefore, all that had been said by philosophers on such subjects as the continuity of space and time and motion must be regarded as sheer error. Cantor freed the conception of infinite number from contradiction, and thus disposed of Kant's antinomies as well as many of Hegel's. Finally Frege showed in detail how arithmetic can be deduced from pure logic, without the need of any fresh ideas or axioms, thus disproving Kant's assertion that '$7 + 5 = 12$' is synthetic—at least in the obvious interpretation of that dictum. As all these results were obtained, not by any heroic method, but by patient detailed reasoning, I began to think it probable that philosophy had erred in adopting heroic remedies for intellectual difficulties, and that solutions were to be found merely by greater care and accuracy. This view I have come to hold more and more strongly as time went on, and it has led me to doubt whether philosophy, as a study distinct from science and possessed of a method of its own, is anything more than an unfortunate legacy from theology.

Frege's work was not final, in the first place because it applied only to arithmetic, not to other branches of mathematics; in the second place because his premises did not exclude certain contradictions to which all past systems of formal logic turned out to be liable. Dr. Whitehead and I in collaboration tried to remedy these two defects, in *Principia Mathematica*, which, however, still falls short of finality in some fundamental points (notably the axiom of reducibility). But in spite of its shortcomings I think that no one who reads this book will dispute its main contention, namely, that from certain ideas and axioms of formal logic, by the help of the logic of relations, all pure mathematics can be deduced, without any new undefined idea or unproved propositions. The technical methods of mathematical logic, as developed in this book, seem to me very powerful, and capable of providing a new instrument for the discussion of many problems that have hitherto remained subject to philosophic vagueness. Dr. Whitehead's *Concept of Nature* and *Principles of Natural Knowledge* may serve as an illustration of what I mean.

When pure mathematics is organized as a deductive system—i.e. as the set of all those propositions that can be deduced from an assigned set of premises—it becomes obvious that, if we are to believe in the truth of pure mathematics, it cannot be solely because we believe in the truth of the set of premises. Some of the premises are much less obvious than some of their consequences, and are believed chiefly because of their consequences. This will be found to be always the case when a science is arranged as a deductive system. It is not the logically simplest propositions of the system that are the most obvious, or that provide the chief part of our reasons for believing in the system. With the empirical sciences this is evident. Electro-dynamics, for example, can be concentrated into Maxwell's equations, but these equations are believed because of the observed truth of certain of their logical consequences. Exactly the same thing happens in the pure realm of logic; the logically first principles of logic—at least some of them—are to be believed, not on their own account, but on account of their consequences. The epistemological question: 'Why should

I believe this set of propositions?' is quite different from the logical question: 'What is the smallest and logically simplest group of propositions from which this set of propositions can be deduced?' Our reasons for believing logic and pure mthematics are, in part, only inductive and probable, in spite of the fact that, in their *logical* order, the propositions of logic and pure mathematics follow from the premises of logic by pure deduction. I think this point important, since errors are liable to arise from assimilating the logical to the epistemological order, and also, conversely, from assimilating the epistemological to the logical order. The only way in which work on mathematical logic throws light on the truth or falsehood of mathematics is by disproving the supposed antinomies. This shows that mathematics *may* be true. But to show that mathematics *is* true would require other methods and other considerations.

One very important heuristic maxim which Dr. Whitehead and I found, by experience, to be applicable in mathematical logic, and have since applied in various other fields, is a form of Ockham's razor. When some set of supposed entities has neat logical properties, it turns out, in a great many instances, that the supposed entities can be replaced by purely logical structures composed of entities which have not such neat properties. In that case, in interpreting a body of propositions hitherto believed to be about the supposed entities, we can substitute the logical structures without altering any of the detail of the body of propositions in question. This is an economy, because entities with neat logical properties are always inferred, and if the propositions in which they occur can be interpreted without making this inference, the ground for the inference fails, and our body of propositions is secured against the need of a doubtful step. The principle may be stated in the form: 'Wherever possible, substitute constructions out of known entities for inferences to unknown entities.'

The uses of this principle are very various, but are not intelligible in detail to those who do not know mathematical logic. The first instance I came across was what I have called 'the principle of abstraction', or 'the principle which dispenses with abstraction.'* This principle is applicable in the case of any symmetrical and transitive relation, such as equality. We are apt to infer that

* *External World*, p. 42.

such relations arise from possession of some common quality. This may or may not be true; probably it is true in some cases and not in others. But all the formal purposes of a common quality can be served by membership of the group of terms having the said relation to a given term. Take magnitude, for example. Let us suppose that we have a group of rods, all equally long. It is easy to suppose that there is a certain quality, called their length, which they all share. But all propositions in which this supposed quality occurs will retain their truth-value unchanged if, instead of 'length of the rod x' we take 'membership of the group of all those rods which are as long as x'. In various special cases—e.g. the definition of real numbers—a simpler construction is possible.

A very important example of the principle is Frege's definition of the cardinal number of a given set of terms as the class of all sets that are 'similar' to the given set—where two sets are 'similar' when there is a one-one relation whose domain is the one set and whose converse domain is the other. Thus a cardinal number is the class of all those classes which are similar to a given class. This definition leaves unchanged the truth-values of all propositions in which cardinal numbers occur, and avoids the inference to a set of entities called 'cardinal numbers', which were never needed except for the purpose of making arithmetic intelligible, and are now no longer needed for that purpose.

Perhaps even more important is the fact that classes themselves can be dispensed with by similar methods. Mathematics is full of propositions which seem to require that a class or an aggregate should be in some sense a single entity—e.g. the proposition 'the number of combinations of n things any number at a time is 2^n'. Since 2^n is always greater than n, this proposition leads to difficulties if classes are admitted because the number of classes of entities in the universe is greater than the number of entities in the universe, which would be odd if classes were some among entities. Fortunately, all the propositions in which classes appear to be mentioned can be interpreted without supposing that there are classes. This is perhaps the most important of all the applications of our principle. (See *Principia Mathematica*, *20.)

Another important example concerns what I call 'definite descriptions', i.e. such phrases as 'the even prime', 'the present King of England', 'the present King of France'. There has always been a difficulty in interpreting such propositions as 'the present King of France does not exist'. The difficulty arose through supposing that 'the present King of France' is the subject of this proposition, which made it necessary to suppose that he subsists although he does not exist. But it is difficult to attribute even subsistence to 'the round square' or 'the even prime greater than 2'. In fact, 'the round square does not subsist' is just as true as 'the present King of France does not exist'. Thus the distinction between existence and subsistence does not help us. The fact is that, when the words 'the so-and-so' occur in a proposition, there is no corresponding single constituent of the proposition, and when the proposition is fully analysed the words 'the so-and-so' have disappeared. An important consequence of the theory of descriptions is that it is meaningless to say 'A exists' unless 'A' is (or stands for) a phrase of the form 'the so-and-so'. If the so-and-so exists, and x is the so-and-so, to say 'x exists' is nonsense. Existence, in the sense in which it is ascribed to single entities, is thus removed altogether from the list of fundamentals. The ontological argument and most of its refutations are found to depend upon bad grammar. (See *Principia Mathematica*, *14.)

There are many other examples of the substitution of constructions for inferences in pure mathematics, for example, series, ordinal numbers, and real numbers. But I will pass on to the examples in physics.

Points and instants are obvious examples: Dr. Whitehead has shown how to construct them out of sets of events all of which have a finite extent and a finite duration. In relativity theory, it is not points or instants that we primarily need, but event-particles, which correspond to what, in older language, might be described as a point at an instant, or an instantaneous point. (In former days, a point of space endured throughout all time, and an instant of time pervaded all space. Now the unit that mathematical physics wants has neither spatial nor temporal extension.) Event-particles are constructed by just the same logical process by which points and instants were constructed. In such constructions, however, we are on a different plane from that of constructions in pure mathematics. The possibility of constructing an event-particle depends upon the existence of sets of events with certain properties; whether the required events exist can only be known empirically, if at all. There is therefore no *a priori* reason to expect continuity (in the mathematical sense), or to feel confident that event-particles can be constructed. If the quantum theory should seem to demand a discrete space-time, our logic is just as ready to meet its requirements as to meet those of traditional physics, which demands continuity. The question is purely empirical, and our logic is (as it ought to be) equally adapted to either alternative.

Similar considerations apply to a particle of matter, or to a piece of matter of finite size. Matter, traditionally, has two of those 'neat' properties which are the mark of a logical construction; first, that two pieces of matter cannot be at the same place at the same time; secondly, that one piece of matter cannot be in two places at the same time. Experience in the substitution of constructions for inferences makes one suspicious of anything so tidy and exact. One cannot help feeling that impenetrability is not an empirical fact, derived from observation of billiard-balls, but is something logically necessary. This feeling is wholly justified, but it could not be so if matter were not a logical construction. An immense number of occurrences coexist in any little region of space-time; when we are speaking of what is not logical construction, we find no such property as impenetrability, but, on the contrary, endless overlapping of the events in a part of space-time, however small. The reason that matter is impenetrable is because our definitions make it so. Speaking roughly, and merely so as to give a notion of how this happens, we may say that a piece of matter is all that happens in a certain track in space-time, and that we construct the tracks called bits of matter in such a way that they do not intersect. Matter is impenetrable because it is easier to state the laws of physics if we make our constructions so as to secure impenetrability. Impenetrability is a logically necessary result of definition, though the fact that such a definition is convenient is empirical. Bits of matter are not among the bricks out of which the world is built. The bricks are events, and bits of matter are portions of the structure to which we find it convenient to give separate attention.

In the philosophy of mental occurrences there are also opportunities for the application of our principle of constructions *versus* inferences. The subject, and the relation of a cognition to what is known, both have that schematic quality that arouses our suspicions. It is clear that the subject, if it is to be preserved at all, must be preserved as a construction, not as an inferred entity; the only question is whether the subject is sufficiently useful to be worth constructing. The relation of a cognition to what is known, again, cannot be a straightforward single ultimate, as I at one time believed it to be. Although I do not agree with pragmatism, I think William James was right in drawing attention to the complexity of 'knowing'. It is impossible in a general summary, such as the present, to set out the reasons for this view. But whoever has acquiesced in our principle will agree that here is prima facie a case for applying it. Most of my *Analysis of Mind* consists of applications of this principle. But as psychology is scientifically much less perfected than physics, the opportunities for applying the principle are not so good. The principle depends, for its use, upon the existence of some fairly reliable body of propositions, which are to be interpreted by the logician in such a way as to preserve their truth while minimizing the element of inference to unobserved entities. The principle therefore presupposes a moderately advanced science, in the absence of which the logician does not know what he ought to construct. Until recently, it would have seemed necessary to construct geometrical points; now it is event-particles that are wanted. In view of such a change in an advanced subject like physics, it is clear that constructions in psychology must be purely provisional.

I have been speaking hitherto of what it is *not* necessary to assume as part of the ultimate constituents of the world. But logical constructions, like all other constructions, require materials, and it is time to turn to the positive question, as to what these materials are to be. This question, however, requires as a preliminary a discussion of logic and language and their relation to what they try to represent.

The influence of language on philosophy has, I believe, been profound and almost unrecognized. If we are not to be misled by this influence, it is necessary to become conscious of it, and to ask ourselves deliberately how far it is legitimate. The subject-predicate logic, with the substance-attribute metaphysic, are a case in point. It is doubtful whether either would have been invented by people speaking a non-Aryan language; certainly they do not seem to have arisen in China, except in connexion with Buddhism, which brought Indian philosophy with it. Again, it is natural, to take a different kind of instance, to suppose that a proper name which can be used significantly stands for a single entity; we suppose that there is a certain more or less persistent being called 'Socrates', because the same name is applied to a series of occurrences which we are led to regard as appearances of this one being. As language grows more abstract, a new set of entities come into philosophy, namely, those represented by abstract words—the universals. I do not wish to maintain that there are no universals, but certainly there are many abstract words which do not stand for single universals—e.g. triangularity and rationality. In these respects language misleads us both by its vocabulary and by its syntax. We must be on our guard in both respects if our logic is not to lead to a false metaphysic.

Syntax and vocabulary have had different kinds of effects on philosophy. Vocabulary has most influence on common sense. It might be urged, conversely, that common sense produces our vocabulary. This is only partially true. A word is applied at first to things which are more or less similar, without any reflection as to whether they have any point of identity. But when once usage has fixed the objects to which the word is to be applied, common sense is influenced by the existence of the word, and tends to suppose that one word must stand for one object, which will be a universal in the case of an adjective or an abstract word. Thus the influence of vocabulary is towards a kind of platonic pluralism of things and ideas.

The influence of syntax, in the case of the Indo-European languages, is quite different. Almost any proposition can be put into a form in which it has a subject and a predicate, united by a copula. It is natural to infer that every fact has a corresponding form, and consists in the possession of a quality by a substance. This leads, of course, to monism, since the fact that there were several substances (if it were a fact) would not have the requisite form. Philosophers, as a rule, believe themselves free from this sort of influence of linguistic forms, but most of them seem to me to be mistaken in this belief. In thinking about abstract matters, the fact that the words for abstractions are no more abstract than ordinary words always makes it easier to think about the words than about what they stand for, and it is almost impossible to resist consistently the temptation to think about the words.

Those who do not succumb to the subject-predicate logic are apt to get only one step further, and admit relations of two terms, such as before-and-after, greater-and-less, right-and-left. Language lends itself to this extension of the subject-predicate logic, since we say '*A* precedes *B*', '*A* exceeds *B*', and so on. It is easy to prove that the fact expressed by a proposition of this sort cannot consist of the possession of a quality by a substance, or of the possession of two or more qualities by two or more substances. (See *Principles of Mathematics*, § 214.) The extension of the subject-predicate logic is therefore right so far as it goes, but obviously a further extension can be proved necessary by exactly similar arguments. How far it is necessary to go up the series of three-term, four-term, five-term . . . relations I do not know. But it is certainly necessary to go beyond two-term relations. In projective geometry, for example, the order of points on a line or of planes through a line requires a four-term relation.

A very unfortunate effect of the peculiarities of language is in connexion with adjectives and relations. All words are of the same logical type; a word is a class of series, of noises or shapes according as it is heard or read. But the meanings of words are of various different types; an attribute (expressed by an adjective) is of a different type from the objects to which it can be (whether truly or falsely) attributed; a relation (expressed perhaps by a preposition, perhaps by a transitive verb, perhaps in some other way) is of a different type from the terms between which it holds or does not hold. The definition of a logical type is as follows: *A* and *B* are of the same logical type if, and only if, given any fact of which *A* is a constituent, there is a corresponding fact which has *B* as a constituent, which either results by substituting *B* for *A*, or is the negation of what so results. To take an illustration, Socrates and Aristotle are of the same type, because 'Socrates was a philosopher' and 'Aristotle was a philosopher' are both facts; Socrates and Caligula are of the same type, because 'Socrates was a philosopher' and 'Caligula was not a philosopher' are both facts. To love and to kill are of the same type, because 'Plato loved Socrates' and 'Plato did not kill Socrates' are both facts. It follows formally from the definition that, when two words have meanings of different types, the relations of the words to what they mean are of different types; that is to say, there is not one relation of meaning between words and what they stand for, but as many relations of meaning, each of a different logical type, as there are logical types among the objects for which there are words. This fact is a very potent source of error and confusion in philosophy. In particular, it has made it extraordinarily difficult to express in words any theory of relations which is logically capable of being true, because language cannot preserve the difference of type between a relation and its terms. Most of the arguments for and against the reality of relations have been vitiated through this source of confusion.

At this point, I propose to digress for a moment, and to say, as shortly as I can, what I believe about relations. My own views on the subject of relations in the past were less clear than I thought them, but were by no means the views which my critics supposed them to be. Owing to lack of clearness in my own thoughts, I was unable to convey my meaning. The subject of relations is difficult, and I am far from claiming to be now clear about it. But I think certain points are clear to me. At the time when I wrote *The Principles of Mathematics*, I had not yet seen the necessity of logical types. The doctrine of types profoundly affects logic, and I think shows what, exactly, is the valid element in the arguments of those who oppose 'external' relations. But so far from strengthening their main position, the doctrine of types leads, on the contrary, to a more complete and radical atomism than any that I conceived to be possible twenty years ago. The question of relations is one of the most important that arise in philosophy, as most other issues turn on it: monism and pluralism; the question whether anything is wholly true except the whole of truth, or wholly real except the whole of reality; idealism and realism, in some of their forms; perhaps the very existence of philosophy as a subject distinct from science and possessing a method of its own. It will serve to make my meaning clear if I take a passage in Mr. Bradley's *Essays on Truth and Reality*, not for controversial purposes, but because it raises exactly the issues that ought to be raised. But first of all I will try to state my own view, without argument.*

Certain contradictions—of which the simplest and oldest is the

---

* I am much indebted ty my friend Wittgenstein in this matter. See his *Tractatus Logico-Philosophicus*, Kegan Paul, 1922. I do not accept all his doctrines, but my debt to him will be obvious to those who read his book.

one about Epimenides the Cretan, who said that all Cretans were liars, which may be reduced to the man who says 'I am lying'—convinced me, after five years devoted mainly to this one question, that no solution is technically possible without the doctrine of types. In its technical form, this doctrine states merely that a word or symbol may form part of a significant proposition, and in this sense have meaning, without being always able to be substituted for another word or symbol in the same or some other proposition without producing nonsense. Stated in this way, the doctrine may seem like a truism. 'Brutus killed Caesar' is significant, but 'Killed killed Caesar' is nonsense, so that we cannot replace 'Brutus' by 'killed', although both words have meaning. This is plain common sense, but unfortunately almost all philosophy consists in an attempt to forget it. The following words, for example, by their very nature, sin against it: attribute, relation, complex, fact, truth, falsehood, not, liar, omniscience. To give a meaning to these words, we have to make a detour by way of words or symbols and the different ways in which they may mean; and even then, we usually arrive, not at one meaning, but at an infinite series of different meanings. Words, as we saw, are all of the same logical type; therefore when the meanings of two words are of different types, the relations of the two words to what they stand for are also of different types. Attribute-words and relation-words are of the same type, therefore we can say significantly 'attribute-words and relation-words have different uses'. But we cannot say significantly 'attributes are not relations'. By our definition of types, since relations are relations, the form of words 'attributes are relations' must be not false, but meaningless, and the form of words 'attributes are not relations', similarly, must be not true, but meaningless. Nevertheless, the statement 'attribute-words are not relation-words' is significant and true.

We can now tackle the question of internal and external relations, remembering that the usual formulations, on both sides, are inconsistent with the doctrine of types. I will begin with attempts to state the doctrine of external relations. It is useless to say 'terms are independent of their relations', because 'independent' is a word which means nothing. Two events may be said to be causally independent when no causal chain leads from one to the other; this happens, in the special theory of relativity, when the separation between the events is space-like. Obviously this sense of 'independent' is irrelevant. If, when we say 'terms are independent of their relations', we mean 'two terms which have a given relation would be the same if they did not have it', that is obviously false; for, being what they are, they have the relation, and therefore whatever does not have the relation is different. If we mean—as opponents of external relations suppose us to mean —that the relation is a third term which comes between the other two terms and is somehow hooked on to them, that is obviously absurd, for in that case the relation has ceased to be a relation, and all that is truly relational is the hooking of the relation to the terms. The conception of the relation as a third term between the other two sins against the doctrine of types, and must be avoided with the utmost care.

What, then, can we mean by the doctrine of external relations? Primarily this, that a relational proposition is not, in general, logically equivalent formally to one or more subject-predicate propositions. Stated more precisely: Given a relational propositional function 'xRy', it is not in general the case that we can find predicates a, β, γ, such that, for all values of x and y, xRy is equivalent to $xa, y\beta, (x, y)\gamma$ (where (x, y) stands for the whole consisting of x and y), or to any one or two of these. This, and this only, is what I mean to affirm when I assert the doctrine of external relations; and this, clearly, is at least part of what Mr. Bradley denies when he asserts the doctrine of internal relations.

In place of 'unities' or 'complexes', I prefer to speak of 'facts'. It must be understood that the word 'fact' cannot occur significantly in any position in a sentence where the word 'simple' can occur significantly, nor can a fact occur where a simple can occur. We must not say 'facts are not simples'. We can say, 'The symbol for a fact must not replace the symbol for a simple, or vice versa, if significance is to be preserved.' But it should be observed that, in this sentence, the word 'for' has different meanings on the two occasions of its use. If we are to have a language which is to safeguard us from errors as to types, the symbol for a fact must be a proposition, not a single word or letter. Facts can be asserted or denied, but cannot be named. (When I say 'facts cannot be named', this is, strictly speaking, nonsense. What can be said without falling into nonsense is: 'The symbol for a fact is not a name'.) This illustrates how meaning is a different relation for different types. The way to mean a fact is to assert it; the way to mean a simple is to name it. Obviously naming is different from asserting, and similar differences exist where more advanced types are concerned, though language has no means of expressing the differences.

There are many other matters in Mr. Bradley's examination of my views which call for reply. But as my present purpose is explanatory rather than controversial, I will pass them by, having, I hope, already said enough on the question of relations and complexes to make it clear what is the theory that I advocate. I will only add, as regards the doctrine of types, that most philosophers assume it now and then, and few would deny it, but that all (so far as I know) avoid formulating it precisely or drawing from it those deductions that are inconvenient for their systems.

I come now to some of Mr. Bradley's criticisms (*loc. cit.*, p. 280 ff.). He says:

'Mr. Russell's main position has remained to myself incomprehensible. On the one side I am led to think that he defends a strict pluralism, for which nothing is admissible beyond simple terms and external relations. On the other side Mr. Russell seems to assert emphatically, and to use throughout, ideas which such a pluralism surely must repudiate. He throughout stands upon unities which are complex and which cannot be analysed into terms and relations. These two positions to my mind are irreconcilable, since the second, as I understand it, contradicts the first flatly.'

With regard to external relations, my view is the one I have just stated, not the one commonly imputed by those who disagree. But with regard to unities, the question is more difficult. The topic is one with which language, by its very nature, is peculiarly unfitted to deal. I must beg the reader, therefore, to be indulgent if what I say is not exactly what I mean, and to try to see what I mean in spite of unavoidable linguistic obstacles to clear expression.

To begin with, I do not believe that there are complexes or unities in the same sense in which there are simples. I did believe this when I wrote *The Principles of Mathematics*, but, on account of the doctrine of types, I have since abandoned this view. To speak loosely, I regard simples and complexes as always of different types. That is to say, the statements 'There are simples' and

'There are complexes' use the words 'there are' in different senses. But if I use the words 'there are' in the sense which they have in the statement 'there are simples', then the form of words 'there are not complexes' is neither true nor false, but meaningless. This shows how difficult it is to say clearly, in ordinary language, what I want to say about complexes. In the language of mathematical logic it is much easier to say what I want to say, but much harder to induce people to understand what I mean when I say it.

When I speak of 'simples' I ought to explain that I am speaking of something not experienced as such, but known only inferentially as the limit of analysis. It is quite possible that, by greater logical skill, the need for assuming them could be avoided. A logical language will not lead to error if its simple symbols (i.e. those not having any parts that are symbols, or any significant structure) all stand for objects of some one type, even if these objects are not simple. The only drawback to such a language is that it is incapable of dealing with anything simpler than the objects which it represents by simple symbols. But I confess it seems obvious to me (as it did to Leibniz) that what is complex must be composed of simples, though the number of constituents may be infinite. It is also obvious that the logical uses of the old notion of substance (i.e. those uses which do not imply temporal duration) can only be applied, if at all, to simples; objects of other types do not have that kind of being which one associates with substances. The essence of a substance, from the symbolic point of view, is that it can only be named—in old-fashioned language, it never occurs in a proposition except as the subject or as one of the terms of a relation. If what we take to be simple is really complex, we may get into trouble by naming it, when what we ought to do is to assert it. For example, if Plato loves Socrates, there is not an entity 'Plato's love for Socrates', but only the fact that Plato loves Socrates. And in speaking of this as 'a fact', we are already making it more substantial and more of a unity than we have any right to do.

Attributes and relations, though they may be not susceptible of analysis, differ from substances by the fact that they suggest a structure, and that there can be no significant symbol which symbolizes them in isolation. All propositions in which an attribute or a relation *seems* to be the subject are only significant if they can be brought into a form in which the attribute is attributed or the relation relates. If this were not the case, there would be significant propositions in which an attribute or a relation would occupy a position appropriate to a substance, which would be contrary to the doctrine of types, and would produce contradictions. Thus the proper symbol for 'yellow' (assuming for the sake of illustration that this is an attribute) is not the single word 'yellow', but the propositional function 'x is yellow', where the structure of the symbol shows the position which the word 'yellow' must have if it is to be significant. Similarly the relation 'precedes' must not be represented by this one word, but by the symbol 'x precedes y', showing the way in which the symbol can occur significantly. (It is here assumed that values are not assigned to x and y when we are speaking of the attribute or relation itself.)

The symbol for the simplest possible kind of fact will still be of the form 'x is yellow' or 'x precedes y', only that 'x' and 'y' will be no longer undetermined variables, but names.

In addition to the fact that we do not experience simples as such, there is another obstacle to the actual creation of a correct logical language such as I have been trying to describe. This obstacle is vagueness. All our words are more or less infected with vagueness, by which I mean that it is not always clear whether they apply to a given object or not. It is of the nature of words to be more or less general, and not to apply only to a single particular, but that would not make them vague if the particulars to which they applied were a definite set. But this is never the case in practice. The defect, however, is one which it is easy to imagine removed, however difficult it may be to remove it in fact.

The purpose of the foregoing discussion of an ideal logical language (which would of course be wholly useless for daily life) is twofold: first, to prevent inferences from the nature of language to the nature of the world, which are fallacious because they depend upon the logical defects of language; secondly, to suggest, by inquiring what logic requires of a language which is to avoid contradiction, what sort of a structure we may reasonably suppose the world to have. If I am right, there is nothing in logic that can help us to decide between monism and pluralism, or between the view that there are ultimate relational facts and the view that there are none. My own decision in favour of pluralism and relations is taken on empirical grounds, after convincing myself that the *a priori* arguments to the contrary are invalid. But I do not think these argumen..s can be adequately refuted without a thorough treatment of logical types, of which the above is a mere sketch.

This brings me, however, to a question of method which I believe to be very important. What are we to take as data in philosophy? What shall we regard as having the greatest likelihood of being true, and what as proper to be rejected if it conflicts with other evidence? It seems to me that science has a much greater likelihood of being true in the main than any philosophy hitherto advanced (I do not, of course, except my own). In science there are many matters about which people are agreed; in philosophy there are none. Therefore, although each proposition in a science may be false, and it is practically certain that there are some that are false, yet we shall be wise to build our philosophy upon science, because the risk of error in philosophy is pretty sure to be greater than in science. If we could hope for certainty in philosophy the matter would be otherwise, but so far as I can see such a hope would be chimerical.

Of course those philosophers whose theories, *prima facie*, run counter to science always profess to be able to interpret science so that it shall remain true on its own level, with that minor degree of truth which ought to content the humble scientist. Those who maintain a position of this sort are bound—so it seems to me—to show in detail how the interpretation is to be effected. In many cases, I believe that this would be quite impossible. I do not believe, for instance, that those who disbelieve in the reality of relations (in some such sense as that explained above) can possibly interpret those numerous parts of science which employ asymmetrical relations. Even if I could see no way of answering the objections to relations raised (for example) by Mr. Bradley, I should still think it more likely than not that some answer was possible, because I should think an error in a very subtle and abstract argument more probable than so fundamental a falsehood in science. Admitting that everything we believe ourselves to know is doubtful, it seems, nevertheless, that what we believe ourselves to know in philosophy is more doubtful than the detail of science, though perhaps not more doubtful than its most sweeping generalizations.

The question of interpretation is of importance for almost every philosophy, and I am not at all inclined to deny that many scientific results require interpretation before they can be fitted into a coherent philosophy. The maxim of 'constructions *versus* inferences' is itself a maxim of interpretation. But I think that any valid kind of interpretation ought to leave the detail unchanged, though it may give a new meaning to fundamental ideas. In practice, this means that *structure* must be preserved. And a test of this is that all the propositions of a science should remain, though new meanings may be found for their terms. A case in point, on a non-philosophical level, is the relation of the physical theory of light to our perceptions of colour. This provides different physical occurrences corresponding to different seen colours, and thus makes the structure of the physical spectrum the same as that of what we see when we look at a rainbow. Unless structure is preserved, we cannot validly speak of an interpretation. And structure is just what is destroyed by a monistic logic.

I do not mean, of course, to suggest that, in any region of science, the structure revealed at present by observation is exactly that which actually exists. On the contrary, it is in the highest degree probable that the actual structure is more fine-grained than the observed structure. This applies just as much to psychological as to physical material. It rests upon the fact that, where we perceive a difference (e.g. between two shades of colour), there is a difference, but where we do not perceive a difference it does not follow that there is not a difference. We have therefore a right, in all interpretation, to demand the preservation of observed differences, and the provision of room for hitherto unobserved differences, although we cannot say in advance what they will be, except when they can be inferentially connected with observed differences.

In science, structure is the main study. A large part of the importance of relativity comes from the fact that it has substituted a single four-dimensional manifold (space-time) for the two manifolds, three-dimensional space and one-dimensional time. This is a change of structure, and therefore has far-reaching consequences, but any change which does not involve a change of structure does not make much difference. The mathematical definition and study of structure (under the name of 'relation-numbers') form Part IV of *Principia Mathematica*.

The business of philosophy, as I conceive it, is essentially that of logical analysis, followed by logical synthesis. Philosophy is more concerned than any special science with relations of different sciences and possible conflicts between them; in particular, it cannot acquiesce in a conflict between physics and psychology, or between psychology and logic. Philosophy should be comprehensive, and should be bold in suggesting hypotheses as to the universe which science is not yet in a position to confirm or confute. But these should always be presented *as* hypotheses, not (as is too often done) as immutable certainties like the dogmas of religion. Although, moreover, comprehensive construction is part of the business of philosophy, I do not believe it is the most important part. The most important part, to my mind, consists in criticizing and clarifying notions which are apt to be regarded as fundamental and accepted uncritically. As instances I might mention: mind, matter, consciousness, knowledge, experience, causality, will, time. I believe all these notions to be inexact and approximate, essentially infected with vagueness, incapable of forming part of any exact science. Out of the original manifold of events, logical structures can be built which will have properties sufficiently like those of the above common notions to account for their prevalence, but sufficiently unlike to allow a great deal of error to creep in through their acceptance as fundamental.

I suggest the following as an outline of a possible structure of the world; it is no more than an outline, and is not offered as more than possible.

The world consists of a number, perhaps finite, perhaps infinite, of entities which have various relations to each other, and perhaps also various qualities. Each of these entities may be called an 'event'; from the point of view of old-fashioned physics, an event occupies a short finite time and a small finite amount of space, but as we are not going to have an old-fashioned space and an old-fashioned time, this statement cannot be taken at its face value. Every event has to a certain number of others a relation which may be called 'compresence'; from the point of view of physics, a collection of compresent events all occupy one small region in space-time. One example of a set of compresent events is what would be called the contents of one man's mind at one time—i.e. all his sensations, images, memories, thoughts, etc., which can coexist temporally. His visual field has, in one sense, spatial extension, but this must not be confused with the extension of physical space-time; every part of his visual field is compresent with every other part, and with the rest of 'the contents of his mind' at that time, and a collection of compresent events occupies a minimal region in space-time. There are such collections not only where there are brains, but everywhere. At any point in 'empty space', a number of stars could be photographed if a camera were introduced; we believe that light travels over the regions intermediate between its source and our eyes, and therefore something is happening in these regions. If light from a number of different sources reaches a certain minimal region in space-time, then at least one event corresponding to each of these sources exists in this minimal region, and all these events are compresent.

We will define a set of compresent events as a 'minimal region'. We find that minimal regions form a four-dimensional manifold, and that, by a little logical manipulation, we can construct from them the manifold of space-time that physics requires. We find also that, from a number of different minimal regions, we can often pick out a set of events, one from each, which are closely similar when they come from neighbouring regions, and vary from one region to another according to discoverable laws. These are the laws of the propagation of light, sound, etc. We find also that certain regions in space-time have quite peculiar properties; these are the regions which are said to be occupied by 'matter'. Such regions can be collected, by means of the laws of physics, into tracks or tubes, very much more extended in one dimension of space-time than in the other three. Such a tube constitutes the 'history' of a piece of matter; from the point of view of the piece of matter itself, the dimension in which it is most extended can be called 'time', but it is only the private time of that piece of matter, because it does not correspond exactly with the dimension in which another piece of matter is most extended. Not only is space-time very peculiar within a piece of matter, but it is also rather peculiar in its neighbourhood, growing less so as the spatio-temporal distance grows greater; the law of this peculiarity is the law of gravitation.

All kinds of matter to some extent, but some kinds of matter (viz. nervous tissue) more particularly, are liable to form 'habits', i.e. to alter their structure in a given environment in such a way that, when they are subsequently in a similar environment, they react in a new way, but if similar environments recur often, the reaction in the end becomes nearly uniform, while remaining different from the reaction on the first occasion. (When I speak of the reaction of a piece of matter to its environment, I am thinking both of the constitution of the set of compresent events of which it consists, and of the nature of the track in space-time which constitutes what we should ordinarily call its motion; these are called a 'reaction to the environment' in so far as there are laws correlating them with characteristics of the environment.) Out of habit, the peculiarities of what we call 'mind' can be constructed; a mind is a track of sets of compresent events in a region of space-time where there is matter which is peculiarly liable to form habits. The greater the liability, the more complex and organized the mind becomes. Thus a mind and a brain are not really distinct, but when we speak of a mind we are thinking chiefly of the set of compresent events in the region concerned, and of their several relations to other events forming parts of other periods in the history of the spatio-temporal tube which we are considering, whereas when we speak of a brain we are taking the set of compresent events as a whole, and considering its external relations to other sets of compresent events, also taken as wholes; in a word, we are considering the shape of the tube, not the events of which each cross-section of it is composed.

The above summary hypothesis would, of course, need to be amplified and refined in many ways in order to fit in completely with scientific facts. It is not put forward as a finished theory, but merely as a suggestion of the kind of thing that may be true. It is of course easy to imagine other hypotheses which may be true, for example, the hypothesis that there is nothing outside the series of sets of events constituting my history. I do not believe that there is any method of arriving at one sole possible hypothesis, and therefore certainty in metaphysics seems to me unattainable. In this respect I must admit that many other philosophies have the advantage, since in spite of their differences *inter se*, each arrives at certainty of its own exclusive truth.

On Order in Time

This paper was written in 1935 and read to the Cambridge Philosophical Society in March of 1936. It first appeared in their PROCEEDINGS. What is known elsewhere as philosophy is Moral Science at Cambridge, and to avoid confusion it is worth noting that it was a scientific organization to which this paper was addressed, not a philosophical one in the usual sense.

Writing of this paper, Russell has told me that he felt it might prove to be important in physics to show that, although instants are generally regarded as mathematical constructions, 'the kind of assumptions one would naturally make do not prove that instants can be constructed'.

Although closely related to another essay of 1936, 'Determinism and Physics' this paper stands apart from Russell's other works of the period. In 1934 he had published FREEDOM AND ORGANIZATION 1814–1914, which, although one of his finest books, failed at first to make the impression it deserved. In RELIGION AND SCIENCE (1935) Russell's argument seems weakened by excessive scepticism and positivism of the overtly narrow sort, while WHICH WAY TO PEACE? (1936) showed him returning to social philosophy to ask the question that dominated the thought of millions of Europeans. It, and the short 'Auto-Obituary' that appeared in the same year (reprinted in UNPOPULAR ESSAYS, 1950), reflect the mood of the times. In 1936 Franklin D. Roosevelt told his countrymen they had a 'rendezvous with destiny' and as European politics moved toward the September days at Munich, two years ahead, the nature of that rendezvous became increasingly clear.

The last thing one might have expected from Russell in 1936 was a technical paper on a mathematical subject, but this is, in fact, a serious and but little-known work with strong ties to his most productive years of mathematical studies. Those who feel inclined to remark that Russell abandoned mathematical philosophy in the twenties are advised to read it with particular diligence.

ON ORDER IN TIME

IT is generally agreed that instants are mathematical constructions, not physical entities. If, therefore, there are instants, they must be classes of events having certain properties. For reasons explained in *Our Knowledge of the External World*, pages 116–20, an instant is most naturally defined as a group of events having the following two properties:

(1) Any two members of the group overlap in time, i.e. neither is wholly before the other.

(2) No event outside the group overlaps with all of them.

We then define one instant as earlier than another if there is some event at the one instant which is earlier than (i.e. wholly precedes) some event at the other. (Note that an event is 'at' an instant when it is a member of the class which is the instant.)

N. Wiener* has shown what conditions are necessary in order that instants should form a series. I have shown (loc. cit.) that every event x has a first instant if every event that begins after x has begun is wholly after some event which exists when x begins.

The present paper investigates further the conditions for the existence of instants, and what happens when they do not exist. It is shown that the existence of instants requires hypotheses which there is no reason to suppose true—a fact which may be not without importance in physics.

For the mathematico-logical treatment of the subject, we need only one fundamental relation, that of *wholly preceding*, which we will call P. Two events overlap, or are contemporaries, or are (at least partially) simultaneous, if neither wholly precedes the other; this relation we call S. Thus we put

* *Proc. Camb. Phil. Soc.*, Vol. 17 (1914), pp. 441–9.

$$P = \text{wholly precedes,}$$

$$S = \doteq P \doteq \breve{P}.$$

It follows that, of any two events that are not contemporaries, one wholly precedes the other. We have

$$S \mid P = \text{begins before,}$$

$$S \mid \breve{P} = \text{ends after,}$$

$$P \mid S = \text{ends before,}$$

$$\breve{P} \mid S = \text{begins after.}$$

We shall assume that P and $S \mid P$ are transitive, and that no event precedes itself; i.e.

$$P \subset \jmath \,.\, P^2 \subset P \,.\, (S \mid P)^2 \subset S \mid P.$$

From $P \subset \jmath$ it follows that, for all values of x, xSx. $S \mid P \subset \jmath$ follows because

$$xS \mid Px \,.\, \supset \,.\, (\exists y) \,.\, xSy \,.\, yPx \,.\, \supset \,.\, (\exists y) \,.\, yPx \,.\, \sim (yPx).$$

Similarly $P \mid S \subset \jmath$.

From xSx it follows that $P \subset S \mid P$ and $P \subset P \mid S$.

From $(S \mid P)^2 \subset S \mid P$ and $S \mid P \subset \jmath$ we have $(S \mid P)^2 \subset \jmath$.
Hence

$$xS \mid P \mid Sy \,.\, \supset \,.\, \sim (yPx), \quad \text{i.e. } S \mid P \mid S \subset \doteq \breve{P}.$$

Now

$$S \mid P \subset S \mid P \mid S \,.\, P \mid S \subset S \mid P \mid S.$$

Thus

$$S \mid P \subset \doteq \breve{P} \,.\, P \mid S \subset \doteq \breve{P}.$$

Hence

$$S \mid P \subset S \cup P \,.\, P \mid S \subset S \cup P.$$

Observe that $S \mid \breve{P} \mid S$ is the converse of $S \mid P \mid S$ (because $S = \breve{S}$).
Thus

$$S \mid P \mid S \subset \doteq \breve{P} \,.\, S \mid \breve{P} \mid S \subset \doteq P.$$

Therefore

$$S \mid P \mid S \dotfrown S \mid \breve{P} \mid S \subset S.$$

Again,

$$zSx \,.\, xP \mid S \mid Py \,.\, \supset \,.\, z(S \mid P)^2 y \,.\, \supset \,.\, z \neq y.$$

Therefore
$$xP\,|\,S\,|\,Py \,.\, \supset .\, \sim(xSy), \quad \text{i.e.} \quad P\,|\,S\,|\,P \,\mathsf{C} \doteq S.$$
Further,
$$S\,|\,P \,\mathsf{C} \doteq \breve{P} \,\mathsf{C}\, S \,\mathbf{\upsilon}\, P.$$
Therefore
$$P\,|\,S\,|\,P \,\mathsf{C}\, P\,|\,S \,\mathbf{\upsilon}\, P^2 \,\mathsf{C} \doteq \breve{P}.$$

Therefore $P\,|\,S\,|\,P \,\mathsf{C}\, P$. Hence $P\,|\,S\,|\,P\,|\,S \,\mathsf{C}\, P\,|\,S$, i.e. $P\,|\,S$ is transitive. Hence also
$$xS\,|\,Py \,.\, \supset .\, \overrightarrow{P^{\iota}}x \subset \overrightarrow{P^{\iota}}y \,.\, \underset{\cdot}{\exists}\,!\, \overrightarrow{P^{\iota}}y - \overrightarrow{P^{\iota}}x.$$
Conversely,
$$\underset{\cdot}{\exists}\,!\, \overrightarrow{P^{\iota}}y - \overrightarrow{P^{\iota}}x \,.\, \supset .\, (\exists z) \,.\, zPy \,.\, z(\breve{P} \,\mathbf{\upsilon}\, S)x :$$
$$\supset : xS\,|\,Py \,.\, \mathsf{v} \,.\, xP^2 y \,.$$
$$\supset .\, xS\,|\,Py.$$
Hence
$$xS\,|\,Py \,.\, \equiv .\, \underset{\cdot}{\exists}\,!\, \overrightarrow{P^{\iota}}y - \overrightarrow{P^{\iota}}x,$$
and
$$\overrightarrow{P^{\iota}}y \subset \overrightarrow{P^{\iota}}x \,.\, \equiv .\, \sim(xS\,|\,Py),$$
and
$$\overrightarrow{P^{\iota}}x = \overrightarrow{P^{\iota}}y \,.\, \equiv .\, \sim(xS\,|\,Py) \,.\, \sim(yS\,|\,Px).$$

And, for all values of x and y,
$$\overrightarrow{P^{\iota}}x \subset \overrightarrow{P^{\iota}}y \,.\, \mathsf{v} \,.\, \overrightarrow{P^{\iota}}y \subset \overrightarrow{P^{\iota}}x.$$

Put $\alpha A\beta$ for $\alpha \subset \beta \,.\, \underset{\cdot}{\exists}\,!\, \beta - \alpha$, i.e. α is a proper part of β. Then
$$xS\,|\,Py \,.\, \equiv .\, \overrightarrow{P^{\iota}}x A \overrightarrow{P^{\iota}}y,$$
$$xS\,|\,\breve{P}y \,.\, \equiv .\, \overleftarrow{P^{\iota}}x A \overleftarrow{P^{\iota}}y,$$
$$xP\,|\,Sy \,.\, \equiv .\, \overleftarrow{P^{\iota}}y A \overleftarrow{P^{\iota}}x \,.\, \equiv .\, yS\,|\,\breve{P}x,$$
$$x\breve{P}\,|\,Sy \,.\, \equiv .\, \overrightarrow{P^{\iota}}y A \overrightarrow{P^{\iota}}x \,.\, \equiv .\, yS\,|\,Px.$$

Classes of the form $\overrightarrow{P^{\iota}}x$, i.e. the members of $D^{\iota}\overrightarrow{P}$, form a series. For
$$(x,y) : \overrightarrow{P^{\iota}}x A \overrightarrow{P^{\iota}}y \,.\, \mathsf{v} \,.\, \overrightarrow{P^{\iota}}x = \overrightarrow{P^{\iota}}y \,.\, \mathsf{v} \,.\, \overrightarrow{P^{\iota}}y A \overrightarrow{P^{\iota}}x.$$
Thus
$$A \upharpoonright D^{\iota}\overrightarrow{P} \,\epsilon\, \text{Ser}.$$
Similarly
$$A \upharpoonright D^{\iota}\overleftarrow{P} \,\epsilon\, \text{Ser}.$$

These series are not each other's converses. The first arranges events by their beginnings, the second by their ends; but one event may begin before and end after another.

Two events x and y for which $\overrightarrow{S}{}^{\prime}x = \overrightarrow{S}{}^{\prime}y$ cover exactly the same period of time; the class $\overrightarrow{S}{}^{\prime}x$ may be defined as the 'duration' of x. Durations can be arranged in a series on the following plan: If two durations do not begin together, put first the one with the earlier beginning; if they begin together, put first the one with the earlier end; i.e.

$$N = \hat{a}\hat{\beta}\{(\exists x,y): a = \overrightarrow{S}{}^{\prime}x \,.\, \beta = \overrightarrow{S}{}^{\prime}y : \overrightarrow{P}{}^{\prime}x A \overrightarrow{P}{}^{\prime}y \,.$$
$$\text{v}\,.\,\overrightarrow{P}{}^{\prime}x = \overrightarrow{P}{}^{\prime}y\,.\,\overleftarrow{P}{}^{\prime}y A \overleftarrow{P}{}^{\prime}x\}.$$

Then

$$N \,\epsilon\, \text{Ser}\,.\,C{}^{\prime}N = \overrightarrow{D}{}^{\prime}S,$$

i.e. N is a series whose terms are all durations.

We now come to the definition of instants and the series of instants. Put

$$\text{In} = \dot{\mu}(\mu = p{}^{\prime}\overrightarrow{S}{}^{\prime\prime}\mu) \quad \text{Df},$$
$$T = (\breve{\epsilon}\,;P)\upharpoonright \text{In} \quad \text{Df}.$$

The first definition states that an instant is a class of events which is identical with the common contemporaries of all the members of the class. The second definition states that one instant is earlier than another if some member of the one wholly precedes some member of another.

We will deal first with the properties of instants, and the series of instants, which do not raise the question of the existence of instants.

$$a,\beta\,\epsilon\,\text{In}\,.\,\beta \subset a\,.\,\supset\,.\,p{}^{\prime}\overrightarrow{S}{}^{\prime\prime}a \subset p{}^{\prime}\overrightarrow{S}{}^{\prime\prime}\beta\,.\,\supset\,.\,a \subset \beta.$$

Hence

$$a,\beta\,\epsilon\,\text{In}\,.\,a \neq \beta\,.\,\supset\,.\,\exists\,!\,a-\beta\,.\,\text{v}\,.\,\exists\,!\,\beta-a.$$

Further,

$$a\,\epsilon\,\text{In}\,.\,\supset\,.\,-a = P{}^{\prime\prime}a \cup \breve{P}{}^{\prime\prime}a.$$

Assume $a,\,\beta\,\epsilon\,\text{In}$. Thus

$$\exists\,!\,\beta-a\,.\,\supset\,.\,(\exists y)\,.\,y\,\epsilon\,\beta\,.\,y\,\epsilon\,P{}^{\prime\prime}a \cup \overrightarrow{P}{}^{\prime\prime}a\,.$$
$$\supset\,.\,(\exists x,y)\,.\,x\,\epsilon\,a\,.\,y\,\epsilon\,\beta\,.\,x(P \cup \breve{P})y\,.$$
$$\supset\,.\,a(T \cup \breve{T})\beta.$$

Hence

$$a, \beta \in \text{In} . \supset : aT\beta . \vee . a = \beta . \vee . \beta Ta.$$

Again,

$$a, \beta \in \text{In} . x \in a . y \in \beta . xPy . \supset . x \sim \in \beta . \supset . a \neq \beta.$$

Hence $T \subseteq J$. Similarly, from $P^2 \subseteq P$, we have $T^2 \subseteq T$. Hence

$$T \in \text{Ser} . C'T = \text{In}.$$

Thus T is a series whose field is all instants.

I come now to the conditions required if the series of instants is to be compact, i.e. if between any two instants there is another, i.e. if $T \subseteq T^2$. This requires

$$a, \gamma \in \text{In} . x \in a . z \in \gamma . xPz .$$
$$\supset . (\exists \beta, a, c, y, y') . a \in a . c \in \gamma . \beta \in \text{In} . y, y' \in \beta . aPy . y'Pc.$$

For this it is necessary (not sufficient) to have

$$P \subseteq S | P | S | P | S,$$

since, in the above, $xSa . aPy . ySy' . y'Pc . cSz$ and xPz. Now in general we shall have $xS | P | Sx$; this only fails if

$$\overrightarrow{S'x} \cap \overrightarrow{P''S'x} = \Lambda . \overrightarrow{S'x} \cap \breve{P}''\overrightarrow{S'x} = \Lambda,$$

i.e. if no contemporary of x ends before x ends or begins after x begins. In that case, $\overrightarrow{S'x} \in \text{In}$, i.e. x lasts only for an instant. If we assume that no event lasts only for an instant, we have always $xS | P | Sx$. Therefore

$$P | S \subseteq S | P | S | P | S.$$

Therefore the above condition reduces to

$$P \subseteq P | S,$$

which is always true. The only further condition required for $T \subseteq T^2$ is, by the above,

$$ySy' . \supset . (\exists \beta) . \beta \in \text{In} . y, y' \in \beta.$$

Thus the series of instants is compact if (a) no event lasts only for an instant, (b) any two overlapping events have at least one instant in common. These conditions are sufficient; the necessary conditions are slightly less stringent.

The existence of instants can be proved on various assumptions. One of these is that events can be well ordered. Others will be given below. There is, however, no reason, either logical or empirical, for supposing these assumptions to be true. If they are not, instants are only a logical ideal, to which, as we shall see, it is possible to approximate indefinitely, but which cannot be reached.

Given any event x, the first instant of its duration, if it exists, must be the class of events existing when x begins, i.e. μ, where

$$\mu = \overrightarrow{S}{}^{\prime}x - \breve{P}{}^{\prime\prime}\overrightarrow{S}{}^{\prime}x.$$

We have

$$\mu \subset p{}^{\prime}\overrightarrow{S}{}^{\prime\prime}\mu.$$

We require also, if μ is to be an instant,

$$-\mu \subset -p{}^{\prime}\overrightarrow{S}{}^{\prime\prime}\mu, \quad \text{i.e.} \quad -\mu \subset P{}^{\prime\prime}\mu \cup \breve{P}{}^{\prime\prime}\mu.$$

Now

$$-\mu = -\overrightarrow{S}{}^{\prime}x \cup \breve{P}{}^{\prime\prime}\overrightarrow{S}{}^{\prime}x.$$

Since

$$x \epsilon \mu \quad \text{and} \quad -\overrightarrow{S}{}^{\prime}x = \overrightarrow{P}{}^{\prime}x \cup \overleftarrow{P}{}^{\prime}x,$$

$$-\overrightarrow{S}{}^{\prime}x \subset P{}^{\prime\prime}\mu \cup \breve{P}{}^{\prime\prime}\mu.$$

Also

$$P{}^{\prime\prime}\mu \subset P{}^{\prime\prime}\overrightarrow{S}{}^{\prime}x - \overrightarrow{S}{}^{\prime}x \subset \overrightarrow{P}{}^{\prime}x.$$

Therefore

$$\breve{P}{}^{\prime\prime}\overrightarrow{S}{}^{\prime}x \subset -\overrightarrow{P}{}^{\prime}x \subset -P{}^{\prime\prime}\mu.$$

Therefore we require, if $\mu \epsilon \text{In}$,

$$\breve{P}{}^{\prime\prime}\overrightarrow{S}{}^{\prime}x \subset \breve{P}{}^{\prime\prime}\mu,$$

i.e. since $\mu \subset \overrightarrow{S}{}^{\prime}x$,

$$\breve{P}{}^{\prime\prime}\overrightarrow{S}{}^{\prime}x = \breve{P}{}^{\prime\prime}(\overrightarrow{S}{}^{\prime}x - \breve{P}{}^{\prime\prime}\overrightarrow{S}{}^{\prime}x).$$

This is the necessary and sufficient condition for μ to have a first instant. It states that, if an event begins after x begins, it is wholly after *some* event which existed when x began; i.e. if y begins after x begins, some event existing when x began stops in the interval between the beginning of x and the beginning of y.

We may put this condition into simpler words by means of the two following definitions:

The *initial contemporaries* of an event x are the events which exist when x begins, i.e. $\overrightarrow{S'}x - \overset{\smile}{P}{}''\overrightarrow{S'}x$.

The *subsequent contemporaries* of an event x are the events which overlap with x but begin later, i.e. $\overrightarrow{S'}x \cap \overset{\smile}{P}{}''\overrightarrow{S'}x$.

Then our condition for the existence of a first instant of x is:

Every subsequent contemporary of x begins after the end of some initial contemporary of x.

To simplify the formal statement of this condition, put

$$M = S \dot{-} \overset{\smile}{P} \mid S.$$

Thus $yMx . = . y$ exists when x begins, and

$$\overrightarrow{M'}x = \overrightarrow{S'}x - \overset{\smile}{P}{}''\overrightarrow{S'}x.$$

Thus the condition for x to have a first instant is

$$xS \mid Py . \supset . xM \mid Py,$$

and the condition that all events have first instants is

$$S \mid P \subset M \mid P.$$

Similarly the condition that all events have last instants is, putting

$$N = S \dot{-} P \mid S,$$
$$S \mid \overset{\smile}{P} \subset N \mid \overset{\smile}{P}.$$

We shall find other forms of the condition for the existence of instants. But first let us consider what happens if x has no first instant. For this purpose, it is convenient to confine our attention as far as possible to the contemporaries of x, i.e. to $\overrightarrow{S'}x$. We therefore put

$$X = P \restriction \overrightarrow{S'}x;$$

that is, X is the relation P confined to contemporaries of x. Then

$$D'X = \overrightarrow{S'}x \cap \overrightarrow{P}{}''S'x,$$
$$\sigma'X = \overrightarrow{S'}x \cap \overset{\smile}{P}{}''\overrightarrow{S'}x,$$
$$\overrightarrow{B'}X = \overrightarrow{S'}x \cap P''\overrightarrow{S'}x - \overset{\smile}{P}{}''\overrightarrow{S'}x,$$
$$\overset{\smile}{X}{}''\overrightarrow{B'}X = \overrightarrow{S'}x \cap \overset{\smile}{P}{}''(\overrightarrow{S'}x - \overset{\smile}{P}{}''\overrightarrow{S'}x).$$

Thus the condition $\breve{P}``\overrightarrow{S}`x=\breve{P}``\mu$ becomes

$$a`X=\breve{X}``\overrightarrow{B}`X.$$

If this condition is not fulfilled, we have

$$\exists!a`X-\breve{X}``\overrightarrow{B}`X.$$

Put

$$\beta=a`X-\breve{X}``\overrightarrow{B}`X.$$

Then

$$y\,\epsilon\,\beta\,.\,\supset\,.\,\exists!\overrightarrow{X}`y\,.\,\overrightarrow{X}`y\subset a`X\,.\,\overrightarrow{X}`y\subset\beta.$$

That is to say, every member of β has predecessors which are β's. Thus in β there are infinite descending series. These series are all contained between the beginning of x and the first stopping-point of events existing when x begins. There must therefore be no lower limit to their duration. They are all contemporary with the whole of μ, i.e.

$$\beta\subset p`\overrightarrow{S}``\mu.$$

In fact,

$$p`\overrightarrow{S}``\mu=\mu\cup\beta=\overrightarrow{S}`x-\breve{P}``(\overrightarrow{S}`x-\breve{P}``\overrightarrow{S}`x).$$

Further,

$$p`\overrightarrow{S}``(\mu\cup\beta)=\mu.$$

Thus μ is too small a class to form an instant, and $\mu\cup\beta$ is too large. For if we have $a\subset p`\overrightarrow{S}``a$, but the two are not equal, we need to enlarge $a$ and therefore diminish (or at least not increase) $p`\overrightarrow{S}``a$ in order to arrive at $a=p`\overrightarrow{S}``a$; but if $p`\overrightarrow{S}``a\subset a$ and the two are not equal, we need to diminish a and therefore increase (or at least not diminish) $p`\overrightarrow{S}``a$ in order to secure equality. These considerations may be illustrated by considering the class λ, where

$$\lambda=\mu\cup(\beta-P``\beta).$$

We have

$$p`\overrightarrow{S}``\beta=\mu;\quad\text{hence}\quad\mu\subset p`\overrightarrow{S}``(\beta-P``\beta).$$

Also

$$p`\overrightarrow{S}``\lambda=p`\overrightarrow{S}``\mu\cap p`\overrightarrow{S}``(\beta-P``\beta),$$
$$=(\mu\cup\beta)\cap p`\overrightarrow{S}``(\beta-P``\beta),$$
$$=\mu\cup\{\beta\cap p`\overrightarrow{S}``(\beta-P``\beta)\}.$$

Thus we shall have $\lambda \epsilon$ In if

$$\beta - P''\beta = \beta \cap p'\overrightarrow{S''}(\beta - P''\beta).$$

Now

$$\beta - P''\beta \subset p'\overrightarrow{S''}(\beta - P''\beta).$$

Therefore if $\lambda \epsilon$ In we require

$$p'\overrightarrow{S''}(\beta - P''\beta) \subset - P''\beta,$$

i.e.

$$P''\beta \subset P''(\beta - P''\beta) \cup \breve{P}''(\beta - P''\beta),$$

i.e.

$$P''\beta \subset P''(\beta - P''\beta).$$

This is a condition exactly analogous (except for the substitution of P for $\breve{P}$) to the previous one, viz.

$$\breve{P}''\overrightarrow{S'}x \subset \breve{P}''(\overrightarrow{S'}x - \breve{P}''\overrightarrow{S'}x),$$

and exactly similar considerations apply to it. If we put

$$\gamma = P''\beta - P''(\beta - P''\beta),$$

and if γ is not null, it contains infinite ascending series of events all contained in a stretch between the end of $P''(\beta - P''\beta)$ and the end of $P''\beta$.

A few general considerations may help to make these possibilities clear. Let the duration of x be represented by XX'. Then the

existence of β implies the existence of a stretch XA such that no event existing at X stops before A, but, given any event which stops in XA, it not only begins in XA, but has predecessors which begin and end in XA, and these have others, and so on *ad infinitum*. The class β consists of events which begin in XA, wherever they may stop.

Now suppose that there is a stretch BA such that every event that begins in BA also stops in BA. All such events are included in $P''\beta$. $\beta - P''\beta$ will be events which begin after X and stop at or after A. By hypothesis, none of these begins in BA. Thus all the events that begin in BA are members of γ.

The hypothesis concerning X was: No event existing at X stops before A. The hypothesis concerning A is: No event existing at A begins after B. If both hypotheses are verified, the duration XA has no instant at the beginning or at the end.

We can, of course, define continually smaller regions, by prolonging the above procedure; but there is no reason to suppose that they approach a point as their limit.

From the above it appears that there must be instants if there is a minimum to duration, i.e. if an infinite series of non-overlapping events must ultimately reach any given region; or, conversely, if a P-series consisting entirely of contemporaries of a given event must be finite. This may be expressed as follows:

$$(R,x): R \subseteq P . C'R \subseteq \overrightarrow{S}'x . \supset . \exists ! \overrightarrow{B}'R.$$

This hypothesis ensures that every event has a first instant. If, for $\overrightarrow{B}'R$, we substitute $\overrightarrow{B}'\breve{R}$, we ensure that every event has a last instant. Thus if, among the contemporaries of x, there are no infinite series of non-overlapping events, x has a first and a last instant.

This matter may be put as follows: If $\overrightarrow{S}'x - \breve{P}''\overrightarrow{S}'x$ is to be an instant, we require, as we have seen,

$$bSx . xS | Pb . \supset . (\exists a) . aSx . \sim(xS | Pa) . aPb.$$

Put

$$a = \overrightarrow{S}'x \cap \overrightarrow{P}'b . a \epsilon a - \breve{P}''a.$$

Then

$$a \epsilon \overrightarrow{S}'x \cap \overrightarrow{P}'b . \overrightarrow{P}'a \subseteq - \overrightarrow{S}'x \cup - \overrightarrow{P}'b . \overrightarrow{P}'a \subseteq \overrightarrow{P}'b . \overrightarrow{P}'a \subseteq P''\overrightarrow{S}'x.$$

Therefore

$$\overrightarrow{P}'a \subseteq - \overrightarrow{S}'x,$$

and therefore $\sim(xS | \breve{P}a)$. Thus $\exists ! a - P''a$ gives the desired result. This follows if $\sim(xS | P^2b)$; and so it does if $\sim(xS | P^nb)$, where n is any finite integer. This leads to the same hypothesis as the above for the existence of instants.

The event x will have a first instant if there is an event a which stops just when x begins. This happens if

$$aSx . P''\overrightarrow{S}'a \subseteq \overrightarrow{P}'x,$$

i.e. if a overlaps x, but nothing that ends sooner does so. In this case,

$$\overrightarrow{S}\text{'}x - \breve{P}\text{''}\overrightarrow{S}\text{'}x \, \epsilon \, \text{In}.$$

For

$$P\text{''}\overrightarrow{S}\text{'}a \subset \overrightarrow{P}\text{'}x \,.\, \supset \,.\, \overrightarrow{P}\text{'}a \subset \overrightarrow{P}\text{'}x \,.\, \supset \,.\, \sim(xS\,|\,Pa).$$

Therefore

$$a \, \epsilon \, \overrightarrow{S}\text{'}x - \breve{P}\text{''}\overrightarrow{S}\text{'}x.$$

Again,

$$xS\,|\,Pz \,.\, \supset \,.\, (\exists y) \,.\, xSy \,.\, yPz.$$

But by hypothesis

$$yPz \,.\, zSa \,.\, \supset \,.\, yPx.$$

Therefore

$$xSy \,.\, yPz \,.\, \supset \,.\, \sim(zSa).$$

Again,

$$\sim(xS\,|\,Pa) \,.\, \supset \,:\, \sim(\exists y) \,.\, xSy \,.\, yPa :$$
$$\supset \,:\, xSy \,.\, yPz \,.\, \supset \,.\, \sim(zPa).$$

Hence

$$xSy \,.\, yPz \,.\, \supset \,.\, aPz.$$

Hence

$$z \, \epsilon \, \breve{P}\text{''}\overrightarrow{S}\text{'}x \,.\, \supset \,.\, z \, \epsilon \, \overleftarrow{P}\text{'}a.$$

But

$$a \, \epsilon \, \overrightarrow{S}\text{'}x - \breve{P}\text{''}\overrightarrow{S}\text{'}x.$$

Therefore

$$z \, \epsilon \, \breve{P}\text{''}\overrightarrow{S}\text{'}x \,.\, \supset \,.\, z \, \epsilon \, \breve{P}\text{''}(\overrightarrow{S}\text{'}x - \breve{P}\text{''}\overrightarrow{S}\text{'}x).$$

Therefore

$$\overrightarrow{S}\text{'}x - \breve{P}\text{''}\overrightarrow{S}\text{'}x \, \epsilon \, \text{In}.$$

The hypothesis

$$aSx \,.\, P\text{''}\overrightarrow{S}\text{'}a \subset \overrightarrow{P}\text{'}x$$

is equivalent to

$$aSx \,.\, \sim(aS\,|\,\breve{P}\,|\,Sx).$$

For

$$P\text{''}\overrightarrow{S}\text{'}a \subset \overrightarrow{P}\text{'}x \,.\, \supset \,.\, P\text{''}\overrightarrow{S}\text{'}a \subset - \overrightarrow{S}\text{'}x \,.\, \supset \,.\, \sim(aS\,|\,\breve{P}\,|\,Sx).$$

And since

$$P\text{''}\overrightarrow{S}\text{'}a \subset - \overleftarrow{P}\text{'}x, \quad P\text{''}\overrightarrow{S}\text{'}a \subset - \overrightarrow{S}\text{'}x \,.\, \supset \,.\, P\text{''}\overrightarrow{S}\text{'}a \subset \overrightarrow{P}\text{'}x.$$

Thus

$$P\text{''}\overrightarrow{S}\text{'}a \subset \overrightarrow{P}\text{'}x \,.\, \equiv \,.\, \sim(aS\,|\,\breve{P}\,|\,Sx) \,.\, \equiv \,.\, \sim(xS\,|\,P\,|\,Sa).$$

Thus a sufficient condition for the existence of instants is

$$\dot{\exists} \, ! \, S \,\dot{-}\, S \mid P \mid S.$$

If this hypothesis is satisfied, there are two events a, x such that

$$aSx \,.\, P``\overrightarrow{S`}a \subset \overrightarrow{P`}x \,.\, \breve{P}``\overrightarrow{S`}x \subset \overleftarrow{P`}a,$$

and the last instant of a is the first of x.

If $S \subset S \mid P \mid S$, then, putting $Q = P \mid S$ and $R = S \mid P$,

$$S \subset S \mid Q \subset S \mid Q^2 \subset S \mid Q^n,$$

where n is any finite integer, and

$$S \subset R \mid S \subset R^2 \mid S \subset R^n \mid S.$$

$S \subset S \mid Q^n$ states that, if two events a and b overlap, there are n events of which the first is a contemporary of a, the second ends later than the first, the third than the second, etc., and b ends later than the nth. $S \subset R^n \mid S$, similarly, states that, if two events a and b overlap, there are n events of which the first begins later than a, the second than the first, etc., and the nth is contemporary with b. If either of these does not happen, one of the events a and b has a first instant and the other a last.

The above sufficient condition may be stated in the form

$$(\exists a,x) : aSx : P``\overrightarrow{S`}a \subset \overrightarrow{P`}x \,.\, \text{v} \,.\, \breve{P}``\overrightarrow{S`}a \subset \overleftarrow{P`}x.$$

Note that

$$aS \mid P \mid Sx \,.\, = \,.\, a \text{ begins before the end of } x,$$

$$aS \mid \breve{P} \mid Sx \,.\, = \,.\, a \text{ ends after the beginning of } x.$$

Thus

$$a(S \,\dot{-}\, S \mid P \mid S)x \,.\, = \,.\, a \text{ begins at the end of } x,$$

and

$$a(S \,\dot{-}\, S \mid \breve{P} \mid S)x \,.\, = \,.\, a \text{ ends at the beginning of } x.$$

Observe that, putting

$$Q = P \mid S \,.\, R = S \mid P,$$

we have

$$a(S \,\dot{-}\, S \mid P \mid S)x \,.\, \equiv \,.\, a \,\epsilon\, \overrightarrow{S`}x - R``\overrightarrow{S`}x,$$

$$a(S \,\dot{\cdot}\, S \mid \breve{P} \mid S)x \,.\, \equiv \,.\, a \,\epsilon\, \overrightarrow{S`}x - \breve{Q}``\overrightarrow{S`}x.$$

We have seen that, if

$$a\,(S \doteq S\,|\,\breve{P}\,|\,S)x, \quad \overrightarrow{S}{}^{\prime}x - \breve{P}{}^{\prime\prime}\overrightarrow{S}{}^{\prime}x \,\epsilon\, \mathrm{In}.$$

In this case,

$$\overrightarrow{S}{}^{\prime}x - \breve{P}{}^{\prime\prime}\overrightarrow{S}{}^{\prime}x = \overrightarrow{S}{}^{\prime}x \cap \overrightarrow{S}{}^{\prime}a,$$

for

$$a \doteq S\,|\,\breve{P}\,|\,Sx\,.\equiv.\,\overrightarrow{S}{}^{\prime}a \subset - \breve{P}{}^{\prime\prime}\overrightarrow{S}{}^{\prime}x.$$

Therefore

$$\overrightarrow{S}{}^{\prime}a \cap \overrightarrow{S}{}^{\prime}x \subset \overrightarrow{S}{}^{\prime}x - \breve{P}{}^{\prime\prime}\overrightarrow{S}{}^{\prime}x.$$

Again,

$$aSx\,.\sim(xS\,|\,Pz)\,.\supset.\sim(aPz),$$

and

$$zPa\,.\supset.\,zPx, \quad \text{so that} \quad xSz\,.\supset.\sim(zPa).$$

Hence

$$xSz\,.\sim(xS\,|\,Pz)\,.\supset.\,zSa,$$

i.e.

$$\overrightarrow{S}{}^{\prime}x - \breve{P}{}^{\prime\prime}\overrightarrow{S}{}^{\prime}x \subset \overrightarrow{S}{}^{\prime}x \cap \overrightarrow{S}{}^{\prime}a.$$

Hence

$$\overrightarrow{S}{}^{\prime}x - \breve{P}{}^{\prime\prime}\overrightarrow{S}{}^{\prime}x = \overrightarrow{S}{}^{\prime}x \cap \overrightarrow{S}{}^{\prime}a.$$

Let μ be an instant for which $\exists!\mu - R{}^{\prime\prime}\mu\,.\,\exists!\mu - \breve{Q}{}^{\prime\prime}\mu$, where $R = S\,|\,P\,.\,Q = P\,|\,S$. That is to say, there is an event a which is a member of μ, and begins not later than any other member of μ; and there is an event b which is a member of μ and ends not earlier than other member.

$$b$$
_____

_____
$$a$$

Thus our hypothesis is

$$a\,\epsilon\,\mu\,.\,b\,\epsilon\,\mu : y\,\epsilon\,\mu\,.\,\supset_y.\sim(aRy)\,.\sim(yQb).$$

Now

$$\sim(aRy)\,.\equiv\,:aSz\,.\,\supset_z.\sim(zPy),$$

$$\sim(yQb)\,.\equiv\,:zSb\,.\,\supset_z.\sim(yPz).$$

Thus

$$y\,\epsilon\,\mu\,.\,\supset_y:aSz\,.\,zSb\,.\,\supset_z.\,zSy,$$

i.e.

$$z\,\epsilon\,\overrightarrow{S}{}^{\prime}a \cap \overrightarrow{S}{}^{\prime}b\,.\,\supset : y\,\epsilon\,\mu\,.\,\supset_y.\,zSy:\supset:z\,\epsilon\,p{}^{\prime}\overrightarrow{S}{}^{\prime\prime}\mu:\supset:z\,\epsilon\,\mu,$$

i.e.

$$\overrightarrow{S}{}^{\prime}a \cap \overrightarrow{S}{}^{\prime}b \subset \mu, \quad \text{i.e.} \quad \overrightarrow{S}{}^{\prime}a \cap \overrightarrow{S}{}^{\prime}b = \mu.$$

In this case,

$$aRc . \supset : c \sim \epsilon \mu : \supset : \sim (cSa) . \mathbf{v} . \sim (cSb),$$
$$aRc . \sim (cSa) . \supset . aPc.$$

But $\sim (aQb)$. Therefore $\sim (cSb)$. Thus

$$aRc . \supset . \sim (cSb), \quad \text{i.e.} \quad \sim (aS|P|Sb).$$

Thus, putting $S|P|S = H$, we have

$$\mu \epsilon \operatorname{In} . \underset{\boldsymbol{\exists}}{} ! \mu - R``\mu . \underset{\boldsymbol{\exists}}{} ! \mu - \breve{Q}``\mu .$$
$$\supset . (\boldsymbol{\exists} a, b) . \mu = \overrightarrow{S}{}^{\prime}a \cap \overrightarrow{S}{}^{\prime}b . a(S \doteq H \doteq \breve{H})b.$$

Conversely, assume $\overrightarrow{S}{}^{\prime}a \cap \overrightarrow{S}{}^{\prime}b \epsilon \operatorname{In}$. Put $\mu = \overrightarrow{S}{}^{\prime}a \cap \overrightarrow{S}{}^{\prime}b$.

$$\mu \epsilon \operatorname{In} \supset : d \epsilon \mu . \equiv . \mu \subset \overrightarrow{S}{}^{\prime}d.$$

Therefore

$$\overrightarrow{S}{}^{\prime}a \cap \overrightarrow{S}{}^{\prime}b \epsilon \operatorname{In} . \supset : d \epsilon \overrightarrow{S}{}^{\prime}a \cap \overrightarrow{S}{}^{\prime}b . \equiv . \overrightarrow{S}{}^{\prime}a \cap \overrightarrow{S}{}^{\prime}b \subset \overrightarrow{S}{}^{\prime}d.$$

Suppose that dQb. Then $\underset{\boldsymbol{\exists}}{} ! \overrightarrow{S}{}^{\prime}b \cap \overleftarrow{P}{}^{\prime}d$. Now

$$c \epsilon \overrightarrow{S}{}^{\prime}b \cap \overleftarrow{P}{}^{\prime}d . dSa . \supset . aRc . \supset . \sim (cPa),$$
$$cSb . bQa . \supset . cHa . \supset . \sim (aPc).$$

Thus

$$c \epsilon \overrightarrow{S}{}^{\prime}b \cap \overleftarrow{P}{}^{\prime}d . dSa . bQa . \supset . cSa . \supset . c \epsilon \mu.$$

Therefore

$$bQa . dQb . dSa . \supset . \underset{\boldsymbol{\exists}}{} ! \mu \cap \overleftarrow{P}{}^{\prime}d . \supset . d \sim \epsilon \mu,$$

whence

$$bQa . \supset . \overrightarrow{Q}{}^{\prime}b \subset - \mu . \supset . b \epsilon - \breve{Q}``\mu.$$

Similarly

$$bRa . \supset . a \epsilon - R``\mu.$$

Now

$$\sim (bQa) . \equiv . \overleftarrow{P}{}^{\prime}b \subset \overleftarrow{P}{}^{\prime}a,$$
$$\sim (bRa) . \equiv . \overrightarrow{P}{}^{\prime}b \subset \overrightarrow{P}{}^{\prime}a.$$

Thus

$$\sim (bQa) . \sim (bRa) . \equiv . \overrightarrow{S}{}^{\prime}a \subset \overrightarrow{S}{}^{\prime}b, \quad \text{whence} \quad \overrightarrow{S}{}^{\prime}a \epsilon \operatorname{In}.$$

Similarly
$$\sim(aQb).\sim(aRb).\equiv.\overrightarrow{S}\text{'}b\subset\overrightarrow{S}\text{'}a,\quad\text{whence }S\text{'}b\,\epsilon\,\text{In}.$$

Hence
$$\overrightarrow{S}\text{'}a\,\epsilon\,\text{In}.\lor.\overrightarrow{S}\text{'}b\,\epsilon\,\text{In}.\lor.\,\exists!\,\overrightarrow{S}\text{'}a-\overrightarrow{S}\text{'}b.\exists!\,\overrightarrow{S}\text{'}b-\overrightarrow{S}\text{'}a.$$

Suppose that
$$y\,\epsilon\,\overrightarrow{S}\text{'}a-\overrightarrow{S}\text{'}b.bPy.z\,\epsilon\,\overrightarrow{S}\text{'}b-\overrightarrow{S}\text{'}a.zPa.$$

Then
$$bQa.bRa.$$

Thus
$$\overrightarrow{S}\text{'}a,\overrightarrow{S}\text{'}b\sim\epsilon\,\text{In}.\overrightarrow{S}\text{'}a\cap\overrightarrow{S}\text{'}b\,\epsilon\,\text{In}.$$
$$\supset:a\,\epsilon-R\text{''}\mu.b\,\epsilon-\breve{Q}\text{''}\mu.\lor.b\,\epsilon-R\text{''}\mu.a\,\epsilon-\breve{Q}\text{''}\mu.$$

Hence
$$\overrightarrow{S}\text{'}a,\overrightarrow{S}\text{'}b\,\epsilon-\text{In}.\mu=\overrightarrow{S}\text{'}a\cap\overrightarrow{S}\text{'}b.\supset:$$
$$\overrightarrow{S}\text{'}a\cap\overrightarrow{S}\text{'}b\,\epsilon\,\text{In}.\equiv:a\,\epsilon-R\text{''}\mu.b\,\epsilon-\breve{Q}\text{''}\mu.\lor.b\,\epsilon-R\text{''}\mu.a\,\epsilon-\breve{Q}\text{''}\mu,$$

and in this case we have $\sim(aS\,|\,P\,|\,Sb).\sim(bS\,|\,P\,|\,Sa)$,

i.e. one stops as the other begins.

It might be thought that, if there is not a first instant when an event exists, there will be a last instant when it does not. But the conditions for the two are independent.

The terms which overlap with x and begin before it are $\overrightarrow{S}\text{'}x$ $\cap S\text{''}\overrightarrow{P}\text{'}x$. The terms which end *just* before x are $\hat{a}(aPx:aP\,|\,Sb.$ $\supset_b.\sim bPx)$, i.e.
$$\overrightarrow{P}\text{'}x-P\text{''}S\text{''}\overrightarrow{P}\text{'}x.$$

Put
$$\lambda=\overrightarrow{S}\text{'}x\cap S\text{''}\overrightarrow{P}\text{'}x.\mu=\overrightarrow{P}\text{'}x-P\text{''}S\text{''}\overrightarrow{P}\text{'}x.R=S\,|\,P.$$

Therefore
$$\lambda\cup\mu=(\overrightarrow{S}\text{'}x\cap S\text{''}\overrightarrow{P}\text{'}x)\cup(\overrightarrow{P}\text{'}x\cap S\text{''}\overrightarrow{P}\text{'}x-P\text{''}S\text{''}\overrightarrow{P}\text{'}x)$$
$$=S\text{''}\overrightarrow{P}\text{'}x-P\text{''}S\text{''}\overrightarrow{P}\text{'}x=\overrightarrow{R}\text{'}x-P\text{''}\overrightarrow{R}\text{'}x,$$

and
$$\lambda=\overrightarrow{S}\text{'}x\cap\overrightarrow{R}\text{'}x.\mu=\overrightarrow{P}\text{'}x-P\text{''}\overrightarrow{R}\text{'}x.$$

Obviously $\lambda\cup\mu\subset p\overrightarrow{S}\text{''}(\lambda\cup\mu)$. We need further
$$-\lambda-\mu\subset P\text{''}\mu\cup\breve{P}\text{''}\mu\cup P\text{''}\lambda\cup\breve{P}\text{''}\lambda.$$

Now

$$-\overrightarrow{R}`x = p`\overleftarrow{P}``\overrightarrow{P}`x \subset p`\overleftarrow{P}``\mu \subset \overset{\smile}{P}``\mu \quad \text{if } \mathrm{\exists}!\mu.$$

Thus it remains to prove

$$P``\overrightarrow{R}`x \subset P``(\lambda \cup \mu).$$

We have

$$\overrightarrow{R}`x = \lambda \cup (\overrightarrow{R}`x \cap \overrightarrow{P}`x) = \lambda \cup \overrightarrow{P}`x.$$

Thus we have to prove

$$P``\overrightarrow{P}`x \subset P``(\lambda \cup \mu).$$

Now

$$P``\overrightarrow{P}`x \subset P``\lambda . \equiv : aP^2x . \supset_a . \mathrm{\exists}! \overleftarrow{P}`a \cap \overrightarrow{R}`x \cap \overrightarrow{S}`x.$$

Since $P \subset R$, we have $\mathrm{\exists}! \overleftarrow{R}`a \cap \overrightarrow{R}`x$. Put $a = \overleftarrow{R}`a \cap \overrightarrow{R}`x$. Assume $b \in a - R``a$. Then

$$aRb . bRx : bRc . \supset_c . \sim (aRc . cRx).$$

But $R^2 \subset R$. Therefore

$$aRb . bRx : bRc . \supset_c . \sim (cRx), \quad \text{i.e. } aRb . bR \dot{-} R^2x.$$

Now $bR \dot{-} R^2x . \supset . bSx$, unless $\overrightarrow{S}`x \in \text{In}$. For

$$b \dot{-} R^2x . \supset : b S | P | Sw . \supset_w . \sim (wPx).$$

Therefore $bS|P|Sb . \supset . \sim (bPx)$. Also $bRx . \supset . \sim (xPb)$. Hence

$$bS|P|Sb . \supset : bR \dot{-} R^2x . \supset . bSx.$$

But

$$\sim (bS|P|Sb) . \supset : \overrightarrow{S}`b \cap P``\overrightarrow{S}`b = \Lambda . \overrightarrow{S}`b \cap \overset{\smile}{P}``\overrightarrow{S}`b = \Lambda :$$
$$\supset : \overrightarrow{S}`b \subset p`\overrightarrow{S}``\overrightarrow{S}`b : \supset : \overrightarrow{S}`b = p`\overrightarrow{S}``\overrightarrow{S}`b :$$
$$\supset : \overrightarrow{S}`b \in \text{In}.$$

Hence

$$\overrightarrow{S}`b \sim \in \text{In} . \supset : bR \dot{-} R^2x . \supset . bSx.$$

Further, $bR \dot{-} R^2x . aP^2x . \supset . aPb$. For

$(\mathrm{\exists}c) . aPc . cPx$, $\therefore bSa . \supset . bRc . \supset . bR^2x$, $\therefore \sim (bSa)$, $\therefore aPb$.

Hence

$$aP^2x . bR \dot{-} R^2x . \supset . b \in \overrightarrow{S}`x \cap \overrightarrow{R}`x . aPb.$$

Thus

$$\mathbf{\exists}!\overrightarrow{R'x}-R''\overrightarrow{R'x}.\supset:P''\overrightarrow{P'x}\subset P''\lambda\,.\,\mathbf{v}\,.\,\overrightarrow{S'x}\,\epsilon\,\mathrm{In}.$$

Hence

$$\mathbf{\exists}!\overrightarrow{P'x}-P''\overrightarrow{R'x}\,.\,\mathbf{\exists}!\overrightarrow{R'x}-R''\overrightarrow{R'x}\,.$$
$$\supset:\overrightarrow{R'x}-P''\overrightarrow{R'x}\,\epsilon\,\mathrm{In}\,.\,\mathbf{v}\,.\,\overrightarrow{S'x}\,\epsilon\,\mathrm{In}.$$

Now

$$\overrightarrow{P'x}\subset P''\overrightarrow{R'x}\,.\,\supset:S''\overrightarrow{P'x}\subset S''P''\overrightarrow{R'x}\,.\,\supset\,.\,\overrightarrow{R'x}\subset R''\overrightarrow{R'x}.$$

Thus

$$\mathbf{\exists}!\overrightarrow{R'x}-R''\overrightarrow{R'x}\,.\,\supset\,.\,\mathbf{\exists}!\overrightarrow{P'x}-P''\overrightarrow{R'x}.$$

Hence

$$\mathbf{\exists}!\overrightarrow{R'x}-R''\overrightarrow{R'x}\,.\,\supset:\overrightarrow{R'x}-P''\overrightarrow{R'x}\,\epsilon\,\mathrm{In}\,.\,\mathbf{v}\,.\,\overrightarrow{S'x}\,\epsilon\,\mathrm{In}.$$

The condition $\mathbf{\exists}!\overrightarrow{R'x}-R''\overrightarrow{R'x}$ is sufficient, but we have not shown it to be necessary; it means that there is a term which begins just before x. Imagining a Dedekind section, x has perhaps no first moment, but the term in question begins at the end of the time before x.

To sum up: When the whole class of events can be well ordered, and also when methods exist of constructing certain kinds of well-ordered series of events, the existence of instants can be proved. But in the absence of such possibilities, I do not know of any way of proving the existence of instants anywhere if it is possible that all the events existing at the beginning of some event (or at the end) continue during a period when others begin and cease (or have previously existed during such a period).

A sufficient condition for the existence of instants is

$$\dot{\mathbf{\exists}}!S\,\dot{-}\,S\,|\,P\,|\,S.$$

Another is, putting $M=S\,\dot{-}\,\breve{P}\,|\,S$,

$$S\,|\,P\subset M\,|\,P,$$

which ensures that every event has a first instant; while, putting $N=S\,\dot{-}\,P\,|\,S$, the condition

$$S\,|\,\breve{P}\subset N\,|\,\breve{P}$$

ensures that every event has a last instant.

Logical Positivism

Few philosophers have altered the thought of their own times as powerfully and directly as Russell, and this has sometimes placed him in the anomalous position of being simultaneously a classic from the antiquity prior to the 1914–18 war and an active and controversial contemporary. His great achievement, the PRINCIPIA MATHEMATICA *was written (with Whitehead) while Russell was, by conventional standards, a young man; he was only forty-one at the time of the appearance of its final volume in 1913. Borrowing from an old joke, we have been obliged in the past three decades to distinguish between the great philosopher Bertrand Russell, whom we all respect, and Mr. B*rtr*nd R*ss*ll, with whom we frequently disagree.*

The whole character of modern British philosophy (and that portion of recent American philosophy which shows its influence) goes back to the revolutionary consequences of the thought of Russell and Moore at Cambridge in the nineties. The concept of philosophy, its problems and methods, developed by Russell and Moore was provided with a rigorous procedure by the formulation, by Russell and Whitehead, of a new logic of greater power and scope than any known previously.

The life-cycles of philosophers are interesting. There are those, such as Hume, who do their greatest work as young men and turn, in later years, to other things; while others, such as Kant, are undistinguished in their youth and only in middle life reveal the unquestionable marks of genius. As Russell grew older his thoughts and writings introduce themes quite removed from those on which he centred his attention in the early years of the century, and many of the ideas he advanced in the years before 1920 were, in the long run, developed by others than himself. The essay on logical positivism reprinted here from the REVUE DES MATHÉMATIQUES *is therefore of considerable interest, since it surveys the chief philosophic tendencies of this century from the vantage point of one who, perhaps more than anyone else, was responsible for them all.*

Portions of this paper were included in the text of HUMAN KNOWLEDGE: ITS SCOPE AND LIMITS (1948). *This is the first republication of the full text.*

LOGICAL POSITIVISM

'LOGICAL POSITIVISM' is a name for a method, not for a certain kind of result. A philosopher is a logical positivist if he holds that there is no special way of knowing that is peculiar to philosophy, but that questions of fact can only be decided by the empirical methods of science, while questions that can be decided without appeal to experience are either mathematical or linguistic. Many members of the school would describe their position briefly as a determination to reject 'metaphysics', but 'metaphysics' is such a vague term that this description has no precise meaning. I should prefer to say that questions of fact cannot be decided without appeal to observation. For example: seventeenth century Continental philosophers would contend that the soul must be immortal because the soul is a substance and substances are indestructible. A logical positivist would reject this argument, but would not necessarily hold that the soul is mortal, since he might think that psychical research gives empirical evidence of survival.

This, however, does not distinguish the logical positivist from earlier empiricists. What is distinctive is attention to mathematics and logic, and emphasis upon linguistic aspects of traditional philosophical problems. British empiricists, from Locke to John Stuart Mill, were very little influenced by mathematics, and had even a certain hostility to the outlook engendered by mathematics. On the other hand, Continental philosophers, down to Kant, regarded mathematics as the pattern to which other knowledge ought to approximate, and thought that pure mathematics, or a not dissimilar type of reasoning, could give knowledge as to the actual world. The logical positivists, though they are as much interested in and influenced by mathematics as Leibniz or Kant, are complete empiricists, and are enabled to combine mathematics with empiricism by a new interpretation of mathematical propositions. It was work on the foundations of mathematics and on mathematical logic that gave the technical basis for the school, and without some understanding of this basis it is impossible to do justice to the grounds for their opinions.

Mathematics, from Pythagoras onward, was mixed up with mysticism. Plato's eternal world was inspired by mathematics. Aristotle, though more empirical and more biological than Plato, still thought the capacity for doing sums so remarkable that the arithmetical part of the soul must be immortal. In modern times, Spinoza took geometry for his model, and hoped to deduce the nature of the universe from self-evident axioms, and Leibniz thought that all questions could be decided by reasoning, as appears in his account of what could be achieved by the Characteristica Universalis: 'If we had it, we should be able to reason in metaphysics and morals in much the same way as in geometry and analysis',* and again: 'If controversies were to arise, there would be no more need of disputation between two philosophers than between two accountants. For it would suffice to take their pencils in their hands, to sit down to their slates, and to say to each other (with a friend as witness, if they liked): Let us calculate'.†

Kant's theory of knowledge cannot be disentangled from his belief that mathematical propositions are both synthetic and *a priori*. My own work on the principles of mathematics was to me, at first, mainly interesting as a refutation of the view that mathematical propositions assert more than can be justified by deductive logic.

Hegel (especially in his *Greater Logic*) made a quite different use of mathematics. The great men of the seventeenth and eighteenth centuries were so much impressed by the *results* of their new methods that they did not trouble to examine their foundations. Although their arguments were fallacious, a special Providence saw to it that their conclusions were more or less true. Hegel fastened upon the obscurities in the foundations of mathematics, turned them into dialectical contradictions, and resolved them by nonsensical syntheses. It is interesting that some of his worst absurdities in this field were repeated by Engels in the *Anti-Dühring*, and that, in consequence, if you live in the Soviet Union

* *Leibnizens gesammelte Werke* (Pertz and Gerhardt's edition, Vol. VII, p. 21.

† Ibid., p. 200.

and take account of what has been done on the principles of mathematics during the last one hundred years, you run a grave risk of being liquidated.

Let us enumerate a few of the errors that infected mathematics in the time of Hegel. There was no defensible definition of irrational numbers, and consequently no ground for the Cartesian assumption that the position of any point in space could be defined by three numerical co-ordinates. There was no definition of continuity, and no known method of dealing with the paradoxes of infinite number. The accepted proofs of fundamental propositions in the differential and integral calculus were all fallacious, and were supposed, not only by Leibniz, but by many later mathematicians, to demand the admission of actual infinitesimals. As regards geometry, it was supposed that the truth of the Euclidean system could be known without any appeal to observation.

The resulting puzzles were all cleared up during the nineteenth century, not by heroic philosophical doctrines such as that of Kant or that of Hegel, but by patient attention to detail. The first step was Lobatchevsky's non-Euclidean geometry, which showed that only empirical observation can decide whether Euclidean geometry is true of actual space, and that geometry as a part of *pure* mathematics throws no more light upon actual space than the multiplication table throws on the population of an actual town.

The next step was Weierstrass's work on the differential and integral calculus, which eliminated infinitesimals and substituted limits. Then came Georg Cantor's definition of continuity and arithmetic of infinite numbers. And last came Frege's definition of cardinal numbers, and his proof that arithmetic requires no concepts and no premises that are not required in deductive logic. It seems strange that, although numbers had been used for many thousands of years, no one could define either 'number' or any particular number until Frege did so in 1884. And what is perhaps even more strange is that no one noticed what Frege had achieved until I read him eighteen years later.

The definition of the number 1 had great importance in clearing up metaphysical confusions. 'One' is a predicate of certain classes, e.g., 'satellite of the earth'; but when a class has only one member, it is nonsense (in the strict sense) to say that that member is one, unless the unit class was a class of classes, in which case it is generally false. E.g. you may say: 'In such-and-such a Parliament there is only one political party', but the party is not one, unless it has only one member. More generally, if I say 'there are three men in the room', the correct statement is 'the class of men in the room is a triad'. This may seem a trivial matter, but it is amazing how much bad metaphysics it refutes.

For example: the scholastics used to say '*One* and *Being* are convertible terms'. It now appears that 'one' is a predicate of concepts, not of the things to which the concepts are applicable; the predicate 'one' applies to 'satellite of the earth' but not to the moon. And for other reasons 'being' applies only to certain descriptions, never to what they describe. These distinctions, it will be found, put an end to many arguments of metaphysicians from Parmenides and Plato to the present day.

This development in the principles of mathematics suggested that philosophical puzzles are to be solved by patience and clear thinking, the result being, in very many cases, that the original question is shown to be nonsensical. Logical positivism arose largely out of this suggestion. Carnap maintained at one time that *all* philosophical problems arise from errors in syntax, and that, when these errors are corrected, the problems either disappear or are obviously not soluble by argument. I do not think he would still maintain quite so extreme a position, but there can be no doubt that correct logical syntax has an importance which was not formerly recognized, and which logical positivists have rightly emphasized.

Wittgenstein's *Tractatus Logico-Philosophicus*, published shortly after the First World War, laid great emphasis upon syntax, and provided a stimulus which helped in the formation of the 'Wiener Kreis', where logical positivism first took the form of a definite school. The Wiener Kreis and the admirable periodical *Erkenntnis* did excellent work, until they were ended by Hitler and the *Anschluss*. It was by the Vienna school that the hierarchy of languages was developed, a doctrine which I had briefly suggested as a way of escaping from Wittgenstein's rather peculiar syntactical mysticism. He had maintained that the *form* of a sentence can only be *shown*, not *stated*. The apprehension of *form*, in his doctrine, was something that was ineffable in the strict sense, and only possible in virtue of some kind of mystical insight. This point of view was very alien to the spirit of logical positivism. It was therefore natural that the Wiener Kreis, admitting Wittgenstein's problem, should seek other ways of solving it.

It appeared that, given any language, it must have a certain incompleteness, in the sense that there are things to be said *about* the language which cannot be said *in* the language. This is connected with the paradoxes—the liar, the class of classes that are not members of themselves, etc. These paradoxes had appeared to me to demand a hierarchy of 'logical types' for their solution, and the doctrine of a hierarchy of languages belongs to the same order of ideas. For example, if I say 'all sentences in the language *L* are either true or false', this is not itself a sentence in the language *L*. It is possible, as Carnap has shown, to construct a language in which many things about the language can be said, but never *all* the things that might be said: some of them will always belong to the metalanguage'. For example, there is mathematics, but however 'mathematics' may be defined, there will be statements *about* mathematics which will belong to 'metamathematics', and must be excluded from mathematics on pain of contradiction.

There has been a vast technical development of logic, logical syntax, and semantics. In this subject, Carnap has done the most work. Tarski's *Der Begriff der Wahrheit in den formalisierten Sprachen* is a very important book, and if compared with the attempts of philosophers in the past to define 'truth' it shows the increase of power derived from a wholly modern technique. Not that difficulties are at an end. A new set of puzzles has resulted from the work of Gödel, especially his article *Über formal unentscheidbare Sätze der Principia Mathematica und verwandter Systeme* (1931), in which he proved that in any formal system it is possible to construct sentences of which the truth or falsehood cannot be decided within the system. Here again we are faced with the essential necessity of a heirarchy, extending upwards *ad infinitum*, and logically incapable of completion.

This whole subject has become so technical, and so capable of quasi-mathematical definiteness, that it can hardly be regarded as belonging to philosophy as formerly understood. True, it solves what *were* philosophical problems, but so did Newton in writing on what he still called 'natural philosophy'. But we do not now regard planetary theory as part of philosophy, and I think that on the same ground much of the recent work on logic, syntax, and semantics should be regarded as definite knowledge, not philosophical speculation.

So far, I have been dealing with topics that arise out of the consideration of mathematics and logic. I come now to what logical positivism has to say about empirical knowledge, and here I find myself, on some important points, no longer in agreement with most members of the school.

There are here two not wholly disconnected questions. The one is as to scientific as opposed to deductive inference; the other is as to what is meant by the 'significance' of a sentence.

The question of scientific inference is one which has been acute ever since the time of Hume. It has been common to include under 'induction' all such inferences as would be considered valid in science but are not justified by the rules of deduction. I think myself that induction has less importance in this problem than is generally thought. What is clear, and generally admitted, is: (1) That scientific as opposed to deductive inference can only make the conclusion probable; (2) That it cannot even do this except by assuming postulates, or a postulate, for which there is, and can be, no empirical evidence. This is an awkward conclusion for an empiricist, but it seems to be unescapable. I shall not in this article deal further with this problem, but shall instead examine the doctrine that 'significance' and 'knowledge' are both confined to experience.

Some modern empiricists—in particular, the majority of logical positivists—have, in my opinion, misconceived the relation of knowledge to experience. This has arisen, if I am not mistaken, from two errors: first, an inadequate analysis of the concept 'experience', and second, a mistake as to what is involved in the belief that some assigned property belongs to some (undetermined) subject. Two specific problems arise, one as regards significance, the other as regards knowledge of what are called 'existence propositions' i.e. propositions of the form 'something has this property'. It is maintained, on the one hand, that a statement is not 'significant' unless there is some known method of verifying it; on the other hand, that we cannot know 'something has this property' unless we can mention a specific subject that has the property. I wish to give reasons for rejecting both these opinions.

Before examining the abstract logic of these two problems, let us consider them, for a moment, from a common-sense point of view.

To begin with verification: There are some who maintain that, if atomic warfare is not checked, it may lead to the extermination of life on this planet. I am not concerned to maintain that this opinion is true, but only that it is significant. It is, however, one which cannot be verified, for who would be left to verify it if life were extinct? Only Berkeley's God, whom, I am sure, logical positivists would not wish to invoke. Going backwards instead of forwards, we all believe that there was a time before there was life on the earth. Those who regard verifiability as necessary to significance do not mean to deny such possibilities, but in order to admit them they are compelled to define 'verifiability' somewhat loosely. Sometimes a proposition is regarded as 'verifiable' if there is any empirical evidence in its favour. That is to say, 'all A is B' is 'verifiable' if we know of one A that is B and do not know of one that is not B. This view, however, leads to logical absurdities. Suppose there is no single member of A concerning which we know whether it is a B, but there is an object x, not a member of A, which we know to be a B. Let A' be the class consisting of the class A together with the object x. Then 'all A' is B' is verifiable in terms of the definition. Since this implies 'all A is B', it follows that 'all A is B' is verifiable if there is, anywhere, a single object known to be a B.

Consider now a generalization of a different sort, such as we may wish to make in connexion with the doctrine of natural kinds. The generalizations I have in mind are those of the form: 'all predicates of the class A are true of the object B'.

Applying the same definition of 'verifiability', this is 'verifiable' if some, or at least one, of the predicates of the class A is empirically known to be true of B. If this is not the case, let P be some predicate known to be true of B, and let A' be the class consisting of the class A together with P. Then 'all predicates of the class A' are true of B' is verifiable, and so, therefore, is 'all predicates of the class A are true of B'.

From these two processes it follows that, if anything is known to have any predicate, all generalizations are 'verifiable'. This consequence was not intended, and shows that the above wide definition of 'verifiability' is useless. But unless we allow some such wide definition, we cannot escape from paradoxes.

Let us next consider propositions containing the word 'some', or an equivalent, e.g. 'some men are black', or 'some quadrupeds have no tails'. As a rule, such propositions are known by means of instances. If I am asked 'how do you know that some quadrupeds have no tails?' I may reply 'because I once had a Manx cat, and it had no tail'. The view which I wish to combat maintains that this is the only way of knowing such propositions. This view has been maintained by Brouwer in mathematics, and is maintained by some other philosophers in regard to empirical objects.

The paradoxes resulting from this opinion are very similar to those resulting from the above doctrine as to verifiability. Take such a proposition as 'rain sometimes falls in places where there is no one to see it'. No sane person would deny this, but it is impossible to mention a raindrop that has never been noticed. To deny that we know that there are occurrences not observed by any one is incompatible with common sense, but is necessary if we never know such propositions as 'there are A's' except when we can mention A's that we have observed. Can any one seriously maintain that the planet Neptune or the Antarctic Continent did not exist until it was discovered? Again only a Berkelian God will enable us to escape from paradoxes. Or again: we all believe that there is iron in the interior of the earth, but we cannot give instances beyond the depth of the deepest mine.

Adherents of the doctrine that I am combating interpret such facts hypothetically. They say that the statement 'there is undiscovered iron' is an abbreviation, and that the full statement should be: 'if I did certain things, I should discover iron'. Suppose, for the sake of precision, we take the statement 'there is iron more than 1,000 kilometres below the surface of the earth'. It is unlikely that anybody will ever find this iron, and, in any case, how can it be known what a person would find? Only by knowing what is there to be found. A hypothetical of which the hypothesis will probably always be false tells us nothing. Or consider: 'there was once a world without life'. This cannot mean: 'if I had been alive then, I should have seen that nothing was alive'.

Let us now consider the above two doctrines more formally, from a strictly logical point of view.

A. MEANING AND VERIFICATION

There is a theory that the meaning of a proposition consists in its method of verification. It follows (a) that what cannot be verified or falsified is meaningless, (b) that two propositions verified by the same occurrences have the same meaning.

I reject both, and I do not think that those who advocate them have fully realized their implications.

First: practically all the advocates of the above view regard verification as a *social* matter. This means that they take up the problem at a late stage, and are unaware of its earlier stages. Other people's observations are not data for me. The hypothesis that nothing exists except what I perceive and remember is for me identical, in all its verifiable consequences, with the hypothesis that there are other people who also perceive and remember. If we are to believe in the existence of these other people—as we must do if we are to admit testimony—we must reject the identification of meaning with verification.

'Verification' is often defined very loosely. The only strict meaning of verification is the following: A proposition asserting a finite number of future occurrences is 'verified' when all these occurrences have taken place, and are, at some moment, perceived or remembered by some one person. But this is not the sense in which the word is usually employed. It is customary to say that a general proposition is 'verified' when all those of its consequences which it has been possible to test have been found to be true. It is always assumed that, in that case, probably the consequences which have not been tested are also true. But this is not the point with which I am concerned at present. The point with which I am concerned at the moment is the theory that two propositions whose verified consequences are identical have the same significance. I say 'verified', not 'verifiable'; for we cannot know, until the last man perishes, whether the 'verifiable' consequences are identical. Take, e.g. 'all men are mortal'. It may be that on 9 February, 1991, an immortal man will be born. The presently verifiable consequences of 'all men are mortal' are the same as those of 'all men born before the time t are mortal, but not all those born later', where t is any time not more than a century before the present.

If we insist upon using the word 'verifiable' rather than

'verified', we cannot know that a proposition is verifiable, since this would involve knowledge of an indefinitely long future. In fact, that a proposition is verifiable is itself not verifiable. This is because to state that all the future consequences of a general proposition are true is itself a general proposition of which the instances cannot be enumerated, and no general proposition can be established on purely empirical evidence except one applying to a list of particulars all of which have been observed. E.g. I may say 'the inhabitants of such-and-such a village are Mr. and Mrs. *A*, Mr. and Mrs. *B*, etc., and their families, all of whom are known to me personally; and all of them are Welsh'.* But when I cannot enumerate the members of a class, I cannot, on purely empirical grounds, justify any generalization about its members except what follows analytically from its definition.

There is however still a point to be made in favour of the verifiers. They contend that there is a distinction between two kinds of cases. In one, we have two propositions whose consequences hitherto have been indistinguishable, but whose future consequences may diverge; e.g. 'all men are mortal' and 'all men born before A.D. 2000 are mortal'. In the other, we have two propositions whose observable consequences can never diverge; this is especially the case with metaphysical hypotheses. The hypothesis that the starry heavens exist at all times, and the hypothesis that they only exist when I see them, are exactly identical in all those of their consequences that I can test. It is specially in such cases that meaning is identified with verification, and that, therefore, the two hypotheses are said to have the same significance. And it is this that I am specially concerned to deny.

Perhaps the most obvious case is other people's minds. The hypothesis that there are other people, having thoughts and feelings more or less like my own, does not have the same significance as the hypothesis that other people are only parts of my dreams, and yet the verifiable consequences of the two hypotheses are identical. We all feel love and hate, sympathy and antipathy, admiration and contempt, for what we believe to be real people. The *emotional* consequences of this belief are very different from those of solipsism, though the *verifiable* consequences are not. I

* Such general enumerative statements involve many difficulties, but I will ignore them.

should say that two beliefs whose emotional consequences differ have substantially distinct significations.

But this is a practical argument. I should go further, and say, as a matter of pure theory, that you cannot, without incurring an endless regress, seek the significance of a proposition in its consequences, which must be other propositions. We cannot explain what is the significance of a belief, or what makes it true or false, without bringing in the concept 'fact', and when this is brought in the part played by verification is seen to be subsidiary and derivative.

B. INFERENTIAL EXISTENCE-PROPOSITIONS

A form of words containing an undetermined variable—for instance, 'x is a man'—is called a 'propositional function' if, when a value is assigned to the variable, the form of words becomes a proposition. Thus 'x is a man' is neither true nor false, but if for 'x' I put 'Mr. Jones' I get a true proposition, and if I put 'Mrs. Jones' I get a false one.

Besides giving a value to 'x', there are two other ways of obtaining a proposition from a propositional function. One is to say that the propositions obtained by giving values to 'x' are all true; the other is to say that at least one of them is true. If '$f(x)$' is the function in question, we will call the first of these '$f(x)$ always' and the second '$f(x)$ sometimes' (where it is understood that 'sometimes' means 'at least once'). If '$f(x)$' is 'x is not a man or x is mortal', we can assert '$f(x)$ always' ; if '$f(x)$' is 'x is a man', we can assert '$f(x)$ sometimes', which is what we should commonly express by saying 'there are men'. If '$f(x)$' is 'I met x and x is a man', '$f(x)$ sometimes' is 'I met at least one man'.

We call '$f(x)$ sometimes' an 'existence-proposition' because it says that something having the property $f(x)$ 'exists'. For instance, if you wanted to say 'unicorns exist', you would first have to define 'x is a unicorn' and then assert that there are values of x for which this is true. In ordinary language, the words 'some', 'a', and 'the' (in the singular) indicate existence-propositions.

There is one obvious way in which we get to know existence-propositions, and that is by means of instances. If I know '$f(a)$', where a is some known object, I can infer '$f(x)$ sometimes'. The question I wish to discuss is whether this is the *only* way in which such propositions can come to be known. I wish to maintain that it is not.

In deductive logic, there are only two ways in which existence-propositions can be proved. One is the above, when '$f(x)$ sometimes' is deduced from '$f(a)$'; the other is when one existence-proposition is deduced from another, for instance 'there are bipeds' from 'there are featherless bipeds'. What other methods are possible in non-deductive inference?

Induction, when valid, gives another method. Suppose there are two classes A and B and a relation R, such that, in a number of observed instances, we have (writing '$a\,R\,b$' for 'a has the relation R to b')

$$a_1 \text{ is an } A. \quad b_1 \text{ is a } B. \quad a_1\,R\,b_1$$
$$a_2 \text{ is an } A. \quad b_2 \text{ is a } B. \quad a_2\,R\,b_2$$

$$a_n \text{ is an } A. \quad b_n \text{ is a } B. \quad a_n\,R\,b_n$$

and suppose we have no contrary instances. Then in all observed instances, if a is an A, there is a B to which a has the relation R. If the case is one to which induction applies, we infer that probably every member of A has the relation R to some member of B. Consequently, if a_{n+1} is the next observed member of A, we infer as probable: 'there is a member of B to which a_{n+1} has the relation R'. We infer this, in fact, in many cases in which we cannot adduce any particular member of B such as we have inferred. We all believe that probably Napoleon III had a father, although no one has ever known who he was. Not even a solipsist, if he allows himself any views as to his own future, can escape from this sort of induction. Suppose, for instance, that our solipsist suffers from intermittent sciatica, which comes on every evening; he may say, on inductive grounds, 'probably I shall be suffering pain at 9 p.m. tonight'. This is an inference to the existence of something transcending his present experience. 'But,' you may say, 'it does not transcend his *future* experience.' If the inference is valid it does not; but the question is: 'how is he to know *now* that the inference is probably valid?'. The whole practical utility of scientific inference consists in giving grounds for anticipating the future; when the future has come and has verified the inference, memory has replaced inference, which is no longer needed. We must, therefore, find grounds for trusting the inference *before* it is verified. And I defy the world to find any such grounds for trusting inferences which will be verified, which are not equally grounds for trusting certain inferences which will be neither verified nor falsified, such as the inference to Napoleon III's father.

We are faced with the question: in what circumstances is induction valid? It is futile to say: 'Induction is valid when it infers something which subsequent experience will verify'. This is futile, because it would confine induction to cases in which it is useless. We must have reasons, in advance of experience, for expecting something, and exactly similar reasons may lead us to believe in something that we cannot experience, for example, the thoughts and feelings of other people. The plain fact is that much too much fuss is made about 'experience'.

Experience is needed for ostensive definition, and therefore for all understanding of the meanings of words. But the proposition 'Mr. *A* had a father' is completely intelligible even if I have no idea who Mr. *A*'s father was. If Mr. *B* was in fact Mr. *A*'s father, 'Mr. *B*' is not a constituent of the statement 'Mr. *A* had a father', or, indeed, of any statement containing the words 'Mr. *A*'s father' but not containing the name 'Mr. *B*'. Similarly I may *understand* 'there was a winged horse' although there never was one, because the statement means that, putting 'fx' for 'x has wings and is a horse', I assert 'fx sometimes'. It must be understood that 'x' is not a constituent of 'fx sometimes' or of 'fx always'. In fact, 'x' means nothing. That is why beginners find it so hard to make out what it means.

When I infer something not experienced—whether I shall or shall not experience it hereafter—I am never inferring something that I can name, but only the truth of an existence-proposition. If induction is ever valid, it is possible to know existence-propositions without knowing any particular instance of their truth. Suppose, for instance, that A is a class of which we have experienced some members, and we infer that a member of A will occur. We have only to substitute 'future members of A' for 'members of A' to make our inference apply to a class of which we cannot mention any instance.

I incline to think that valid inductions, and, generally, inferences going beyond my personal past and present experience, always depend upon causation, sometimes supplemented by analogy. But, in the present article, I wished only to remove certain *a priori* objections to a certain kind of inference—objections which, though *a priori*, are urged by those who imagine themselves able to dispense with the *a priori* altogether.

There is, I think, a danger that logical positivism may develop a new kind of scholasticism, and may, by being unduly linguistic, forget the relation to fact that makes a statement true. I will give one illustration of what I should regard as scholasticism in the bad sense. Carnap, and others of the same school, have very rightly pointed out the confusions that arise when we do not distinguish adequately between using a word and naming it. In ordinary cases this danger does not arise. We say: Socrates was a man, 'Socrates' is a word of eight letters. We can go on to say: 'Socrates' is the name of a man, but ' "Socrates" ' is the name of a word. The usual method of designating a word by putting it in inverted commas is useful, presupposing that we know what a word is. But difficulties arise when we carry on the same process as regards sentences or propositions. If the words 'To-day is Tuesday' occur without quotes, the sentence is used, not named. But when the sentence occurs in quotes, what am I naming? Do I include sentences, in other languages, which have the same meaning, e.g. 'aujourd'hui est mardi'? Conversely, suppose that in the Hottentot language the noise 'to-day is Tuesday' means 'I like cheese'. Clearly this should not be included in what I designate by the phrase in quotes. We must say: a sentence in quotes designates the class of those utterances, in no matter what language, that have the significance that I attach to the sentence when I *use* it: we must include the Frenchman's phonetically dissimilar remark, and exclude the Hottentot's phonetically similar remark. It follows that we cannot tell what is designated by a sentence in quotes without first investigating what is meant by saying that two utterances have the same significance. At any rate, we cannot do so if the sentences, when used, are to be possible values of the propositional variables used in logic, e.g. when we say 'if p implies q, then not-q implies not-p'. This shows that what is meant when a set of words is put in quotes is not such a simple matter as one would sometimes suppose from the works of some logical positivists. In this way, there is danger of a technique which conceals problems instead of helping to solve them.

Absorption in language sometimes leads to a neglect of the connexion of language with non-linguistic facts, although it is this connexion which gives meaning to words and significance to sentences. No one can understand the word 'cheese' unless he has a non-linguistic acquaintance with cheese. The problem of meaning and significance requires much that is psychological, and demands some understanding of pre-linguistic mental processes. Most logical positivists fight shy of psychology, and therefore have little to say about meaning or significance. This makes them, in my opinion, somewhat narrow, and not capable of producing an all-round philosophy. They have, however, the great merit that their method allows them to tackle problems one by one, and that they are not obliged, as philosophers used to be, to produce a complete theory of the universe on all occasions. Their procedure, in fact, is more analogous to that of science than to that of traditional philosophy. In this respect I am wholly at one with them. I value their rigour, exactness, and attention to detail, and speaking broadly, I am more hopeful of results by methods such as theirs than by any that philosophers have employed in the past. What can be ascertained, can be ascertained by methods such as theirs; what cannot be ascertained by such methods we must be content not to know.

There is one matter of great philosophic importance in which a careful analysis of scientific inference and logical syntax leads—if I am not mistaken—to a conclusion which is unwelcome to me and (I believe) to almost all logical positivists. This conclusion is, that uncompromising empiricism is untenable. From a finite number of observations no general proposition can be inferred to be even probable unless we postulate some general principle of inference which cannot be established empirically. So far, there is agreement among logical positivists. But as to what is to be done in consequence there is no agreement. Some hold that truth does not consist in conformity with fact, but only in coherence with other propositions already accepted for some undefined reason. Others, like Reichenbach, favour a posit which is a mere act of will and is admitted to be not intellectually justified. Yet others make attempts

—to my mind futile—to dispense with general propositions. For my part, I assume that science is broadly speaking true, and arrive at the necessary postulates by analysis. But against the thoroughgoing sceptic I can advance no argument except that I do not believe him to be sincere.